CAMBRIDGE TEXTS IN THE
HISTORY OF POLITICAL THOUGHT

LOCKE
Political Essays

D0763684

CAMBRIDGE TEXTS IN THE
HISTORY OF POLITICAL THOUGHT

Series editors

RAYMOND GEUSS

Lecturer in Social and Political Sciences, University of Cambridge

QUENTIN SKINNER

Regius Professor of Modern History in the University of Cambridge

Cambridge Texts in the History of Political Thought is now firmly established as the major student textbook series in political theory. It aims to make available to students all the most important texts in the history of western political thought, from ancient Greece to the early twentieth century. All the familiar classic texts will be included but the series seeks at the same time to enlarge the conventional canon by incorporating an extensive range of less well-known works, many of them never before available in a modern English edition. Wherever possible, texts are published in complete and unabridged form, and translations are specially commissioned for the series. Each volume contains a critical introduction together with chronologies, biographical sketches, a guide to further reading and any necessary glossaries and textual apparatus. When completed, the series will aim to offer an outline of the entire evolution of western political thought.

For a list of titles published in the series, please see end of book.

LOCKE

Political Essays

EDITED BY

MARK GOLDIE

Lecturer in History,
University of Cambridge,
and Vice-Master of Churchill College

CAMBRIDGE
UNIVERSITY PRESS

PUBLISHED BY THE PRESS SYNDICATE OF THE UNIVERSITY OF CAMBRIDGE
The Pitt Building, Trumpington Street, Cambridge CB2 1RP, United Kingdom

CAMBRIDGE UNIVERSITY PRESS
The Edinburgh Building, Cambridge, CB2 2RU, United Kingdom
40 West 20th Street, New York, NY 10011–4211, USA
10 Stamford Road, Oakleigh, Melbourne 3166, Australia

First published 1997

Printed in the United Kingdom at the University Press, Cambridge

Typeset in Ehrhardt 9.5/12 pt

A catalogue record for this book is available from the British Library

Library of Congress Cataloguing in Publication data

Locke, John, 1632–1704.
[Selections. 1997]
Locke: political essays/edited by Mark Goldie.
p.   cm. – (Cambridge texts in the history of political thought)
Includes bibliographical references (p.   ) and index.
ISBN 0 521 47269 5 (hard) – ISBN 0 521 47861 8 (pbk.)
1. Political science – Early works to 1800.   2. Locke, John, 1632–1704 – Contributions in political science.   I. Goldie, Mark.
II. Title.   III. Title: Political essays   IV. Series.
JC153.L79 1997
320.51'2 – dc21   96–45153 CIP
ISBN 0 521 47269 5 hardback
ISBN 0 521 47861 8 paperback

Contents

Acknowledgements

Whether Locke would have welcomed this volume is not quite clear. On the one hand he pronounced that 'What I cannot at all approve of . . is the absurd industry of editors whose way it is to collect with the greatest care everything that learned men have written, and to give it to the world' (Letter 1262). But on the other hand he also wrote, for the plaque to stand over his tomb: 'learn from his writings; which will show you what is to be said about him more faithfully than the doubtful eulogies of an epitaph'.

My own editorial industry has fallen short of absurdity by having had the good fortune to stand on the shoulders of other Locke scholars. To have started such a volume as this from scratch would have entailed many years' work. The project has only been feasible because of the labours of earlier editors of Locke's texts, especially Lord King and H. R. Fox Bourne, who in the nineteenth century laid the foundations of modern Locke scholarship, and, in more recent times, Philip Abrams and Wolfgang Von Leyden, who edited the longest texts printed here, as well as others who have put Locke's manuscripts into print: R. I. Aaron and J. Gibb, J. L. Axtell, John Biddle, Maurice Cranston, Esmond De Beer, E. A. Driscoll, John Dunn, James Farr, Kimimasa Inoue, Patrick Kelly, Peter Laslett, John Lough, John Milton, Philip Milton, M. E. Parker, Clayton Roberts, Mario Sina, and John and Jean Yolton. I am indebted to them all. I particularly thank the Delegates of Oxford University Press for permission to use copyright material from Wolfgang Von Leyden's edition of the *Essays on the Law of Nature*.

I would like to record my warmest thanks to those who have made comments, offered suggestions, answered questions, or helped with editorial chores: the late Richard Ashcraft, Virginia Catmur, Conal Condren, John Dunn, James Farr, Richard Fisher, Ian Harris, Kimimasa Inoue, Clare Jackson, Patrick Kelly, Matthew Kramer, Christine MacLeod, John Marshall, Joshua Petersen, John Rogers, Quentin Skinner, Sandy Stewart, Sylvana Tomaselli, James Tully, Ian Wei, Jean Wilkins, David Wootton, and John and Jean Yolton. I must single out John Milton, who generously shared his remarkable knowledge of Locke's papers, saved me from several errors and transcribed some passages of Locke's shorthand.

Introduction

I

We know more about the development of John Locke's ideas than we do about almost any other philosopher's before modern times. At his death in 1704 he left behind an immense collection of unpublished papers, many of which remained in his own escritoire until the Second World War, by which time they were in the possession of the Earl of Lovelace. They were moved from a furniture store in Tunbridge Wells to the Bodleian Library in Oxford in 1942. Consequently we have not only Locke's published works, which fill ten volumes in their nineteenth-century edition, but also more than one hundred volumes of manuscripts. Besides the Lovelace Collection, there are important materials in the Shaftesbury Papers in the Public Record Office and elsewhere. Locke's papers include drafts of treatises, memoranda, commonplace books, journals, account books, library lists and medical prescriptions. As well as these, there are some 3,500 extant letters written by or to Locke. These writings cover all of Locke's major intellectual preoccupations: ethics, epistemology, politics, economics, theology, ecclesiology and medicine.

Except for some items put into print by Lord King in 1829 and copied by H. R. Fox Bourne in 1876, the Lovelace Collection was virtually unknown until the Bodleian acquired formal possession in 1947. In the half century since then, much (though not all) that is of theoretical significance has been published. But it is scattered among a host of often inaccessible journals, or contained in volumes long out of print. The purpose of this book is to bring together for the first time Locke's writings on politics and society, apart from the canonical works published during his lifetime, in a collection as full as is practicable within a single volume.

That the eighteenth- and nineteenth-century editions of Locke's *Works* contain only a tiny fraction of the material printed in the present volume is a measure of the modern transformation in Locke scholarship. It is also a measure of the gap between the writings Locke chose to publish and the private working papers known only to his closest friends. His was a life of relentless intellectual activity, yet he published virtually nothing until he was fifty-seven years old. In the immediate aftermath of the 'Glorious Revolution' of 1688–9 were published, in close sequence, the three works by which is chiefly known: his political philosophy in the *Two Treatises of Government*, his exploration of the foundations of knowledge in *An Essay Concerning Human Understanding*, and his plea for religious liberty in *A Letter Concerning Toleration*. Within a few years he also published *Some Thoughts Concerning Education* and *The Reasonableness of Christianity*, together with polemical defences of the *Essay* and of *A Letter Concerning Toleration* and a series of treatises on economics and theology. Most of these works had a lengthy pre-history, their topics the object of his thoughts over three decades. Many items in the present volume were preparatory or parallel reflections: they form a palimpsest of Locke's intellectual development.

One thing, however, immediately strikes the reader. Locke's seminal publications are not equally well represented in his surviving papers. Just as the *Essay* was the book to which Locke put his name, which he fiercely defended, and which made him famous, so it was the philosophical investigations which lay behind it that leave the most frequent footprints in his papers. Closely behind follow his preoccupations with religious liberty and the relationship between secular and ecclesiastical authority. By contrast, the student in search of deep-laid foundations for the *Two Treatises* will be disappointed. Certainly there are pertinent materials here, such as his anthropological notes concerning government among native American peoples and the essay on allegiance written in the aftermath of the Glorious Revolution. But on the evidence of the extant materials, the *Two Treatises* appears to be an unexpected eruption, a sudden deviation from his characteristic concerns – or, alternatively, a book of which its author was keen to destroy any trace, for he did not confess his authorship until his last days.

This is not to say that the present volume is any the less 'political' in its content. Readers of the *Two Treatises* need to adjust their expectations of the character of Locke's politics in order to take account of the salience for him of questions concerning the philosophical foundations of morality and sociability and the proper boundaries of church and state. Moreover, the present volume reveals a Locke whose sense of the political was more practical than might be deduced from the theoretical abstractions of the *Two Treatises*, for he frequently addressed constitutional, administrative and policy matters. 'True politics', he told Lady Peterborough, 'I look on as a part of moral philosophy, which is nothing but the art of conducting men right in society' (Letter 2320).

The longest and most important texts printed here are Locke's earliest treatises, the *Two Tracts on Government* (1660–2), which argue for the magistrate's right to impose a uniform religion upon his people, and the *Essays on the Law of Nature* (1663–4), which investigate the grounds for speaking of a universally binding moral law. These are joined by three further substantial essays, *An Essay on Toleration* (1667), which marked a decisive shift in Locke's views on religious liberty; *The Fundamental Constitutions of Carolina* (1669), a meticulous scheme for North America which reproduced the aristocratic, participatory and localist features of English government; and *An Essay on the Poor Law* (1697), a memorandum prepared for the Board of Trade, which aimed to harness the productive powers of the indigent. These treatises are contained in the first section, 'Major Essays'. The second section, 'Minor Essays', contains seventy shorter pieces, memoranda and fragments. Fifteen of these have not previously been printed. The appendix contains brief extracts from a further four works. The texts have been arranged chronologically within each section, both because a division by subject matter would artificially designate and segregate Locke's concerns and because an understanding of the evolution of his ideas over time has long been at the heart of the investigation of his philosophy.

A caveat should be entered about this volume. Locke wrote these texts over a span of half a century and generally without any intention to publish. The materials are of diverse sorts, including university lectures, polemical treatises, government position papers, philosophical meditations, notes on reading, epigrams, communications to friends, journal entries written in shorthand, and discarded drafts. Those who have looked at the original manuscripts know that the pages are often riddled with deletions and interlinear insertions. Some of his briefer texts have been wrested from a flow of diary entries or from a patchwork of comments and quotations prompted by books which he was reading. Printing such variegated and imperfect manuscripts in a single sequence and in a standardised typography and format is apt to lend to the whole a spurious impression of coherence, completeness and purposiveness. The reader should be aware that the contents of this book are more like a collection of shards from an archaeologist's dig than the revelation of a Lockean *Summa*.

II

Locke was born in Somerset in 1632. In 1661 he reflected, 'I no sooner perceived myself in the world but I found myself in a storm.' He was ten when his father and his patron took up arms against King Charles I. He was fifteen when his uncle helped evict the Anglican minister of a local parish. He was sixteen when Charles I was executed. And he was twenty-one when he saluted the ruler of the English republic, Oliver Cromwell, in verse: 'You, Sir, from Heav'n a finish'd hero fell.' Locke's roots lay firmly among the Puritans who fought the Civil War in the name of a parliamentary constitution and a godly church. A generation later, early in the 1680s, he wrote the *Two Treatises of Government*, when it seemed to him and to his fellow Whigs that once again Englishmen might have to resist the forces of monarchical absolutism.

In between, however, Locke recoiled from many of the convictions that inspired the Civil War, and he shared in the visceral cultural reaction that marked Restoration England. Arguably his political development is best described as a gradual rediscovery of the principles of 1642, but in successive modifications of sensibility by which godly Puritanism was transformed into Enlightenment Whiggery. The latitudinarian Anglicanism of his later life contained within it characteristic attitudes of the moderate Puritanism of the 1640s: a rejection of divine right claims, whether of doctrinaire monarchists or republicans, or of Episcopalians or Presbyterians; an 'anti-formalism' that accented virtuous conduct rather than credal or ceremonial dogma; a distaste for sectarians and 'enthusiasts' (whatever their legitimate claims to toleration); and a horror of Roman Catholicism both as a theological monstrosity and a threat to civilised society.

Locke's adult life can be divided into four phases, the first three of which fill the period of the Restoration, between the return of Stuart monarchy in 1660 and its second overthrow in 1688. At first he was an Oxford don. He took pastoral care of gentlemen's sons and taught them Latin, Greek and moral philosophy. He evaded the normal expectation that he would became a clergyman; he studied medicine, which he thereafter practised informally, and he ventured into public life as secretary to an embassy to Cleves.

In 1667 Locke abandoned the academic seclusion of Christ Church and joined the household of Lord Ashley, who was Charles II's Chancellor of the Exchequer and later became Earl of Shaftesbury and Lord Chancellor. Locke acted as Ashley's political confidant and secretary and as tutor to his grandchild. Ashley was a great landed magnate, his income several hundred times that of a labourer. Locke served him when he was in power, acting as secretary to the Proprietors of Carolina and to the Council of Trade. He served him in opposition, when, at the end of the 1670s, the earl attacked the growth of 'popery and arbitrary power' and rallied a political movement that acquired the name Whig. He served him in defeat, when opposition turned to treason. Finally, when his master fled to Holland, Locke followed.

From 1683 until the beginning of 1689 Locke lived in the Dutch republic, among the community of fugitive English and Scottish Whigs and religious Dissenters. Sometimes he went into hiding, for fear of kidnap by English government agents. Had he died at this time, he would have left scarcely a mark on the historical record, a suspect servant of a fallen aristocratic courtier.

In the last phase, after returning to England in February 1689, Locke's life was transformed. He became a doyen of the republic of letters, an internationally renowned philosopher, an adviser to government, the 'great Mr Locke'. He lived most of the time in the Essex household of Damaris Masham, a clever woman with a dull husband. He corresponded with a circle of Whig politicians and courtiers who called themselves 'the College' and who were closely involved in the ending of press censorship in 1695 and the national recoinage of 1696. He served on the Board of Trade, deliberating on such matters as the Irish textile industry and the grievances of Virginia. He wrote commentaries on the Scriptures and puzzled over biblical chronology with Isaac Newton. Damaris Masham was reading the Psalms to him when he died on 28 October 1704.

III

Since the discovery of the *Two Tracts on Government* it has become common to see Locke as arriving belatedly at radical political views, the early conservative becoming the revolutionary Whig. And indeed, Locke gives the impression of being reluctantly driven to new positions against the grain of his temperament, which was cautious, anxious and painfully sensitive to the fragility of social order. The mood of ideological exhaustion that most English gentlemen felt after twenty years of turmoil is palpable in the preface to the *Two Tracts*. 'War, cruelty, rapine, confusion' have 'wearied and wasted this poor nation'; the world tumbles between tyranny and anarchy; the passionate multitude is armed with cries of liberty and conscience.

The *Two Tracts* addressed a crucial unresolved aspect of the process of restoration. Monarchy had returned, but the character of the re-established Church of England was not yet settled. Episcopalians and Presbyterians quarrelled over whether Christ intended his church to be governed by bishops. Some thought that the rituals laid down in the old Book of Common Prayer were popish superstitions. The new sects, such as the Quakers and Baptists, demanded liberty of conscience. Locke's Christ Church colleague, Edward Bagshaw, opposed the re-imposition of ceremonies and formularies. Locke responded with the *Two Tracts*.

Locke's procedure in the *Two Tracts* is not unlike that of the later *Two Treatises*. The first part clears the ground by a combative and minute refutation of his opponent's interpretation of Scripture. The second part presents his own position in more synoptic and less polemical terms. Locke's subject matter is apt now to seem arcane. Readers have searched for fleeting reflections on the nature of political authority. Locke agnostically says that there is no need to 'meddle with that question whether the magistrate's crown drops down on his head immediately from heaven or be placed there by the hands of his subjects'. However, he does assert that 'the supreme magistrate of every nation . . . must necessarily have an absolute and arbitrary power'. He was not here defending monarchical 'absolutism', but the juridical view that in every state there must be an ultimate legislative power, since, he goes on, it is no different in a 'pure commonwealth' (a republic), 'the same arbitrary power being there in the assembly'.

These were incidental remarks. The main topic is the legitimacy of the ruler's imposition of forms of religious worship. The key term of art is 'things indifferent', or 'adiaphora', a subject of intense debate in English Reformation thought. In an authoritative tradition, pre-eminently represented in Richard Hooker's *Laws of Ecclesiastical Polity*, it was held that although God must be worshipped, he was not unduly prescriptive about how this should be done. Hence, while some matters of ritual (and of morality and church government) had been prescribed by divine law and were 'things necessary' to salvation, there was a broad array of ritual performances (and of behaviour and jurisdiction) which were nonprescriptive and were 'things indifferent' to salvation. In this latter sphere, it was argued, the magistrate had discretion to impose outward forms of public ritual and ecclesiastical government for the sake of decency and good order. The magistrate was still visibly the Lutheran Godly Prince, in whose hands lay the external arrangements of religious as of secular life. Arguably, adiaphorism was the sustaining doctrine of the Church of England as an inclusive national church. It entailed a strong sense that while some things were *jure divino* (by divine right) and hence not subject to human choice, most things were *jure humano* (by human law) and were legitimately subject to such human arrangements as seemed practical.

It followed that zealots who thought that every iota of human life was governed by divine revelation – all actions being either commanded or forbidden by God – were dangerously misguided. They were apt to challenge the magistrate as ungodly at every turn, either demanding particular impositions, or claiming a Christian liberty of exemption from superstitious human contrivances. Such were the fanatics who, Locke wrote, had brought England to 'the tyranny of a religious rage'. Locke's line of thought was a conventional piece of Anglican (and moderate Presbyterian) adiaphorism. In less palatable form, it was also Hobbes's view, for *Leviathan* was a deliberate *reductio* of the adiaphorist position, in that what is *jure humano* almost entirely occludes what is *jure divino*.

Locke's *Essay on Toleration* (1667) marked a decisive change of mind. He now repeatedly asserted that the magistrate's sole concern was the 'peace, safety, or security of the people'. Any law not driven by this criterion was 'meddling'. Since no particular ritual could be said to endanger the state, it was no business of the state to impose. Thus not only must speculative theological opinion be free, but also 'the place, time, and manner of worshipping'. Locke began to attempt to erect a theoretical barrier between the ecclesiastical sphere and 'civil concernments'. The Lutheran Godly Prince disappeared. Locke conceded that religious symbols could become rallying cries for 'factiousness and turbulency' and he continued to believe that an empirical assessment of threat would yield the conclusion that Papists and some Protestant fanatics were dangerous. The magistrate might suppress them as underminers of the commonwealth, but he advised the magistrate that persecution, where it is not necessary, is a sure way of turning innocent sectaries into seditious rebels. He also began to adopt the language of the political economists, advising that toleration would promote the 'number and industry' and the 'riches and power' of the nation.

There were, again, incidental remarks on the origins of political authority. Locke now said that those who preach *jure divino* monarchy had 'forgot what country they are born in'. But he remained emphatic that even those people with affronted consciences, wrongly coerced in religious matters, should quietly 'submit to the penalty the law inflicts'. Outside the *Two Treatises* it seems impossible to find Locke unequivocally endorsing a right of armed resistance.

Locke's new position is also visible in his critique of Samuel Parker's adiaphorist and Hobbesian *Discourse of Ecclesiastical Polity* (1669). In a series of further fragments in the 1670s and 1680s, such as 'Civil and Ecclesiastical Power', 'Ecclesia', 'Pacific Christians' and several headed 'Toleration', the lineaments of Locke's mature position are visible. Above all, he decisively removed temporal magistracy from the sphere of religion: the security of the commonwealth and the saving of souls were distinct. It could not be supposed that we gave to civil society a power to coerce us in matters concerning salvation. Membership of churches should be voluntary; their disciplinary instrument was excommunication, but without civil penalties attached. Locke came to find the adiaphorist case implausible. In 'Toleration D' he wrote that particular modes of worship 'cannot be indifferent to him that thinks them not so'. However tiresomely wrongheaded zealots might be, a profound injury is done to them when they are compelled. Locke had an increasingly anthropological appreciation of the rootedness of custom and of culturally embedded ritual. One nation's barbarism was another's civility, and some people will die for a custom which others find silly. Locke also became increasingly anticlerical in his hostility to churchmen who meddled in politics and sought to govern doctrine and practice.

IV

In the *Two Tracts* Locke wrote that 'God hath made known his will either by the discoveries of reason, usually called the law of nature, or the revelations of his word.' In the *Essays on the Law of Nature* (*ELN*) Locke turned from the latter to the former. Nothing troubled him more persistently than the problem of the rational foundations of morality and their relationship to God's will. The *Essay Concerning Human Understanding* (*ECHU*) had its origins early in the 1670s, as James Tyrrell tells us, in conversations concerning morality and revealed religion. There is a complex history of textual continuity running from the 1660s to the 1690s. The *ELN* broached the subject; some aspects reappear in Drafts A and B (1671) of the *ECHU*; part of 'Ethic in General' (*c.* 1686–8?) derives almost verbatim from Draft B; and as late as 1690 Tyrrell suggested that Locke should publish the *ELN*. One remarkable continuity is Locke's example of the atheistic natives of Soldania Bay in Southern Africa: it occurs in the *ELN*, Draft B, the *ECHU* and in one version of the *Two Treatises*.

In the *ELN* Locke worked within the inheritance of the neo-Scholastic treatment of natural law, familiar to university scholars chiefly through Aquinas and Suárez. The *Essays* are more properly *Quaestiones*, lectures which address disputed questions. Having asserted that there is a law of nature, Locke turns to consider what reliable knowledge we can have of it. It is striking that he decisively rejects two conventional grounds for moral knowledge, the Platonist notion of innate ideas and the Ciceronian or Grotian *sensus communis*, the common consent or tradition of mankind. The ground is already laid for the critique of innatism and for the anthropologically supported scepticism about the cultural universality of moral assumptions, which are at the heart of the *ECHU*. In the *ELN* (and in the *ECHU*) Locke's theism is indispensable to the alternative approach he offers.

The Scholastic treatment of God's nature produced a tension between conceiving of God as an omnipotent agent whose will constituted the good, and an omniscient agent whose reason apprehended the good. This was the tension between voluntarism and rationalism. Like most of his contemporaries, Locke adopted a Suarezian middle way, for God is 'not only powerful but also wise'. In 'God's Justice' (1680) Locke wrote that God's 'unlimited power cannot be an excellency without it be regulated by wisdom and goodness'. But his fundamental position was voluntarist: the law of nature was created by the contingent will of God, and ethics was a matter of having adequate knowledge of divine law. Locke repeatedly stressed that moral concepts were meaningless without the idea of law, and that law entailed the command of someone who has power to attach penalties to its breach. In 'Virtue A' (1681) he reiterated that virtue must be construed as deriving from the will of God and hence as having the force of law. In 'Of Ethic in General' he urged that, unless we construe morality judicially, 'morality' becomes merely descriptive of the fashions and mores of particular societies.

Locke's position in the *ELN* is similar, but more complex. He stresses that God's will is not arbitrary and meaningless, and therefore it is something about which we can reason and about which we do not have to rely upon the contingent utterances of Scripture. Although the law of nature is a 'decree of the divine will', it is 'discernible by the light of nature', for God 'has not created this world for nothing and without purpose'. There can be a 'rational apprehension of what is right'. This cannot be done purely by introspective contemplation, in the manner of the Cambridge Platonists or the Civil War mystics. That way leads to 'enthusiasm', to false and facile enlightenments. Our knowledge of the mind of God involves an effortful and hard-won inspection of his works, of the natural order he has created. Locke concludes that the only plausible route to moral knowledge is through reason working upon sense experience. Reason therefore does not (blasphemously) *constitute* the natural law, but *finds* it in the world around us. Inspection of God's design of the world will show that we are impelled to social life and the virtues which sustain it. God's 'footsteps' are visible enough. In 'Understanding' (1677) Locke derides empty metaphysical enquiries: our epistemological purposes lie in discovering how we should behave and in 'experimental natural philosophy' to improve our earthly felicity.

Locke's voluntarism and empiricism render all the more puzzling his apparently rationalist and hubristic claims about the demonstrability of moral certainties. In 'Knowledge B' (1681) he first stated that 'morality as well as mathematics [is] capable of demonstration', whereas, by contrast, 'physic' and 'polity' are not capable of demonstration, but rest on opinion and prudent judgement in the light of the 'history of matter of fact'. In 1692 William Molyneux urged Locke to fulfil his aspiration, voiced in the *ECHU*, to explain morality 'demonstrable according to the mathematical method' (Letter 1530). The weaker sense of Locke's claim is that we can elaborate a formal framework consisting in tautological propositions, like 'Where there is no property, there is no injustice', and 'No government allows absolute liberty' (*ECHU*, bk IV, chs. 3, 17). The stronger version is that we can demonstrate substantive moral imperatives. Perhaps something of this sort is intended in his remark, in 'Law' (*c.* 1693), that since laws involve the dependency of one agent upon another, we can deduce our obligations to our Maker and our parallel obligations to our parents. In this sense perhaps, experiential moral knowledge, which must be partial and contingent, is compatible with a type of demonstrability.

No less puzzling, in the face of Locke's rejection of innatism, is his penchant for continuing to refer to moral knowledge in apparently innatist terms. In the *Two Treatises* he writes of the law of nature as 'writ in the hearts of all mankind' (II, §11); elsewhere he talks of what conscience immediately teaches. Locke either failed to resolve his difficulties or was inclined to think of adequate ratiocination in moral matters as amounting to intuitions of such force as to seem like innate ideas. To further compound the difficulties, there are signs that, despairing of the enterprise of demonstrability, he turned, in *The Reasonableness of Christianity* (1695), to an increasing reliance on revelation: the New Testament must supply what reason fails to deliver.

One imperative behind Locke's insistence that nature and reason can teach God's purposes is plain enough: Locke's rejection of innatism and the *sensus communis* imperilled his respectability. Upon reading the *ECHU*, Isaac Newton exclaimed, 'I took you for a Hobbist' (Letter 1659). Locke was at pains to avoid the conclusion (originally sketched in its fiercest form by Thrasymachus in Plato's *Republic*) that morality is a human construct and hence relative to different times and places. The law of nature, he stressed, is perpetual, universal and visible. He was anxious not to be associated with a view which contemporaries attributed to Hobbes: that natural law is so ineffable and ineffectual that it must dissolve into positive law, into the magistrate's sanctions. In the *Two Treatises* Locke even suggested that the law of nature is plainer than positive law (II, §12).

Moreover, for Locke, moral knowledge is available to *any* diligent investigator without reliance upon the authority of princes or priests. The burden of individual responsibility for epistemic effort was great. It could not be usurped by, or sloughed off on to, those who undertook to do our thinking for us. Nonetheless, plainly not everybody embarked upon the requisite rational investigation. Ploughmen and dairymaids were not economically at leisure to do so: it was for them especially, Locke seems to suggest in *The Reasonableness of Christianity*, that Christ's 'republication' of the law of nature in the New Testament offered a readier rule of right conduct.

If the problem of moral knowledge was in principle tractable, not only was it in practice not so, but, worse, knowledge alone would never solve the problem of motivation and obedience. In 'Ethica B' (1693) Locke repeats a crucial distinction between knowledge and motive: we can know what we ought to do, but lack the will to do it; sometimes we neither know nor will – ignorance conspires with depravity. Locke's pessimism about ordinary capacities for reasoning and self-discipline provoked febrile images of moral mayhem, of the 'robberies, murders, rapes, and the sports of men set at liberty from punishment and censure' (*ECHU*, bk I, ch. 3). It was this which made the state of nature, without settled government, so unstable. Locke never underestimated the pressing need for coercive social discipline.

From the mid-1670s he came increasingly to believe that God had structured human psychology as a system of desires and aversions. He was influenced by the Epicurean revival and by his work in translating Nicole's *Moral Essays*. The hedonic turn became starkly visible in 'Pleasure, Pain, the Passions' (1676) and remained a persistent theme in 'Morality' (*c.* 1677–8) and in the important essays, 'Thus I Think' (*c.* 1686–8) and 'Of Ethic in General'. Pleasure and pain are the springs of human action. People 'only and always' desire happiness and the avoidance of misery. With a resolute subjectivism, Locke determines that 'good is what gives or increases pleasure'. Good and bad are 'relative terms' which 'do not denote anything in the nature of the thing' but only an 'aptness and tendency' to produce pleasure and pain ('Of Ethic in General'). This was not to say that happiness is reducible to transitory sensual pleasure or material gain: we are led to complex ideas of happiness which value health, reputation, knowledge, benefiting others and anticipating eternity. Nobody is to be condemned for seeking pleasure, but only for preferring transient worldly pleasures. Since there is, Locke believed, an overwhelming probability of an afterlife and of eternal happiness or misery, we have good and apparent motives to act according to God's will. The pursuit of happiness and avoidance of misery are the levers in the system of rewards and punishments by which the deity, the magistrate and society at large, through opinion and reputation, secure compliance. Similarly, it is the task of educators to break the untutored passions of children and 'by habits establish a contrary pleasure', so that reason, conscience and desire are brought into mature harmony ('Ethica B'). Above all, Locke clung steadfastly, although precariously, to the conviction that there is a divine lawgiver who punishes and rewards and has 'sufficiently promulgated' his will to mankind.

V

In 'Concerning Reading and Study for a Gentleman' (1703) Locke distinguished two aspects of the science of politics, 'the one containing the original of societies, and the rise and extent of political power, the other, the art of governing men in society'. In several

'Adversaria', which laid out a map of the human and physical sciences, Locke likewise contrasted the study of the foundations of the polity with 'prudence', which included the power of the state, its economy and administration and its military might. The *Two Treatises* concerns political legitimacy; in other writings Locke addressed political prudence. Although his authorship of the *Two Treatises* was not commonly known in the 1690s, he was, quite independently, regarded as having 'great judgement' and as being 'very communicative' in 'politics' (Letter 2880).

The *Two Treatises* is nearly silent on the matter, but there is no mystery about the type of polity that Locke thought it prudent to adopt. It was old England's 'Ancient Constitution', comprising monarch, nobility and representatives of the commonalty. This is the regime he presumes in paragraph 213 of the Second Treatise. It is the regime elaborately reproduced for export to North America in *The Fundamental Constitutions of Carolina*, which, under a nominal monarchy, envisaged rule by an hereditary nobility and landed gentlemen, 'that we may avoid erecting a numerous democracy'. It is the regime which the *Letter from a Person of Quality* (1675) pronounced to be under threat from the absolutist aspirations of Charles II's ministers. It is the regime Locke urged upon the Convention which debated the Revolution settlement in February 1689: he told Edward Clarke that the 'settlement of the nation upon the sure grounds of peace and security . . . can no way so well be done as by restoring our ancient government, the best possibly that ever was if taken and put together all of a piece in its original constitution' (Letter 1102). The paradoxical conclusion of the *Two Treatises* is that while a people, in a condition of the dissolution of government, may erect any form of government they think best, it would be sensible for them to recur to the tried and trusted ancient form. When correcting the 1698 edition he adjusted the final sentence so that instead of reading 'place it in a new form, or new hands', it now read 'erect a new form, or under the old form place it in new hands'. Locke was well satisfied that the Glorious Revolution achieved the latter. The new hands were those of King William III, whose servant Locke became.

Locke was endorsing a Whig commonplace. The idea of the Ancient Constitution was a happy fusion of the classical wisdom that the best sort of polity is a mixture of the three pure forms, monarchy, aristocracy and democracy, with a Teutonic mythology about the putative liberties enjoyed by Saxon freemen. Locke felt no need to write a treatise about it: instead he recommended other treatises. In *Some Thoughts Concerning Education* and 'Concerning Reading' he recommended wide reading in English legal history, for 'history ... is the great mistress of prudence and civil knowledge' (*Some Thoughts*, §182). For example, gentlemen should read James Tyrrell's *History of England* and John Sadler's *Rights of the Kingdom*.

Locke's enthusiasm for the finer details of ancient English governance is readily overlooked. Parishes had constables, an office held in rotation by members of village elites; in the West Country they were called tithingmen. In 'Atlantis' Locke specified that each tithing, as the word properly implied, should be constituted by ten households. The tithingman is to register citizens, control vagrancy and visit every household once a month 'to see what lives they lead'. He is also to ensure public assistance for those who are needy through age, sickness, or burden of children. *The Constitutions of Carolina* stipulates a complex structure of local government officers: justices, sheriffs, stewards, jurymen, constables and registrars.

Under the Elizabethan Poor Laws, parishes chose overseers of the poor, who disciplined the idle and succoured the deserving indigent. In *An Essay on the Poor Law* Locke sought to improve Poor Law administration. The guardians of the poor were to create working-schools and require local craftsmen and farmers to employ apprentices when pupils left the schools. Locke pictures a commonwealth of virtuous and industrious rate-payers, 'virtue and industry being ... constant companions'. These citizens are distinguished from those who are 'utter strangers to industry, morality and religion', whom they are to reform. They govern their communities, but also take on a burden of obligations, for they should be fined if they negligently let poor people die. They elect churchwardens and guardians, the latter serving for a fixed term of three years, one third standing down each year.

Locke's vision of English local administration mirrors the extensive practice of neighbourhood self-government which historians have discovered in early modern England. In the interstices of the monarchical polity, a plurality of small-scale quasi-republican 'commonwealths' flourished. They gave practical expression to the twin ideals of citizen participation (drawn chiefly from Cicero's *Offices*) and godly 'reformation of manners'. In 'Concerning Reading' Locke specified two books to be read on morality: Cicero's *Offices* and the New Testament.

There is, however, a contrasting aspect to Locke's reflections on political prudence. He envisaged using traditional methods of self-government as instruments of national economic regeneration. From his notes on 'Trade' (1674) through to his memoranda for the Board of Trade and his papers on coinage and the naturalisation of immigrants in the 1690s, Locke sought to give strength to what the mercantilists saw as the twin pillars of national statecraft, the advancement of trade and the maximisation of labour power. In a late addition to the *Two Treatises* he wrote that 'the increase of hands and the right employing of them is the great art of government' (II, §42). In *An Essay on the Poor Law* parishes were to establish a network of textile workshops. The poor were to be made 'useful to the public', for 'things should be so ordered' that no labour 'should be lost'. Locke did not conceive of market constraints on the availability of work: those who did not labour were either idle or physically unable. He used a national calculus which the new practitioners of 'political arithmetic' were establishing. This showed that 100,000 semi-able poor, currently idle, put to work for six days a week, and earning threepence a day, would gain the kingdom £400,000 per annum.

For the political arithmeticians, a state's productive powers were directly correlated with its population. Locke's energetic commitment to government action to increase population is an unexpected aspect of his thought. In 'Atlantis' he wrote that a 'multitude of strong and healthy people bring the riches of every country'. Progenitiveness was to be encouraged by tax concessions and exemptions from public office. Unmarried men over forty were to have their inheritance rights curtailed. Barren women might be divorced. In a deleted passage, men were permitted bigamy. In 'Virtue B' (1681) Locke wrote of the female sex that 'the chief end of her being [is] the propagation of mankind'.

In the domain of Lockean political prudence, ancient communalism sits alongside modern state-building. The English state after the Glorious Revolution had the same cross-grained character. After 1689 prolonged war with France prompted unprecedented growth of the 'fiscal–military state', which increasingly brought the imperatives of political economy and imperial commerce within the ambit of government. Locke was an agent of the most ambitious programme of state-building yet undertaken by England's rulers. As a Commissioner for Appeals in Excise he was a servant of the growing fiscal civil service; as a member of the Board of Trade he was a busy drafter of memoranda on imperial and commercial policy.

Locke's polity, both at parish and national level, was a much governed one. He was a patron of minimal government only in certain, if crucial, ways. He stressed what government was not about: it did not exist to save souls, nor to censor intellectual speculation. But it did exist to create the circumstances of earthly well-being. Propitious circumstances did not come about by accident: they required an effort of public policy-making. The Glorious Revolution defeated absolute monarchy but strengthened executive power. As a theorist of political prudence Locke harnessed the 'Ancient Constitution' on behalf of the Whig state-builders who seized the reins of government in the 1690s.

By placing the writings contained in the present volume alongside the *Two Treatises*, these characteristics of Locke's political thought become visible. For, to understand Locke aright, some demanding juxtapositions must be made between the private papers generated during half a century's reflection upon human sociability and governance and the canonised text of modern liberal constitutionalism.

Principal events in Locke's life

1671?–5   Serves as secretary to the Lords Proprietors of Carolina (perhaps from 1669).

1671   Begins *An Essay Concerning Human Understanding.*

1672   Lord Ashley created Earl of Shaftesbury and appointed Lord Chancellor. The King issues his Declaration of Indulgence (an edict of religious toleration).

1672–3   Serves as Secretary for Presentations (to church livings).

1673–4   Secretary to the Council of Trade and Plantations.

1673   The conversion to Catholicism of the King's brother and heir, James, Duke of York, made public. Shaftesbury ousted from office.

1675   The Shaftesburian manifesto published: *A Letter from a Person of Quality to his Friend in the Country.*

1675–9   Travels in France, residing chiefly in Montpellier; from mid-1677 to mid-1678 in Paris.

1676   Translates Nicole's *Essais de Morale.*

1678   Popish Plot revealed.

1679   Death of Thomas Hobbes. Locke returns to London.

1679–81   Exclusion Crisis: attempt to exclude James, Duke of York, from succession to the throne. Party names 'Whig' and 'Tory' coined.

1680   Publication of Sir Robert Filmer's *Patriarcha.*

1680–3   Resides in Oxford, London and Oakley, James Tyrrell's seat in Buckinghamshire. Writes *Two Treatises of Government.*

1681   Meeting and abrupt dismissal of Charles II's last parliament, at Oxford. Shaftesbury charged with treason, a Whig grand jury dismisses the charge. Locke writes a defence of toleration against Edward Stillingfleet.

1682   Tory coup against Whig leadership in the City of London. Flight of Shaftesbury to Holland.

1683   Rye House Plot. Execution of Algernon Sidney and Lord William Russell; suicide of the Earl of Essex in the Tower; death of Shaftesbury in Holland.

1683–9   In exile in Holland, mainly in Utrecht and Amsterdam until early 1687, then in Rotterdam.

1684   Expelled from Studentship of Christ Church. Writes his first letter to Edward Clarke concerning his son's education.

1685 Death of Charles II; accession of James II. Rebellion of the Duke of Monmouth, who is defeated at Sedgemoor and executed. Locke in hiding in Amsterdam. He writes the *Epistola de Tolerantia.*

1686 *An Essay Concerning Human Understanding* substantially finished during this year.

1687 Publication of Isaac Newton's *Principia.*

1688 Glorious Revolution: invasion of England by Prince William of Orange and flight of James II. The *Abrégé* of Locke's *Essay* published.

1689 Accession of William III and Mary II. Declaration and Bill of Rights. Act of Toleration. War against Louis XIV of France. Locke returns to England in February. Appointed Commissioner of Excise Appeals. Publication in the autumn of *Two Treatises* (dated 1690), *Essay Concerning Human Understanding* (dated 1690) and *Letter Concerning Toleration.*

1690 Battle of the Boyne: William defeats James in Ireland. Locke settles at Oates in Essex in Damaris Masham's household.

1691 Publication of *Some Considerations of the Consequences of the Lowering of Interest and Raising the Value of Money* (dated 1692).

1692 Publication of *A Third Letter for Toleration.* Opens a correspondence with William Molyneux.

1693 Publication of *Some Thoughts Concerning Education.*

1694 Triennial Act, requiring regular general elections. Foundation of the Bank of England.

1695 Advises on the ending of press censorship and on the great recoinage. Publication of *The Reasonableness of Christianity* and of its first *Vindication.*

1696 Appointed a member of the Board of Trade and Plantations; serves until 1700. Publication of *Further Considerations concerning Raising the Value of Money.*

1697 Publication of *A Second Vindication of the Reasonableness of Christianity.* His controversy with Bishop Edward Stillingfleet over the *ECHU* at its height.

1700 Pierre Coste's French translation of the *ECHU* published.

1701   The Act of Settlement ensures the Protestant (Hanoverian) succession.

1702   Death of William III; accession of Queen Anne.

1704   Duke of Marlborough's victory over France at Blenheim. Locke completes his *Paraphrase and Notes on the Epistles of St Paul*. Dies at Oates, 28 October. Buried in High Laver churchyard, Essex.

Further reading

No complete edition of Locke's *Works* has been published since the nineteenth century: the tenth edition of 1801 is most often cited. Volumes published so far in the Clarendon Edition of the Works of John Locke are: De Beer 1976–89, Kelly 1991, Nidditch 1975, Nidditch and Rogers 1990, Wainright 1987, Yolton and Yolton 1989. The Cambridge Texts in the History of Political Thought series will include three volumes of Locke's writings: the *Two Treatises of Government* (Laslett 1960, reissued 1988), the present volume, and writings on toleration, edited by James Tully. Besides Laslett's there are many editions of the *Two Treatises*; the most recent is Goldie 1993. For the *Essay Concerning Human Understanding* see editions by Nidditch 1975 and Yolton 1976. There are several editions of the *Letter Concerning Toleration*, but see especially Tully 1983 and Horton and Mendus 1991. Other modern editions of Locke's writings are: Aaron and Gibb 1936, Abrams 1967, Axtell 1968, Klibansky and Gough 1968, Lough 1953, Montuori 1963, Viano 1961, Von Leyden 1954, Wootton 1993. A volume of selected correspondence will be published by Oxford University Press in 1998.

The major biographies are King 1829, Fox Bourne 1876, and Cranston 1957; see also Dewhurst 1963 and Ashcraft 1986. The political and intellectual background can be explored in Appleby 1978, Burns and Goldie 1991, Daly 1979, Dunn 1980, Haley 1968, Horne 1990, Kenyon 1977, Phillipson and Skinner 1993, Pocock 1957, 1975 and 1985, Schochet 1975, Scott 1991, Skinner 1978, Tuck 1979, and Western 1972.

Introductions to Locke's ideas can be found in Yolton 1993 and

Chappell 1994. Short surveys of Locke's political thought are Parry 1978 and Dunn 1984; a longer account is Ashcraft 1987. The most challenging re-interpretations in recent times were offered by Macpherson 1962 and Dunn 1969. Macpherson's vision of the bourgeois Locke is modified in Wood 1983 and 1984 and McNally 1988. Dunn's emphasis on the centrality of Locke's religious commitments and their implications for his thinking on ethics, toleration and civil society are pursued in Harris 1994 and Marshall 1994. For Locke as a theorist of natural rights and private property see Schouls 1992, Simmons 1992 and 1993, Tully 1980 and 1993, Von Leyden 1981, Waldron 1988. For the 'Chicago school' view of Locke as a conservative liberal see Cox 1960, Grant 1987, Tarcov 1984. For a feminist approach see Pateman 1988. For Locke on toleration see Horton and Mendus 1991.

The circumstances in which Locke wrote and published the *Two Treatises* and the extent of his personal involvement in radical politics are considered in Laslett 1960 and Wootton 1993, in greatest depth in Ashcraft 1986, and also in Franklin 1978 and Marshall 1994. For Locke on, and in, America see Dworetz 1990 and Tully 1993. Valuable collections of essays are Yolton 1969, Brandt 1981, and Rogers 1994.

Scholarly articles on Locke appear at the rate of about one a week: a small selection is listed in the Bibliography. Recent debates are best approached through *The Historical Journal, History of Political Thought, The Journal of the History of Ideas, Political Studies,* and *Political Theory.* Ashcraft 1991 gathers over one hundred articles on Locke, Blaug 1991 gathers articles on the background to his economic thought. Works which pay close attention to the material in Locke's journals and notebooks are: Cox 1960, Driscoll 1972, Dunn 1967, 1968 and 1969, Gough 1950, Harris 1994, Marshall 1994, and Tully 1980.

Fuller bibliographies of works about Locke are: Attig 1985, Christopherson 1930, Hall and Woolhouse 1983, Yolton and Yolton 1985; there is an annual update in *The Locke Newsletter.* For descriptions of Locke's manuscripts see: Long 1959 and 1964, Lough 1953 (Appx C), Milton 1996b, Schankula 1973. Other items in the Bibliography print texts by Locke or provide technical discussion of such texts: they are cited at appropriate points throughout this book.

A note on the selection

Evidence for Locke's opinions on politics and society can be gleaned from practically everything he wrote. Once we step beyond the *Two Treatises of Government* and the *Letter Concerning Toleration* we might turn in several directions, particularly to the *Essay Concerning Human Understanding* (and its earlier versions, known as Drafts A, B and C), to *Some Thoughts Concerning Education*, and to the series of writings on economics and the coinage. (The political implications of the *Essay* are discussed in Tully 1980 and Wood 1983, of *Education* in Tarcov 1984, and of the economic writings in Kelly 1991.) It is not, however, the purpose of this volume to anthologise from Locke's major works.

Constraints of space have forced the exclusion of some important texts with a bearing on politics, church government and human conduct. One significant victim is *The Conduct of the Understanding* (written in 1697, first published in 1706), a work often overlooked. Sections 8, 10 and 23, on Religion, Prejudice and Theology, are especially illuminating. Another serious omission (except for a brief extract in the Appendix) is the tolerationist *Critical Notes on Stillingfleet* (*c.* 1681). It is a long treatise and by far the most important of Locke's works never yet published. It will in due course appear in the Clarendon Edition of the Works of John Locke. A further omission is the essay on *The Grievances of Virginia*, which offers prescriptions for colonial government (see Ashcraft 1969, Farr 1986, Kammen 1966). Another is *Some Consequences that are Like to Follow upon Lessening of Interest to 4 per cent* (1668), which laid the groundwork for Locke's tracts on money published in the 1690s and casts considerable light on his economic thought (see Kelly

1988, 1991; Letwin 1963). Absent too, and thus perpetuating its almost total neglect, is Locke's *Memoir of the Life of Lord Shaftesbury* (*Works* 1801, IX, 266–81).

Another self-denying ordinance has been the exclusion of any of Locke's letters. Many of these are of great importance for understanding his political thought. However, a volume of *Selected Correspondence* will be published by Oxford University Press shortly after the appearance of this collection and may fruitfully be read in conjunction with this. (There is some textual overlap between Locke's 'letters' and 'essays': for example, 'Enthusiasm' (1682), printed here, overlaps with letters written to Damaris Masham, while the 'essays' on recreation and scrupulosity formed letters to Dennis Grenville and appear in the *Selected Correspondence*.)

Many of Locke's surviving essays and memoranda lie at the boundaries between politics, philosophy and theology. In selecting from among these I have chosen the philosophical pieces which have greatest bearing on ethics, rather than on epistemology, and from the religious pieces those which have most to do with toleration and ecclesiology rather than soteriology or Scriptural hermeneutics. I have tried to include all Locke's discussions of the topic that constantly vexed him, the demonstrability of moral knowledge. How many of the journal entries written during the 1670s and 1680s were intended to be preparatory drafts towards the *Essay Concerning Human Understanding* is a complex question which I do not attempt to resolve. Of Locke's guidance on political education I have selected his 'Thoughts concerning Reading' and, in the Appendix, an extract from 'Study'.

I have included several items that have not hitherto appeared in print. There remain others yet to be disinterred from Locke's journals and notebooks, although most of them are brief and epigrammatic – such as his sardonic pronouncement that 'When anyone boasts or makes a show of anything he can do or has done 'tis a sign 'tis new or unusual to him and that he has it not in perfection' (MS Locke, c. 33, fo. 23); or, that the Biblical date of Creation (4004 BC) must be accurate because it is improbable that 'philosophy [would] not be found out by the inquisitive mind of man till a little before Tully's [Cicero's] time' (MS Locke, f. 7, pp. 35–6).

There remain doubts about the reliability of the attribution of some texts to Locke. As with other great authors, the canon was apt to grow, especially at the hands of eighteenth-century editors. I hope to have included only items which can with reasonable certainty be assigned to Locke and to have signalled any doubts in the headnotes. The most problematic cases are *The Fundamental Constitutions of Carolina*, printed here in full, and the *Letter from a Person of Quality to his Friend in the Country*, extracts from which are in the Appendix. The presence here of the *Carolina* essay is, in my view, fully justified by the evidence that Locke strongly associated himself with it. The issue of authorship also arises in the case of Locke's position papers prepared for the Board of Trade in the late 1690s. We can be confident of his authorship of the *Essay on the Poor Law*, but other papers are less securely attributed to him because they were signed by several members of the Board. This is the case with a paper on the Irish linen industry (printed in the *Journals of the House of Commons*, 1803, pp. 427–30; and Fox Bourne 1876, II, 263–72; discussed in Kearney 1959 and Kelly 1988). The *Poor Law* essay is the only Board of Trade paper included here.

The most treacherous area of authorial doubt lies in the Shaftesbury Papers in the Public Record Office. This jumble of material deriving from different sources and including position papers prepared within the Earl of Shaftesbury's entourage makes attribution difficult. Many papers crossed Locke's desk in his capacity as secretary. For example, 'The Particular Test for Priests' is not in Locke's hand but is endorsed by him: I have included this because in fact it is found in the less problematical Lovelace Collection. Some scholars have attached views about church power to Locke on the basis of two papers concerning ecclesiastical jurisdiction, which are Erastian in tone, and date from around 1670: they are in the Shaftesbury Papers (PRO 30/24/6B/429–30). There is no persuasive reason to attribute them to Locke and I have not included them. In the Shaftesbury Papers also is the medical text most often cited in more general discussions of Locke's philosophy, 'De Arte Medica' (1669), though it may have been written by Thomas Sydenham (Dewhurst 1966, pp. 79–84; Fox Bourne 1876, I, 222–7).

There are other apocrypha too. In 1876 Fox Bourne attributed the *Reflections upon the Roman Commonwealth* to Locke; it is in fact by Walter Moyle and is printed in Robbins 1969; the mistake was copied in the *Dictionary of National Biography*. Fox Bourne also wrongly ascribed to Locke an essay on *Old England's Legal Constitution* (1695), a mistake still occasionally repeated. Likewise, the item called 'Philosophy' that occurs in his father's notebook is not by Locke (BL, Add. MS 28,273; Fox Bourne 1876, I, 70–1): it is a précis from William Baldwin's Puritan classic, *A Treatise of Moral Philosophy* (1620). In Locke's own time other works were falsely ascribed to him, either out of political animus, such as the seditious Whig tract, *No Protestant Plot* (1681), probably by Robert Ferguson, or from presumed similitude of thought, such as Damaris Masham's *Discourse Concerning the Love of God* (1696). On Locke apocrypha see Attig 1985, pp. 159–65; Milton 1996a.

Attribution is difficult even within Locke's own papers in the Lovelace Collection for another reason. His notebooks are full of material gleaned from his reading and, although he generally marked his own thoughts with his initials, it is not always clear when a piece of text is his. Moreover, he often used an amanuensis, so that some texts that are assumed to be his do not exist in his own hand.

Textual scholars will continue to fret about attribution. Meanwhile other scholars are busy dissolving the concept of authorship. Without succumbing to Pyrrhonian doubt, it is worth concluding with the thought that, like all of us, Locke spoke to different audiences in different ways, modulated his thoughts according to circumstances, uttered what was apposite within the dynamic of particular disputes, and collaborated with colleagues in formulating 'his' ideas. Furthermore, by the scholastic protocols practised in seventeenth-century universities, the pedagogic business of commenting upon and elaborating others' texts was sometimes scarcely distinguishable from what we might today call plagiarism. It is not always helpful to think of Locke's writings as solitary and unmediated inventions.

A note on the texts

Almost nothing about Locke is uncontroversial and this is as true for the transcription, dating and entitling of his texts as it is for the interpretation of his thought. This edition is designed to make Locke's texts accessible to students and scholars. It aims to provide a reliable version, but it does not aspire to offer the apparatus of a critical edition. Hardly any of the texts printed here was published in Locke's lifetime and we rely upon his often unpolished and heavily corrected manuscripts, the proper rendering of which is a complex and vexed matter. Moreover, Locke sometimes wrote in shorthand. I necessarily rely upon editors who have gone before me, as most of the texts included here have been published previously. The texts of the *Tracts on Government* and the *Essays on the Law of Nature* are derived from the Abrams and Von Leyden editions, respectively, without recourse to the original manuscripts. In most other cases texts have been transcribed from printed editions but have been checked and corrected against the manuscripts: this has yielded a significant crop of corrections to earlier editions, and in some cases missing passages have been restored. Except for what is in the Appendix, no texts have been abridged.

The spelling and capitalisation of Locke's texts have been modernised (except in the case of poetry). Contractions have been expanded (e.g. 'ye', 'yt'). Compounds have been elided (e.g. 'every one', 'any one'). Punctuation has sometimes been adjusted to improve the sense. In a handful of cases, slips of the pen have been silently corrected, where Locke's intention is obvious. Marginal and interlinear insertions are generally silently incorporated, and deleted passages are not recorded except where they seem especially significant. Square brackets indicate editorial interpolations.

Each text is preceded by a headnote. These record the provenance of the text, together with information on previous English-language printings. Where appropriate, the headnotes provide a summary of the text and a brief explanation of the context of its writing. They also indicate any peculiarities as to the titles of texts. Often Locke provided no title and this generates confusion where scholars have ascribed differing titles: I have tried not to multiply this confusion. In the case of Locke's journals, titles are constituted by the keywords he wrote in the margins.

The first modern attempt to print substantial extracts from Locke's unpublished papers was made by Lord King. I give citations to the 1829 and 1830 editions, which are differently paginated. To have provided extensive references to modern discussions of Locke's texts in the headnotes would have consumed an inordinate amount of space and over-extended the bibliography. However, I indicate all cases where texts have been cited by Peter Laslett in the notes to his authoritative edition of the *Two Treatises of Government*. I also indicate items in Locke's correspondence which have bearing on the texts.

The dating of some of Locke's essays is not secure. The most vexed area is the material in the notebook 'Adversaria 1661' (see Milton 1993). Despite its title, it includes material down to the 1690s. Earlier scholars were led to place the items much earlier in time, with consequent distortions in interpretation. Fox Bourne's picture of Locke (1876) as a 'liberal' from an early age stems partly from this error. Material in MS Locke, c. 28 is also difficult to date.

Footnoting has been minimised. The notes aim only to explicate puzzling words and phrases and allusions to books, persons and events. Occasionally they record textual variants. They do not offer analytic commentary and only very rarely provide cross-references to passages elsewhere in Locke's writings. I follow Locke's own injunction: he preferred editors to record 'the design of each [text] and the time when it was writ' and not to 'tire the reader with a useless ostentation of pedantic citations or contentions' (MS Locke, c. 33, fo. 25).

Abbreviations and conventions

Throughout this book the author–date system of referencing is used: full publication details are given in the bibliography at the end. References to Locke's letters follow the numeration supplied by Esmond De Beer in *The Correspondence of John Locke* (1976–89). 'MS Locke' refers to papers in the Lovelace Collection in the Bodleian Library, Oxford. 'PRO' refers to the Shaftesbury and Board of Trade papers in Public Record Office, London. 'BL' refers to the British Library, London. 'Adversaria 1661' (also known as the '1661 Commonplace Book') is in private hands (previously owned by Arthur A. Houghton, Jr, New York, and now by Henri Schiller of Paris); it is available in the Bodleian Library, MS Film 77. Locke, *Works* refers to the edition of 1801. *ECHU* stands for *An Essay Concerning Human Understanding* (Nidditch 1975 is the standard edition). *ELN* stands for *Essays on the Law of Nature*.

The conventional form of reference to statutes was by regnal year and chapter in that year's enrolment of Acts. In the seventeenth century one pound (£) was made up of twenty shillings (s), and one shilling of twelve pennies (d).

Major Essays

First Tract on Government

1660 (September–December; preface added *c*. May 1661). The title is a modern usage, ascribed by Philip Abrams; also known as 'the English tract'. MS headed: 'Question: Whether the Civil Magistrate may lawfully impose and determine the use of indifferent things in reference to Religious Worship'. MS Locke, e. 7; the preface is in MS Locke, c. 28, fos. 1–2. Printed in Viano 1961, pp. 14–61; Abrams 1967, pp. 117–75; extracts in King 1829, pp. 8–9; 1830, I, 13–15; Gough 1950, pp. 179–80; Wootton 1993, pp. 141–51. Discussed in Cranston 1957, pp. 59–63; Von Leyden 1954, pp. 21–30; Abrams 1967; Dunn 1969, ch. 2. Cited by Laslett, *First Treatise*, §§125, 131. The text printed here is reproduced from the Abrams edition. Locke's quotations from Edward Bagshaw are placed in inverted commas, with page references supplied in brackets. His incomplete or mistaken citations from Scripture are silently corrected. Locke's distinctions and divisions are complex: I have augmented his numeration to clarify the structure of the argument. Several items in Locke's correspondence relate to this tract: Letters 43, 66, 75, 81, 106, 108, 115, 118, 123, 127, 129. The antepenultimate paragraph of the Preface repeats verbatim the second half of Letter 108 (11 December 1660). Locke's colleagues urged him to publish his tract and he seriously considered doing so.

Locke's tract is a reply to Edward Bagshaw, *The Great Question Concerning Things Indifferent in Religious Worship* (September 1660), who is 'our author' referred to throughout; Locke's heading repeats the subtitle of Bagshaw's tract. 'Things indifferent' (also called 'adiaphora') were those aspects of worship (or belief) which were held not to have been prescribed by God in Scripture, and hence could legitimately be varied or used permissively, or prescribed by the civil magistrate without injury to conscience; they stood in contrast to 'things necessary' for salvation. Many Puritans objected to the set formularies of the Book of Common Prayer, and to the 'popish' practices of wearing the surplice and kneeling before the eucharistic sacrament. Some of the earlier treatises in the debate were: Richard Hooker, *Of the Laws of Ecclesiastical Polity* (1593–1661); William Ames, *Conscience* (1634); Henry Hammond, *Of Conscience* (1644); and Jeremy Taylor, *The Liberty of Prophesying* (1647). At the Restoration the debate intensified, the chief tracts being: Henry Jeanes, *A Treatise Concerning Indifferency* (1659); Henry Hammond, *A Vindication of Uniformity* (1659); Robert Sanderson, *De Obligatione Conscientiae* (1660); Edward Stillingfleet, *Irenicum* (1660). Locke mentions Hooker and Sanderson in his text. At the Restoration, the character of the re-established church at first remained unresolved, and many people hoped for a 'comprehensive' settlement which would be tolerant of both Puritan and Anglican practices. The matter was settled by the narrowly Anglican Act of Uniformity of 1662, which drove the Puritans from the fold of the established church. Locke's tract, though a technical treatise on ecclesiology, reveals much about his early political thinking.

He proceeds as follows. He begins with some premises and a general claim for magisterial imposition in indifferent things. Then the main body of the tract counters four of Bagshaw's claims: (I) if Christian magistrates cannot impose their religion on Jews and Muslims, they cannot impose on Christians either; (II) impositions are contrary to Gospel injunctions; (III) impositions are contrary to the practice of Jesus Christ and the apostles; (IV) impositions are politically and socially imprudent.

The Preface to the Reader

Reader

This discourse which was written many months since, had not been more than written now but had still lain concealed in a secure privacy, had not importunity prevailed against my intentions, and forced it into the public. I shall not trouble thee with the history or occasion of its original, though it be certain that thou here receivest from me a present, which was not at first designed thee. This confession how little soever obliging, I the more easily make since I am not very solicitous what entertainment it shall receive, and if truth (which I only aim at) suffer not by this edition, I am very secure as to everything else. To bespeak thy impartial perusal were to expect more from thee than books, especially of this nature, usually meet with; and I should too fondly promise myself the good hap [fortune] to meet with that temper that this age is scarcely blessed with; wherein truth is seldom allowed a fair hearing, and the generality of men, conducted either by chance or advantage, take to themselves their opinions as they do their wives, which when they have once espoused them think themselves concerned to maintain, though for no other reason but because they are theirs, being as tender of the credit of one as of the other, and if 'twere left to their own choice, 'tis not improbable that this would be the more difficult divorce.

My design being only the clearing a truth in question, I shall be very glad if I have said anything that may satisfy her impartial followers, being otherwise very careless how little soever I gratify the interests, or fancies of others. However that I may not give any advantage to this partial humour I shall take the same way to prevent it that the gentleman whom I trace hath trod before me, and by concealing my name leave thee concerned for nothing but the arguments themselves.

And indeed besides the reasons that persuaded my author to conceal himself there be many other that more strongly oblige me to it. Amongst others I should be sure to incur the censure of many of my acquaintance. For having always professed myself an enemy to the scribbling of this age and often accused the pens of Englishmen of as much guilt as their swords, judging that the issue of blood from whence such an inundation hath flowed had scarce been opened, or at least not so long unstopped had men been more sparing of their ink, and that these furies, war, cruelty, rapine, confusion, etc., which have so wearied and wasted this poor nation have been conjured up in private studies and from thence sent abroad to disturb the quiet we enjoyed. This objection then will lie against me, that I now run upon the same guilt I condemned in others, disturbing the beginnings of our happy settlement by engaging in a quarrel, and bandying a question which it would be well if it were quite forgotten, and hath been but too loudly disputed already. But

I hope I shall deserve no more blame than he that takes arms only to keep the peace and draws his sword in the same side with the magistrate, with a design to suppress, not begin a quarrel.

I could heartily wish that all disputes of this nature would cease, that men would rather be content to enjoy the freedom they have, than by such questions increase at once their own suspicions and disquiets, and the magistrate's trouble; such discourses, however cautiously proposed, with desire of search and satisfaction being understood usually rather to speak [of] discontents than doubts, and increase the one rather than remove the other. And however sincere the author may be, the interested and prejudiced reader not seldom greedily entertains them as the just reproaches of the state, and hence takes the boldness to censure the miscarriages of the magistrate and question the equity and obligation of all laws which have not the good luck to square with his private judgement.

I confess it cannot be thought, but that men should fly from oppression, but disorder will give them but an incommodious sanctuary. 'Tis not without reason that tyranny and anarchy are judged the smartest scourges [that] can fall upon mankind, the plea of authority usually backing the one and of liberty inducing the other: and between these two it is, that human affairs are perpetually kept tumbling. Nor is it to be hoped that the prudence of man should provide against these, beyond any fear of their return, so long as men have either ambitious thoughts or discontented minds, or till the greatest part of men are well satisfied in their own condition; which is not to be looked for in this world. All the remedy that can be found is when the prince makes the good of the people the measure of his injunctions and the people without examining the reasons, pay a ready and entire obedience, and both these founded on a mutual confidence each of [the] other, which is the greatest security and happiness of any people, and a blessing, if ever, to expect now, and to be found amongst those many miracles that have restored (and we hope will continue) his majesty to us, very pregnant assurances whereof we have received in that great tenderness and affection to his people which his majesty beyond parallel hath shown in the transactions of the late and [the] opening of the present parliament.[1]

---

[1] The 'late parliament' is the Convention Parliament (1660–1), which restored the monarchy; 'the present parliament' is the Cavalier Parliament, which opened on 8 May 1661.

As for myself, there is no one [that] can have a greater respect and veneration for authority than I. I no sooner perceived myself in the world but I found myself in a storm, which hath lasted almost hitherto, and therefore cannot but entertain the approaches of a calm with the greatest joy and satisfaction; and this methinks obliges me, both in duty and gratitude to be chary of such a blessing, and [to do] what lies in me to endeavour its continuance, by disposing men's minds to obedience to that government which hath brought with it that quiet and settlement which our own giddy folly had put beyond the reach, not only of our contrivance, but hopes. And I would men would be persuaded to be so kind to their religion, their country and themselves as not to hazard again the substantial blessings of peace and settlement in an over-zealous contention about things, which they themselves confess to be little and at most are but indifferent.

Besides the submission I have for authority I have no less a love of liberty without which a man shall find himself less happy than a beast. Slavery being a condition that robs us of all the benefits of life, and embitters the greatest blessings, reason itself in slaves (which is the grand privilege of other men) increasing the weight of their chains and joining with their oppressions to torment them. But since I find that a general freedom is but a general bondage, that the popular assertors of public liberty are the greatest engrossers of it too and not unfitly called its keepers, and I know not whether experience (if it may be credited) would not give us some reason to think that were this part of freedom contended for here by our author generally indulged in England it would prove only a liberty for contention, censure and persecution and turn us loose to the tyranny of a religious rage; were every indifferent thing left unlimited nothing would be lawful and 'twould quickly be found that the practice of indifferent things not approved by dissenting parties, would then be judged as anti-Christian and unlawful as their injunction is now, and engage the heads and hands of the zealous partisans in the necessary duty of reformation, and it may well be feared by any that will but consider the conscientious disorders amongst us that the several bands of saints would not want their Venners[2] to animate and lead them on in the work of the Lord:

---

[2] On 6 January 1661 the Fifth Monarchist Thomas Venner staged a minor uprising in London: it exacerbated the national backlash against the sects.

Summus utrimque
Inde furor vulgo, quod numina vicinorum
Odit uterque locus, quum solos credat habendos
Esse deos, quos ipse colit.[3]

And he must confess himself a stranger to England that thinks that meats and habits, that places and times of worship, etc., would not be as sufficient occasion of hatred and quarrels amongst us, as leeks and onions and other trifles described in that satire by Juvenal was amongst them, and be distinctions able to keep us always at a distance, and eagerly ready for like violence and cruelty as often as the teachers should alarm the consciences of their zealous votaries and direct them against the adverse party.

I have not therefore the same apprehensions of liberty that I find some have or can think the benefits of it to consist in a liberty for men at pleasure to adopt themselves children of God, and from thence assume a title to inheritance here and proclaim themselves heirs of the world; not a liberty for ambition to pull down well-framed constitutions, that out of its ruins they may build themselves fortunes; not a liberty to be Christians so as not to be subjects; nor such a liberty as is like to engage us in perpetual dissension and disorder. All the freedom I can wish my country or myself is to enjoy the protection of those laws which the prudence and providence of our ancestors established and the happy return of his majesty hath restored: a body of laws so well composed, that whilst this nation would be content only to be under them they were always sure to be above their neighbours, which forced from the world this constant acknowledgement, that we were not only the happiest state but the purest church of the latter age.

'Tis therefore in defence of the authority of these laws that against many reasons I am drawn to appear in public, the preservation whereof as the only security I can yet find of this nation's settlement I think myself concerned in, till I can find other reasons than I have yet met with to show their non-obligation as long as unrepealed, and dispense with my obedience. After this I hope I need not assure thee that neither vanity nor any pique against the

---

[3] 'Each party is filled with fury against the other because each hates its neighbours' gods, believing that none can be holy but those it worships itself': Juvenal, *Satires*, xv.

author put the pen into my hand, the concealment we both lie under having sufficiently provided against that suspicion. I dare say could his opinion have ever won upon me, it would have been in that handsome dress and those many ornaments his pen hath bestowed upon it with all the advantages it was capable of. But I cannot relinquish the contrary persuasion whilst truth (at least in my apprehension) so strongly declares for it, and I believe he cannot take it ill that whilst he pleads so earnestly for liberty in actions I should be unwilling to have my understanding, the noblest part, imposed on, and will not be so forgetful of his own principles as to deny me the liberty of dissenting; and if he will permit himself to peruse these answers with the same desire of satisfaction wherewith he professes himself to have proposed his doubts, and I assure him I read them, it may be hoped he will be persuaded if not to alter his judgement yet at least not to think them blind who cannot see in his spectacles or cannot find themselves by his arguments freed from that obedience to the civil magistrate in all things indifferent, which obedience God in his infinite wisdom hath made necessary and therefore not left free.

I have chose[n] to draw a great part of my discourse from the sup-position of the magistrate's power, derived from, or conveyed to him by, the consent of the people, as a way best suited to those patrons of liberty, and most likely to obviate their objections, the foundation of their plea being usually an opinion of their natural freedom, which they are apt to think too much entrenched upon by impositions in things indifferent. Not that I intend to meddle with that question whether the magistrate's crown drops down on his head immediately from heaven or be placed there by the hands of his subjects, it being sufficient to my purpose that the supreme magistrate of every nation what way soever created, must necessarily have an absolute and arbi-trary power over all the indifferent actions of his people. And if his authority must needs be of so large an extent in the lowest and nar-rowest way of its original (that can be supposed) when derived from the scanty allowance of the people, who are never forward to part with more of their liberty than needs must, I think it will clearly follow, that if he receive his commission immediately from God the people will have little reason thereupon to think it more confined than if he received it from them until they can produce the charter of their own liberty, or the limitation of the legislator's authority, from the same

God that gave it. Otherwise no doubt, those indifferent things that God hath not forbid or commanded, his vicegerent may, having no other rule to direct his commands than every single person hath for his actions, viz.: the law of God; and it will be granted that the people have but a poor pretence to liberty in indifferent things in a condition wherein they have no liberty at all, but by the appointment of the great sovereign of heaven and earth are born subjects to the will and pleasure of another.

But I shall not build upon this foundation, but allowing every man by nature as large a liberty as he himself can wish, shall yet make it appear that whilst there is society, government and order in the world, rulers still must have the power of all things indifferent which I hope (Reader) thou wilt find evident in the following pages whither I remit thee.

Only give me leave first to say that it would be a strange thing if anyone amongst us should question the obligation of those laws which are not ratified nor imposed on him but by his own consent in parliament.

Question: Whether the civil magistrate may lawfully impose and determine the use of indifferent things in reference to religious worship

In order to the clearer debating this question, besides the granting my author's two suppositions, viz.: (i) that a Christian may be a magistrate, (ii) that there are some things indifferent, it will not be amiss to premiss some few things about these matters of indifferency, viz.:

(1) That were there no law there would be no moral good or evil, but man would be left to a most entire liberty in all his actions, and could meet with nothing which would not be purely indifferent, and consequently, that what doth not lie under the obligation of any law is still indifferent.

(2) That nobody hath a natural original power and disposure of this liberty of man but only God himself, from whose authority all laws do fundamentally derive their obligation, as being either immediately enjoined by him, or framed by some authority derived from him.

(3) That wherever God hath made known his will either by the discoveries of reason, usually called the law of nature, or the revel-

ations of his word, there nothing is left man but submission and obedience, and all things within the compass of this law are necessarily and indispensably good or evil.

(4) That all things not comprehended in that law are perfectly indifferent and as to them man is naturally free, but yet so much master of his own liberty, that he may by compact convey it over to another and invest him with a power over his actions, there being no law of God forbidding a man to dispose of his liberty and obey another. But on the other side, there being a law of God enforcing fidelity and truth in all lawful contracts, it obliges him after such a resignation and agreement to submit.

(5) That supposing man naturally owner of an entire liberty, and so much master of himself as to owe no subjection to any other but God alone (which is the freest condition we can fancy him in), it is yet the unalterable condition of society and government that every particular man must unavoidably part with this right to his liberty and entrust the magistrate[4] with as full a power over all his actions as he himself hath, it being otherwise impossible that anyone should be subject to the commands of another who retains the free disposure of himself, and is master of an equal liberty. Nor do men, as some fondly conceive, enjoy any greater share of this freedom in a pure commonwealth, if [such is] anywhere to be found, than in an absolute monarchy, the same arbitrary power being there in the assembly (which acts like one person) as in a monarch, wherein each particular man hath no more power (bating [excepting] the inconsiderable addition of his single vote) of himself to make new or dispute old laws than in a monarchy; all he can do (which is no more than kings allow petitioners) is to persuade the majority which is the monarch.

Having laid down these things, which I think my author will not deny me, I shall content myself with one only argument rising from thence, sufficient to persuade me that the magistrate may lawfully determine the use of indifferent things relating to religion, viz.:

---

[4] Locke has a footnote: 'By magistrate I understand the supreme legislative power of any society, not considering the form of government or number of persons wherein it is placed. Only give me leave to say that the indelible memory of our late miseries, and the happy return of our ancient freedom and felicity, are proofs sufficient to convince us where the supreme power of these nations is most advantageously placed, without the assistance of any other arguments.'

because it is lawful for the magistrate to command whatever it is lawful for any subject to do. For, (1) [if][5] you suppose him immediately commissioned by God and by him entrusted with the care of the society, it is impossible to set any other bounds to his commands than what God himself by a superior law (to which with other men he owes an equal obedience) hath already prescribed him, all other things having an equal indifferency being left to the free determination of his will to be enjoined or forbidden, as he shall think most conducing to the good and peace of his people whereof he alone is the sole judge, else could there be no law made which could not be disputed, and all magistracy would have only an opportunity to persuade, not an authority to command obedience. Or, (2) if the supreme authority and power of making laws be conferred on the magistrate by the consent of the people (since 'tis pleaded nature gives no superiority of dominion, but all men seem equal till someone's eminent virtues, or any other advantages hath directed the choice of the people to advance him, or custom and the general agreement hath affixed the supremacy to a certain person, line or election) then it is evident that they have resigned up the liberty of their actions into his disposure, and so all his commands are but their own votes, and his edicts their own injunctions made by proxy which by mutual contract they are bound to obey, whence it clearly follows, that whatever any man hath the liberty of doing himself, one may consent and compact that another should enjoin him. And here I cannot but wonder how indifferent things relating to religion should be excluded more than any other, which though they relate to the worship of God are still but indifferent and a man hath as free a disposure of his liberty in these as any other civil actions till some law of God can be produced, that so annexes this freedom to every single Christian that it puts it beyond his power to part with it; which how much those places[6] urged by our author do, will be considered in their order. I shall in the way only take notice of his distinction of indifferent things into such 'as are purely so, viz.: time and place of meeting for religious worship, and other things that are commonly supposed indifferent but by abuse have become occasions of superstition such as are bowing at the name of Jesus,

---

[5] MS has 'whether': 'if' makes more sense.
[6] I.e. citations from Scripture.

the cross in baptism, surplice in preaching, kneeling at the sacrament, set forms of prayer and the like' (p. 2). But how time and place are more purely indifferent, how less liable to superstitious abuse, and how the magistrate comes by a power over them more than the other, the law of God determining neither, they all equally relating to religious worship, and being equally obnoxious to superstition, I cannot possibly see.

[I] The author's first argument is 'that because 'tis agreed that a Christian magistrate cannot force his religion on a Jew or Mahomedan, therefore much less can he abridge his fellow Christian in things of lesser moment' (p. 2) i.e. indifferent, a conclusion no way following from that supposition, as will evidently appear by these following reasons.

(1) From the end and intention of penalties and force especially in matters of religion, which are designed only to work obedience, outward violence being never to be applied but when there is hopes it may bend the dissenter to a submission and compliance. But the understanding and assent (whereof God hath reserved the disposure to himself, and not so much as entrusted man with a liberty at pleasure to believe or reject) being not to be wrought upon by force, a magistrate would in vain assault that part of man which owes no homage to his authority, or endeavour to establish his religion by those ways which would only increase an aversion and make enemies rather than proselytes. But in things of indifferency it is far otherwise, which depending freely upon the choice of the doer will be entertained or neglected proportionally as the law shall annex rewards or punishments to them, and the magistrate may expect to find those laws obeyed which demand not any performance above the power of the subject, so that though it be true that severity loses its end which is to remove the offence not the man (and is therefore not to be made use of) when it is employed to plant religion, which cannot be wrought into the hearts of men by any other power but that of its first author, nor any other way than what he hath prescribed, yet it is able to reach the external and indifferent actions of men, and may in them be applied with success enough. And though the magistrate ought not to torture poor creatures whom he hath no hopes to amend, and so to discredit and abuse punishments, the great instruments of government and remedies of disorders, as

to set them upon impossibilities where they are sure to be ineffectual, yet this doth no way tie up his hands from prosecuting those faults which may be thereby amended. 'Twould be tyranny in a father to whip a child, because his apprehensions were less quick, or his sight not so clear, or the lineaments of his face perhaps not so like his own as the rest of his brethren, who yet with equity enough might chastise the disobedience of his actions, and take this way to reclaim his wilful disorders. To conclude, rigour which cannot work an internal persuasion may [work] notwithstanding an outward conformity, all that is here required, and may be as necessary in the one as useless in the other.

⟨2⟩⁷ Upon supposition of the magistrate's power derived from the people (which is a question I shall not here dispute but only by allowing this hypothesis to those patrons of freedom as the ground of all their pleas and arguments show that it will afford but a very weak foundation to their opinion, and that placing the original of the magistrate's power as low as they can yet will it reach all indifferent things).

[2] A second reason against my author's conclusion will be from the extent of the power and authority of the magistrate which, being received from the resignation of the people, can pretend to a jurisdiction only over those actions whereof they themselves were the masters; but religion is none of these which is not to be assumed or laid down at pleasure. God in this wherein he hath a nearer communion with men retaining a more immediate dominion over their minds, which are brought to an assent to such truths proportionably as God either by the wise contrivance of his providence, or a more immediate operation of his spirit shall please to dispose or enlighten them and as Christ himself tells us, 'he reveals to babes what he hides from the wise and prudent' (Matt. 11:25), and therefore these discoveries and a consequent belief being not in their own power, 'twould be as irrational for men to engage to be of the same religion or persuasion with their magistrate, as to promise to have the same looks or constitution. Indeed education, custom and conversation have no small influence on the persuasions of men, and are usually by laws provided for, but these work not by violence, they insinuate

---

⁷ This paragraph, an alternative opening to 'the second reason', is a late insertion, intended to qualify the apparent endorsement of the contractarian thesis in the following paragraph.

only, not compel. But the liberty God hath naturally left us over our exterior, indifferent actions must and ought in all societies be resigned freely into the hands of the magistrate, and it is impossible there should be any supreme legislative power which hath not the full and unlimited disposure of all indifferent things, since if supreme it cannot be bounded by any superior authority of man and in things of indifferency God hath left us to ourselves. It is as certain, then, that the magistrate hath an absolute command over all the actions of men whereof they themselves are free and undetermined agents, as that beyond this he hath no authority, and therefore though he cannot enforce religion, which they never had the liberty to give up to another's injunctions, yet all things which they had a power to do or omit, they have made him the judge, when, where, and how far they ought to be done, and are obliged to obey.

[II] The author's second reason is because 'this imposing things indifferent is directly contrary to Gospel precepts' [p. 3]. Indeed, were this proved the controversy were at an end and the question beyond doubt, but amongst those many places produced I find not one command directed to the magistrate to forbid his intermeddling in things indifferent, which were to be expected if his determinations were against God's commands. 'Tis strange that in imposing things indifferent he should sin against Gospel precepts, and yet in the whole Gospel not one precept be found that limits or directs his authority. 'Tis strange that that doctrine that enjoins submission to a Nero, should be thought to free us from subjection to a Constantine,[8] that that which doth advance the throne and establish the authority of a heathen and a tyrant should weaken and pull down that of a good man and a good Christian. Had that monster commanded the Christians either out of prudence or peevishness, either to distinguish or expose that sect, to have worn white or black garments in the time of worship, to have assembled in this or that place, how would his injunctions have been unlawful, any more than for a Christian magistrate to prescribe either time or place or habit to a Mahomedan for his worship if his Alcoran [Koran] hath

---

[8] St Paul's injunction to 'obey the powers that be' (Rom. 13:1–2) was believed to have been written in the reign of the tyrannical pagan emperor Nero (54–68). Constantine (*c.* 274–337) was the first Christian emperor.

left them undetermined; indeed in those that are determined he ought not to be forced as being made by the doctrine of his religion no longer indifferent. Had the first Christians received such commands from Nero, who can think they would have scrupled at his orders and by disobedience in these indifferent things disturbed their own quiet and the progress of the Gospel? 'Tis true as my author says, p. 15,[9] their writings are full of arguments for liberty but it was for that liberty which was then encroached on and far different from what is here in question; 'twas for the substantials of their profession and not against the addition of ceremonies; their oppression was from those from whom they feared the subversion of the very foundations of their religion and not too gaudy and curious a superstructure; they complained not of being burdened with too many habits, but of being stripped stark naked. They would have taken any garments so they might have been permitted with them to have put on Christ Jesus too. But an exemption from the power of the magistrate though an infidel neither the Gospel nor they ever pleaded for; and shall a Christian magistrate find his authority weakened by that doctrine which strengthens a heathen's; must he first renounce his own kingdom before he enters into Christ's, cannot he be a convert and a king at once, and must our author's first supposition be still in doubt whether a Christian may be a magistrate?

The texts produced inform Christians in general of the liberty purchased them by our saviour, and there appears not in one of them any precept to magistrates to forbid their imposing indifferent things. But whether that liberty be to be understood as an exemption from the magistrate's injunctions in religious worship, the word being used indefinitely without application to things either religious or civil and so not to be limited by the fancy of every interpreter unless the scope of the place shall favour it, we shall see in their particular examination.

[1] The first is that 'our saviour doth in many places inveigh against the rigid and imposing pharisees for laying yokes upon others and therefore invites all to come unto him for freedom, "Take my yoke upon you", said he, "for it is easy and my burden

---

[9] Bagshaw: 'all the writings of the Christians for the first two hundred years are full of nothing else but such arguments as evince a liberty, more absolute and universal than I contend for'.

is light" ' (p. 3; Matt. 11:24–30, Matt. 23:1–36, John 8:36). To this may be replied:

(i) That though Christ inveighed against the encroaching pharisees when they joined their traditions to the law of God and pressed them as equally sacred and obliging, as Matt. 15, which was clearly contrary to the command of God – Deut. 4:2, Deut. 12:32 – therefore it follows not that he forbade the lawful magistrate to limit things indifferent. Christ might check those proud and meddling people who would be busy beyond their power, and though they took upon them to interpret the old law had no authority to add to it, and yet leave the magistrate free in the exercise of his power, it being no argument that because Christ condemned the impositions of the pharisees on the Jewish church to which God had set down an unalterable platform, and as our author confesses, p. 14, 'in the minutest circumstances had provided for uniformity of worship', that therefore he prohibited the Christian magistrate to determine those things which now he had left indifferent, that so their uses might be suited to the several exigences of times and tempers of people to whom the unchangeable and necessary doctrine of the Gospel should be revealed.

But, (ii), we may take notice that Christ in this place [Matt. 23:3] at the same time that he dislikes the pharisees' impositions he commands the multitude nevertheless to observe what they bid them, v. 3; and in the same breath that he reproves their hypocritical rigour he commands the people obedience.

And the reason he gives for it, v. 2, is because they sit in Moses' chair. Whereby is meant that either they expounded Moses' law and so all that came within the compass of that law, though heavy burdens yet, was to be submitted to by the people; or else they sat in Moses' chair, i.e. supplied his room and were the governors of the people, and then they are meant as the Sanhedrin, who our author says, p. 5, were then not only the ecclesiastical but civil rulers of the Jews, and then Christ's discourse runs thus, that the Jews were to obey the pharisees, as their civil governors to whose commands they were to pay a ready obedience though they were heavy and burdensome; and so this place will make against our author. In which sense soever it be taken the people were to obey, and the pharisees reproved not so much for imposing burdens as not bearing their part with others because they tied up others with strict rules of duty, and contented themselves with broad phylac-teries[10] and other outside easy performances.

And if we will observe these and other places [e.g. Mark 12:38–40; Luke 11:39–52] where Christ speaks to and of the scribes and pharisees, he levels his reproof against their hypocrisies, their affec-ted outside worship, neglecting the inward and substantial (which nobody defends) and their usurping a liberty to mingle their tra-ditions with the law of God, obtruding them as of equal authority with the divine injunctions and so binding burdens upon men's consciences which could not but be extremely criminal in a worship which God himself had framed and that with so much caution against any innovation or addition, that he descended to the lowest actions and most trivial utensils, not leaving out the very snuffers and firepans of the sanctuary – but of this I shall have occasion to speak hereafter. Though here we may observe concerning all those places relating to Christ and the pharisees:

(i) That where the pharisees enjoin things as magistrates and make laws as men, there Christ commands obedience though it were burdensome, as Matt. 23:3.

(ii) That where they urge their traditions as the laws of God, Christ denies the obligation of such traditions as traditions and proves it by the opposition of some of those traditions to the law of God, Matt. 15:1–6, but yet doth not even there deny washing of hands to be lawful because they commanded it, though it seems his disciples neglected it in their practice that they might not seem to countenance irregular injunctions of pretended divine traditions, which were contrary to the law of God which prohibited all additions.

That those places, Matt. 11:28–30, John 8:36, are to be under-stood of a freedom from sin and the devil and not from laws, the freedom of Christ's subjects being of the same nature with the king-dom whereof they were subjects, that is, not of this world or of the outward but inward man, is clear not only from the general current of interpreters but the places themselves; for where Christ invites them to submit their necks to his yoke because it is easy, he tells them what ease it is they must expect, viz.: rest to their souls, v.

---

[10] Parchments inscribed with Scriptures carried about the person; hence also, osten-tatious display of religiosity.

29 – the whole antecedent discourse being of the internal work of the Gospel upon the heart, of faith and repentance, and the happiness of those to whom God revealed the Gospel, and not relating at all to their outward privileges or in the least glancing at any exemption from the dominion and rule of the magistrate.

[2] The next Scripture urged is 'stand fast in the liberty wherewith Christ hath made you free and be not again entangled with the yoke of bondage' (Gal. 5:1), and here I shall consent with the author, that this verse, as also the greatest part of the epistle is the doctrine of Christians' enfranchisement from the ceremonial law. But how he will 'from thence draw an unanswerable argument against the urging of any other now' I cannot see. His words are, 'since that the Mosaical ceremonies which had so much to plead for themselves, upon the account of their divine original, and which even after they were fulfilled by our saviour still remained indifferent in their use and were so practised by Paul, yet when once they were imposed and a necessity pleaded for their continuance, the apostle writes so sharply against them, exhorting the Galatians to stand fast in their liberty, as part of our saviour's purchase; if this I say was the case with those old rites, then much less can any now impose an invented form of worship, for which there cannot be pretended the least warrant that ever God did authorise it' [p. 3]. I confess they had their original from divine authority, but 'tis as true that they had their end, too, from the same divine appointment, and it was as sinful to urge them as obliging after God had abolished them, as it was to neglect them whilst he enjoined their observation; they were a law till Christ, not after, types and promises of the messiah's coming and kingdom, but not to be rules of obedience under it; those shadows vanished upon the rising of our sun of righteousness, and therefore, though their use were indifferent afterwards and lawful and their practice allowed both by the permission of the apostles and their example too when it would [in] any way advantage the Gospel, or be any means of gaining converts or securing the peace of the church, but to allow their imposition and to acknowledge that law still in force which was to be abrogated by the coming of the messiah was to contradict their own doctrine, and deny that Christ was come which was their great design to establish, so that the things were left but the law that formerly made them necessary removed, and for a man to think himself under the

obligation of the ceremonial law and at the same time entertain the doctrine of the Gospel, was as impossible as to be a Jew and a Christian at once which St Paul, ch. 1, makes inconsistent [Gal. 1:10–24]. So that it is no wonder he should so vigorously oppose the doctrine of subjection to the ceremonial law, which would ruin and undermine the very foundations of that religion he was then building; and so smartly handle St Peter his fellow apostle when by his carriage he seemed to confirm it [Gal. 2:11–21]. But I think it will not follow that because that law ceased which was inconsistent with the Gospel that therefore the Christian magistrate's authority doth too, that because a law repealed by God himself could not be urged as in force, therefore no other law can be enacted. Those injunctions were rejected because the law from which they were urged was inconsistent with the Gospel and so will the magistrate's be also when they can be proved inconsistent too, which must be by some other argument than that of the ceremonial laws being antiquated. In vain, therefore, shall anyone from hence plead for any other liberty than what the apostle asserts, which was nothing but a freedom from the ceremonial law which after Christ was bondage, as is evident from the whole epistle, and the Galatians and all Christians 'shall stand fast enough in their liberty' if they preserve it from the encroachments and corrupt doctrines of false brethren, ch. 2, v. 4, and not the injunctions of the lawful magistrate. It was the false brethren that were most dangerous to Christian liberty, and ensnared the consciences with a bondage to that as a necessary law and of divine authority and so obliging the consciences which God himself had repealed and nulled by sending the messiah; the magistrate is not at all touched at in the whole epistle: who, notwithstanding the ceremonial law hath lost its obligation as the law of God, may enforce his own laws as the laws of a man who is the steward and judge of the public good.

But the author goes on, 'it seems altogether needless that the Jewish ceremonies should as to their necessity at least expire and be abrogated if others might succeed in their room, and be as strictly commanded as ever the former were' [p. 3]. Who would not presently reply that it seems altogether needless that the Jewish tithes should as to their necessity at least expire and be abrogated if other might succeed in their room and be as strictly commanded as ever the former were. Things are then needless when God removes them, not when our fancies dislike or perhaps our conveniences oppose them. The ceremonial law began then to be needless when God thought fit it should be abrogated, and when he shall either abolish magistracy or restrain its power from things of the sanctuary it will then so far be needless too, till then it will better become the temper of a Christian patiently to obey than to presumptuously complain and murmur that God hath not put human affairs into a posture suited to his humour or squared the economy of the world or frame of the temple according to the model of his brain.

'Our religion is styled the perfect law of liberty (James 1:25), which liberty I understand not wherein it consists if in things necessary we are already determined by God, and in things indifferent we may still be tied up to human ordinances and outside rites at the pleasure of our magistrate' [pp. 3–4]. A plea which if granted doth at one stroke dissolve all human laws or the greatest part of them, our liberty consisting in the free use of all indifferencies as well civil as ecclesiastical and the authority of the magistrate (as I have proved) extending itself as much to one as to the other, I know not why a rebellious subject may not under the patronage of this text cast off his allegiance as well as a dissenting Christian forbear conformity, Christianity being called a law of liberty without any limitation to this or that sort of indifferent things.

[3] 'To those Scriptures which deny all imposition may be added all those texts which consequently do it, such as are "do to others as you would have others do to you" [Matt. 1:12; John 6:31]. And who is there would have his conscience imposed upon?' (p. 4). If private men's judgements were the moulds wherein laws were to be cast 'tis a question whether we should have any at all. If this be the rule that must measure the equity and obligation of all edicts I doubt whether any can challenge [claim] a universal obedience, when it is impossible that any law should be by human prudence so contrived which whilst it minds the good of the whole will not be inconvenient to several of the members, and wherein many will not think themselves hardly and unequally dealt with. The magistrate in his constitutions regards the public concernment and not private opinions which, biased by their own interest, or misled by their ignorance and indiscretion, are like to make them but ill judges of reasons of state or the equity of laws; and when we find the greatest part of men usually complaining, we may easily conclude,

that they think that precept of 'do as thou wouldst be done unto' but ill observed by their superiors. Were magistrates to gratify the desires of men in all things to which by a partial interpretation they would extend this rule, they would quickly stand in need of a power not to make laws but worlds, and provide enlargements not restraints for the liberty of their subjects. And hence rises one of those necessities of government – that since men were not like (being favourable judges in their own cause) to be well satisfied with the equity of others, and would be ready to judge that others made use of their liberty, to their prejudice with neglect of this rule of equity, it was requisite to settle a peace and society amongst men that they should mutually agree to give up the exercise of their native liberty to the disposure and prudence of some select person or number of men who should make laws for them which should be the rule of their actions one towards another and the measure of their enjoyments; but this by the by.

'Tis true, 'who would have his conscience imposed upon?' and 'tis as true, who would pay taxes? who would be poor? who almost would not be a prince? And yet these (as some think them) burdens, this inequality, is owing all to human laws and those just enough, the law of God or nature neither distinguishing their degrees nor bounding their possessions. I grant all agree that conscience is tenderly to be dealt with, and not to be imposed on, but if the determining any indifferent outward action contrary to a man's persuasion (conscience being nothing but an opinion of the truth of any practical position, which many concern any actions as well moral as religious, civil as ecclesiastical), be imposing on conscience and so unlawful, I know not how a Quaker should be compelled by hat or leg[11] to pay a due respect to the magistrate or an Anabaptist [Baptist] be forced to pay tithes, who if conscience be a sufficient plea for toleration (since we in charity ought to think them as sincere in their profession as others than whom they are found less wavering), have as much reason not to feel constraint as those who contend so much for or against a surplice, for not putting off the hat grounded upon a command of the Gospel, though misunderstood, is as much an act of religion and matter of conscience to those so persuaded as

---

[11] Quakers, believing all people to be equal under Christ, refused 'hat honour', the removal of their hats in front of social superiors. 'Making a leg' is a formal bow.

not wearing a surplice.[12] Imposing on conscience seems to me to be, the pressing of doctrines or laws upon the belief or practice of men as of divine original, as necessary to salvation and in themselves obliging the conscience, when indeed they are no other but the ordinances of men and the products of their authority; otherwise, if you take it in our author's sense every lawful command of the magistrate, since we are to obey them for conscience sake, would be an imposing on conscience and so according to his way of arguing unlawful.

[4] ' "You that are strong bear with the infirmities of the weak" (Rom. 15:1) – whereas this practice will be so far from easing the burdens of the weak, that if men are at all scrupulous, it only lays more load upon them' [p. 4]. What was meant by imposing or burdening the conscience I showed but now. But this text relating to scandal, which the author makes one of his arguments, will be there more fitly spoken to;[13] I shall here only say that 'bear with the infirmities' signifies no more than 'not despise' in the beginning of the foregoing chapter, and so is a rule to private Christians not to slight or undervalue those their brethren who being 'weak in the faith', i.e. not so fully informed and satisfied of the extent of their Christian liberty, scruple at matters indifferent, and are ready, as they are there described, to judge those that allow and practise them; and this a magistrate may do whilst he makes laws for their observance, he may pity those whom he punishes, nor in his thoughts condemn them because not so strong in the faith as others. So that 'this kind of rigour' is not 'utterly inconsistent' as our author would persuade us 'with the rules of Christian charity', prescribed in this place, 'which no Christian magistrate ought to think himself absolved from. Since though as a magistrate he hath a power in civil things; yet as a Christian he ought to have a care that in things of spiritual concernment he grieves not the minds of any, who are upon that relation not his subjects so much as his brethren' [p. 4]. If outward indifferent things be things of spiritual concernment I wish our author would do us the courtesy to show us the bounds of each and tell us where civil things end and spiritual

---

[12] Strict Presbyterians objected to the Anglican surplice as popish and preferred the black Geneva gown.

[13] Locke takes up this point towards the end of the tract.

begin. Is a courteous saluting, a friendly compellation,[14] a decency of habit according to the fashion of the place, and indeed subjection to the civil magistrate, civil things, and these by many are made matters of conscience and there is no action so indifferent which a scrupulous conscience will not fetch in with some consequence from Scripture and make of spiritual concernment, and if nothing else will scandal at least shall reach him. 'Tis true a Christian magistrate ought to deal tenderly with weak Christians, but must not so attend the infirmities and indulge the distempers of some few dissatisfied as to neglect the peace and safety of the whole. The Christian magistrate is a brother to his fellow Christians and so may pity and bear with them but he is also their magistrate and must command and govern them, and if it be certain that to prescribe to the scrupulous be against this Scripture and be to lay load upon the weak, he will find it impossible not to offend, and burden a great part, some being as conscientiously earnest for conformity as others for liberty, and a law for toleration would as much offend their consciences as of limitation others. The magistrate he 'confesseth may bound not abridge their liberty', a sentence very difficult to be understood and hard to be put into other words.

[5] 'Decency and order when it is of constraint not of consent is nothing else but in the imposer tyranny, in the person imposed upon bondage, and makes him to be what in things appertaining to religion we are forbidden to be, "the servants of men"' (1 Cor. 7:23) [p. 4]. Which text cannot without force be applied to any other but a civil bondage. The apostle in that chapter gives them a resolution of some doubts which it seems they had proposed to him concerning the several relations and conditions of men, as the married and unmarried, the servant and the free, and in general tells them, v. 20, that conversion to Christianity did not dissolve any of those obligations they were tied in before but that the Gospel continued them in the same condition and under the same civil obligations it found them. The married were not to leave their consorts, nor the servant freed from his master, but because they were such as Christ had purchased with his blood and free men of his kingdom he thinks them fitter to be free, and advises them if they could to gain their

---

[14] Greeting, address. Identical phrases occur in Henry Stubbe, *A Light Shining out of Darkness* (1659), in reference to the fashion in Oxford to challenge even ordinary greetings on conscientious grounds.

liberty and not debase themselves to slavery and that too for the same reasons he counsels virgins to continue single, that they might the more freely attend the business of religion and not be entangled in the avocations and concernments of the world. Nor can those words 'be ye not the servants of men' be possibly understood of obedience to the injunctions of the magistrate in matters of religion or be any answer to their question, Christianity being scarce then known to the heathen magistrate, who was more likely to persecute the profession than prescribe forms of worship in a religion new and opposite to his own. Nor could 'servant' in this sense relate (as our author would have it [p. 4]) 'to the master extending his rule over the conscience', who, 'if a heathen', might possibly forbid [but] would never fashion the worship of a Christian, 'if a Christian', ⟨the argument at best would be but against the master not against the magistrate in prescribing rules of worship⟩.[15] Though it is very improbable that the Corinthians should at the very first approaches of this religion be so inquisitive after the smallest things of discipline, whereof all sects in their beginnings are not very curious as we find the first Christians were not, or that Paul in answer to their demands should provide against an evil wherewith they were not threatened, for who can think that masters that could not but know their servants' privileges and freedom in the Gospel to be equal with their own should take upon them presently so magisterially to chalk out a way of worship to their servants, when yet they were scarcely acquainted with the particulars of the doctrine itself, and it is known that masters and servants, all the converts did usually assemble with their fellow Christians and join in the same worship with the church they were of; I shall not therefore fear to affirm the 'be you not the servants of men', v. 23, is but repeating the advice he gave, v. 21, 'if thou mayst be made free use it rather'.

[III] The third argument is 'because it is contrary to Christian practice' [pp. 4–5]. To this I answer in general that precepts are the rule of our duty and not practice which is to be judged of by them. God hath made his commands the measure of our obedience and not the lives of his saints, who were men and might and did err, and therefore are to be tried by the law they were to approve

---

[15] This passage is deleted in the MS but restored here to improve the sense.

themselves to. 'Be ye followers of me as I am of Christ' was St
Paul's rule [1 Cor. 4:16]. Indeed the life of Christ is a perfect
example of holiness but yet there are many things in it above, and
in the lives of all his followers many things besides and some, *sit
verbo venia* [if I may say so], beneath our imitation. For who thinks
he ought to imitate St Peter in that which St Paul opposed him in
[Matt. 26:70–5]? Or in denying his master? 'Tis by the command
we are to learn where they walked right, I'm sure where we ought
to tread in their steps.

[1] 'The first shall be that of our saviour Christ who was of a
most sweet and complying disposition, yet when his Christian liberty came once to be invaded he laid aside gentleness, and proved
a stiff and peremptory assertor of it. To omit many passages of
which his story is full, I shall mention but one that was his refusing
to wash his hands before meat' (p. 5; Matt. 15:2). What Christ did
here I know not how it could be said to be in defence of his 'Christian liberty'. Indeed he came to promulge the great law of liberty
to believers, to redeem men from the slavery of sin and Satan and
subjection to the ceremonial law, but he himself was made under
the law, lived under it, and fulfilled it, and therefore it appears to
me rather a vindication of his national Jewish liberty which was
very much encroached on by the traditions of the pharisees, who
thought they 'sat in Moses' chair' [Matt. 23:2] yet went beyond the
bounds he had set them. God had delivered to the Jews an entire
and complete platform of worship, prescribed and limited, too, all
the circumstances and ceremonies of it, and so strictly tied them to
that rule he had given that Moses himself was not permitted to
deviate in the least from it, 'look that thou make them after the
pattern that was showed thee in the mount' (Exod. 25:40). It could
not then but be a horrid impiety and presumption for the pharisees
not only to step into Moses' chair but also to ascend into Mount
Sinai, and dare to mingle their wisdom with God's and take upon
them to correct or perfect that frame which the great architect of
heaven and earth had erected for his sanctuary. This usurpation
might well draw sharp rebukes from the meekest and most complying temper. Christ bore with the infirmities of the weak but not
with the open rebellion of the haughty and obstinate; these were
those who truly bound burdens on men's consciences by stamping
a divine impression on their own counterfeit inventions and tra-

ditions and enjoined them under the penalties of God's displeasure
and the curses of the law. But I think it will be no very good consequence that because Christ opposed the usurpation of the pharisees,
therefore a Christian may dispute the dominion of his magistrate;
that because the traditions of the elders (which were such too as
made the commandment of God of none effect, Matt. 15:6) were
unlawful in a religion tied to a certain and set form which was to
receive neither alteration nor addition, 'you shall not add unto the
word that I command you neither shall you diminish aught from it'
(Deut. 4:2, Deut. 12:32; Prov. 30:6), wherein God had left nothing
arbitrary or indifferent, therefore all impositions are unlawful in a
religion wherein almost all the outward actions are left undetermined and free; that because it was a part of the Jewish liberty not
to be fettered with pharisaical traditions, therefore it is part of the
Christian liberty not to submit to legal injunctions, and therefore it
is no wonder that Christ should not prefer 'arguments from decency' [p. 5] before those from duty, nor wash his hands when he could
not do it without contracting guilt, nor pay obedience to that law
which God had condemned and provided against by a repeated
prohibition – such traditions as they delivered to the people not as
their own injunctions but as part of the law of God, being properly
additions to it and so consequently unlawful; but Christ, who here
denied the obligation of forbidden traditions, did not thereby
destroy either the indifferency of the action or the magistrate's
power of enjoining it, and had Caesar commanded washing of hands
at any time of the day I have no reason to think that Christ would
have denied him this any more than tribute.

'And Christ leaves two unanswerable arguments which are of
equal validity in things of the same nature as, [i] first, that this was
not a plant of his father's planting and therefore it should be rooted
up; from whence, I gather this rule, that when once human inventions become impositions and lay a necessity upon that which God
hath left free, then may we lawfully reject them as plants of man's
setting and not of God's owning' [p. 5; Matt. 15:13]. In arguments
drawn from examples the condition of the persons and nature of
things ought well to agree, but in this case they are all far different.
The Elders, though perhaps as our author says the Sanhedrin and
so their rulers, yet did not impose these as lawmakers but pretended
only to be the conveyors of the law of God by a tradition as sacred

as any written precepts, whereas the magistrate urges his decrees in indifferent things as no otherwise binding than by virtue of his own authority as having the same original and obligation with all his other laws. The things there were prohibited traditions, for to urge anything as the law of God and a divine rule of his worship was clear against those positive commands of God in Deuteronomy, but here they are things free and indifferent so that what Christ here so sharply reproves was the hypocrisy of the teachers not the authority of lawmakers – their prohibited traditions not any impositions in indifferent things. From whence may be gathered this rule and no other; that when human inventions are pretended to be of divine original and imposed as such contrary to the positive commands of God, and lay a dogmatical and divine necessity upon that which God hath left free, then we may lawfully reject them as plants of man's setting and not of God's owning.

[ii] 'The second argument our saviour uses is that those things did not defile a man, from whence I infer that in the worship of God we are chiefly to look after the substance of things, and as for circumstances they are not worth our notice' [p. 5; Matt. 15:20]. Which possibly is true of those that are left by the magistrate to our choice and not those which cannot be disregarded without disobedience to him and affront to his authority. 'They who press outward conformity in divine worship, endeavour to serve God the wrong way, and oftentimes do only force carnal and hypocritical men to present God a sacrifice which his soul abhors' (p. 6). The magistrate's laws make none 'carnal and hypocrites' but find them so. He hath no commission to examine the hearts, but to take care of the actions of his subjects and though possibly he may increase their sin, whilst he endeavours to amend their lives (an inconvenience which he must not hope to avoid since Christ's own sermons and edicts were not exempt from it, which as much increased the damnation of the obstinate made thereby the more odious in the sight of God, as they advanced the happiness and privileges of the obedient), yet the same God that abhors the sacrifice of the hypocritical compliant, would not approve the magistrate's neglect of duty, should he by too much forbearance indulge the growth of contention and disorder, where a restraint in things indifferent might prevent it, the consequential miscarriages of others not at all

lessening the obligation of his duty which is a care of the public quiet.

'Whilst to others that are more tender and scrupulous they make the sacrifice itself unpleasant, because they will not let it be what God would have it, a free will offering' [p. 6]. The service of the inward man which God looks after and accepts may be a 'free will offering', a sincere and spiritual performance under what shape soever of outward indifferent circumstances; the heart may be lift up to heaven, whilst the body bows. And I know not how any habit can lie heavier on the spirits of any man and hinder its free motion towards God, than the stocks did Paul and Silas (Acts 16:25), or why anyone should pray less fervently, or doubt more of being heard in a church, and near an organ than Daniel in the den amidst the roaring of the lions [Dan. 6:16–22]. All that God looks for in his worship now under the Gospel is the sacrifice of a broken and contrite heart, which may be willingly and acceptably given to God in any place or posture, but he hath left it to the discretion of those who are entrusted with the care of the society to determine what shall be order and decency which depend wholly on the opinions and fancies of men, and 'tis as impossible to fix any certain rule to them as to hope to cast all men's minds and manners into one mould. He that will open his eyes upon any country or age but his own will presently see that they are ready to fight and venture their lives for that in some places which we should laugh at here. Our deformity is others' beauty, our rudeness others' civility, and there is nothing so uncouth and unhandsome to us which doth not somewhere or other find applause and approbation; and should the eastern and turbanned nations embrace Christianity 'twould be as uncomely to them to be bare in the public worship of God as to us to be covered. And this is so not only in different places, but if we survey the several ages of the church we shall find religion sometimes gay and glorious, beset with pomp and ceremony, sometimes plain and negligent, stripped of all show and outside, but always decent and in order because suited to the present opinion of the age; esteem in this as well as many putting all the difference of value, and why should not the magistrate's stamp and allowance make the one current as well as the other, why should anyone complain his heart and affections (the only free will offering) were more taken off from God than his friend, by the circumstantial determinations of the magistrate? What obedient son would less willingly (if it were so appointed him) meet his father in the church than in the chamber, or find his piety slacken by consideration of the place? Or what malefactor would complain of the injunction, or pretend that he could not as fervently beg his life of his prince in a cassock as in a cloak, were that the habit wherein he were commanded to approach his presence? 'Tis true 'tis not unusual to fright the weak and scrupulous with the terrible name of superstition, to clap disgraceful appellations upon innocent actions to deter men from them, a practice (as a learned man says well) not unlike the cruelty of the barbarous heathens that covered the Christians with those skins they had taken off from ravenous beasts that under that disguise they might the better bait them. But superstition if I understand it aright is a false apprehension of God, or of a false god, attended with a slavish fear of severity and cruelty in him, which they hope to mitigate by a worship of their own invention, and such sacrifices either of the lives of men or beasts or tortures on themselves, as their fears persuaded them are most like to expiate and satisfy the displeasure of the deity. But that superstition in this sense cannot be applied to the limitation of indifferent things is clear; which are not understood to be designed for atonement.

But our author here opposes free will offerings to commanded services and seems to make them inconsistent, which if true I know not how any Gospel duty can be acceptably performed and if 'in the worship of God to make the sacrifice such as God would have it a free will offering' [p. 6] it be necessary to follow no other rule but the various dictates of our own wills or fancies I hope hereafter we shall be secured from the fear of will-worship when whatsoever our own choice shall lead us to will be most acceptable because a 'free will offering'.

[2] 'My second instance shall be the resolution of the apostles in that famous and important query concerning the Jewish ceremonies, whether they were to be imposed or not. After a long dispute to find out the trust St Peter directly opposes those rites; "why do ye", says he, "tempt God by putting a yoke upon the necks of the disciples" – intimating that to put a yoke upon others (and to impose in things indifferent is certainly a great one) from which either God had expressly freed us, by commanding the contrary or

else tacitly freed us by not commanding them, this is nothing but to tempt God and to pretend to be more wise and holy than he' [p. 6].[16] The case is almost the same here with that of the Galatians above, only the resolution was given there only by St Paul alone, here by a synod. The dispute here seems to be between some converted pharisees wedded to an opinion of their old ceremonies and the rest of the church, and the answers given in the former case will serve here, only the author's deductions ought to be taken a little asunder and considered.

St Peter might well oppose the 'putting on this yoke on the necks of the disciples' not only because it so galled the Jews, but also being taken off and broken by God himself was not to be renewed; but this will not concern other things of indifferency. If we grant that things indifferent may be called yokes, it will follow from the metaphor that they are heavy perhaps but not unlawful, troublesome not criminal, and so are taxes and tributes and all penal laws, which if yokes are not to be put upon the necks of Christians they may upon the same score plead for forbearance. But who knows not that the stubborn necks of the people do often call for yokes and those strong and heavy without which it would be impossible they should be kept in order? But the yoke here spoken of is of far another nature than the imposition of indifferent things, [and] the question was, as appears v. 1, whether the ceremonial law was still in force and obliged the converted Gentiles, [and] whether circumcision were necessary to salvation. This the believing pharisees plead for, v. 5, but St Peter opposes and confutes, vv. 7, 8, 9, showing that God put no difference between the circumcised and uncircumcised but that they equally believed and received the Holy Ghost; the synod therefore by a decree quits them from subjection to the ceremonial law, and only forbids them fornication (which was then generally in those countries esteemed a very trivial and almost indifferent thing and therefore might well be ranked amongst eating of things strangled which were thought to carry as much guilt in them) and some other things which were necessary (not in their own nature) for the better uniting believers, Jews and Gentiles, and to prevent scandal and offence between the strong and weak brethren. All the inference that can be drawn from hence is, that though

---

[16] The Scriptural texts quoted in the next few paragraphs are all from Acts 15.

the ceremonial law was a heavy yoke and is not now to be put upon the necks of Christians, yet the exigences of the church and the condition of Christians may make the imposition of many things (that are in their own nature indifferent) necessary.

'From which God hath either expressly', etc. – if God hath tacitly freed us from those things which he hath not expressly commanded I can acknowledge no book of statutes but the Bible, and acts of Parliament can have no obligation. 'This is nothing else but to tempt', etc. – 'tis so if we interpose in matters forbidden or commanded by him already, in the rest the magistrate may use his authority without incurring this censure.

'Again James decries those ceremonies upon this score, lest they should be troublesome to the converted Gentiles' [p. 7]. It could not but become their Christian prudence to open as easy a passage as they could to the conversion of the Gentiles, to remove all possible rubs out of their way and not cumber the progress of the yet infant Gospel with unnecessary ceremonies, but the magistrate when his already converted people shall trouble themselves and him too about things indifferent and from thence grow into dangerous factions and tumults, may determine the business by injunctions or prohibitions without any prejudice to the doctrines of Christianity. The magistrate indeed ought not to be troublesome by his injunctions to the people, but he alone is judge [of] what is so and what not.

'Upon the hearing of those two the result of the synod is very observable. [i] First from the style they use, "It seems good to the Holy Ghost and to us", so that whoever exercises the same imposing power had need [to] be sure he hath the same divine authority for fear he only rashly assumes what was never granted him' (p. 6). The magistrates now, as the apostles then, have an authority, though far different. Those gave rules that obliged the conscience only by the dictates and inspirations of the holy spirit of God, having no secular authority and so were only deliverers not makers of those laws which they themselves could not alter. Whereas the magistrate commands the obedience of the outward man by an authority settled on him by God and the people, wherein he is not to expect immediate inspirations but is to follow the dictates of his own understanding, and establish or alter all indifferent things as he shall judge them conducing to the good of the public.

[ii] 'Secondly from the things they impose: (a) they call them a weight which is not unnecessarily to be laid on the shoulders of any.' But the magistrate is the sole judge of that necessity. '(b) They forbid only those very necessary things, to show that necessary things only and not indifferent should be the matter of our imposition' [p. 7]. I answer:

(i) That things may be necessary, (a) in their own nature and so are all comprehended within the law of God; (b) *ex suppositione*, as being the means to some requisite end, so meat is necessary to him that would live, etc., such were the things necessary here – and so things indifferent may become necessary before they are enjoined and oblige the prince before they are commanded the people, and such a necessity (which I say still the magistrate is judge of) is sufficient for their imposition.

(ii) I answer against what he here contends for, that those things enjoined to the churches by the synod, excepting only fornication, were not in themselves necessary, as appears, because no law then in force commanded them[17] since the positive moral law of God nowhere mentions them but only the same ceremonial law which was now abolished. Indeed eating of blood was forbidden Noah [Gen. 4:4] which precept our author thinks is 'still obligatory to all his posterity', p. 8, though contrary to the doctrine of St Paul, 1 Cor. 8, concerning things offered to idols, and Rom. 14:14, where he clears the doubt concerning them all, 'I know and am persuaded by the Lord Jesus that there is nothing unclean of itself but to him that esteems it', and v. 20, 'all things indeed are pure', i.e. defile not the eater but are indifferent in their use. And St Paul, 1 Tim. 4, calls the commanding to abstain from meats the doctrine of devils, giving the reason, v. 4, 'for every creature of God is good and nothing to be refused if it be received with thanksgiving'. The same is also clear from 1 Cor. 10:27, 'the apostle's scope was to ease and free not tie up their brethren' [p. 7]. 'Twas indeed here as in all other places where it came into question the apostle's intention to enlarge converts from a subjection to the ceremonial law; but

---

[17] Locke here has a significant deleted passage, which maintains that the law of nature can be known by the general consent of humankind: 'for we have no reason to think them any part of the law of nature, since the practice and doctrine of all the world, the usual and best interpreter of that law, was wanting, bating [excepting] only the Jews in obedience to their ceremonial laws and'.

whatever was the reason 'tis certain they did tie up their brethren by those injunctions in things that were in themselves most of them indifferent – if St Paul's judgement be to be taken before our author's.

After a large consideration of the circumstances of the decree [Acts 15] and a discourse of the particulars contained in it he thus closes: 'Hence I conclude for persons (a) who have no such authority' (p. 9), the magistrate may have another authority and that sufficient though not such; as I have above proved. '(b) In things much more indifferent'; those were not then under the obligation of any law and therefore as much in their own nature indifferent as any. '(c) And where the necessity of conforming is nothing near so pressing'; the lawmaker alone is the judge of that necessity and its urgency in those laws that he establishes and therefore from thence we can take no rise to question the equity of his injunctions. 'For such I say to take upon themselves an arbitrary and an imposing power is altogether unwarrantable and therefore sinful' [p. 9]. It is not requisite he should have such an authority as the apostles had. Then all our laws must be necessarily the dictates of the spirit of God, nor could the magistrate appoint so much as a fast or determine any indifferent thing without a special revelation. It suffices if he have any authority at all nor is it requisite he should make known the reasons of his edicts, 'tis enough if he himself be satisfied of them. Indeed should anyone without authority impose on others he might well be ranked with the greatest offenders and expect the sentence of the law as well as our author's censure to lay hold upon him, but the case is far otherwise with the magistrate, whose authority I have proved already. Or should anyone make use of the lawful authority he hath needlessly to burden his subjects, and without a necessity appearing to him sport himself with the liberties of his brethren, and confine them narrowly in the use of indifferent things, he would not perhaps be innocent and though he should not be liable to the censures of men, yet would not [e]scape the tribunal of God. However, this would not discharge our obedience. And I think 'tis no paradox to affirm that subjects may be obliged to obey those laws which it may be sinful for the magistrate to enact.

[3] All that the author says in his third instance from Paul's opposing the false brethren is no more than hath been urged and answered above in the same case of the Galatians, only there it is

brought as a precept, here as an example [p. 10; 1 Cor. 9:19–23, Acts 16:3, Gal. 2:4]. From whence in the close he comes to lay down a very strange position, viz.: 'When any shall take upon them to make a thing indifferent necessary, then the thing so imposed presently loses not its liberty only, but likewise its lawfulness. And we may not without breach of the apostle's precept submit to it.' A conclusion that by no means can be drawn from his instance, Gal. 2, where those the apostle disputes against were not any that pretended a power to make laws, or imposed those as their own injunctions, but urged them as necessary doctrines and the laws of God which obliged their consciences. The Scripture, that almost everywhere commands submission though contrary to the whole bent of our inclinations, could never be thought to teach us disobedience and that too contrary to our wills; this is an opinion so monstrous that it cannot without a very great injury be fathered upon the apostles. Who can believe that the magistrate's authority should make anything unlawful by enjoining it; that if in those things we are cheerfully doing ourselves his command should come and encourage us we ought presently to stop, to turn about and resist him and at once oppose his and our own wills too, alone, as if a child going to church of his own accord being by the way commanded by his father to go on ought straight to return back again? If this doctrine be true, I know not how any law can be established by the magistrate or obeyed by the subject, indifferent things of civil as well as religious concernment being of the same nature, and will always be so, till our author can show where God hath put a distinction between them, this I'm sure that according to his own rule the observation of a fast enjoined by the magistrate must needs be a sin, it being an imposition relating to the worship of God in indifferent things. An anniversary thanksgiving day[18] will be but an anniversary provocation, and those that assemble in obedience to such a command instead of returning a praise to God for a blessing, would call down on their heads a curse. This is truly to ensnare the consciences of men and put them under a necessity of sinning, a doctrine which strikes at the very root and foundation of all laws and government and opens a gap so wide to disobedience and

---

[18] An Act passed in 1660 (12 Car. II, c. 14) established an anniversary thanksgiving every 29 May to mark the king's restoration day.

disorder as will quickly ruin the best founded societies. Let the people (whose ears are always open to complaints against their governors, who greedily swallow all pleas for liberty) but once hear that the magistrate hath no authority to enjoin things indifferent in matters of religion, they will all of an instant be converts, conscience and religion shall presently mingle itself with all their actions and be spread over their whole lives to protect them from the reach of the magistrate, and they will quickly find the large extent of *inordine ad spiritualia* [what is excluded from the spiritual order]. Let but the ruler's power be excluded out of the sanctuary and it will prove an asylum for the greatest enormities, tithes will be as unlawful as sacrifice, and civil respect to a man as impious as if it were divine adoration, the stubborn servant will beard his master with a charter of freedom under Paul's hand, 'Be ye not the servants of men' [1 Cor. 7:23]. Nor will our author's interpretation be able to prevent it. Magistracy itself will at last be concluded anti-Christian (as the author himself confesses many do, p. 1). Let the multitude be once persuaded that obedience to impositions in indifferent things is sin and it will not be long ere they find it their duty to pull down the imposer. Do but once arm their consciences against the magistrate and their hands will not be long idle or innocent. But of inconveniences I shall have more occasion to speak in his next argument.

[IV] 'My last argument against impositions shall be taken from inconveniences that attend such a practice' (p. 10). If inconveniences make things unlawful as well as sometimes unpleasant I know nothing could be innocent, all our blessings would have their seasons of being curses, we cannot doubt there can be anything so good or innocent which the frail nature or improved corruption of man may not make use of to harm himself or his neighbour since the apostle tells us we may abuse the grace of God into wantonness. Ever since man first threw himself into the pollution of sin, he sullies whatever he takes into his hand, and he that at first could make the best and perfectest nature degenerate cannot fail now to make other things so too.

'In principles on which moral actions are grounded the inconveniences do use [are usually] to be weighed, and that doctrine for the most part seems most true, at least most plausible which is attended by fewest inconveniences' [p. 10]. Principles ought to be of unalterable verity and therefore are not to be established upon our uncertain and commonly partial judgement of their consequences, which are usually so many, so various and cross, that nothing then could stand firm, if every little inconvenience should shake it. The question being of lawful or unlawful we are to be judged by some law and not by supposed inconveniences which nobody can miss of, that will seek to discredit and dissuade any constitution, and study as he says to render the contrary doctrine plausible. If popular arguments were proofs I know no principles could stand secure, and the Gospel itself would not be free from question, in which the heathens found inconveniences and arguments enough to render it less plausible than their own absurdities and irrational superstitions. Who might not this way declaim government itself out of the world and quickly insinuate into the multitude that it is beneath the dignity of a man to enslave his understanding and subject his will to another's pleasure, to think himself so ignorant or imprudent as to stand in need of a guardian, and not to be as God and nature made him, the free disposer of his own actions? To fight to support greatness and a dominion over himself, and rob his own necessities to maintain the pomp and pleasure of one that regards him not, to hold his life as a tenant at will and to be ready to part with his head when it shall be demanded, these and many more such are the disadvantages of government, yet far less than are to be found in its absence as [for example] no peace, no security, no enjoyments, enmity with all men and safe possession of nothing, and those stinging swarms of miseries that attend anarchy and rebellion.[19] This I grant is a ready but not a fair way to decry any doctrine, to point out all the dangers that may follow from it and not at all to touch its advantages or obligation, and by showing only the black side of the cloud persuade the beholder that even the Israelites are in darkness and error whereas a better prospect would discover them guided by a brighter illumination. 'Tis true everyone in those things that fall under his choice ought well to balance the conveniences and inconveniences on both sides, and to be poised on that side on which the weightier consequences shall hang, and he sins at least against discretion that shall do otherwise. And thus the magistrate is to consider the

---

[19] A passage often cited as evidence of Locke's 'Hobbism' at this period.

consequences of those things which God hath left free before he determine them by his public decrees, and the subject to consider the consequences of those things which the magistrate hath left free before he determine them by his private resolution; and would all men thus limit their motions within their own sphere they would not be so turbulent and troublesome.

'The opposers of liberty have very little else to urge for themselves besides inconveniences' [p. 10]. But the defenders of the magistrate's power offer something more when they tell you that a man cannot part with his liberty and have it too, convey it by compact to the magistrate and retain it himself.

[1] 'The first inconvenience is the impossibility to fix a point where the imposer will stop. For do but once grant that the magistrate hath a power to impose, and then we lie at his mercy how far he will go' [p. 10]. An inconvenience as strong against civil as ecclesiastical jurisdiction: do but once grant the magistrate a power to impose taxes and we then lie at his mercy whether he will leave us anything. Grant him a power to confine anyone, and we cannot be long secure of any liberty: who knows how soon he will make our houses our prisons. Grant him a power to forbid assemblies and conventions, and who knows how long he will allow us the company of our friends, or permit us to enjoy the conversation of our relations. A practice not unknown to the Presbytery of Scotland, who took on them a pleasure to forbid the civil and innocent meeting of friends in any place but the church or market, under pretence to prevent evil and scandal.[20] So far will religious and spiritual jurisdiction be extended even to the most indifferent of common actions when it falls into busy and unskilful hands. Grant once that the magistrate hath a power to command the subject to work, and limit his wages too,[21] and who can secure us that he will not prove rather an Egyptian taskmaster than a Christian ruler, and enforce us to make brick without straw to erect monuments of his rigour and our slavery.

---

[20] Locke provides a marginal reference, '*vide* Burden of Issachar', the only specific reference to a book in the tract: James Maxwell, *The Burden of Issachar . . . or the Tyrannical Power and Practices of the Presbytericall Government in Scotland* (1646). Locke exaggerates what even Maxwell complains of in the Scottish prohibitions.

[21] Locke's marginal reference: '*vide* Stat: 5 Eliz., c. 4., 1 Jac., c. 6': the Statutes of Artificers, 1564 and 1603.

These are inconveniences whose speculation following from the constitution of polities may often fright but their practice seldom hurt the people. Nor will the largeness of the governor's power appear dangerous or more than necessary if we consider that as occasion requires it is employed upon the multitude that are as impatient of restraint as the sea, and whose tempests and overflows cannot be too well provided against. Would it be thought dangerous or inconvenient that anyone should be allowed to make banks and fences against the waves for fear he should too much encroach upon and straighten the ocean? The magistrate's concernments will always teach him to use no more rigour than the temper of the people and the necessity of the age shall call for, knowing that too great checks as well as too loose a rein may make this untamed beast to cast his rider. Who would decline embarking himself because the pilot hath the sole guiding of the ship, out of fear lest he should be too busy and impertinently troublesome at the helm, and disturb the voyage with the ill management of his place; who would rather be content to steer the vessel with a gentle than a stiff hand would the winds and waves permit him; he increases his forces and violence only with the increase of the storm and tumult; the tossings and several turns of the ship are from without and not begotten in the steerage or at the helm? Whence is most danger to be rationally feared, from ignorant or knowing heads? From an orderly council or a confused multitude? To whom are we most like to become a prey, to those whom the Scripture calls gods, or those whom knowing men have always found and therefore called beasts? Who knows but that since the multitude is always craving, never satisfied, that there can be nothing set over them which they will not always be reaching at and endeavouring to pull down, those constitutions in indifferent things may be erected as the outward fences to secure the more substantial parts of religion which experience tells us they will be sure to be tampering with when these are gone which are therefore fit to be set up, because they may be with least danger assaulted and shaken and that there may be always something in a readiness to be parted with to their importunity without injuring the indispensable and more sacred parts of religion when their fury and impatience shall make such an indulgence necessary. But I too forwardly intrude myself into the council chamber, and like an impertinent traveller, which am concerned only which way the hand of the dial points, lose time in searching after the spring and wheels that give it motion. It being our duty not curiously to examine the counsels but cheerfully to obey the commands of the magistrate in all things that God hath left us free.

But to my author's inconvenience I shall oppose another I think greater, I'm sure more to be provided against because more pressing and oftener occurring. Grant the people once free and unlimited in the exercise of their religion and where will they stop, where will they themselves bound it, and will it not be religion to destroy all that are not of their profession? And will they not think they do God good service to take vengeance on those that they have voted his enemies? Shall not this be the land of promise, and those that join not with them be the Canaanites to be rooted out [Num. 33:51–5]? Must not Christ reign and they prepare for his coming by cutting off the wicked? Shall we not be all taught of God and the ministry cast off as needless? They that have got the right use of Scripture and the knack of applying it with advantage, who can bring God's word in defence of those practices which his soul abhors and do already tell us we are returning to Egypt, would, were they permitted, as easily find us Egyptians and think it their right to despoil us. Though I can believe that our author would not make this large use of his liberty, yet if he thinks others would not so far improve his principles, let him look some years back [and] he will find that a liberty for tender consciences was the first inlet to all those confusions and unheard of and destructive opinions that overspread this nation. The same hearts are still in men as liable to zealous mistakes and religious furies, there wants but leave for crafty men to inspirit and fire them with such doctrines. I cannot deny but that the sincere and tender-hearted Christians should be gently dealt with and much might be indulged them, but who shall be able to distinguish them, and if a toleration be allowed as their right who shall hinder others who shall be ready enough to lay hold on the same plea?

Indeed [I have][22] observed that almost all those tragical revolutions which have exercised Christendom these many years have turned upon this hinge, that there hath been no design so wicked which hath not worn the vizor of religion, nor rebellion which hath

[22] MS has 'having'.

not been so kind to itself as to assume the specious name of reformation, proclaiming a design either to supply the defects or correct
the errors of religion, that none ever went about to ruin the state
but with pretence to build the temple, all those disturbers of public
quiet being wise enough to lay hold on religion as a shield which if
it could not defend their cause was best like to secure their credit,
and gain as well pity to their ruin as partisans to their success, men
finding no cause that can so rationally draw them to hazard this life,
or compound for the dangers of a war, as that which promises them
a better, all other arguments, of liberty, country, relations, glory,
being to be enjoyed only in this life, can give but small encouragements to a man to endanger that and to improve their present enjoyments a little, run themselves into the danger of an irreparable loss
of all. Hence have the cunning and malice of men taken occasion to
pervert the doctrine of peace and charity into a perpetual foundation
of war and contention, all those flames that have made such havoc
and desolation in Europe, and have not been quenched but with the
blood of so many millions, have been at first kindled with coals
from the altar, and too much blown with the breath of those that
attend the altar, who, forgetting their calling, which is to promote
peace and meekness, have proved [to be] the trumpeters of strife
and sounded a charge with a 'curse ye Meros'.[23] I know not therefore how much it might conduce to the peace and security of mankind if religion were banished the camp and forbid[den] to take
arms, at least to use no other sword but that of the word and spirit,
if ambition and revenge were disrobed of that so specious outside
of reformation and the cause of God, [and] were forced to appear
in their own native ugliness and lie open to the eyes and contempt
of all the world, if the believer and unbeliever could be content as
Paul advises to live together, and use no other weapons to conquer
each other's opinions but pity and persuasion (1 Cor. 7:12–13), if
men would suffer one another to go to heaven everyone his own
way, and not out of a fond conceit of themselves pretend to greater
knowledge and care of another's soul and eternal concernments than
he himself, how much I say if such a temper and tenderness were
wrought in the hearts of men our author's doctrine of toleration
might promote a quiet in the world, and at last bring those glorious

---

[23] Judges 5:23: regularly invoked by radical Puritan preachers.

days that men have a great while sought after the wrong way, I shall leave everyone to judge.

But it is like to produce far different effects among a people that are ready to conclude God dishonoured upon every small deviation from that way of his worship which either education or interest hath made sacred to them and that therefore they ought to vindicate the cause of God with swords in their hands, and rather to fight for this honour than their own; who are apt to judge every other exercise of religion as an affront to theirs, and branding all others with the odious names of idolatry, superstition or will-worship, and so looking on both the persons and practices of others as condemned by God already, are forward to take commission from their own zeal to be their executioners, and so in the actions of the greatest cruelty applaud themselves as good Christians, and think with Paul they do God good service. And here, should not the magistrate's authority interpose itself and put a stop to the secret contrivances of deceivers and the passionate zeal of the deceived, he would certainly neglect his duty of being the great *conservator pacis* [guardian of the peace], and let the very foundations of government and the end of it lie neglected, and leave the peace of that society [which] is committed to his care open to be torn and rent in pieces by everyone that could but pretend to conscience and draw a sword.

After some enlargement and an enumeration of certain particulars and ceremonies of the Church of Rome, which whether indifferent or no concerns not our question, he comes to make the imposing of indifferent things the mark of Antichrist: 'If I understand anything of Antichrist his nature seems to me to consist in this, that he acts in a way contrary to Christ (Rev. 13:17), instead of a spiritual he brings in a devised worship, and instead of freedom lays a constraint even upon our devotion, so that as John in his Revelation says of him, "Men shall neither buy nor sell which have not his mark", i.e. who do not serve God in that outward way which he commands' [pp. 10–11]. St John, who alone names and more than once describes Antichrist, gives another character of him, and if he will take his authority we shall find his nature to consist in denying Jesus to be the Christ, 1 John 2:18, 22; 1 John 4:3; 2 John 7. And here would we content ourselves with those discoveries the Scripture allows us, we should not grope for Antichrist in the dark prophecies of the revelations, nor found arguments upon our own interpretation wherein the mistakes of eminent men might teach us to be wary and not over-peremptory in our guesses.

'I know very well that the argument is specious and often urged why should men be so scrupulous? Most pleading for ceremonies as Lot did for Zoar [Gen. 19:20], are not they little things? But I answer, (i) That a little thing unwarrantably done is a great sin' (p. 11). Unwarrantably against a positive precept, not unwarrantably without a special commission. '(ii) That a little thing, unjustly gained makes way for a greater.' Though little things make way for greater yet still they will be within the compass of indifferent, beyond that we plead for no allowance and whether a power to impose these be 'unjustly gained' must be judged by the arguments already urged.

[2] 'The second inconvenience is that it quite inverts the nature of Christian religion not only by taking away its freedom but likewise its spirituality' [pp. 11–12]. Our author here had forgot that rule, what God hath joined let no man put asunder. That an outward set form of worship should necessarily take away the spirituality of religion I cannot think, since God himself that did then demand the worship of the heart and spirit no less than now and made that the only way to please him, did once erect an outward form of worship cumbered with more ceremonies and circumstances than I believe ever any in the world besides, which could yet no way shut out or clog the operations of his spirit where he pleased to enter and enliven any soul.

'Our saviour says that God will now be worshipped not in show and ceremony but in spirit and in truth' [p. 12]. Show and ceremony are not in the text, and might here have been spared without any injury to the discourse of Christ which doth not usually need such supplements. The words of our saviour are, John 4, v. 24, 'The hour cometh and now is when the true worshippers shall worship the Father in spirit and in truth'; the discourse is to a woman of Samaria, the people whereof contended with the Jews about the right place of worship, preferring their Mount Gerezime to Mount Sion, between whom the controversy had bred such dislike and aversion that it broke off all civil commerce as appears by the woman's words, v. 9, who being zealous for the religion of her country maintains it against that of the Jews; but Christ to put an end to the controversy and to prepare her for his doctrine, tells her first indeed that her religion was false, but that of the Jews too which was true, was then to cease and that therefore they should no longer contest which mountain stood nearest heaven nor in which place the worship of God was most acceptable, since God was now publishing a religion to the world not confined to any place, but wherever there were a heart inflamed with love to him and a spirit rightly disposed to his service there was a sacrifice acceptable to him [John 4:9–21]. All that can be drawn hence is that the great business of the Christian religion lies in the heart, that wherever there is a well set spirit there God may be worshipped wherever it be, but this excludes not an outward form, nor can it be from hence concluded inconsistent with it. God may be worshipped in spirit and in truth as well where the indifferent circumstances are limited as where they are free, a gracious heart may pray as fervently in the ancient form of the church as the extemporary form of the minister, and an humble soul may receive instruction as well from the pulpit as the state; a surplice indeed will add but little heat to the body, but I know not why it should chill our devotions. There is no necessity why David should be thought less zealous when he danced with all his might in a linen ephod[24] than when he was clad in his shepherd's coat [1 Chron. 15:27]. He that judges that where he finds ceremony and show there spirit and truth are necessarily wanting may as rationally conclude that where he observes an uniform structure with a stately outside there is no fire or inhabitants within, or that handsome bodies have no souls.

'Whereas the doctrine of impositions places it (viz.: religion) in such things in the observance of which superstition will be sure to outdo devotion' [p. 12]. This doctrine that the magistrate hath power to impose indifferent things places it in none, but leaves it to his arbitrary and uncertain determination, and should the magistrate prescribe such a form wherein superstition (a word always sounding ill and not seldom applied to very innocent actions) would perhaps outdo devotion, yet this would be no better an argument against such injunction than if he should endeavour to prove that the magistrate should not command truth and justice because they are things wherein Turks will be sure to outdo Christians. That the superstitious should be more zealous than the devout or a Turk

---

[24] A surplice worn by Jewish priests.

honester than a Christian might indeed well shame the professors but could not at all discredit the doctrine of either.

'But true religion like the spirits of wine or subtle essences whenever it comes to be opened and exposed to view runs the hazard of being presently dispirited and lost' [p. 12]. Christ who best understood the nature of Christian religion hath fitted it with another simile, Matt. 5:15, he fears not to trust it to the open view, nor thinks that the profession of the Gospel would have less heat or light upon an hill than in a corner, and makes it a kind of absurdity to endeavour to conceal that which was to be a light to those that sit in darkness and was to shine over all the world, this would be to confine the sun to a cave, and not to light or set up a candle for fear it should go out, which runs a greater hazard in a close confinement.

'There is a vast difference between purity and pomp, between spirit and splendour' [p. 12]. Not so vast a distance but that they may meet. The priest's robes many and specious did not make Aaron guilty, nor the whiteness of his garment diminish the innocence of his heart [Exod. 28]. Spirit and splendour are so far different as life and clothes, yet no man is persuaded to strip himself naked because his life consists in the inward motion of his heart and not the outward fashion of his habit, and those ornaments that make not a man more strong and vigorous in himself may render him more comely and acceptable to others.

'Whereas the imposer only drives at and improves the latter (viz.: splendour) but of the former (viz.: spirit) is altogether secure and careless as is evident in those places where uniformity is most strictly practised' [p. 12]. The imposer carries his religion as far as he can, and being not able to reach beyond the outside he must necessarily stop there, neither his commission nor power extending any further, but that he is secure and careless of an inward purity, that he doth not wish and pray for that too, is a very severe censure. The miscarriages of those where uniformity is most strictly practised are no more to be imputed to his law than the formality of the Jews to the ceremonial. As long as the greatest part of men shall be the worst, and outward profession shall be more easy and cheaper than inward conversion, it will be no more wonder to find want of spirit with splendour, formality under uniformity, than ambition and faction, pride and hypocrisy under a toleration, and generally want of sincerity in all professions. And 'tis not to be doubted that many may find admittance in a church as well as conventicle here who will scarce get admittance into heaven hereafter.

[3] 'Thirdly this doctrine making no provision at all for such as are scrupulous and tender supposes the same measure of faith in all' [p. 12]. This inconvenience was touched at above, page 4 [of Bagshaw's tract], and generally this plea of scandal and offence is made use of by all sorts of men as a sufficient reason against whatever suits not with their humour, who cannot but be well pleased to find themselves always furnished with this argument against whatever cannot gain their approbation, and to think anything unlawful and ought to be removed because they dislike it. This is an inconvenience that Christ himself and his doctrine could not escape, this cornerstone which was a sure footing to some, was also a stumbling block whereat many stumbled and fell and were broken in Israel. Were offences arguments against anything, I know not who might not clap on a tender conscience and therewith sufficiently arm himself against all the injunctions of the magistrate, and no law could lay hold on him without encroaching on this law of charity and his just freedom. How far we ought to part with our own liberty to gratify another's scruple is a question full of niceness and difficulty. But this I dare say, that of what value soever the inward and private peace of a Christian be, it ought not to be purchased at the settled and public peace of the commonwealth, especially where it will not remove the offence and only cast the scandal on the other side and disturb the peace of the contrary persuasion, since some men will be as much offended at the magistrate's forbearance as others at his injunctions and be as much scandalised to see a hat on in the public worship as others a surplice.

'As the apostle says of things offered to idols so concerning ceremonies I may say that all have not knowledge. But to this day many there are utterly unsatisfied with the lawfulness of any, and most are convinced of the uselessness of them all' [p. 12; 1 Cor. 8:7]. Many too are unsatisfied of the lawfulness of a Christian magistrate, and yet who besides themselves think they are not obliged whilst they live within his dominions to submit to his laws, and may without any inconvenience be punished if they offend against them? And who will think a prince ought to betray his right

and lay by his sceptre as often as anyone shall scruple at his power
and plead conscience against his authority?

[4] 'The last inconvenience is that by impositions, especially
when the penalty is severe, we seem to lay as much weight and
stress upon these indifferent things as upon any the most material
parts of our religion' [p. 12]. If the magistrate employ his power
only within those bounds that are set to his authority he doth not
thereby slight or undervalue those things that are out of his reach.
Were faith and repentance, the substantial parts of religion,
entrusted to his jurisdiction and open to his knowledge we might
possibly find his penalties severer in those things than in any other.
But God, the judge of hearts, hath reserved both the knowledge
and censure of these internal acts to himself, and removed those
actions from the judgement of any tribunal but his own. We may
well spare the magistrate the exercise of his sovereignty in those
things wherein God doth not allow it, and we have as little reason
to accuse him of usurpation because he makes use of the authority
that is put into his hands as of negligence and lukewarmness because
he goes not beyond his commission. Nor doth human impositions
in indifferent things advance them above the more substantial and
necessary which stand above them by the appointment of a superior
law enjoined by divine authority, and therefore challenges [claims]
the first and chiefest part of our homage and obedience, so that
though he say 'that this rigid irrespective obtruding of small things
makes no difference at all between ceremony and substance', 'tis
certain it puts as much difference as is acknowledged between a
human and a divine law, as between the commands of God and the
injunctions of man. The magistrate whilst he reverently forbears to
interpose his authority in these things lays a greater stress upon
them by acknowledging them to be above his authority, and he that
in all other things stands above and commands his people, in these
descends to their level and confesses himself their fellow subject.

'So that a man who were not a Christian at all would find as
good, nay perhaps better usage from the imposer, than he who
labouring and endeavouring to live up to other parts of Christian
faith, shall yet forbear to practise those ceremonies: which is not
only harsh and cruel but very incongruous dealing, that a Jew or
Mahomedan should be better regarded than a weak or scrupulous

Christian' [p. 12]. Whatever other country do, England is clear of this imputation. Yet I shall further add that he who thinks he ought to allow a Turk as well as a Christian the free use of his religion, hath as little reason to force or abridge the one contrary to his Alcoran as the other contrary to his Gospel, and can as little forbid circumcision to the one as baptism to the other. But yet nevertheless he retains an absolute authority over all those indifferent actions which the respective law of each hath left undetermined, but the reason why perhaps he determines the indifferent things of his own profession whilst he leaves those which he disregards free is (by the example of the great lawmaker who though he strictly tied up his own people to ceremony in the true worship yet never prescribed a form to the idolators in their false) lest by enjoining positive ceremonies in their religion he might seem to countenance and command its profession and by taking care for their worship acknowledge something good and right in it; it being irrational that the magistrate should impose (possibly he might forbid) any indifferent actions in that religion wherein he looks on the whole worship as false and idolatrous. The Christian prince that in any public calamity should enjoin a fast and command the Christians in their public place of worship to send up their prayers to God and implore his mercy might perhaps at the same time prohibit his subject Turks the ordinary works of their vocations, but would never send them in sackcloth and ashes to their mosques to intercede with Mahomed for a blessing (which he might be well supposed to do were he of their persuasion) and so encourage their superstition by seeming to expect a blessing from it; this would be to condemn his own prayers, to affront his own religion and to provoke God whom he endeavours to appease, and proclaim his distrust of him whilst he seeks help from another. Though those of different religions have hence small occasion to boast of the advantage of their condition, whatsoever is bated [excepted] in ceremonies being usually doubled in taxes, and the charge their immunity puts them to in constant tributes will be found far heavier than the occasional penalties of nonconforming offenders.

Another reason why the magistrate possibly doth more severely tie up the liberty of those of his own profession, and exercise his power in indifferent things especially over them, may be because they are most likely to disturb the public peace, the state religion

being usually the state trouble, which is[25] seldom found to arm the
subjects against the prince but when he is of the same profession,
either because men generally, when their fears are removed and
have a free exercise of their religion allowed, are apt to grow wanton
and know not how to set bounds to their restless spirits if persecution hang not over their heads; they will be ready to advance
them too high, and if the fear of losing divert not their thoughts,
they will employ them in getting; where nothing checks them, they
will be sure to mount still and not stop so long as anything is above
them, and those perhaps who under the Turks would be well content to be subjects so they might be Christians will in England
scarce digest that condition but be ready to think if the magistrate
be their fellow Christian he is their brother too and will hence
expect, as our author pleads, p. 4, to be used rather as brethren
than subjects, equals than inferiors. Nor is the subtlety of malicious
men wanting to make the magistrate's religion troublesome to him,
wherein they will be sure to search out those arguments and spin
those consequences (which a different profession could never afford
them) which shall lay hold on the actions and, as they will represent
them, mal-administrations of the prince. They will offer proofs
from Scripture that he is not true to his own profession, that he
either superstitiously innovates the worship, or is supinely careless
of reformation or tyrannically abridges them of that liberty, which
the law of their God, and that doctrine which he cannot deny freely
and equally bestows on them, and pretend him as disobedient to
the law of God as they will hence take leave to be to his, and at last
will arrive at this, if he will not reform what they think amiss, they
themselves may, or at last conclude that he cannot be a Christian
and a magistrate at once. Thus are the public religions of countries
apt by the badness of the professors to become troublesome to the
magistrate and dangerous to the peace, if not carefully eyed and
directed by a strong and steady hand, whilst underling and tolerated
professions are quiet, and the professors content themselves to com-
mend their doctrine by the strictness and sobriety of their lives
and are careful not to rend their unity by needless disputes about
circumstances and so lay themselves open to the reproach of their

---

[25] Locke inserted 'not' after 'is', but that destroys his meaning; when inserting 'not'
he must have intended to delete 'but' after 'prince'.

enemies; or if any difference creep in, mutual consent closes it, without appealing to force or endeavouring to carve out a reformation with the sword, an argument never made use of but when there are hands enough prepared to wield it.

The remaining part of his discourse is taken up with answers to some objections which they are concerned to defend that first urged them; amongst others he mentions the learned and reverend Mr Hooker and Dr Sanderson, two such eminent champions of truth that it would be an high presumption in me to take upon me to be their second and adventure to make good their arguments which I am the more unfit to do as having never yet had the opportunity to peruse the writings of the former beyond his preface, and the lectures of the latter at their first appearance in public I run over with that haste and inadvertency that I could be able to give but a very slender account of their reasonings.[26] Yet I shall take the boldness to say that their argument mentioned by our author is not so slight as he makes of it. Their argument as it is quoted by him stands thus: 'That since things necessary to the worship of God be already determined by God, and over them the magistrate hath no power; if likewise he should have no power in indifferent things, then it would follow that in things appertaining to religion, the Christian magistrate would have no power at all. Which they think to be absurd' (p. 14), which well they might that the magistrate should have no power at all, for if you once deny his power in any sort of indifferent things you take it away in them all for they are all of the same nature, and there is no law of God which confines his power to this or that kind of them. But let us see the author's answer:

'(1) That it is no absurdity at all that princes should have no more power in ordering the things of God than God himself hath allowed them. And if God nowhere hath given them such an imposing power they must be content to go without it.' If they have no imposing power till God by a positive express commission somewhere hath given it them, they will be found to have as little in civil as religious indifferent things and no right of tying up our liberty in either. But that they have a power in both and how they

---

[26] Locke refers to Richard Hooker, *Of the Laws of Ecclesiastical Polity* (1594–7), and Robert Sanderson, *De Obligatione Conscientiae* (1660).

came by it I have shown above. 'But in this case where will the
Christian magistrate find his warrant?' In whatever text of Scripture
the magistrate's charter for jurisdiction in civil indifferent things is
to be found, in the very same or next verse is his warrant for impositions in religious. 'The Scriptures being utterly silent that he is
now to take such authority upon him which because the things
concern not man but the worship of God had it been thought necessary and fit would certainly not have been omitted.' The Scripture
speaks very little of polities[27] anywhere (except only the government
of the Jews constituted by God himself over which he had a particular care) and God doth nowhere by distinct and particular prescriptions set down rules of governments and bounds to the magistrate's
authority, since one form of government was not like to fit all
people, and mankind was by the light of nature and their own conveniences sufficiently instructed in the necessity of laws and government and a magistrate with power over them, who is no more to
expect a commission from Scripture which shall be the foundation
and bounds of his authority in every particular and beyond which
he shall have none at all, than a master is to examine by Scripture
what power he hath over his servant,[28] the light of reason and nature
of government itself making evident that in all societies it is
unavoidably necessary that the supreme power (wherever seated in
one or more) must be still supreme, i.e. have a full and unlimited
power over all indifferent things and actions within the bounds of
that society. Whatever our author saith there 'tis certain there be
many particular things necessary and fit now, that are yet omitted
in Scripture and are left to be determined by more general rules.
Had the questions of paedobaptism, church government, ordination, excommunication, etc. been as hotly disputed in the days of
the apostles as in ours, 'tis very probable we should have had as
clear resolutions of those doubts and as positive rules as about eating
thing[s] strangled and blood[y]. But the Scripture is very silent in
particular questions, the discourses of Christ and his apostles

---

[27] Locke deleted 'government' and replaced it with 'polities', or perhaps 'politics'.

[28] There is a significant deleted passage here: 'it being the consent of parties and
not an immediate grant from God that confers it on both, hence it is that one
princes hath a different powers [sic] – some larger, others narrower, according to
their different constitutions of their countries, which could not be were there laid
down in Scripture one stand-charter for them all. Only this I say'

seldom going beyond the general doctrines of the messiah or the duties of the moral law, but where either the condition of the persons or their enquiry made it necessary to descend to particulars, and possibly had there not some miscarriages sprung up in the church of Corinth we had never received that command of decency and order, and 'twas their enquiry that occasioned Paul's resolution of those their private doubts, 1 Cor., ch. 7, ch. 8. It was not therefore requisite that we should look for the magistrate's commission to be renewed in Scripture who was before even by the law of nature and the very condition of government sufficiently invested with a power over all indifferent actions. Nor can we rationally conclude he hath none because we cannot find it in the Bible.

[2] His second answer is no more but an affirmation that things indifferent cannot be determined which is the question between us and no proofs of it.

[3] 'Lastly it is much more suited to the nature of the Gospel that Christian princes should reform religion rather by the example of their life than the severity of their laws' (p. 15). (i) I answer that it is not easy to be guessed what our author means here by 'reformation of religion'. The outward moral acts of virtue and obedience to the second table[29] he makes no part of religion, at least in the sense we dispute of, which is the worship of God. Or if he will grant them to be religion and within the compass of our question he will not, I believe, deny the magistrate a power of making laws concerning them, unless instead of pleading for tender consciences he become a patron of hardened and deboshed [debauched] offenders. And as for the observance of outward ceremonies in the worship (they being in his opinion 'either unlawful or useless'), he will readily exclude them from reformation, and how the magistrate's example of life can any way reform except in one of these two is beyond my apprehension. Since 'true religion', i.e. the internal acts of faith and dependence on God, love of him and sorrow for sin, etc., are (as our author says) 'like the spirits of wine or subtle essences' I'm sure in this that they cannot be seen and therefore cannot be an example to others. (ii) I answer that it is a very good way, for the prince to teach the people the service of God by his own example, and 'tis very likely the paths of virtue

[29] The second half of the Ten Commandments.

and religion will be trodden by many when they lead to credit and preferment and the prince will be sure to have a large train of followers which way soever he goes. But all men live not within the influence of the court, nor if they did are all so ingenuous to be thus easily won over to goodness. This is one but not the only means of drawing men to their duty, nor doth it forbid the magistrate the rigour of laws, and the severer applications of his authority where the stubbornness and peevishness of the people will not be otherwise reclaimed.

Second Tract on Government

c. 1662. The title is a modern usage, ascribed by Philip Abrams; the work is also known as 'the Latin tract'. MS headed: 'An Magistratus Civilis possit res adiaphoras in divini cultus ritus asciscere, easque populo imponere? Affirmatur.' ('Whether the civil magistrate may incorporate indifferent things into the ceremonies of divine worship and impose them on the people: Confirmed.') MS Locke, c. 28, fos. 3–20. There is a draft, with some variations, in MS Locke, e. 6, fos. 91–69 (retro). The tract was composed some time between autumn 1660 and the beginning of 1663, most likely late in 1662. Printed in Viano 1961, pp. 62–80; Abrams 1967, pp. 185–209, with English translation at pp. 210–41; Wootton 1993, pp. 152–77. Cited by Laslett, First Treatise, §129. The text given here is Abrams' translation.

Locke takes up the same themes he discussed by way of point-by-point refutation in the *First Tract* and now presents them in the more formal mode of an academic presentation or oration. He draws heavily upon Bishop Robert Sanderson's *De Obligatione Conscientiae*, published in 1660 but based on lectures given in 1647. Locke proceeds as follows. After a preamble, he turns to define (I) magistracy; (II) religious worship (with an excursus on the magistrate's right and the subject's duty); and (III) indifferent things, this last turning into an account of the nature of law. Next he considers the foundations of political authority, and, finally, the arguments from Scripture used against the magistrate's imposition of indifferent things.

If only this truth which is now drawn into dispute and which has already been the subject of so many hot debates, and has been band-

54

ied about in such bitter party quarrels, would finally stop being challenged! If only, having achieved the place that it deserves in every mind, it would, being settled, at last grant security to each and peace to all! If only it might demand advocates no longer, but rather recognise worshippers! Exhausted as we are by so bitter a clash of opinions and of arms, we ought to rest content with our liberty and quiet. But when I remind myself what disasters this one issue has caused, what tempests, military no less than civil, it has provoked – tempests of which distant rumblings are heard even now, and of which the whole ferment has hardly yet subsided; when I consider that this exceedingly provocative question, in connection with which deeds almost always follow words, is hardly raised in public but it is attended by a train of as many violent acts as there are points of view, and that it does not permit of calm or passive listeners, but inspires, excites and arms them and sets them, bitter and incensed, against one another; when I consider all this, it looks to me as though I am not approaching a gymnasium and a private fencing-match so much as a public arena and a field of battle, and not so much proposing a thesis as raising a war-cry.

For there is hardly anyone who can contain himself on this subject, or bear to take part soberly in controversies of this sort without imagining that his own interests are seriously at stake and must be defended with the greatest energy, not to say by force of arms, when, their enthusiasms driven this way and that by opinion, hope or conscience, some here anxiously complain that peace, religion and the church are imperilled by excessive licence, and there others vehemently cry out that the liberty of the Gospel, that greatest privilege of Christians, is despotically suppressed and the right of conscience violated. And hence follows the belittling of the magistrate, the violation of laws; all things sacred as well as profane are held as nothing and so long as they march under the banners of liberty and conscience, those two watchwords of wonderful effect in winning support, they assert that each may do what he will. And certainly the overheated zeal of those who know how to arm the rash folly of the ignorant and passionate multitude with the authority of conscience often kindles a blaze among the populace capable of consuming everything.

Germany, which is notorious for civil disasters, provides evidence of this. And I only wish that this age and country of ours, so happy in other respects, had been content with foreign examples and had not provided such wretched evidence of this truth in its own domestic misfortunes or wished to learn by experiment on its own body how many calamities a predatory lust under the guise of Christian liberty and religion brings in its wake – calamities of which the very memory would in truth be thoroughly distressing did not our present good fortune, the new posture of affairs and the well-composed order of society reassure us. Nor do we now look back at those miseries but as men who, standing safely on the shore, gaze, not unsatisfied, at the tossing and vain threats of the waves from which they have just escaped. And now that almighty God has restored peace to us – which was not to be hoped for without a long chain of miracles, the discord of the immediate past making its arrival still more welcome – it is to be hoped that nobody will be so obstinate and stiff-necked as to attempt further civil changes or to disparage the magistrate's power in respect of indifferent things. Rather, it is to be hoped that now that that chaos has abated along with the heady ferment of passions, a more sober view will eventually recognise that civil obedience, even in the indifferent things of divine worship, is not to be counted among the least duties of the Christian religion, and that there is no other help but in eagerness to obey. And I hope that in future this controversy will excite no further conflict, unless it be a mock battle of the present sort. And in order that we may the better undertake such a combat we must set forth the debate and define its terms in such a way that we shall understand what is meant here by 'magistrate', what by 'religious worship', and what by 'things indifferent'.

(1) By 'magistrate' we here understand one who has responsibility for the care of the community, who holds a supreme power over all others and to whom, finally, is delegated the power of constituting and abrogating laws; for this is that essential right of command in which alone resides that power of the magistrate by which he rules and restrains other men and, at will and by any means, orders and disposes civil affairs to preserve the public good and keep the people in peace and concord. Nor is there any need to enumerate the particular tokens of sovereignty and the rights defined as regal, such as the final appeal, the right of life and death, of making war and peace, the authority to coin money, to raise revenue and taxes, and many things of that sort, since it is certain that all these are adjuncts

of the power of making law and may be prescribed on the authority of that power in different ways in different commonwealths according to the custom of the people. Nor, above all, is it necessary in this context to review the forms of government or prescribe the numbers of the governors. It is sufficient for our purpose, in effect, and we may take it as settled that that [institution] may be called 'magistrate' which can, of its own right, impose laws on subjects and sanction them, whether it be an assembly – as some desire – or a monarch.

(II) 'Divine worship' has several meanings.

(1) There are some for whom the phrase has the same meaning as 'religion' and they take both expressions in a very general sense as referring to the whole of that obedience which we owe to divine laws. Whatever in any way binds the conscience, anything we perform as commanded by God, all this they declare – not at all correctly, however – to be 'religion' and a part of 'divine worship', taking the definition so far that almost all human actions turn into divine worship, and we worship God in eating, drinking and sleeping, since there can be some degree of righteousness in these actions. And I conclude that in this sense of the phrase, surely, no one will deny that the magistrate can determine indifferent things in the worship of God and impose them on his subjects. Although when this is granted, it will not perhaps be altogether clear why the same right is necessarily denied in the remaining ceremonial trappings and the public gatherings of religion, since the same argument of indifferency applies in each case, as God, the supreme legislator, has nowhere excluded the power of the magistrate from these matters. But more of this below.

(2) 'Divine worship' is more correctly understood as being the actions of the inner virtues of all of which God is the object, as the love of God, reverence, fear, faith, etc.; this is that inner worship of the heart which God demands, in which the essence and soul of religion consists, and in the absence of which all the other observations of religious worship provoke God rather than propitiate him, offering a sacrifice no more pleasing to the divine will than the mutilated carcasses of slaughtered beasts would be. And this is why God so frequently and so particularly claims the heart and spirit for himself, and calls the mind and the inner depths of the soul shrines dedicated to his worship, and requires a spirit obedient to himself

as if it were the only worshipper that he prizes. But this worship, wholly silent and secret as it is, completely hidden from the eyes and observation of men, is neither subject to human laws, nor indeed capable of such subjection. God who lays bare the most secret corners of the mind, and who can alone either know the private deliberations of the mind or pass judgement upon them, is the only examiner of men's hearts.

(3) The outward acts of religion are also called 'divine worship'. Since God ordained that man should be composed of body as well as soul, he orders that he alone should be served by one of these, while by means of the other he has secured society and mutual association for mankind; for men cannot express the sentiments of their mind or benefit from mutual good will without the mediation and service of the body. But God requires the obedience of both, and he exacts from each the tribute it is able to pay; and since he seeks due service and recognition for himself on earth he is not satisfied with that silent and almost furtive form of worship alone, but he has required his worshippers – taught by whose example the rest of mankind are to be roused to the worship and reverence of his divine majesty – to acknowledge his name openly. And therefore he demands those outward performances by which that inner worship of the spirit is expressed, and indeed enlarged, such as public prayers, acts of thanksgiving, the singing of psalms, participation in the holy sacraments and the hearing of the divine word, by all of which we either bear witness here and now to the love, faith and obedience of the soul, or else strengthen it for the future; and this is the worship called external which is everywhere ordained by God in his law, and which by holy writ we are bound to fulfil, nor does the magistrate possess any right over this worship since it can be altered by none but the divine Lawgiver himself.

(4) Since there are no actions without a host of circumstances which always attend them, such as time, place, appearance, posture, etc., even divine worship cannot be free from this attendance; and thus these attributes of actions, by virtue of the necessary association they have with divine affairs, and because they everywhere and always in some way serve the end of the solemn and public forms of religious worship, are therefore themselves popularly taken for worship itself and styled devotion. But God in his great wisdom and beneficence has relinquished these rites to the discretion of the

magistrate and entrusted them to the care of him who holds power and has the right of governing the church, to be amended, abolished, renewed, or in whatever way soever enjoined as he should judge best in the light of the times and the customs of the people, and as the needs of the church should demand. And so long as his injunctions concerning the true and spiritual worship are kept inviolate, so long as the substance of religion is secure, he has allowed everything else to the churches themselves, that is, to their governors, to be established as it should seem necessary under this single law and token, namely that dignity, decency and order be sought after; for in different places different customs prevail, and a constant rule and standard could not possibly have been laid down in the divine law which would make clear what was proper for the several nations and what was not. Therefore, to make the path to the Christian religion as free of obstacles as possible for all the various nations, and in order that the approach to Christ and the new religion might lie more easily in the Gospel, God in his great mercy appointed that Christian doctrine should be embraced by the soul and faith alone and that true worship should be fulfilled in public gatherings and outward actions. But he by no means looked for so onerous an obedience from proselytes as that all men should forthwith abandon the customs and practices of their race, which are so generally agreeable, so dear to them through long use, and so honoured through education and esteem that you shall wrest fortune, life, liberty and all from most of them sooner than their respect and use of these things. How reluctantly, how bitterly, the Jews, when converted to Christianity, laid down that grievous and burdensome train of ceremonies already familiar to their race by custom; nor when freed by Christ did they want the heavy yoke to be shaken off their necks. We have recently heard reports of a city, situated in the East, among the Chinese, which after a prolonged siege was driven at last to surrender. The gates were thrown open to the enemy forces and all the inhabitants gave themselves up to the will of the triumphant victor. They had abandoned to their enemy's hands their own persons, their wives, families, liberty, wealth, and in short all things sacred and profane, but when they were ordered to cut off the plait of hair which, by national custom, they wore on their heads, they took up their arms again and fought fiercely until, to a man, all were killed. These men, although they

59

were ready to allow their whole civil existence to be reduced to slavery by their enemies, were so unable to allow them even the least interference with their hair, worn according to an ancestral custom, that the slightest of things and one of no significance, a mere excretion of the body, but all but sacrosanct by general esteem and the custom of their race, was easily preferred to life itself and the solid benefits of nature.[1]

And, certainly, whoever cares to contemplate our own civil commotions will confess that perhaps even among us war has at times been waged by some with equal barbarity and similar bitterness over issues of no greater weight.

But to return to the point: clearly, these ceremonies, these concomitant circumstances of actions, are so diverse and so unlike in practice among all peoples that you would look in vain, and comb the Gospel to no purpose, for a single common standard of propriety. You would not easily persuade an inhabitant of the East or a devotee of the Mahomedan profession to embrace the faith of a Christian worshipping his God (as he would consider) offensively with a bare head. It would seem no lighter an offence to them, the custom being unknown among them, than praying with the head covered would to us. And certainly, no one would consider going over to a religion as ridiculous in its ceremonies as all the customs of every nation are to every other. Therefore God, indulging the weakness of mankind, left his worship undetermined, to be adorned with ceremonies as the judgement of men might determine in the light of custom; and he no more judges his worshippers by these things than a king judges his subjects and their loyalty and obedience by their physical condition or the style of their clothes. But neither as Christians nor as subjects are those to be considered more faithful who are carelessly or meanly arrayed.

It seems, then, to be agreed by all that the magistrate is the judge of what constitutes order and of what is to be considered decent, and that he and he alone is able to determine what is appropriate and seemly. Nor, indeed (whatever some may assert to the contrary), do I think it the least part of Christian liberty that the magistrate is permitted to consult at the same time the interests of

---

[1] The probable source for this story is Martinus Martini, *Bellum Tartaricum*, published in Alvarez Semmedo's *History of that Great and Renowned Monarchy of China* (1655).

both public peace and the growth and dignity of religion, and to provide by the same laws for them both. So much may suffice regarding 'divine worship'.

We shall next explain what is to be understood here when it is said that the magistrate 'can impose on his subjects'. It is an axiom with the lawyers that we 'can' do that which we do by law, but I think two things are indicated by the terms of our question: (1) the right of the magistrate and his lawful power, and (2) the obligation of subjects – that is to say, what the magistrate can do without fault on his own part, and what he can do given the obligation of his subjects. In order that these may be more clearly defined we must start with a number of distinctions.

(1) A double power can be observed in the sanctions of the magistrate which I may call the material power and the preceptive power, a power over the object and a power in the act. (i) Power is material when the thing itself which is commanded is lawful and indifferent and contrary to no divine precept. (ii) Power is preceptive when the command is itself lawful; for, on the one hand, it is possible that the magistrate may sin in commanding unrestricted things, and, on the other hand, it is not lawful for him to bind all free and indifferent things and enclose them within the boundaries of the laws and impose them on the people, since in truth a magistrate is set above a people that governs them for this reason, that he may provide for the common good and the general welfare; he holds the helm so that he may guide the ship into harbour and not on to the rocks. The measure of this power is to be taken from the end or intention of the legislator; that is to say, the magistrate can impose whatever he judges to serve the well-being of the community but, on the other hand, he cannot – without sin, that is – impose that which he does not consider to serve or be subordinate to this end.

(2) As to the obligation of subjects, it must be understood that the power of the magistrate is on the one hand regulatory and on the other coercive, to which corresponds a double obligation, (i) the obligation to act, (ii) the obligation, if I may put it thus, to suffer; or, as it is commonly put, an active and a passive obedience.

On which premisses I hold:

(1) That the subject is bound to a passive obedience under any decree of the magistrate whatever, whether just or unjust, nor, on any ground whatsoever may a private citizen oppose the magistrate's

decrees by force of arms, though indeed if the matter is unlawful the magistrate sins in commanding.

(2) That if a law is 'lawful' in respect of its matter as well as its precept, the magistrate can legitimately sanction it and the subject is bound to execute obedience in all its forms, active as well as passive.

(3) That if a law is 'lawful' as to its matter but in the precept and intention is unlawful, that is, if it is designed not for public but for private benefit, as for instance when the magistrate, indulging his own cruelty or greed or vanity, introduces a law only to enrich himself, to abuse his subjects or to flatter himself, then, though such a law certainly renders the magistrates guilty and liable to punishment before the divine tribunal, yet, nevertheless, it binds the subject even to an active obedience, for where the matter is lawful the standard of obedience is not the intention of the legislator, which cannot be known, but his expressed will, which establishes obligation.

[III] Lastly,[2] it remains to say something of 'indifferent things' and what they are, since this is a hotly disputed subject. Now things are said to be indifferent in respect of moral good and evil, so that all things which are morally neither good nor evil are called indifferent. Since, however, moral actions imply a law as a standard of good and evil, against which we ought to measure and test our life and actions (for it is certain that if no law were provided all things and actions would be entirely indifferent and neutral, so that they could be done or left undone at the will of each individual), therefore, in order that indifferent things may be more clearly understood, some account must be given of laws, the general nature of which the learned Hooker describes, [*The Laws of Ecclesiastical Polity*] book I, ch. 2, thus: 'That which doth assign the force and power, that which doth appoint the form and measure of working, the same we term a law.'

Definitions of law occur in the writings of the authorities disagreeing in the way they are expressed but not in their substance – in the sense that there are manifold divisions and distinctions, for example, into natural and positive, human and divine, civil and

---

[2] Referring back to Locke's promise, at the beginning, to define 'magistrate', 'religious worship', and 'things indifferent'.

ecclesiastical and so forth. Leaving these on one side I may perhaps be allowed in the present controversy to venture a new way of sub-dividing law – into divine, or moral; political, or human; fraternal, or the law of charity; and monastic, or private. And although this distinction may be less familiar than others, and is less exact than is proper, it will perhaps be more suited to our present purpose for all that, and far from useless in the explanation of indifferent things. This mode of distinguishing between laws is derived mainly from the authors; for we call that law 'divine' which is instituted by God, and that 'human' which is instituted by a man invested with power; and these authors of laws are, by their power, superior to the laws themselves and to the subjects they govern. The fraternal law, or law of charity, also owns God as its author, but the occasion of its obligation can and usually does spring from some equal or even inferior fellow Christian. The author of the last law, which we call 'private', is any single individual, who is neither superior, he himself being obliged by this law, nor does he have the authority, in respect of a law relating to himself, to abrogate it once it has been intro-duced. But the grounds of these distinctions will appear more clearly in what follows:

(1) The divine law is that which, having been delivered to men by God, is a rule and pattern of living for them. And according as it either becomes known by the light of reason which is natural and implanted in men, or is made manifest in divine revelation, it is in turn divided into natural and positive law. And each of these I describe under the same head as 'moral' since each is exactly the same in its content and matter and they differ only in the manner of their promulgation and the clarity of their precepts. For this is that great rule of right and justice and the eternal foundation of all moral good and evil and which can be discovered even in things indifferent by the mediation of an inferior law. Whatever, then, this law reaches, either by prohibition or command, is always and everywhere necessarily good or evil, and all other things which are not confined within the bounds of this law are indifferent by nature and their use is free.

(2) Human law is that which is enacted by anyone maintaining law and command over others. Or, rather, I should say that any command of a superior to his inferior over whom he holds legitimate power, for instance of parents to children, of master to

servant, can come under the head of human law and requires obedience, although the public ordinances of societies enacted by the magistrate, as they are particularly important and either abolish or confirm or alter private rights at will, are what we specially want to be understood here under the title of human law. Its proper matter is indifferent things which are not comprised within the limits of a higher, that is, of the divine, law, and are to that extent not already bound up and determined. For although the magistrate can forbid theft and demand chastity this is to act superfluously and seems to be not so much to make new law as to declare and enforce the old. For things of this sort are necessary and oblige the conscience of subjects even if he is silent. But since the responsibility for society is entrusted to the magistrate by God and since on the one hand all the evils likely to befall a commonwealth could not be guarded against by an unlimited number of laws, while on the other to have exactly the same constitution would not always be an advantage to a people, God left many indifferent things untrammelled by his laws and handed them to his deputy the magistrate as fit material for civil government, which, as occasion should demand, could be commanded or prohibited, and by the wise regulation of which the welfare of the commonwealth could be provided for.

(3) That law is styled fraternal or the law of charity by which our liberty is confined within an even narrower compass and we lose the use of things left free both by divine and civil law. This happens when a weak brother, holding no power over us, can in his own right tie up our liberty in indifferent things although allowed us both by God and the magistrate, and consequently cause that to be unlawful for us 'here and now' – as they say – which might be entirely lawful elsewhere and for another. This is commonly known as the law of scandal, which we obey when, taking account of the welfare and innocence of any Christian not fully informed of his liberty, we are unwilling to make public use of our liberty in things lawful lest he, perchance unacquainted with his Christian liberty, and led into error by our example, performs that which he is far from convinced is lawful for him to do and thus becomes guilty of a crime. For example, eating meat offered to idols was lawful for Christians, nor did any divine or human law forbid it, and the action was accordingly indifferent and entirely lawful. But since many were unaware of this liberty and in the words of the Apostle Paul,

1 Cor. 8:7, 'in all men there is not that knowledge', etc., he even warns us in that passage to abstain from free things lest we provide a stumbling-block for our brother[3] – the sum of which precept comes simply to this: that things indifferent and altogether lawful should be refrained from if there is any fear that a brother may be offended by that liberty. That is, not lest he is angered or takes it ill or is enraged because another sins or appears to sin, but lest on our example he should do that which is not lawful for him because he himself does not consider it lawful for him.

(4) Besides the above-named laws there remains the other called monastic or private, which a man imposes on himself and by a new, superinduced obligation renders necessary things hitherto indifferent and not bound by previous laws. And this law is twofold, either of conscience or of contract, the one originating from the judgement, the other from the will. The law of conscience we call that fundamental judgement of the practical intellect concerning any possible truth of a moral proposition about things to be done in life. For it is not enough that a thing may be indifferent in its own nature unless we are convinced that it is so. God implanted the light of nature in our hearts and willed that there should be an inner legislator (in effect) constantly present in us whose edicts it should not be lawful for us to transgress even a nail's breadth. Thus our liberty in indifferent things is so insecure and so bound up with the opinion of everyone else that it may be taken as certain that we do indeed lack the liberty which we think we lack. That injunction of the apostle to the Romans, ch. 14, v. 5, is to the point here: 'Let each man be fully assured in his own mind', and verse 14, 'I know and am persuaded in the Lord Jesus, that nothing is unclean of itself' (he is speaking of things to be eaten); 'save that to him who accounteth anything to be unclean, to him it is unclean', and v. 23, 'But he that doubteth is damned if he eat, because he eateth not of faith; and whatsoever is not of faith, is sin' – this faith being nothing but a fixed opinion of one's own liberty, as appears from the context.

The other private law is derived from the will and takes the form of compact, which we enter into with God or with our fellow man.

---

[3] Verse 13: 'Wherefore, if meat make my brother to offend, I will eat no flesh while the world standeth, lest I make my brother to offend.'

The former is called by a special name, a vow, an example of which was that of Jacob, Genesis, ch. 28, 'And Jacob vowed a vow, saying, If God will be with me, and will keep me in this way that I go, and will give me bread to eat, and raiment to put on, then this stone, which I have set up for a pillar, shall be God's house; and of all that thou shalt give me I will surely give the tenth unto thee.' And the obligation of a vow is shown in Deuteronomy, ch. 23, vv. 21, 22, 'When thou shalt vow a vow unto the Lord thy God, though shalt not be slack to pay it; for the Lord thy God will surely require it of thee; and it would be sin in thee. But if you shalt forbear to vow, it shall be no sin in thee.' And this is here described as a freewill offering. Promises between men bind in the same way and in both cases our liberty is in our own hands so that we may abandon or preserve it as we will.

These points being made, I argue:

(1) That all these laws are, in respect of their obligation, plainly divine, that is, that no other law immediately and of itself binds the consciences of men except for the divine, since the others do not bind men by virtue of their own innate force but by virtue of some divine precept on which they are grounded; nor are we bound to obey magistrates for any other reason than that the Lord has commanded it, saying, 'Let every soul be in subjection to the higher powers', and that 'it is necessary to be subject, not only because of the wrath but also for conscience sake' [Rom. 13:1, 5].[4]

(2) That human laws and the others detailed just now, with the single exception of the divine, do not change the nature of indifferent things so far that, on the authority of these laws, from being altogether indifferent they become, of themselves, necessary, but only so far as we are concerned, 'here and now', and with regard to the obligation which a new and human injunction may have temporarily induced and by which we are bound to obey, to act or to abstain. However, when that law is abolished or is in any way inoperative, we are restored to our former liberty, the thing itself remaining unchanged.

(3) That the subordination of these laws one to another is such that an inferior law cannot in any way remove or repudiate the

---

[4] Locke refers to this famous text for political obedience in the First Treatise of Government, §92.

obligation and authority of a superior. For this would be to overturn the order of things and subject master to servant, to establish not order and government in the world but anarchy, and to own no other legislator than the meanest and most ignorant member of the mob.[5] To appeal from the divine tribunal to man is not lawful, nor can a subject's vow or a private error of conscience nullify the edicts of the magistrate, for, if this is once granted, discipline will be everywhere at an end, all law will collapse, all authority will vanish from the earth and, the seemly order of affairs being convulsed and the frame of government dissolved, each would be his own law-maker and his own God.

(4) And lastly I hold: that all the things that are indifferent so far as a higher law is concerned are the object and matter of a lower, and the authority of the individual prevails in all matters that are not wholly prescribed by a superior law, and whatever is left, as it were, in the balance, inclining neither to this side nor to that, towards neither good nor evil, can be adopted and appropriated to either class by an adjoining and subordinate power. For where the divine law sets bounds to its action, there the authority of the magistrate begins, and whatever is classed as indeterminate and indifferent under that law is subordinate to the civil power. Where the edicts of the commonwealth are wanting, the law of scandal will find a place; and only when all these are silent are the commands of conscience and the vow observed. Nor does anything remain free from the higher laws which each individual as master of his own liberty cannot, by opinion, vow or contract, make necessary for himself.

And it is indeed to be wondered for what reason the very men who freely allow this arrangement and extent of power in all other respects wish it to be denied exclusively to the magistrate and the civil authority if, as one must suppose, they believe that public power ought to be ranked above that of the individual and that there either can or should be some government and political society among men. In addition to that supreme power of almighty God they have no doubts either about the other laws listed here. They readily own as extensive and absolute an authority as you please of

---

[5] The Latin is 'plebs'; the word 'mob' was not yet in English usage, but became so by the end of the century.

scandal, conscience, oath and compact in the determination and limiting of indifferent things. But they firmly maintain that there is no right over indifferent things on the part of the magistrate – whom they call a contemptible little creature governing with a power obtained by entreaty and not (as holy Scripture holds) ordained by God with the power of command – at least not over those concerning the worship of God. But we would argue that the opposite conclusion is confirmed in this matter, by, for instance, the analogy and subordination of the laws mentioned above, as, too, by the precepts of the apostle where he commands all creatures to be obedient to the higher powers [Rom. 13:1], and again by the [first] Epistle of Saint Peter, ch. 2, v. 13, 'Be subject to every ordinance of man for the Lord's sake: whether it be to the king as supreme.' And one might be permitted to add some other evidence to this. From which instances it would appear that the magistrate does have some power in indifferent things, for where obedience is required, and subjection, there must necessarily be power, nor can anyone be subjected unless there is some superior personage endowed with public authority – a personage who can not only impose things already good or evil under the divine law on his subjects, as some would have it, but things indifferent as well.

And this is apparent from the fact: (i) That the apostle in that place commands the performance of obedience to the magistrate, not to God. And if his only duty were to repeat the commandments of God, and as a herald rather than a legislator only to declare the divine commands and impress them on the people, the power of the magistrate seems to be no greater than that of any private citizen. For divine law possesses the same force and the same grounds for obligation whether it is made known through the mouth of the prince or through that of the subject; and neither of them commands but rather teaches. (ii) That he commands subordination for conscience sake, which would be a pointless addition unless magistrates have some power in indifferent matters. For no Christian could doubt that in necessary things even when the magistrate is silent the conscience obliges – because things are 'necessary' just because they do bind the conscience. And therefore what ought to be understood here is something that obliges by virtue of the command of a superior power, and this can be nothing but a thing indifferent. (iii) Because the apostle takes indifferent things as an example. Tribute, he says, to whom tribute is due [Rom. 13:7], although it is certain that no tribute is due unless the magistrate commands it, both ownership and the rights of property being in general entirely free, it being open to everyone individually either to harvest his wealth or to give away his riches to anyone else and, as it were, to transfer them; and whether they are ours or another's is a matter of complete indifference.

But[6] what is the point of all this? Who, you will ask, denies the power of the magistrate in civil indifferent things? I will tell you: the fact is that he who denies either of these powers denies them both. And there are indeed some who flatly and openly do this, denying what others admit when pressed, although they [too] deny it when disputing; so true is it that either both [powers] must be kept or both must be abandoned.

We must therefore start by establishing that general principle from which, once it is proved, it will follow with perfect justice that indifferent things, even those regarding divine worship, must be subjected to governmental power. Now as the indifferency of all things is exactly the same and on both sides we find the same arguments and indeed the same matter, the only difference being in the way they are viewed, there being no greater distinction than there is between a gown worn in the market-place and the self-same gown worn in church, it is clear that the magistrate's authority embraces the one type of indifferent things as much as the other unless God by some decree of his own has circumscribed the magistrate's power within narrower limits, not allowing his sanctuary to be set within the bounds of the civil jurisdiction.

But for the truth to be more clearly evident the subject must be examined a little more profoundly. The sources of civil power must be investigated and the very foundations of authority uncovered.

Now I find that there are, among the authors who discuss this question, commonly two such foundations. It is not impossible for our present thesis to be grounded on either of these foundations or to be established whichever of the two is accepted. For some suppose men to be born in servitude, others, to liberty. The latter assert an equality between men founded on the law of nature, while the

---

[6] This paragraph is not in Locke's first draft; it underscores his animus against the radical sects.

former maintain a paternal right over children and claim that government originates thence. However that may be, this much is certain, that, if the magistrate is born to command, and if he possesses the throne and sceptre by divine institution and by the distinction of his character and nature, then it is beyond dispute that he is the sole ruler of the land and its inhabitants without contract or condition and that he may do whatever is not forbidden by God, to whom alone he is subjected and from whom alone he received his title to live and to rule. Nor can anyone deny that all indifferent actions, of whatsoever sort they may be, lie under the power of him to whose discretion are delivered the liberty, fortunes and the life itself of every subject. But, if men enjoy a right to an equal liberty, being equal by virtue of their common birth, then it is clear that no union could occur among men, that no common way of life would be possible, no law, nor any constitution by which men could, as it were, unite themselves into a single body unless each one first divests himself of that native liberty – as they suppose it to be – and transfers it to some other, whether a prince or a senate (depending on the constitution on which they happen to agree) in whom a supreme power must necessarily reside. For a commonwealth without human laws never has existed and never could, and laws derived from any but the highest power cannot bind; for who would have the right to determine anything against his superiors, or those who were equally free? Now that power is sovereign which has no superior on earth to which it is bound to give an account of its actions. But such a power can never be established unless each and every individual surrenders the whole of this natural liberty of his, however great it may be, to the legislator, granting it to him who with the authority of all (by proxy, as it were), empowered by the general consent of each, makes valid laws for them. Whence it follows that whatever any individual is permitted to do that, too, the magistrate is permitted to command. For he concentrates in his person the authority and natural right of every individual by a general contract; and all indifferent things, sacred no less than profane, are entirely subjected to his legislative power and government.

To these a third way of constituting civil power may perhaps be added. One in which all authority is held to come from God but the nomination and appointment of the person bearing that power is thought to be made by the people. Otherwise a right to govern will not easily be derived from the paternal right nor a right of life and death from the popular.

However, I offer no conclusion about these theories, nor do I consider it of any relevance to our present controversy whether one or other of them be true. Rather I say: God wished there to be order, society and government among men. And this we call the commonwealth. In every commonwealth there must be some supreme power without which it cannot truly be a commonwealth; and that supreme power is exactly the same in all government, namely, legislative. The object and matter of legislative power we have shown above to be all indifferent things, and we repeat once more that either the power of the supreme magistrate is over these, or else it is nothing. But since it is certainly agreed that the magistrate has power over civil things indifferent, and most people grant this to be so, it would follow from their own arguments that if religion did not exist all indifferent things would be subject to the authority of the magistrate, and therefore, since our religion is Christian, it follows that if no law can be deduced from the Christian religion by which any part of indifferent things is withdrawn from the magistrate's control, and by which the magistrate is forbidden to determine this or that sort of indifferency in this or that respect, then power in all indifferent things is of exactly the same extent as if there were no religion at all, since the authority of the magistrate is denied in many indifferent things only on the pretext of a Christian law of this sort.

But whether any law of this sort opposed to civil power can in fact be found established among the precepts of the Gospel will appear from the following arguments of the dissenting schools.

(1) The first among them are those who, proceeding directly, maintain that the law of the Gospel takes this authority from the magistrate to itself and keeps the civil governor at a distance from holy matters. They claim that the New Testament forbids him to presume to intermingle himself and his power with holy worship. They exult in their present emancipation from this slavery and chatter about nothing but their Christian liberty. Determined to make good their case, they pile up Scriptural texts, quote the testimony of the apostles, marshal an army of instances and, with complete faith in these forces, look for an easy and certain victory. As it would be tedious to go through each of these cases individually, let

alone to discuss and refute them in detail, I shall briefly reply thus: truly, great liberty is given to mankind by our Saviour and is often proclaimed in the Gospel, but on looking at that evidence a little more carefully it will be agreed that this liberty provides very little support for their argument. For that liberty of which mention is so frequently made in the Gospel has two senses only. One is that Christ frees his subjects from the dominion and slavery of the devil. The other is that he removed from the necks of the Jews that grim yoke of the ceremonial law which, as the Apostle Peter observes [Acts 15], neither they nor their fathers could support; and, after nullifying that law under which, straitened and oppressed, they had long groaned, he set them free to enjoy the common destiny of his subjects and of his most welcome kingdom.

However, the New Testament nowhere makes any mention of the controlling or limiting of the magistrate's authority since no precept appointed for the civil magistrate appears either in the Gospel or in the Epistles. In truth it is for the most part silent as to government and civil power, or rather Christ himself, often lighting on occasions of discussing this matter, seems to refuse deliberately to involve himself in civil affairs and, not owning any kingdom but the divine spiritual one as his own, he let the civil government of the commonwealth go by unchanged. And the Apostle Paul, the teacher of the Gentiles, confirms the point, 1 Cor., ch. 7, where he teaches that the civil condition of men is not to be altered at all by Christian religion and liberty, but that bondservants, even though they were made subject to Christ, should still continue bondservants in their civil state and owe the same obedience as before to their masters. Nor is the argument at all different in the case of the prince and his subjects, since there appears not the faintest trace in holy Scripture of any commandment by which the power of the magistrate is diminished in any indifferent matters.

(2) Others deny that the magistrate is allowed to impose indifferent things in divine worship on the ground that Scripture itself is a perfect rule both of life and conduct. I reply: that by this argument the perfection of Scripture abolishes the magistrate's power in civil as much as in ecclesiastical things. For if Scripture is so far a perfect rule of conduct that it is an offence to introduce other laws regarding the reform and discipline of conduct, civil edicts would, on this account, be as unlawful henceforth as religious ones. Nor would it

be right for the magistrate to enact a law about anything at all, since no law can be introduced which is not in some sort a rule of life and conduct. By what greater right could he prescribe a style of dress to judges and lawyers than to priests and ministers of religion? Or how should he presume to determine place, manner and time of speaking for a lecturer any more than for a preacher of the Gospel, since the argument is the same in each case and that perfect rule of life neither needs nor allows any other rule for determining the conduct of the Christian lecturer or public speaker? But I suggest that this rule can be called perfect in two ways. First, Scripture can be called a perfect rule in so far as it provides general standards of conduct from which all other particular rules derive and can be deduced. Nor can any just command be discovered, whether of magistrate, parent or master, which is not contained and grounded in Scripture, as, for example, that precept, 'Let all things be done decently and in order' [1 Cor. 14:40], [which] encompasses the particular laws regarding the ceremonies of divine worship subsequently to be enacted by the governors of the church. Secondly, that may be called a perfect rule of conduct which embraces each particular duty of our lives and prescribes what should be done and what left undone by each of us in every circumstance – a perfect rule of life such as there never was or could be. Or, if they like, Scripture is a perfect rule of the inward and necessary worship, but it has nowhere delivered or described the number and kind of ceremonies and circumstances but has left them to the churches themselves so that the custom of each place might be taken into account and all things established in the light of the necessity of the times, the opinions of men and the dignity of the things themselves.

(3) It is objected that to mix the contrivances of human wit with divine worship is 'superstition'; that acts of worship which ought to be performed according to the purpose and rule of the divine will do not allow of human ceremonies, nor are presumptuous men lightly permitted to violate that holy sphere and the realm in which God is sole legislator. Hence if any rite is prescribed in divine worship which is distasteful to their palate, they at once launch a bitter attack on the legislator and pass sentence with severe censure on both the thing itself and its author. But because 'superstition' is a word which has an evil sound, by this means, as though with some spectre, those who seek either to decry or to change the

outward worship of God are accustomed to alarm the ignorant minds of the crowd, and they apply this designation as a mask to things that are quite inoffensive and proper.

In Latin the word means the worship of those remaining alive after death and it corresponds to the word *daemonia*, which has various meanings in Greek: first, it is synonymous with the worship of demons, that is, of spirits: second, the worship of heroes; third, fear (which they consider slavish) of the one true God, as a result of which, terrified no doubt, we represent the deity as harsh, implacable and cruel; fourth, the worship of each sect and religion is called 'superstition' by others since the initiates of every sect, condemning all other ways of worshipping the deity but their own, are in the habit of labelling them 'superstition'. Thus, Festus calls the Christian religion a superstition, Acts 25:19, 'But had certain questions against him of their own superstition, and of one Jesus, who was dead, whom Paul affirmed to be alive'. Whence we conclude that the same liberty is granted to these objectors as was allowed Festus: they may call the institutions of the church and the religious ceremonial prescribed by law 'superstition', but the worship itself is not thereby rendered in any way less lawful. Nor is it any more to be repudiated on that account than the Christian faith had to be abandoned by blessed Paul once he had heard it called 'superstition'. When, in short, they claim that God is the sole legislator this is to be understood in the same way as the argument that Scripture is the only and perfect rule of life. Namely, that God alone has power over the consciences of men, that he alone enacts laws on his own authority, and that all just commands, public as well as private, proceed from his will and are founded on it. However, that text, 'One only is the Lawgiver able to save and to destroy', taken from the Epistle of St James [4:12], is not wholly relevant to the present issue, as appears from the context.

(4) Scandal is raised as an objection; that is to say, the magistrate is not allowed to impose ceremonies because they are stumbling-blocks.

(i) I reply that that is not a scandal which annoys another, or which another considers improper to be performed – which is habitually the state of mind of those who take the opposite view and who usually sin, not by imitating, in which the nature of scandal consists, but by taking offence.

(ii) I hold that all that which is called scandalous, at which a man may stumble and so fall, is not directly evil; for Christ himself is often called a stumbling-block and many are said to have been offended by him.

(iii) I hold that he who takes offence always errs, but not so he who gives it.

(iv) I say that if the magistrate were not allowed to establish anything but what cannot offend anyone he could not justly enact any law at all, since nothing is so pleasing to everyone, nothing seems so just and reasonable to every eye, that someone will not discover in it something which he will denounce and consider in his judgement unlawful.

(v) I hold that because it may happen that a man is genuinely offended by ceremonies established by the magistrate it does not therefore follow that the law is sinful and on that account does not oblige, since the ill will of an individual inferior or a private opinion or scruple does not in the least prejudice the public right of the magistrate. Nor can any condition of an inferior possibly suspend the power of a superior. For in such a case the obligation of laws would depend not on the will of the magistrate but on our assent, and a subject might at will nullify all the laws enacted by the magistrate. It can never be that the magistrate should know the minds and wishes of all his subjects, since the perverting influence of customs, the frivolity of opinions, the allurements of pleasures, the violence of passions and the enthusiasm of parties confuse and mislead our feeble minds in such diverse ways. Nor, even if he did know, could he or should he consult the opinion and scruples of all concerned. It suffices for the legality and obligation of a law if in free and indifferent contexts he establishes whatever appears to him, as bearing responsibility for the commonwealth, to be in some way conducive to public peace and the welfare of the people.

(5) Others, to withdraw themselves from the reach of the magistrate and to flout the obligation of the laws established by him, retire into themselves and seek an asylum where they may safely hide in the depths of their own conscience, not to be profaned in the least degree by the laws and ceremonies of the church. This liberty of conscience is altogether divine and under obligation only to the will of God, so that if the magistrate asserts that it lies within the scope of his power, he culpably perpetrates an affront to the

divine majesty and does violence and injustice to his fellow men. Hence all laws which in any way constrain or circumscribe this liberty are held to be *ipso facto* unlawful and void.

But, in order to understand what laws are indeed opposed to the liberty of conscience – it being apparent that all the just laws of the magistrate, civil as well as ecclesiastical, do oblige the consciences of subjects – some distinction must first be made between obligation and liberty.

I maintain, then, that the obligation of human laws may be of two sorts, material, or formal. (i) Obligation is 'material' when the thing itself which is the subject-matter of a human law obliges the conscience of itself; when, that is, it was already unquestionably necessary by virtue of the force of the divine law before the intro-duction of a human law. (ii) Obligation is 'formal' when a thing otherwise indifferent is imposed on the people by the lawful power of the magistrate and obliges the conscience. One of these obliges of its own nature, the other by virtue of the extent of the magistrate's command.

It follows that the liberty with which we are concerned here is also twofold: a liberty of the judgement, and a liberty of the will. (i) Liberty of the judgement exists when the approbation of the judgement is not necessarily required that this or that is in its own nature 'necessary'; and in this consists the whole liberty of the con-science. (ii) Liberty of the will exists when the assent of the will is not required to this or that act; and this can be removed without infringing the liberty of the conscience.

These points being made, I now hold:

(i) That if the magistrate commands what has already been enjoined by God – for example, that a subject should refrain from theft or adultery – the obligation of this law is both material and formal so that the liberty of both the judgement and the will is removed and thereby that of the conscience itself. Such a law, how-ever, is not unjust, since it throws no new shackles on the con-science, nor does the magistrate set other or narrower limits to the liberty of the conscience than does God himself.

(ii) That if the magistrate, in so far as he is provided with legisl-ative power, on his own authority commands a free and indifferent action of his subjects by decree, then that law – since its obligation is merely formal and not material, that is, the matter is made necessary not of its own nature but by virtue of the command of the civil magistrate – certainly binds the conscience. But it does not remove its liberty since to be obeyed it requires the assent of the will only. It does not require the assent of the judgement that it has any necessity in itself. And hence I say that all the magistrate's laws, civil as well as ecclesiastical, those that concern divine worship as much as those that concern civil life, are just and valid, obliging men to act but not to judge; and, providing for both at the same time, unite a necessity of obedience with a liberty of conscience.

(iii) That if the magistrate chooses to impose a thing indifferent by material obligation on his subjects; that is to say, if he legislates as if the thing was in itself necessary before the law was proposed by him when in fact it was not but was quite indifferent, then by such a law he ensnares the liberty of the conscience and sins in commanding it. But in truth ecclesiastical laws, by which acts are transformed into ceremonial practices, are not proposed in this manner, nor so much ordered because they are necessary as called necessary because they are ordered.

[6] Finally, at the end of the column, come those who for[e]bode ill of the authority of the magistrate and say that so great a power is neither lawful nor tolerable on this ground: that it can be extremely productive of misfortune, that it can be full of hazards, that it is impossible to know where the magistrate will finally restrain himself. What burden or absurdity, they repeatedly cry, may not a headstrong magistrate impose on us, if he is endowed with an almost infinite power of this sort? Why has God bestowed reason on us, and why religion, to what purpose are we born human, to what end made Christians, if neither our reason nor our religion will suffice to establish practices for fulfilling the worship of God? And a great many similar complaints and bugbears of various kinds are conjured up in the empty heads of these foolish men.

But it is appropriate to observe here, that these objections, as those mentioned before, oppose and uproot the power of the magistrate in civil indifferencies as much as in those of religion, whence again we may perceive how close the affinity and association is between all things indifferent, those regarding ceremonies no less than those regarding manners. So that if the authority of the magistrate is withdrawn, even in part, from the one, it collapses in the other. But, briefly, I reply: in the nature of things there is nothing so utterly perfect and harmless that from it no evil can, or is accustomed to, derive, or at least be feared; and many just and lawful things are regularly felt by some to be senseless and onerous. But in truth those inconveniences which befall me, or can befall me, from the right of another in no way impede his right.

And so I have now displayed and described the forces of the enemy in this slight sketch and in passing have touched lightly on the heads of their arguments. To review all their devices and examples and authorities would be a tedious business, nor does time allow, or the weight of the arguments demand, a detailed examination. Whoever now takes arms against us will find his place in the ranks set out above.

Essays on the Law of Nature

c. 1663–4. Nine essays in Latin, of which I–VIII are printed here.
There is no general title, each essay being individually titled. MS
Locke, e. 6 is in Locke's hand but contains only Essays IV–IX; f. 31
is a copy of the whole text in the hand of an amanuensis with
corrections and additions by Locke; there is a later copy in f. 30,
pp. 122–84 (which Locke marked 'Lex Na[tur]ae'). Printed in Von
Leyden 1954; Horwitz *et al.* 1990 (under the title *Questions Concerning the Law of Nature*); extracts in Raphael 1969, I, 160–66;
Wootton 1993, pp. 177–83. Discussed in Von Leyden 1954 and
1956; Singh 1961; Seliger 1963; Abrams 1967, pp. 84–107; Dunn
1969, chs. 3, 14; Snyder 1986. Cited by Laslett, First Treatise,
§86; Second Treatise, §§12, 14, 51, 57, 77, 93. Letters 104, 106, 932
and 957 are pertinent. The present text reproduces Von Leyden's
translation (1954, pp. 109–215). He used MS f. 31 as his copy-text;
arguably he should have used MS e. 6 for Essays IV–IX. For criti-
cism of his edition see Horwitz *et al.* 1990 and Stewart 1992. Horwitz argues, inter alia, that Von Leyden's use of such Christian
terms as 'Almighty God' and 'Adam' is not warranted by the Latin
text. I have retained Von Leyden's numbering of the essays: in
fact, Locke numbered from I to XII, but left three as titles only,
without corresponding text.

Locke delivered these essays as lectures in his capacity as Censor
of Moral Philosophy at Christ Church, Oxford. The term 'essays'
is misleading: they are disquisitions which follow the traditional
scholastic format of posing arguments for, and objections against,
disputed questions. I have omitted Essay IX, his Valedictory
Address as Censor (printed in Von Leyden, pp. 221–43), which is
distinct in purpose and tone, being a light-hearted adieu to his

office and to his colleagues. In the essays Locke made many distinctions and divisions: I have occasionally inserted numeration to make the structure of his argument more visible. The essays prefigure later discussion in the *Essay Concerning Human Understanding*, especially the critique of innate ideas in bk I, the discussion of morality in bk II, ch. 28, and the discussion of the grounds and kinds of knowledge in bk IV; Essay VIII is closest to the later concerns of the *Two Treatises*. Von Leyden suggests several sources for Locke's ideas. The most tangible are the silent borrowings from Richard Hooker's *Laws of Ecclesiastical Polity* in Essay I, and from Robert Sanderson's *De Juramenti Promissorii Obligatione* (1646) and *De Obligatione Conscientiae* (1660) in Essay VI. Also detectable is Nathaniel Culverwell's *Discourse of the Light of Nature* (1652). Locke's citations include Aristotle, Seneca, Augustine, Aquinas, and Grotius.

Locke proceeds as follows. Having asserted that there is a law of nature (I), he turns to consider how we can know it (II–V): he delineates kinds of knowledge (II), denies that the law of nature can be known intuitively (III), or from the common consent of humanity (V), and argues that, rather, it is known through reason working upon the data of sense-experience (IV). He then discusses what makes the law of nature obligatory. This entails consideration of God's justice, the concept of lawmaking, and the role of punishment (VI). Next it entails reflection upon the ways in which law, while being universally binding, is modified by circumstances and by particular moral relations (VII). Finally, Locke challenges the sceptical claim that the only ground for human action is self-interest and personal pleasure (VIII).

Locke never published his essays, though James Tyrrell urged him to do so. They were known within his circle, and their influence is marked in his friend Gabriel Towerson's *An Explication of the Decalogue* (1676) and in Tyrrell's *Brief Disquisition of the Law of Nature* (1692), which includes extracts, almost verbatim, from Essay VI. Locke's own doubts about his arguments may be reflected in a remark he made in his Valedictory Address: 'I took part this year in your disputations on such terms that I always went out at once beaten and enriched. Such indeed was the grace of your victory that your arguments, to which I so often yielded, added as much to my knowledge as they detracted from my reputation. That law about which was all our strife had often eluded my fruitless quest, had not your way of life restored that very same law which your tongue had wrested from me. Hence it can be doubted

whether your disputations assaulted the law of nature or your
behaviour defended it, more keenly' (Von Leyden 1954, pp. 237–
9).

I

Is there a Rule of Morals, or Law of Nature given to us? Yes

Since God shows himself to us as present everywhere and, as it
were, forces himself upon the eyes of men as much in the fixed
course of nature now as by the frequent evidence of miracles in
time past, I assume there will be no one to deny the existence of
God, provided he recognises either the necessity for some rational
account of our life, or that there is a thing that deserves to be called
virtue or vice. This then being taken for granted, and it would be
wrong to doubt it, namely, that some divine being presides over the
world – for it is by his order that the heaven revolves in unbroken
rotation, the earth stands fast and the stars shine, and it is he who
has set bounds even to the wild sea and prescribed to every kind of
plants the manner and periods of germination and growth; it is in
obedience to his will that all living beings have their own laws of
birth and life; and there is nothing so unstable, so uncertain in this
whole constitution of things as not to admit of valid and fixed laws
of operation appropriate to its nature – it seems just therefore to
inquire whether man alone has come into the world altogether
exempt from any law applicable to himself, without a plan, rule, or
any pattern of his life. No one will easily believe this, who has
reflected upon Almighty God,[1] or the unvarying consensus of the
whole of mankind at every time and in every place, or even upon
himself or his conscience. But before we come to speak of the law
itself and those arguments whereby its existence is proved, it seems
to me worthwhile to indicate the various names by which it is
denoted.

[1] First then, we can equate with our law that moral good or
virtue which philosophers in former times (and among them
especially the Stoics[2]) have searched for with so much zeal and

---

[1] MS has 'Deum O.M.', i.e. 'Deum Optimum Maximum'.

[2] A school of Greek and Roman philosophers, chiefly Seneca, Cicero, Epictetus,
and Marcus Aurelius.

adorned with so many praises; we can equate with it that single good which Seneca says man ought to be content with, to which appertains so much dignity, so much glory, that even those among mortals who are corrupted by vice recognise it and, while shunning it, approve it.

[2] Secondly, there is the title of right reason, to which everyone who considers himself a human being lays claim, and this it is about which the various parties of men contend so fiercely among themselves, and which each one alleges to be the foundation of its doctrine. By reason, however, I do not think is meant here that faculty of the understanding which forms trains of thought and deduces proofs, but certain definite principles of action from which spring all virtues and whatever is necessary for the proper moulding of morals. For that which is correctly derived from these principles is justly said to be in accordance with right reason.

[3] Others, and they are many, refer to a law of nature, by which term they understand a law of the following description: i.e. a law which each can detect merely by the light planted in us by nature, to which also he shows himself obedient in all points and which, he perceives, is presupposed by the principle of his obligation; and this is the rule of living according to nature which the Stoics so often emphasise.

This law, denoted by these appellations, ought to be distinguished from natural right: for right is grounded in the fact that we have the free use of a thing, whereas law is that which enjoins or forbids the doing of a thing.

Hence, this law of nature can be described as being the decree of the divine will discernible by the light of nature and indicating what is and what is not in conformity with rational nature, and for this very reason commanding or prohibiting. It appears to me less correctly termed by some people the dictate of reason, since reason does not so much establish and pronounce this law of nature as search for it and discover it as a law enacted by a superior power and implanted in our hearts. Neither is reason so much the maker of that law as its interpreter, unless, violating the dignity of the supreme legislator, we wish to make reason responsible for that received law which it merely investigates; nor indeed can reason give us laws, since it is only a faculty of our mind and part of us. Hence it is pretty clear that all the requisites of a law are found in natural law. For, in the first place, it is the decree of a superior will, wherein the formal cause of a law appears to consist; in what manner, however, this may become known to mankind is a question perhaps to be discussed later on. Secondly, it lays down what is and what is not to be done, which is the proper function of a law. Thirdly, it binds men, for it contains in itself all that is requisite to create an obligation. Though, no doubt, it is not made known in the same way as positive laws, it is sufficiently known to men (and this is all that is needed for the purpose) because it can be perceived by the light of nature alone.

So much being assumed, the existence of such a law is made acceptable by the following arguments:

[1] The first argument can be derived from a passage in Aristotle's *Nicomachean Ethics*, bk I, ch. 7, where he says that 'the special function of man is the active exercise of the mind's faculties in accordance with rational principle' [1098a7]. For since in the preceding passages he had shown by various examples that there is a special sort of work each thing is designed to perform, he tried to find out what this may be in the case of a human being also. Thus, having taken account of all the operations of the vegetal and sentient faculties which men have in common with animals and plants, in the end he rightly concludes that the proper function of man is acting in conformity with reason, so much so that man must of necessity perform what reason prescribes. Likewise in bk v, ch. 7, where he draws a distinction between legal justice and natural justice, Aristotle says 'A natural rule of justice is one which has the same validity everywhere' [1134b18]. Hence it is rightly concluded that there is a law of nature, since there is a law which obtains everywhere.

⟨For[3] there are some moral principles which the whole of mankind recognises and which all men in the world accept unanimously; but this could not happen if the law were not a natural one. Though there are indeed some principles about which men disagree among themselves, nevertheless the definitions of virtues are fixed and invariable among them all. But if these laws were positive and

---

[3] This paragraph was deleted by Locke, but not before he had made corrections in it. The passage takes a more sanguine view of the argument from the consent of humankind than is expressed in Essay v.

arbitrarily laid down by men without any concept or obligation antecedent to such laws, they would not be everywhere so similar to one another, nor would there be so much agreement among them: virtue would be one thing among the Indians, another among the Romans, for in nothing do men differ and diverge from one another more than in their civil laws and their positive regulations of manners and customs. This argument is also demonstrated by the fact that the theory of virtues can be comprised within the limits of a science, for it is by this that 'whatever depends on convention is highly distinguished from things natural; for things concerning nature, being always the same, can readily be gathered into a science, while those which are the outcome of convention form no part of science, because they often change and are different in different places'.[4] Hence it is rightly concluded that there is a law laid down by nature. Nor, in fact, is the general consent of men a matter without meaning and of no importance at all; for this general consent cannot be derived from any other source than some principle which is common to all men and of which nature itself is the source. Surely, when many men in different times and places affirm one and the same thing as a certain truth, this thing must be related to a universal cause which can be nothing else but a dictate of reason itself and a common nature. For there cannot be anything else which is capable of instilling into the minds of all the same principles and forcing them to think alike. Indeed, from this general consent of men in agreement with one another conclusions can be drawn not only as to what action man may do, since men do not seem likely to do what is against nature, but also as to what they ought to do, since we see that most men when not urged by expediency or enticed by the attraction of some pleasure, both do, and declare that they must do, that for which the only reason is the obedience which they feel they ought to pay to the law of nature. And furthermore such an action, when performed, they all applaud, so that by their own reckoning they affirm that this law exists; for they applaud an act which would seem rather to be a fit object of ridicule, so long as they are not doing it themselves; for, without such a law, it would be the mark not so much of a virtuous as of a

---

[4] Hugo Grotius, *De Jure Belli ac Pacis*, Prolegomenon, §30.

foolish man to do good to others and so harm himself (and this thing often happens in keeping faith).⟩

Some people here raise an objection against the law of nature, namely that there is no such law in existence at all, since it can nowhere be found, for most people live as though there were no rational ground in life at all nor any law of such a kind that all men recognise it; on the contrary, on this point men appear to disagree most of all. If indeed natural law were discernible by the light of reason, why is it that not all people who possess reason have knowledge of it?

[i] My answer to this is, first, that, as in civil affairs, it does not follow that a law does not exist or is not published, because it is impossible for a blind man, and difficult for one who sees badly, to read a legal notice displayed in a public place, so, in other circumstances, a man who is occupied is not free, nor an idle or bad man disposed, to lift his eyes to the notice-board and learn from it the nature of his duty. I admit that all people are by nature endowed with reason, and I say that natural law can be known by reason, but from this it does not necessarily follow that it is known to any and every one. For there are some who make no use of the light of reason but prefer darkness and would not wish to show themselves to themselves. But not even the sun shows a man the way to go, unless he opens his eyes and is well prepared for the journey. There are others, brought up in vice, who scarcely distinguish between good and evil, because a bad way of life, becoming strong by lapse of time, has established barbarous habits, and evil customs have perverted even matters of principle. In others, again, through natural defect the acumen of the mind is too dull to be able to bring to light those secret decrees of nature. For how few there are who in matters of daily practice or matters easy to know surrender themselves to the jurisdiction of reason or follow its lead, when, either led astray by the violence of passions or being indifferent through carelessness or degenerate through habit, they readily follow the inducements of pleasure or the urges of their base instincts rather than the dictates of reason. Who, as I might almost say, is there in a commonwealth that knows the laws of his state, though they have been promulgated, hung up in public places, are easy to read and to understand, and are everywhere exposed to view? And how much

less will he be acquainted with the secret and hidden laws of nature? Hence, in this matter, not the majority of people should be consulted but those who are more rational and perceptive than the rest.

[ii] Secondly, I answer that, although even the more rational of men do not absolutely agree among themselves as to what the law of nature is and what its true and known precepts are, it does not follow from this that there is no law of nature at all; on the contrary it follows rather that there is such a law, when people contend about it so fiercely. For just as in a commonwealth it is wrong to conclude that there are no laws because various interpretations of laws are to be met with among jurisprudents, so likewise in morality it is improperly inferred that there is no law of nature, because in one place it is pronounced to be this, in another something different. This fact rather establishes the existence of the law more firmly, seeing that all the disputants maintain the same idea about the law itself (for they all know that there is something evil and something good by nature), and they differ only in their interpretations of it. However, this argument will have to be discussed again a little further on, when we shall have to deal with the way in which this law is known.

[2] The second argument which proves the existence of a law of nature can be derived from men's consciences; from the fact, namely, that 'no one who commits a wicked action is acquitted in his own judgement'.[5] Thus the sentence which everyone passes on himself testifies that there is a law of nature. For if there were no law of nature which reason declares we must show ourselves obedient to, how does it come to pass that the conscience of people who recognise the precepts of no other law whereby they are either guided or bound in duty, nevertheless passes judgement upon their life and conduct and either acquits or declares guilty, seeing that without some law no judgement can be pronounced? This law, then, is not written, but innate, i.e. natural.

[3] The third argument is derived from the very constitution of this world, wherein all things observe a fixed law of their operations and a manner of existence appropriate to their nature. For that which prescribes to everything the form and manner and measure of working is just what law is. Aquinas says that all that happens in

---

[5] Juvenal, *Satires*, XIII, 2–3.

things created is the subject-matter of the eternal law, and, following Hippocrates, 'each thing both in small and in great fulfilleth the task which destiny hath set down', that is to say nothing deviates even by an inch from the law prescribed to it.[6] This being so, it does not seem that man alone is independent of laws while everything else is bound. On the contrary, a manner of acting is prescribed to him that is suitable to his nature; for it does not seem to fit in with the wisdom of the Creator to form an animal that is most perfect and ever active, and to endow it abundantly above all others with mind, intellect, reason, and all the requisites for working, and yet not assign to it any work, or again to make man alone susceptible of law precisely in order that he may submit to none.

[4] The fourth argument is taken from human society, since without this law men can have no social intercourse or union among themselves. Indeed there are two factors on which human society appears to rest, i.e. firstly, a definite constitution of the state and form of government, and, secondly, the fulfilment of pacts. Every community among men falls to the ground if these are abolished, just as they themselves fall to the ground if the law of nature is annulled. In fact, what is to be the shape of a body politic, the constitution of a state, and the security of its interests, if that part of a community which has the power to do most harm may do everything as it pleases, if in the supreme authority there is the most unrestrained liberty? For since the rulers, in whose power it is to make or remake laws at their will and as the masters of others to do everything in favour of their own dominion, are not, and cannot be, bound either by their own or by other people's positive laws, supposing there is no other, superior, law of nature, i.e. one which they are bound to obey, in what condition, pray, would be men's interests, what would be the privileges of society, if men united in a commonwealth only to become a more ready prey for the power of others? Nor indeed would the condition of the rulers be better than that of the subjects, if there were no natural law, for without it the people could not be restrained by the laws of the state. Certainly, positive civil laws are not binding by their own nature or force or in any other way than in virtue of the law of

---

[6] Aquinas, *Summa Theologica*, Ia IIae, qu. 93, art. 4. Locke is closely following Hooker here: *Of the Laws of Ecclesiastical Polity*, bk I, ch. 3, §§1–4. Hippocrates: an ancient Greek physician.

nature, which orders obedience to superiors and the keeping of public peace. Thus, without this law, the rulers can perhaps by force and with the aid of arms compel the multitude to obedience, but put them under an obligation they cannot. Without natural law the other basis also of human society is overthrown, i.e. the faithful fulfilment of contracts, for it is not to be expected that a man would abide by a compact because he has promised it, when better terms are offered elsewhere, unless the obligation to keep promises was derived from nature, and not from human will.

[5] The fifth argument is that without natural law there would be neither virtue nor vice, neither the reward of goodness nor the punishment of evil: there is no fault, no guilt, where there is no law. Everything would have to depend on human will, and, since there would be nothing to demand dutiful action, it seems that man would not be bound to do anything but what utility or pleasure might recommend, or what a blind and lawless impulse might happen perchance to fasten on. The terms 'upright' and 'virtuous' would disappear as meaningless or be nothing at all but empty names. Man would not be able to act wrongfully, since there was no law issuing commands or prohibitions, and he would be the completely free and sovereign arbiter of his actions. Granted that, undisciplined as he would then be, he would seem, perhaps, to have taken but little thought for his life and health, yet he seems in no way to have disregarded honour and duty, since whatever honour or baseness our virtues and vices possess they owe it all to this law of nature; for the nature of good and evil is eternal and certain, and their value cannot be determined either by the public ordinances of men or by any private opinion.

II
Can the Law of Nature be Known by the Light of Nature? Yes

Since some principle of good and evil is acknowledged by all men, and since there is no nation so savage and so far removed from any humane feelings that it does not have some notion of virtue and vice, some consciousness of praise and blame, it seems we must next inquire in what ways men come to know the law of nature to which they pay deference by so general a consent, and of which they cannot eradicate all feeling without at the same time eradicating humanity itself; for nature must be altogether negated before one can claim for oneself absolute liberty. Now we maintain that the way in which we arrive at the knowledge of this law is by the light of nature as opposed to other ways of knowledge. But while we assert that the light of nature points to this law, we should not wish this to be understood in the sense that some inward light is by nature implanted in man, which perpetually reminds him of his duty and leads him straight and without fail whither he has to go. We do not maintain that this law of nature, written as it were on tablets, lies open in our hearts, and that, as soon as some inward light comes near it (like a torch approaching a notice-board hung up in darkness), it is at length read, perceived, and noted by the rays of that light. Rather, by saying that something can be known by the light of nature, we mean nothing else but that there is some sort of truth to the knowledge of which a man can attain by himself and without the help of another, if he makes proper use of the faculties he is endowed with by nature.

However, there are three kinds of knowledge which, without an over-careful choice of terms, I may call [1] inscription, [2] tradition, and [3] sense-experience.[7] To these may be added a fourth kind, namely supernatural and divine revelation, but this is no part of our present argument. For we do not investigate here what a man can experience who is divinely inspired, or what a man can behold who is illuminated by a light from heaven, but what a man who is endowed with understanding, reason, and sense-perception can by the help of nature and his own sagacity search out and examine. For all this sort of learning, whatever its extent (and it certainly has made great progress), traverses the whole world and is not confined within any of its limits but leads even to the contemplation of the sky, and has inquired with no little care into the nature and functions of spirits and minds and the laws that apply to them; all this learning, I repeat, reaches the mind altogether from those three ways of knowing, and besides these there exist no other principles and foundations of knowledge. For whatever we know is all either inscribed in our hearts by a gift of nature and a certain privilege of

---

[7] 'Inscriptionem, traditionem, et sensum', i.e. innate knowledge, received or inherited knowledge, and sense data.

birth, or conveyed to us by hearsay, or drawn by us from the senses.

However, since I have proposed to deal with ways of knowing, someone perhaps may wonder in this connection why I have omitted to mention reason, that great and, as it seems, chief light of all knowledge, especially because the law of nature is most often called right reason itself and the dictate of right reason. Our explanation is that we investigate here the first principles and sources of all kinds of knowledge, the way in which primary notions and the elements of knowledge enter the mind. Yet all these, we maintain, are not apprehended by reason: they are either stamped on our minds by inscription, or we receive them second-hand, or they enter by the senses. Nothing indeed is achieved by reason, that powerful faculty of arguing, unless there is first something posited and taken for granted. Admittedly, reason makes use of these elements of knowledge, to amplify and refine them, but it does not in the least establish them. It does not lay a foundation, although again and again it raises a most majestic building and lifts the summits of knowledge right into the sky. As easily, indeed, will a man be able to construct a syllogism without premises as find use for his reason without anything first being known and admitted as true. It is, however, the actual origin of knowledge we are inquiring into just now.

[1] As regards inscription, there are some who are of the opinion that this law of nature is inborn in us and is so implanted by nature in the minds of all, that there is none who comes into the world whose mind does not carry these innate characters and marks of his duty engraved upon it, who has not in his thoughts these moral precepts and rules of conduct born with him and known to him; and that it is not necessary to seek information from any other source, consulting moral laws borrowed from somewhere without oneself, since man has his pandects[8] within himself and always open before his eyes, and they contain all that constitutes his duty. Admittedly this is an easy and very convenient way of knowing, and the human race would be very well off if men were so fully informed and so endowed by nature that from birth they were in no doubt as to what is fitting and what is less so. If this view is accepted, the truth of our assertion is firmly established, namely that the law of nature can be known by the light of nature. Whether

---

[8] I.e. a whole digest of laws.

in fact there is any such imprint of the law of nature in our hearts, and whether it becomes known to mankind in the manner described, will perhaps be discussed at another place [Essay III]. As regards the present question, it will suffice to have proved that, if man makes use properly of his reason and of the inborn faculties with which nature has equipped him, he can attain to the knowledge of this law without any teacher instructing him in his duties, any monitor reminding him of them. However, if we shall hereafter prove that this law is known otherwise than by tradition, it will be certain that it is known by the light of nature and by an inward principle, since, whatever a man knows, he necessarily learns it all either from others or from himself.

[2] We come next to tradition,[9] which we distinguish from sense-experience not because traditions do not enter the mind by sense – for it is through hearsay that they are received – but because the ears hear the sound only, and it is belief which embraces the fact. For example, provided we place confidence in Cicero when he speaks of Caesar, we believe that Caesar, whom Cicero knew to have lived, has lived. Now, of tradition we say that it is not a way of knowing whereby the law of nature comes to us; and this we do not say because we deny that some, nay almost all, precepts of that law are transmitted to us by parents, teachers, and all those who busily fashion the manners of young people and fill the still tender souls with the love and knowledge of virtue. For, indeed, that we must take special care lest human souls become too prone to pleasure, or get caught by the enticements of the body, or are led aside by bad examples that occur everywhere, and thus make light of the more wholesome precepts of reason, is held by all those who reflect a little on the education of young minds and who indeed early in that as yet youthful age lay the foundations of the moral virtues and do their best to inculcate sentiments of respect and love for the deity, obedience to superiors, fidelity in keeping promises and telling the truth, mildness and purity of character, a friendly disposition, and all the other virtues. Since all these are precepts of the law of nature,

---

[9] Locke originally intended a separate essay on tradition, since at the close of this essay he added a title for an unwritten essay: 'Does the law of nature become known to us through tradition? No.' The idea of 'tradition' carried resonances of anti-Catholic controversy, since the Catholic Church taught that Christian truth was known through the tradition of the Church's teaching.

we do not deny that such precepts can be transmitted to us by others, but only this: that tradition is a primary and certain way of knowing the law of nature. For what we take over from other people's talk, if we embrace it only because others have insisted that it is good, may perhaps direct our morals well enough and keep them within the bounds of dutiful action, yet it is not what reason but what men tell us. And I am in no doubt that most persons, content with these second-hand rules of conduct which they derive from tradition, build up their morals after the manner and belief of those among whom they happen to be born and educated, and that they have no other rule of what is right and good than the customs of their society and the common opinion of the people with whom they live. And for this reason they least of all strive to derive the law of nature from its very fountainhead and to investigate on what principles the ground of their duty rests, in what manner it creates obligations, and what its first origin is; for they are, after all, guided by belief and approval, not by the law of nature. But that the law of nature, in so far as it is a law, does not become known to us by means of tradition, is shown, if I mistake not, by the following arguments.

[i] First, in the presence of so much variety among conflicting traditions it would be impossible to determine what the law of nature is, and it would be difficult to decide completely what is true and what is false, what is law and what is opinion, what is commanded by nature and what by utility, what advice reason gives and what instructions are given by society. For since traditions vary so much the world over and men's opinions are so obviously opposed to one another and mutually destructive, and that not only among different nations but in one and the same state – for each single opinion we learn from others becomes a tradition – and finally since everybody contends so fiercely for his own opinion and demands that he be believed, it would plainly be impossible – supposing tradition alone lays down the ground of our duty – to find out what that tradition is, or to pick out truth from among such a variety, because no ground can be assigned why one man of the older generation, rather than another maintaining quite the opposite, should be credited with the authority of tradition or be more worthy of trust; except it be that reason discovers a difference in the things themselves that are transmitted, and embraces one opinion while

rejecting another, just because it detects more evidence recognisable by the light of nature for the one than for the other. Such a procedure, surely, is not the same as to believe in tradition, but is an attempt to form a considered opinion about things themselves; and this brings all the authority of tradition to naught. Thus there are three possibilities: either that in trying to become acquainted with the law of nature as promulgated by tradition one has to employ reason and understanding, and then the whole of tradition becomes void, or that the law of nature cannot become known by tradition, or that it does not exist at all. For since the law of nature is everywhere one and the same, but traditions vary, it follows either that there is no law of nature at all, or that it cannot be known by means of tradition.

[ii] Secondly, if the law of nature could be learnt from tradition, it would be a matter of trust rather than of knowledge, since it would depend more on the authority of the giver of information than on the evidence of things themselves, and would therefore be a derived rather than an inborn, i.e. natural, law.

[iii] Thirdly, those who maintain that the law of nature is known by tradition apparently contradict themselves. For anyone who is willing to look back and trace a tradition to its very source must necessarily come to a stand somewhere and in the end recognise someone as the original author of this tradition, who either will have found the law of nature inscribed within his heart or come to know it by reasoning from the facts perceived by the senses. These ways of knowing, however, are equally open to the rest of mankind also, and there is no need of tradition as long as everyone has within himself the same basic principles of knowledge. But if that first author of the tradition in question has laid down a law to the world, because he was instructed by some oracle or inspired by a divine message, then a law of this kind and promulgated in this manner is by no means a law of nature, but a positive law.

Therefore we conclude that, if there is a law of nature (and this nobody has denied), it cannot be known in so far as it is a law by means of tradition.

[3] The last way of knowledge that remains to be discussed is sense-perception, which we declare to be the basis of our knowledge of the law of nature. However, this must not be understood in the sense that the law of nature appears somewhere so conspicuously

that we can either read it off with our eyes, examine it with our hands, or hear it proclaiming itself. But since we are searching now for the principle and origin of the knowledge of this law and for the way in which it becomes known to mankind, I declare that the foundation of all knowledge of it is derived from those things which we perceive through our senses. From these things, then, reason and the power of arguing, which are both distinctive marks of man, advance to the notion of the maker of these things (there being no lack of arguments in this direction such as are necessarily derived from the matter, motion, and the visible structure and arrangement of this world) and at last they conclude and establish for themselves as certain that some deity is the author of all these things. As soon as this is laid down, the notion of a universal law of nature binding on all men necessarily emerges; and this will become clear later on [Essay IV]. From what has been said, however, it is quite certain that there is a law of nature that can be known by the light of nature. For whatever among men obtains the force of a law, necessarily looks to God, or nature, or man as its maker; yet whatever man has commanded or God has ordered by divine declaration, all this is positive law. But since the law of nature cannot be known by tradition, all that remains is that it becomes known to men by the light of nature alone.

Against this conclusion of ours the following objection readily presents itself: if the law of nature becomes known by the light of nature, how does it happen that where all are enlightened there are so many blind, since this inward law is implanted by nature in all men? How does it arise that very many mortals are without knowledge of this law and nearly all think of it differently, a fact that does not seem possible if all men are led to the knowledge of it by the light of nature?

This objection would have some force in it if we asserted that the law of nature is inscribed in our hearts. For, if this were assumed, it would necessarily follow that what is thought about this law would be everywhere the same, since this law would be written down in all men and be disclosed to the understanding as one and the same. Our answer, however, is that, granted that our mental faculties can lead us to the knowledge of this law, nevertheless it does not follow from this that all men necessarily make proper use of these faculties. The nature and properties of figures and numbers appear obvious and, no doubt, knowable by the light of nature; yet from this it does not follow that whoever is in possession of mental faculties turns out a geometer or knows thoroughly the science of arithmetic. Careful reflection, thought, and attention by the mind is needed, in order that by argument and reasoning one may find a way from perceptible and obvious things into their hidden nature. Concealed in the bowels of the earth lie veins richly provided with gold and silver; human beings besides are possessed of arms and hands with which they can dig these out, and of reason which invents machines. Yet from this we do not conclude that all men are wealthy. First they have to equip themselves; and it is with great labour that those resources which lie hidden in darkness are to be brought to the light of day. They do not present themselves to idle and listless people, nor indeed to all those who search for them, since we notice some also who are toiling in vain. But if in matters that relate to the practice of ordinary life we meet but few who are directed by reason, since men only seldom delve into themselves in order to search out from thence the condition, manner, and purpose of their life, then it is not to be wondered at that of the law of nature, which is much less easy to know, men's opinions are so different. For most people are little concerned about their duty; they are guided not so much by reason as either by the example of others, or by traditional customs and the fashion of the country, or finally by the authority of those whom they consider good and wise. They want no other rule of life and conduct, being satisfied with that second-hand rule which other people's conduct, opinions, and advice, without any serious thinking or application, easily supply to the unwary. It does not therefore follow that the law of nature cannot be known by the light of nature because there are only few who, neither corrupted by vice nor carelessly indifferent, make a proper use of that light.

III
Is the Law of Nature Inscribed in the Minds of Men? No

Since we have proved earlier that there is a law of nature and that this law can be known, not indeed by tradition but by the light of nature, doubts can be raised as to what this light of nature is: for while like sunlight it reveals to us by its rays the rest of reality, it is itself unknown and its nature is concealed in darkness. Since in fact nothing is known to man without the principle of that knowledge being either imprinted in the original nature of the soul or imparted from outside through the senses, it appears worth our labour to investigate the first beginning of this knowledge and to inquire whether the souls of the newly-born are just empty tablets[10] afterwards to be filled in by observation and reasoning, or whether they have the laws of nature as signs of their duty inscribed on them at birth. But by our inquiry whether the law of nature is written in the souls of men we mean this: namely, whether there are any moral propositions inborn in the mind and as it were engraved upon it such that they are as natural and familiar to it as its own faculties, the will, namely, and the understanding, and whether, unchangeable as they are and always clear, they are known to us without any study or deliberate consideration. The following arguments, however, show that there exists no such imprint of the law of nature in our hearts.

[1] It has been only an empty assertion and no one has proved it until now, although many have laboured[11] to this end, that the souls of men when they are born are something more than empty tablets capable of receiving all sorts of imprints but having none stamped on them by nature.

[2] If this law of nature were stamped by nature upon the minds of men as a whole at their very birth, how does it come about that human beings, who would have their souls furnished with that law, do not forthwith all to a man agree about it without hesitation and show readiness to obey it? For in respect to this law they differ so very widely, one rule of nature and right reason being proclaimed here, another there, one and the same thing being good with some people, evil with others, some recognising a different law of nature, others none; but all see in it something obscure. If anyone at this juncture should reply (and I know that several have done so) that this law which nature has inscribed in our hearts has, on account

---

[10] 'Rasae tabulae'. Locke is famous for his use of the phrase 'tabula rasa', which occurs in Draft B of the *Essay Concerning Human Understanding* (Nidditch and Rogers 1990, p. 128) but is not in fact in the *Essay* itself ('white paper': bk II, ch. I; 'empty cabinet': bk I, ch. 2).

[11] Locke deleted a phrase which specifies Descartes as having laboured to demonstrate the doctrine of innate ideas.

of the Fall, been either partly erased or absolutely and altogether effaced (an argument which, to be sure, is wholly unknown to the majority of men, who may not even once have thought about Adam[12] and his fall), such an answer, besides being one that does not particularly concern philosophers, would by no means remove the difficulty nor take away the doubt. For since they maintain that this law originally written in the hearts of men has been effaced, they must affirm one or the other of two things, namely that this law of nature has been either partly lost, that is to say that some of its precepts have entirely perished, or that all its precepts have become lost. If only some of the precepts of this law have been utterly effaced from the hearts of men, those that remain inscribed therein are either the same in all or are different. If it is said that they are the same, then all men in the world would easily agree among themselves about these precepts, for they would readily be known; but this we can see is by no means the case. If it is said that the decrees of nature which are left behind in the souls of men are different and that these innate impressions are unlike one another, what I ask here is the cause of this difference, since nature in its works is everywhere the same and uniform? And then, does it not seem unreasonable to assert that the minds of men differ from one another about the very first principles? Again, by what means could the law of nature and a definite rule of moral rectitude and goodness be known, if it is once admitted that the dictates of nature and the principles of action vary from person to person? But if it is asserted that this law originally impressed is altogether effaced, where, pray, will be that law of nature for which we search? Surely on this admission it will be nothing, unless we can find a way of knowledge other than by inscription.

[3] If this law of nature is inscribed in the minds of men, how does it happen that younger boys, illiterate people, and those primitive races which, having no institutions, laws, and knowledge, are said to live in accordance with nature, do not best of all know and understand this law? They are all free from notions coming from without which may divert their minds elsewhere; they do not imbibe opinions borrowed from some other source, which can either corrupt, or blot out or destroy the dictates of nature; for they have

---

[12] MS has 'primo homine', first man.

no other teachers than themselves and follow nothing but nature. If the law of nature were written in the hearts of men, one would have to believe that among these people it will be found undiminished and unspoiled. But yet anyone who consults the histories both of the old and the new world, or the itineraries of travellers, will easily observe how far apart from virtue the morals of these people are, what strangers they are to any humane feelings, since nowhere else is there such doubtful honesty, so much treachery, such frightful cruelty, in that they sacrifice to the gods and also to their tutelary spirit by killing people and offering kindred blood. And no one will believe that the law of nature is best known and observed among these primitive and untutored tribes, since among most of them there appears not the slightest trace or track of piety, merciful feeling, fidelity, chastity, and the rest of the virtues; but rather they spend their life wretchedly among robberies, thefts, debaucheries, and murders. Thus the law of nature does not appear to be written in the hearts of men, if those who have no other guide than nature itself and among whom the decrees of nature are least spoiled by arbitrary moral customs live in such ignorance of every law, as though there were no principle of rightness and goodness to be had at all.

I myself admit that among the peoples which are better mannered and polished through training and moral instruction there exist some definite and undoubted views about morals, but although they may take these for the law of nature and believe that they are written in their hearts by nature, nevertheless I hardly think they are derived from nature but suppose that they have come from some other source. Though they may be perhaps some of the precepts of the law of nature, they are not learned from nature but from men. For these opinions about moral rightness and goodness which we embrace so firmly are for the most part such as, in a still tender age, before we can as yet determine anything about them or observe how they insinuate themselves, stream into our unguarded minds and are inculcated by our parents or teachers or others with whom we live. For since these believe that such opinions are conducive to the well ordering of life, and perhaps have also themselves been brought up in them in the same manner, they are inclined to inure the still fresh minds of the young to opinions of this kind, which they regard as indispensable for a good and happy life. For in this matter the most cautious and zealous are those who think that the whole hope of an after-life rests upon the moral foundations which are laid in the beginning. And at last, because in this way and without our notice these opinions have crept into our minds with but little attention on our part, striking roots in our breasts while we are unaware either of the manner or the time, and also because they assert their authority by the general consent and approval of men with whom we have social intercourse, we immediately think we must conclude that they are inscribed in our hearts by God and by nature, since we observe no other origin of them. And since by daily practice we are firmly establishing these opinions as rules to live by, we should both be uncertain of our future life and repent of our past life, if we were to doubt that these represent the law of nature. For if the law of nature were not what we have hitherto observed, it would be necessary to conclude that thus far we have lived badly and without reason. On that account, therefore, we embrace as firmly as possible these opinions of early youth which have been instilled into us by others, we think of them the more highly, believe in them obstinately, and do not suffer them to be called in question by anybody. And since we proclaim them as principles, we do not allow ourselves either to doubt them or to argue about them against anyone denying them (for we believe them to be first principles). From all this, therefore, it is clear that there can exist many things which anyone may believe to be inscribed in his mind by nature, which nevertheless derive their origin from some other source, and that it does not follow that, just because we eagerly believe in something and cherish it as a principle, though we are ignorant of its source, this is the law of nature, written in our hearts by nature.

[4] If this law of nature were written in our hearts, why do the foolish and insane have no knowledge of it, since the law is said to be stamped immediately on the soul itself and this depends very little upon the constitution and structure of the body's organs. Yet therein admittedly lies the only difference between the wise and the stupid.

[5] If the law of nature were written in our hearts, it would have to be inferred that speculative as well as practical principles

are inscribed. But this seems difficult to prove; for if we try to search out the first and best known principle of the sciences (namely, that it is impossible that the same thing should at the same time both be and not be), it will be readily agreed that this principle is not inscribed by nature as an axiom in our hearts nor taken for granted by anyone before he has either learned it from another or (which is the proper method of establishing principles) proved it to himself by induction and by observing particulars. Thus it appears to me that no principles, either practical or speculative, are written in the minds of men by nature.

IV
Can Reason Attain to the Knowledge of Natural Law through Sense-Experience? Yes

We have proved above that natural law can be known by the light of nature, which, indeed, is our only guide when we are entering the course of this life, and which, amid the various intricacies of duty, avoiding the rough roads of vice on one side and the by-ways of error on the other, leads us to that height of virtue and felicity whereto the gods invite and nature also tends. But since, I say, this light of nature lies hidden in darkness and it seems far more difficult to know what it is than whither it leads, it appears worth our labour both to dispel this darkness also and to be no longer blind in the light of the sun itself. Certainly it is fitting not only, like beasts, to derive advantage from light for the service of life and to use it to guide one's steps, but also to inquire by deeper investigation what is this light, its nature and its source. But since, as has been shown elsewhere [Essays II–III], this light of nature is neither tradition nor some inward moral principle written in our minds by nature, there remains nothing by which it can be defined but reason and sense-perception. For only these two faculties appear to teach and educate the minds of men and to provide what is characteristic of the light of nature, namely that things otherwise wholly unknown and hidden in darkness should be able to come before the mind and be known and as it were looked into. As long as these two faculties serve one another, sensation furnishing reason with the ideas of particular sense-objects and supplying the subject-matter of discourse, reason on the other hand guiding the faculty of sense, and arranging together the images of things derived from sense-perception, thence forming others and composing new ones, there is nothing so obscure, so concealed, so removed from any meaning that the mind, capable of everything, could not apprehend it by reflection and reasoning, if it is supported by these faculties. But if you take away one of the two, the other is certainly of no avail, for without reason, though actuated by our senses, we scarcely rise to the standard of nature found in brute beasts, seeing that the pig and the ape, and many of the quadrupeds, far surpass men in the sharpness of the senses. On the other hand, without the help and assistance of the senses, reason can achieve nothing more than a labourer can working in darkness behind shuttered windows. Unless the ideas of objects penetrate the mind there will be no subject-matter of reasoning, nor could the mind do more towards the construction of knowledge than an architect can towards the building of houses if he falls short of stones, timber, sand, and the rest of building material.

By reason here we do not mean some moral principles or any propositions laid up in the mind such that, if the actions of our life fitly correspond to them, these are said to be in accordance with right reason; for right reason of this sort is nothing but the law of nature itself already known, not the manner whereby, or that light of nature whereby, natural law is known; it is only the object of reason, not reason itself; that is to say, it is such truths as reason seeks and pursues as necessary for the direction of life and the formation of character. On the contrary, reason is here taken to mean the discursive faculty of the mind, which advances from things known to things unknown and argues from one thing to another in a definite and fixed order of propositions. It is this reason by means of which mankind arrives at the knowledge of natural law. The foundations, however, on which rests the whole of that knowledge which reason builds up and raises as high as heaven are the objects of sense-experience; for the senses primarily supply the entire as well as the chief subject-matter of discourse and introduce it into the deep recesses of the mind. In fact, at all times every argumentation proceeds from what is known and taken for granted, and the mind cannot discourse or reason without some truth that is given and perceived, any more than the swiftest animal whatsoever among the quadrupeds can move or advance from place to place without something stable to uphold its steps. I admit it is astonishing what reason finds and tracks out in mathematical science, but all this is dependent upon a line, is built within a plane, and has a solid substance as foundation to rest on. Surely mathematics presupposes these objects of its operations together with other general principles and axioms as its data; it does not discover them nor prove them true. Reason, plainly, adopts the same way of procedure also in the transmission and investigation of other forms of knowledge and in the embellishment and perfecting of anything whatsoever. And if there are things obscure, sublime, and noble, which even reason itself may marvel at and bring forth and proclaim as a discovery, yet, if you would run through each single speculative science, there is none in which something is not always presupposed and taken for granted and derived from the senses by way of borrowing. Every conception in the mental, no less than in the physical, sense always arises out of some pre-existing material, and reason proceeds in the same manner in the moral and practical sciences also and demands to be allowed this material. But in order that we may know how sense-experience and reason, as long as they assist one another mutually, can lead us to the knowledge of natural law, certain facts must first be set forth, because they are necessarily presupposed in the knowledge of any and every law. [1] First, in order that anyone may understand that he is bound by a law, he must know beforehand that there is a lawmaker, i.e. some superior power to which he is rightly subject. [2] Secondly, it is also necessary to know that there is some will on the part of that superior power with respect to the things to be done by us, that is to say, that the lawmaker, whoever he may prove to be, wishes that we do this but leave off that, and demands of us that the conduct of our life should be in accordance with his will. In what follows it will become clear what sense-experience contributes and what reason does, in order that these two presuppositions, which are required for knowledge of the law of nature, may become known to us.

[1] [i] In the first place, then, we say it is evident from sense-experience that in the natural world there are perceptible objects, i.e. that there really exist solid bodies and their conditions, namely lightness and heaviness, warmth and coldness, colours and the rest of the qualities presented to the senses, which can all in some way

be traced back to motion; that this visible world is constructed with wonderful art and regularity, and of this world we, the human race, are also a part. We certainly see the stars turning round in an unbroken and fixed course, rivers rolling along into the sea, and the years and changes of the seasons following one another in a definite order. This and almost infinitely more we learn from the senses.

[ii] Secondly, we say that the mind, after more carefully considering in itself the fabric of this world perceived by the senses and after contemplating the beauty of the objects to be observed, their order, array, and motion, thence proceeds to an inquiry into their origin, to find out what was the cause, and who the maker, of such an excellent work, for it is surely undisputed that this could not have come together casually and by chance into so regular and in every respect so perfect and ingeniously prepared a structure. Hence it is undoubtedly inferred that there must be a powerful and wise creator of all these things, who has made and built this whole universe and us mortals who are not the lowest part of it. For, indeed, all the rest of it, inanimate things and brute beasts, cannot create man who is far more perfect than they are. Nor, on the other hand, can man create himself; for that we do not owe our origin to ourselves is surely undisputed, not merely for the reason that nothing is its own cause – for obviously this axiom does not prevent us, if we are willing to acknowledge God, from believing that something exists which does not depend upon another – but also because man does not find in himself all those perfections which he can conceive in his mind. For (omitting perfect knowledge of all things and a greater authority over things in nature) if man were the maker of himself, able to give himself being, then he who could bring himself forth into the world of nature would also give himself an existence of everlasting duration. For it cannot be conceived that anything will be so unfriendly, so hostile to itself that, while able to bestow existence on itself, it would not at the same time preserve it, or would willingly let it go, when a little life's brief course had ended; for without it all other precious, useful, agreeable, and blessed things cannot be retained and are sought for in vain. Certainly it requires a lesser power to preserve something than to create it, or at any rate only the same power, and whoever at any moment has ordered something to come into being, he can effect that it does not cease to exist at some other moment. After the case has been

put thus it necessarily follows that above ourselves there exists another more powerful and wiser agent who at his will can bring us into the world, maintain us, and take us away. Hence, having inferred this on the evidence of the senses, reason lays down that there must be some superior power to which we are rightly subject, namely God who has a just and inevitable command over us and at his pleasure can raise us up or throw us down, and make us by the same commanding power happy or miserable. And since he has himself created the soul and constructed the body with wonderful art, and has thoroughly explored the faculties and powers of each, as well as their hidden constitution and nature, he can fill and stir the one with sorrow or delight, the other with pain or pleasure; he also can lift both together to a condition of the utmost happiness or thrust them down to a state of misery and torment. Hence it appears clearly that, with sense-perception showing the way, reason can lead us to the knowledge of a lawmaker or of some superior power to which we are necessarily subject. And this was the first thing needed for the knowledge of any law.

Certainly I grant that some have undertaken to prove from the testimony of conscience that there is a deity presiding over this world; others have done so from the idea of God, regarded as innate in us, either of which ways of argument would certainly prove that God exists, even if (and this will perhaps become clear to anyone considering the case more carefully) the argument of neither method derives its whole force from our inborn faculties, i.e. from sense-perception and reason, operating upon objects of sense, and from points of arguments thence deduced. However, for the purpose of confirming the truth of our argument it suffices that man, as has been shown above, by exercising the senses and reason at the same time, can attain to the knowledge of some supreme godhead. Let me for the present abstain from pointing out that it can be justly doubted whether that idea of God pertains to all men by nature, because, if travellers abroad are to be trusted, there are in the world, as the records of their journeys testify, some peoples which recognise no deity at all, whereas there is nowhere a nation so uncivilised and so far removed from any culture as not to rejoice in the use of the senses and not to surpass brute animals in the use of reason and the faculty of arguing, though perhaps it has not sufficiently perfected those inborn faculties by training as well. In fact, all men everywhere are sufficiently prepared by nature to discover God in his works, so long as they are not indifferent to the use of these inborn faculties and do not refuse to follow whither nature leads. Thus it is clear that men can infer from sense-experience that there exists some powerful superior who has right and authority over themselves; for who will deny that the clay is subject to the potter's will, and that a piece of pottery can be shattered by the same hand by which it has been formed?

[2] In the second place, then, since on the evidence of the senses it must be concluded that there is some maker of all these things, whom it is necessary to recognise as not only powerful but also wise, it follows from this that he has not created this world for nothing and without purpose. For it is contrary to such great wisdom to work with no fixed aim; nor indeed can man believe, since he perceives that he has an agile, capable mind, versatile and ready for anything, furnished with reason and knowledge, and a body besides which is quick and easy to be moved hither and thither by virtue of the soul's authority, that all this equipment for action is bestowed on him by a most wise creator in order that he may do nothing, and that he is fitted out with all these faculties in order that he may thereby be more splendidly idle and sluggish. Hence it is quite evident that God intends man to do something, and this was the second of the two things required for the knowledge of any and every law, namely, the will on the part of a superior power with respect to the things to be done by us; that is, God wills that we do something. But what it is that is to be done by us can be partly gathered from the end in view for all things. For since these derive their origin from a gracious divine purpose and are the work of a most perfect and wise maker, they appear to be intended by him for no other end than his own glory, and to this all things must be related. Partly also we can infer the principle and a definite rule of our duty from man's own constitution and the faculties with which he is equipped. For since man is neither made without design nor endowed to no purpose with these faculties which both can and must be employed, his function appears to be that which nature has prepared him to perform. That is to say, when he in himself finds sense-experience and reason, he feels himself disposed and ready to contemplate God's works and that wisdom and power of his which they display, and thereupon to assign and render praise, honour,

and glory most worthy of so great and so beneficent a creator. Further, he feels himself not only to be impelled by life's experience and pressing needs to procure and preserve a life in society with other men, but also to be urged to enter into society by a certain propensity of nature, and to be prepared for the maintenance of society by the gift of speech and through the intercourse of language, in fact as much as he is obliged to preserve himself. But since man is very much urged on to this part of his duty by an inward instinct, and nobody can be found who does not care for himself or who disowns himself, and all direct perhaps more attention to this point than is necessary, there is no need for me here to admonish. But there will be room perhaps elsewhere to discuss one by one these three subjects which embrace all that men owe to God, their neighbour, and themselves.[13]

V
Can the Law of Nature be Known from the General Consent of Men? No

'The voice of the people is the voice of God'.[14] Surely, we have been taught by a most unhappy lesson[15] how doubtful, how fallacious this maxim is, how productive of evils, and with how much party spirit and with what cruel intent this ill-omened proverb has been flung wide lately among the common people. Indeed, if we should listen to this voice as if it were the herald of a divine law, we should hardly believe that there was any God at all. For is there anything so abominable, so wicked, so contrary to all right and law, which the general consent, or rather the conspiracy, of a senseless crowd would not at some time advocate? Hence we have heard of the plunder of divine temples, the obstinacy of insolence and immorality, the violation of laws, and the overthrow of kingdoms. And surely, if this voice were the voice of God, it would be exactly the opposite of that first fiat whereby he created and furnished this

---

[13] Locke here added the title of an unwritten essay: 'Can the law of nature be known from man's natural inclination? No.'

[14] 'Vox populi, vox Dei': an ancient saying ubiquitous in seventeenth-century political commentary. Locke also used it in *The Conduct of the Understanding*: *Works*, III, 226.

[15] I.e. the Civil War and Interregnum.

world, bringing order out of chaos; nor does God ever speak to men in such a way – unless he should wish to throw everything into confusion again and to reduce it to a state of chaos. In vain, therefore, should we seek the dictates of reason and the decrees of nature in the general consent of men.

But the general consent of men can be considered in different ways, for, firstly, it can be divided into [1] positive and [2] natural consent.

[1] We call positive consent one that arises from a contract, either from a tacit contract, i.e. prompted by the common interests and convenience of men, such as the free passage of envoys, free trade, and other things of that kind; or from an expressly stated contract, such as the fixed boundary-lines between neighbouring peoples, the prohibition of the purchase and import of particular goods, and many other such things. Neither form of general consent, since both wholly depend on a contract and are not derived from any natural principle, proves at all a law of nature. For, to take an example, it is evident that the agreement about envoys having safe passage which is kept among almost all nations is positive and does not imply a law of nature, precisely because according to the law of nature all men alike are friends of one another and are bound together by common interests, unless (as is maintained by some) there is in the state of nature a general war and a perpetual and deadly hatred among men. But whether you decide for this alternative or for that, whether you would have it that men are hostile or friendly to one another, no reason can yet be given by natural law why the passage of an envoy among foreign peoples is safer, or his position more important, than that of some private person, unless this is brought about by a tacit agreement among men, arising out of a pressing need – an agreement, that is, that men should be able to reclaim property unjustly taken from them at the request of a single man rather than by open force on the part of great numbers. While, however, the law of nature altogether forbids us to offend or injure without cause any private person as well as an envoy, I for my part admit of course that, if a contract such as we have described is assumed, the crime of doing violence to envoys is worse than that of injuring any private person: for the guilt is twofold, i.e. wrong is done and an agreement is violated. Thus, although an envoy in foreign countries is held more inviolable than another

person, this rule is not ordained by the law of nature; for this law neither supposes nor allows men to be inflamed with hatred for one another and to be divided into hostile states. Nor indeed is that consent, which we have called positive, so general in other matters that it would apply to all nations. For what perhaps is firmly believed in among the neighbouring and kindred nations of Europe and wholly approved of by all is utterly disregarded and set at nought by other peoples both of Asia and America, who do not consider themselves to be bound by the same laws, separated from us as they are by long stretches of land and unaccustomed to our morals and beliefs. Therefore, all this general consent derived from contract does not prove a natural law, but should rather be called the law of nations, which is not imposed by the law of nature but has been suggested to men by common expediency.

[2] Secondly, natural consent, namely one to which men are led by a certain natural instinct without the intervention of some compact, can be of three kinds. [i] In customs or actions, that is, the conformity to be found in the moral conduct of men and in the practice of social life. [ii] In those opinions to which men give assent in various ways, firmly and invariably to some, feebly and unsteadily to others. [iii] In first principles, which are precisely such as to elicit ready assent from any man of sound mind, and such that there is no sane person who could be doubtful of their truth after having understood their terms.

[i] First, then, concerning general consent in matters of morals, we say that it by no means proves a natural law. For if what is rightful and lawful were to be determined by men's way of living, moral rectitude and integrity would be done for. What immorality would not be allowable and even be inevitable, if the example of the majority gave us the law? Into what disgrace, villainy, and all sorts of shameful things would not the law of nature lead us astray, if we had to go whither most people go? In fact, how many are there among the more civilised nations, brought up under definite laws recognised and acknowledged by all as binding, who do not by their way of life set the mark of their approval upon vices and very often by bad example teach others to go astray, and whose frequent lapses are not innumerable? Nay, by this time every kind of evil has grown up among men and spread over the world and become mixed with everything. In the past, men have already shown so much ingenuity

in the corruption of morals and such a variety of vices that nothing has been left for posterity to invent or add, and it is impossible for anyone to commit any crime whatsoever of which there has not been an example already. It comes to this, that if anyone wants to judge moral rectitude by the standard of such accordance of human actions among themselves, and thence to infer a law of nature, he is doing no more than if he bestowed his pains on playing the fool according to reason. No one, therefore, has attempted to build up a law of nature upon this most unfortunate agreement among men. It may be said, however, that the law of nature is to be inferred not from men's behaviour but from their innermost ways of thinking – we must search not the lives of men but their souls – for it is there that the precepts of nature are imprinted and the rules of morality lie hidden together with those principles which men's manners cannot corrupt; and that, since these principles are the same in every one of us, they can have no other author than God and nature. And it is for this reason that the internal law, whose existence is often denied by vices, is acknowledged by men's conscience and the very men who act perversely feel rightly. Let us pass therefore to that general consent which we hope will be found in men's opinions.

[ii] We say, then, [a] in the first place, that no universal and general consent is found among men about morals. [b] In the second place, we say that, if there did exist an invariable and unanimous consent concerning dutiful actions among all men in the world, still from this the law of nature could not be inferred and known for certain.

[a] First, then, there does not occur among men a general consent concerning moral rectitude. And here, before I proceed to details, I shall say briefly that there is almost no vice, no infringement of natural law, no moral wrong, which anyone who consults the history of the world and observes the affairs of men will not readily perceive to have been not only privately committed somewhere on earth, but also approved by public authority and custom. Nor has there been anything so shameful in its nature that it has not been either sanctified somewhere by religion, or put in the place of virtue and abundantly rewarded with praise. Hence it is easy to see what has been the opinion of men in this matter, since they believed that by such deeds they either reverently honoured the gods or were themselves made godlike. I shall say nothing here of the various religions of

the nations, some of which are ridiculous in their ceremonies, others irreverent in their rites and impious in respect of the cult itself, so that the other nations shudder at the very name of them and believe that the sacred rites of those peoples, since they are clearly at variance with natural law itself, are to be purged by fresh sacrifices. All this, I repeat, I shall pass over, because we must believe that religion becomes known to men not so much by the light of nature as by divine revelation. But if we would review each class of virtues and vices – and nobody doubts that this classification is the actual law of nature – it will easily appear that there is none of them of which men do not form different opinions buttressed by public authority and custom. Hence, if the general consent of men is to be regarded as the rule of morality, there will either be no law of nature at all or it will vary from place to place, a thing being morally good in one place and wrong in another, and the vices themselves will become duties. But this no one will maintain. For while men, led by the prevailing opinion, have performed this or that according to the moral practice of their country (though perhaps, and not without reason, it appeared to others wrong and wicked) they did not think they had transgressed the law of nature but rather had observed it; they felt no pangs of conscience nor that inward mental scourge which usually punishes and torments the guilty, for they believed that their action, whatever it may have been, was not only lawful but laudable. From this review, evidently, one can infer not only what were the morals of men, but also what men thought about those morals.

What are we to believe has been men's notion of justice, that chief law of nature and bond of every society, when we have learned from reliable authors that whole nations have professedly been pirates and robbers? 'Among the ancients piracy was not of ill repute but of good', Didymus says in a marginal note by him on Homer.[16] Aristo, in a passage quoted by Aulus Gellius, maintains that 'among the ancient Egyptians, a race of men known to have been both ingenious in the invention of the arts and shrewd in pursuing the knowledge of things, thefts of all kinds were lawful and free from punishment'. And Gellius himself says, 'Among the

---

[16] Homer, *Odyssey*, III, 71; Didymus (attrib.), *Scholia minora*.

Spartans too, temperate and brave men they (a matter for which the evidence is not so far back in time as in the case of the Egyptians), many, nay, distinguished writers affirm that stealing was lawful and customary.'[17] In what way, in fact, have even the Romans, who are alleged to present to the whole world examples of virtue, procured for themselves honours, triumphs, glory, and the memory of their immortal name, if not by the robbery and brigandage by means of which they devastated the whole earth? What else did that virtue, so highly praised and celebrated, mean to them – what else, I say, but force and violence? And this injurious view of justice has not yet disappeared, since even now for most nations desert consists precisely in plunder, deceit, oppression, assault, and in gaining as many possessions as they can by force of arms: all this is regarded as true glory and the height of generalship. They also believe that justice, such as they have come to conceive it, is blind and armed with a sword. 'Thieves committing private theft', says Cato, 'spend their lives in prison and in chains; public thieves, in gold and in purple.'[18]

What is one to say of modesty and chastity, if among the Assyrians women were accustomed and encouraged to take part in banquets stark naked and exposed to the view of all present, while among other nations it is unlawful for women to go out in public, even though veiled, or to show their faces, or be seen by strangers? Among others it is lawful for unmarried girls to live dissolutely, and it is thought that chastity belongs only to married women, and that females are restrained from lust only by matrimony. There are others who consecrate the bridal bed by lechery and kindle the nuptial torches with the flames of lust, and where the bride lies with all the wedding guests, having in her first night as many adulterers as Messalina had.[19] There are some where it is the custom that the prince, others that the priest, obtains the spoil of the bride's virginity. According to Solinus, 'the Garamantes in Ethiopia do not know of private marriage, on the contrary all may form promiscuous

---

[17] Aulus Gellius, *Noctes Attica*, XI.18.16–17. Aristo: Roman jurist, early second century AD.

[18] *Ibid.*, XI.18.18. Cato of Utica, the Younger: Roman statesman, first century BC.

[19] Messalina: wife of Emperor Claudius, first century AD, notorious for lust and cruelty.

unions', and this immorality is also ascribed to them by Pomponius Mela[20] (and the mother of the gods would be placated by such rites as would give offence to a decent woman!).[21] Let me pass over polygamy, which here is regarded as a right, there as a sin, which in one place is commanded by law, in another is punished by death.

What is one to believe about duty towards parents, if whole nations have been met with where grown-up offspring kill their parents, where children, fiercer even than the goddesses of Fate, take away the life which the Fates continue to bestow, where it is not only ordained that all must die but a particular time of death is appointed beforehand, where no ripe old age and no lingering on of slowly declining years are to be expected, where each is the executioner of his parent and parricide is considered as one of the duties of piety. Aelianus says, 'There is a custom in Sardinia that children kill their aged fathers by beating them with sticks, and then bury them, believing that it would be wrong if those who are already too old remained alive any longer.' He says in the same place that the Derbices kill all those who have advanced beyond the age of seventy, and other tribes show no more concern for their children, since at their will they expose the newly-born, and seem to have given life only in order that they may take it away.[22] There are others who utterly discard their female progeny as if it were bastard and a mistake of nature, and purchase wives from their neighbours in hope of offspring from them. Thus men do not regard a law which nature seems to have established even in the souls of animals as binding on themselves, and they surpass brutes in savageness.

But if any law of nature would seem to be established among all as sacred in the highest degree, which the whole of mankind, it seems, is urged to observe by a certain natural instinct and by its own interest, surely this is self-preservation, and therefore some lay this down as the chief and fundamental law of nature. But in fact the power of custom and of opinion based on traditional ways of life is such as to arm men even against their own selves, so that

[20] Solinus, *Collectanea Rerum Memorabilium*, ch. 30; Pomponius Mela, *De Chorographia*, I, 8.
[21] The phrase is Augustine's: *The City of God*, II, 5.
[22] Claudius Aelianus, *Varia Historia*, IV, I. Derbices: an ancient people of the Caspian Sea.

they lay violent hands upon themselves and seek death as eagerly as others shun it. Subjects have been met with who not only worship and defend their king while alive but also follow him into death. And there are slaves who attend their masters beyond the grave and desire to discharge their duty of obedience in a place where all are equal. Nor have only male persons, the more spirited portion of mortals, the courage to do this, for among the Indians the weak and timid female sex dares to make light of dying and to hasten to rejoin departed husbands by passing through the flames and through the gate of death. They allow the nuptial torches to be extinguished only in the flames of the funeral pyre, and they prefer to seek a new marriage-chamber in the grave itself rather than to endure a widow's couch and mourning for a lost spouse. Of this fact Mandelslo, in the recently published itinerary of Olearius, declares himself an eye-witness. As he himself relates, he saw a beautiful young woman who after the death of her husband could not be prevailed upon, or restrained from murdering herself, by the advice, entreaties, and tears of her friends. At length, after an involuntary delay of six months, with the permission of the magistrate, she dressed as if for a wedding, triumphantly and with a joyous face ascended a pyre set up in the middle of the market-place, and cheerfully perished in the flames.[23]

It would be tedious to describe further instances. Nor is it surprising that men think so differently about what is right and good, since they differ even in the matter of first principles, and doubt is thrown upon God and the immortality of souls. Even if God and the soul's immortality are not moral propositions and laws of nature, nevertheless they must be necessarily presupposed if natural law is to exist. For there is no law without a lawmaker, and law is to no purpose without punishment. For example, some nations in Brazil and the inhabitants of Soldania Bay[24] acknowledge or worship no god at all, as is reported by those who have considered it worth while to go to these places. But even if no one had ever been so devoid of every sense, so destitute of reason and humane feelings

---

[23] Adam Olearius, *The Voyages and Travels of the Ambassadors . . . whereto are added the Travels of John Albert de Mandelslo into the East Indies* (1662).

[24] In southern Africa. A favourite reference for Locke. He used it in the first state of the first edition of the *Two Treatises*, II, §14; in Draft B of *ECHU*; in *ECHU* (bk I, ch. 4, §§8, 12); and in the second reply to Stillingfleet (*Works*, IV, 496–7).

as not to have a god in his heart, to what extent, pray, is the belief of polytheists in a better position? What sort of thing is the opinion of the Greeks, the Romans, and the whole heathen world concerning the gods? For since all these have conceived of many gods and represented them as fighting among themselves, as they did in the Trojan War, as being variously affected towards one another, as cruel, thieves, adulterers, it does not appear surprising if they were unable to derive the ground of their duty from the will of such gods. What rule of life would that religion teach, where each person picked out for himself any sort of god and worship he liked, where deities grew up in gardens, where a harvest of gods was to be expected every year, and where ox and dog received divine honours? Is it surprising that such a general consent about gods on the part of men has contributed nothing at all to the proper foundation of morals? What are these people, pray, if not disguised atheists? For it is just as impossible that many gods either exist or can be apprehended, as that there is no God. In fact, to increase the number of gods means to abolish divinity. Nor will you gain anything if you appeal to more civilised peoples or to philosophers of a sounder mind. For to the Jews all the other nations are heathen and unholy, to the Greek they are barbarous, and while Sparta, that austere nation, approves of theft, Roman religion approves of the atrocious sacrifices of the Latin Jupiter. What use is it to turn to philosophers? For Varro produces more than two hundred of their notions about the highest good, and there can be no fewer opinions about how to reach happiness, that is, about the law of nature.[25] And also such philosophers as Diagoras of Melos, Theodorus of Cyrene, and Protagoras were notorious for atheism.[26] If you wish to consult those professing Christianity, what is one to think of those who break the great bond of humanity by their teaching that faith is not to be kept with heretics, that is, with people who do not recognise the supremacy of the pope and join in the one society? They go so far as to believe that faith is to be kept perhaps with their own fellow citizens, but that fraud and cunning are permissible if directed against foreigners. What sort of men, to say nothing of many others,

---

[25] Marcus Terentius Varro, *De Philosophia*: Locke is doubtless repeating Augustine here: *City of God*, XIX, 1.

[26] Diagoras of Melos, poet; Theodorus of Cyrene, mathematician, teacher of Plato; Protagoras, Sophist philosopher; all fifth century BC.

were Socrates and Cato, the wisest of the Greeks and Romans? They admitted others to their bridal-bed, they lent their wives to friends and made themselves abettors of another man's lust. From all this it is quite evident that natural law can in no wise be inferred from the general consent to be found among men.

[b] In the second place, we say that if there existed among men a unanimous and universal consent in some opinion, that consent would not prove this opinion to be a natural law. For surely, each single person has to infer the law of nature from the first principles of nature, not from another person's belief. Besides, such a consent can be about a thing which is in no wise a law of nature; for instance, if among all men gold were more highly valued than lead, it would not follow that this is decreed by natural law. If all men, following the practice of the Persians, were to expose human corpses to be eaten by dogs, or, along with the Greeks, were to burn them, this would not prove that either the one or the other practice is a law of nature nor that it is binding on men, for such a general agreement is by no means a sufficient reason for creating an obligation. Admittedly, such a general consent might point to a natural law, but it could not prove it; it might make me believe more ardently, but could not make me know with greater certainty, that this opinion is a law of nature. For I can never know for certain whether this is the opinion of every individual. That would be a matter of belief, not of knowledge. For [α] if I discover this opinion in my own mind before ascertaining the fact of such general consent, then the knowledge of the general consent will not prove to me what I knew already from natural principles; and [β] if I cannot be sure that it really is the opinion of my own mind until I have first ascertained that there is such a general consent among men, then I can also reasonably doubt whether it is the opinion of others; since it is impossible to suggest a reason why something should be accorded by nature to all other men which I feel to be wanting in myself. Nor, indeed, can those very people who think alike know that something is good because they think alike; rather they think alike because from natural principles they know that something is good. And truly, knowledge precedes general consent, for otherwise the same thing would at the same time be cause and effect, and the consent of all would give rise to the consent of all, a thing which is plainly absurd.

[iii] Lastly, it is not necessary for me to say much about the third kind of general consent, i.e. agreement in first principles, because speculative principles do not pertain to the matter under discussion and do not affect moral facts in any respect whatsoever. From what has been said above, however, it is easy to gather what is the nature of the general consent of men with regard to practical principles.

VI
Are Men Bound by the Law of Nature? Yes

Since there are some who trace the whole law of nature back to each person's self-preservation and do not seek its foundations in anything greater than that love and instinct wherewith each single person cherishes himself and, as much as he can, looks to his own safety and welfare, and since everyone feels himself zealous and industrious enough in self-preservation, it seems worth our labour to inquire what and how great is the binding force of the law of nature. For if the source and origin of all this law is the care and preservation of oneself, virtue would seem to be not so much man's duty as his convenience, nor will anything be good except what is useful to him; and the observance of this law would be not so much our duty and obligation, to which we are bound by nature, as a privilege and an advantage, to which we are led by expediency. And thus, whenever it pleases us to claim our right and give way to our own inclinations, we can certainly disregard and transgress this law without blame, though perhaps not without disadvantage.

But in order that it may be known how and to what extent the law of nature is binding, a few facts concerning obligation must first be set forth. The jurists define obligation in the following manner, namely that it is the bond of law whereby one is bound to render what is due, and by law they mean the civil code. Yet this definition also describes well enough all kinds of obligation, if by law you understand that particular law the binding force of which you propose to define. Hence, by the bond of law we must mean here the bond of natural law whereby one is bound to discharge a natural obligation, that is, to fulfil the duty which it lies upon one to perform by reason of one's nature, or else submit to the penalty due to a perpetrated crime. But in order that we may know whence this bond of law takes its origin, we must understand that no one can oblige or bind us to do anything, unless he has right and power over us; and indeed, when he commands what he wishes should be done and what should not be done, he only makes use of his right. Hence that bond derives from the lordship and command which any superior has over us and our actions, and in so far as we are subject to another we are so far under an obligation. But that bond constrains us to discharge our liability, and the liability is twofold:

First, a liability to pay dutiful obedience, namely what anyone is bound to do or not to do at the command of a superior power. For when the will of a lawmaker is known to us, or so sufficiently promulgated that it can be known unless there is some impediment on our part, then we are bound to obey it and to submit to it in everything, and it is this which is called liability to pay dutiful obedience, namely to conform our actions to the rule imposed upon them, i.e. the will of a superior power. And this obligation seems to derive partly from the divine wisdom of the lawmaker, and partly from the right which the creator has over his creation. For, ultimately, all obligation leads back to God, and we are bound to show ourselves obedient to the authority of his will because both our being and our work depend on his will, since we have received these from him, and so we are bound to observe the limits he prescribes; moreover, it is reasonable that we should do what shall please him who is omniscient and most wise.

Secondly, a liability to punishment, which arises from a failure to pay dutiful obedience, so that those who refuse to be led by reason and to own that in the matter of morals and right conduct they are subject to a superior authority may recognise that they are constrained by force and punishment to be submissive to that authority and feel the strength of him whose will they refuse to follow. And so the force of this obligation seems to be grounded in the authority of a lawmaker, so that power compels those who cannot be moved by warnings. However, not all obligation seems to consist in, and ultimately to be limited by, that power which can coerce offenders and punish the wicked, but rather to consist in the authority and dominion which someone has over another, either by natural right and the right of creation, as when all things are justly subject to that by which they have first been made and also are constantly preserved; or by the right of donation, as when God, to whom all things belong, has transferred part of his dominion to someone and granted the right to give orders to the first-born, for example, and to monarchs; or by the right of contract, as when someone has voluntarily surrendered himself to another and submitted himself to another's will. Indeed, all obligation binds conscience and lays a bond on the mind itself, so that not fear of punishment, but a rational apprehension of what is right, puts us under an obligation, and conscience passes judgement on morals, and, if we are guilty of a crime, declares that we deserve punishment. Assuredly, the poet's saying is true that 'no one who commits a wicked action is acquitted in his own judgement';[27] but it would clearly be otherwise, if fear of punishment alone imposed an obligation. Anyone would easily discern in himself that this is so and perceive that there was one ground of his obedience when as a captive he was constrained to the service of a pirate, and that there was another ground when as a subject he was giving obedience to a ruler; he would judge in one way about disregarding allegiance to a king, in another about wittingly transgressing the orders of a pirate or robber. For in the latter case, with the approval of conscience, he rightly had regard only for his own well-being, but in the former, though conscience condemned him, he would violate the right of another.

Further, regarding obligation, it must be noted that some things bind 'effectively', others only 'terminatively', i.e. by delimitation. That thing binds 'effectively' which is the prime cause of all obligation, and from which springs the formal cause of obligation, namely the will of a superior. For we are bound to something for the very reason that he, under whose rule we are, wills it. That thing binds 'terminatively', or by delimitation, which prescribes the manner and measure of an obligation and of our duty and is nothing other than the declaration of that will, and this declaration by another name we call law. We are indeed bound by Almighty God[28] because he wills, but the declaration of his will delimits the obligation and the ground of our obedience; for we are not bound to anything except what a lawmaker in some way has made known and proclaimed as his will.

Besides, some things bind of themselves and by their intrinsic force, others indirectly and by a power external to themselves:

[27] Juvenal, *Satires*, XIII, 2–3.
[28] MS has 'Deo . . . optimo maximo'.

[1] Of itself and by its intrinsic force (and only so) is the divine will binding, and either it can be known by the light of nature, in which case it is that law of nature which we are discussing; or it is revealed by God-inspired men or in some other manner, in which case it is the positive divine law.

[2] Indirectly and by delegated power the will of any other superior is binding, be it that of a king or a parent, to whom we are subject by the will of God. All that dominion which the rest of lawmakers exercise over others, both the right of legislation and the right to impose an obligation to obey, they borrow from God alone, and we are bound to obey them because God willed thus, and commanded thus, so that by complying with them we also obey God.

The case having been put thus, we say that the law of nature is binding on all men primarily and of itself and by its intrinsic force, and we shall endeavour to prove this by the following arguments:

[1] Because this law contains all that is necessary to make a law binding. For God, the author of this law, has willed it to be the rule of our moral life, and he has made it sufficiently known, so that anyone can understand it who is willing to apply diligent study and to direct his mind to the knowledge of it. The result is that, since nothing else is required to impose an obligation but the authority and rightful power of the one who commands and the disclosure of his will, no one can doubt that the law of nature is binding on men.

For, in the first place, since God is supreme over everything and has such authority and power over us as we cannot exercise over ourselves, and since we owe our body, soul, and life – whatever we are, whatever we have, and even whatever we can be – to him and to him alone, it is proper that we should live according to the precept of his will. God has created us out of nothing and, if he pleases, will reduce us again to nothing: we are, therefore, subject to him in perfect justice and by utmost necessity.

In the second place, this law is the will of this omnipotent lawmaker, known to us by the light and principles of nature; the knowledge of it can be concealed from no one unless he loves blindness and darkness and casts off nature in order that he may avoid his duty.

[2] If natural law is not binding on men, neither can positive divine law be binding, and that no one has maintained. In fact, the

basis of obligation is in both cases the same, i.e. the will of a supreme Godhead. The two laws differ only in method of promulgation and in the way in which we know them: the former we know with certainty by the light of nature and from natural principles, the latter we apprehend by faith.

[3] If natural law is not binding on men, neither can any human positive law be binding. For the laws of the civil magistrate derive their whole force from the constraining power of natural law, certainly so far as the majority of men is concerned. In fact, since the definite knowledge of a divine revelation has not reached them, they have no other law, both divine and binding by its very nature, than natural law; so that, if you abolish the law of nature among them, you banish from among mankind at the same time the whole body politic, all authority, order, and fellowship among them. For we should not obey a king just out of fear, because, being more powerful, he can constrain (this in fact would be to establish firmly the authority of tyrants, robbers, and pirates), but for conscience' sake, because a king has command over us by right; that is to say, because the law of nature decrees that princes and a lawmaker, or a superior by whatever name you call him, should be obeyed. Hence the binding force of civil law is dependent on natural law; and we are not so much coerced into rendering obedience to the magistrate by the power of the civil law as bound to obedience by natural right.[29]

VII
Is the Binding Force of the Law of Nature Perpetual and Universal? Yes

The only thing, perhaps, about which all mortals think alike is that men's opinions about the law of nature and the ground of their duty are diverse and manifold – a fact which, even if tongues were silent, moral behaviour, which differs so widely, would show pretty well. Men are everywhere met with, not only a select few and those in a private station but whole nations, in whom no sense of law, no moral rectitude, can be observed. There are also other nations, and they are many, which with no guilty feeling disregard some at least

---

[29] Locke here inserted the title of the third unwritten essay: 'Are animals bound by the law of nature? No.'

of the precepts of natural law and consider it to be not only customary but also praiseworthy to commit, and to approve of, such crimes as are utterly loathsome to those who think rightly and live according to nature. Hence, among these nations, thefts are lawful and commendable, and the greedy hands of robbers are not debarred from violence and injury by any shackles of conscience. For others there is no disgrace in debauchery; and while in one place there are no temples or altars of the gods, in another they are found spattered with human blood. Since such is the case, it may be justly doubted whether the law of nature is binding on all mankind, unsettled and uncertain as men are, accustomed to the most diverse institutions, and driven by impulses in quite opposite directions; for that the decrees of nature are so obscure that they are hidden from whole nations is hard to believe. That some men are born defective in mind as well as in eyesight, and are in need of a guide and do not know whither they ought to go, can readily be admitted; but who will say that entire nations are born blind, or that a thing is according to nature, of which whole nations and a multitude of men are absolutely ignorant, or that the light infused into human hearts either differs not at all from darkness or like an *ignis fatuus*[30] leads into error by its uncertain gleam? To say this would be to insult nature, for while praising her gentleness we should be experiencing her most terrible tyranny. For has there ever been cruelty, even Sicilian cruelty,[31] so savage as that nature should demand of her subjects observance of a law which in the meantime she would conceal – that they should be obedient to a will which they could have no knowledge of? Draco's laws,[32] we read, were written in blood, but even so they were written so that they could be known. Surely, nature, the mother of all things, cannot be so cruel that she would bid mortals submit to a law which she has not taught and sufficiently promulgated. Hence it seems necessary to conclude, either that there is no law of nature in some places, or that some nations at least are not bound by it, so that the binding force of natural law is not universal.

In spite of these objections, we maintain that the binding force of the law of nature is [1] perpetual and [2] universal.

---

[30] Literally a foolish fire: a delusive illumination that leads one astray.

[31] Possibly refers to Phalaris, tyrant of Agrigentum.

[32] The severe laws of Draco, archon at Athens in 621 BC; hence Draconic.

[1] We have already proved that this law is given as morally binding, and we must now discuss to what extent it is in fact binding. We say then that in the first place the binding force of the law of nature is permanent, that is to say, there is no time when it would be lawful for a man to act against the precepts of this law; no interregnum is provided here, in this realm there are no Saturnalian holidays given to either freedom or licence. The bonds of this law are perpetual and coeval with the human race, beginning with it and perishing with it at the same time. However, this permanently binding force must not be supposed to be such that men would be bound at all times to perform everything that the law of nature commands. This would be simply impossible, since one man is not capable of performing different actions at the same time, and he can no more observe several duties at once than a body can be in several places. Still, we say that the binding force of nature is perpetual in the sense that there neither is, nor can be, a time when the law of nature orders men, or any man, to do something and he is not obliged to show himself obedient; so that the binding force is continuous though it is not necessary that the action be so. The binding force of the law never changes, though often there is a change in both the times and the circumstances of actions, whereby our obedience is defined. We can sometimes stop acting according to the law, but act against the law we cannot. In this life's journey rest is sometimes allowed, but straying at no time. However, the following points must be noted concerning the binding force of the law of nature:

[i] There are things which are altogether forbidden and to these we are bound – as the Schoolmen[33] are wont to say – for ever; in other words, there is no single moment when one is at liberty to perform anything of this kind without incurring guilt; for example theft, murder, and other acts of that sort. Thus to force or cheat a man out of his property is at all times a crime, and no one can stain himself with another man's blood without incurring guilt. From these and other such acts we are for ever bound to abstain.

[ii] There are other things towards which the law of nature requires us to maintain certain sentiments, such as reverence and fear of the deity, tender affection for parents, love of one's neigh-

---

[33] I.e. the Scholastic theologians of the medieval church.

bour, and other such sentiments. To these, too, we are obliged for ever, and there is no single moment when one is allowed to throw off these mental dispositions or be disposed towards those objects otherwise than the law of nature prescribes.

[iii] There are things of which the outward performance is commanded, for example the outward worship of the deity, the consoling of a distressed neighbour, the relief of one in trouble, the feeding the hungry: in these matters we are not under obligation continuously, but only at a particular time and in a particular manner. For we are not obliged to provide with shelter and to refresh with food any and every man, or at any time whatever, but only when a poor man's misfortune calls for our alms and our property supplies means for charity.

[iv] Lastly, there are cases where the action in itself is not commanded but only circumstances accompanying it. For example, in customary intercourse among men and in communal life who is bound to hold a conversation about his neighbour and to meddle with other people's affairs? No one, surely. Anyone can without harm either talk or be silent. But if perchance one wants to talk about another person, the law of nature undoubtedly enjoins that one's talk be candid and friendly and that one should say things that do not harm that other person's reputation and character. In cases like these, the 'matter' of the action is neither good nor bad, but the circumstances accompanying it are so determined. We are not bound here absolutely, but only conditionally, and it depends on our ability, and is entrusted to our prudence, whether or not we care to undertake some such actions in which we incur obligation. In all these cases, as is obvious, the binding force of the law is equally permanent; the requirements of our duty, however, are not equally permanent. In the cases I mentioned in the first two sections we are always bound to actual obedience; in cases mentioned in the last two sections we are likewise always bound to undertake the things which we have to do, but these things occur at intervals only and successively, and regard is paid to place, time, and circumstances, so that while the action comes to an end at some time, the obligation never does.

[2] Next we say that the binding force of natural law is universal, but not because any and every law of nature is binding on any and every man, since this is impossible. For most precepts of this law

have regard to the various relations between men and are founded on these. Princes have many privileges which are not granted to the common people, and subjects, in their capacity as subjects, have many duties which cannot be appropriate to a king. While it is a general's duty to assign soldiers their posts, it is the soldiers' duty to hold them; and it would not become a parent to salute his children ceremoniously and humbly. Of these matters we have to lay down our view briefly thus: those precepts of the law of nature which are absolute and which embrace thefts, debaucheries, and slanders, and on the other hand religion, charity, fidelity and the rest, these I say, and others of that kind, are binding on all men in the world equally, kings as well as subjects, noblemen as well as the common people, both parents and children, barbarians no less than Greeks. And no nation or human being is so removed from all humanity, so savage and so beyond the law, that it is not held by these bonds of law. But those decrees of nature which are concerned with the various conditions of men and the relations between them are binding on men exactly in proportion as either private or public functions demand; the duty of a king is one thing, the duty of a subject is another. Each single subject is bound to obey the prince; but each single man is not bound to be a subject, for certain men are born kings. It is a father's duty to feed and bring up his children, but no one is compelled to be a father. The result is that the binding force of natural law is everywhere the same, only the circumstances of life are different. Clearly, the duty of a subject is the same among the Garamantes[34] and the Indians as among the Athenians or the Romans.

On these assumptions we say that the binding force of the law of nature holds its power undiminished and unchanged both throughout all ages and over the whole world. Because if this law is not binding on all men the reason is either that [i] it has never been given at all to any part of mankind, or that [ii] it has been repealed. Neither of these two things, however, can be maintained.

[i] For, in the first place, it cannot be said that some men are born so free that they are not in the least subject to this law, for this is not a private or positive law created according to circumstances and for an immediate convenience; rather it is a fixed and

---

[34] See above, p. III.

permanent rule of morals, which reason itself pronounces, and which persists, being a fact so firmly rooted in the soil of human nature. Hence human nature must needs be changed before this law can be either altered or annulled. There is, in fact, a harmony between these two, and what is proper now for the rational nature, in so far as it is rational, must needs be proper for ever, and the same reason will pronounce everywhere the same moral rules. Since therefore all men are by nature rational, and since there is a harmony between this law and the rational nature, and this harmony can be known by the light of nature, it follows that all those who are endowed with a rational nature, i.e. all men in the world, are morally bound by this law. Hence, if natural law is binding on at least some men, clearly by the same right it must be binding on all men as well, because the ground of obligation is the same for all men, and also the manner of its being known and its nature are the same. In fact, this law does not depend on an unstable and changeable will, but on the eternal order of things. For it seems to me that certain essential features of things are immutable, and that certain duties arise out of necessity and cannot be other than they are. And this is not because nature or God (as I should say more correctly) could not have created man differently. Rather, the cause is that, since man has been made such as he is, equipped with reason and his other faculties and destined for this mode of life, there necessarily result from his inborn constitution some definite duties for him, which cannot be other than they are. In fact it seems to me to follow just as necessarily from the nature of man that, if he is a man, he is bound to love and worship God and also to fulfil other things appropriate to the rational nature, i.e. to observe the law of nature, as it follows from the nature of a triangle that, if it is a triangle, its three angles are equal to two right angles, although perhaps very many men are so lazy and so thoughtless that for want of attention they are ignorant of both these truths, which are so manifest and certain that nothing can be plainer. Hence, no one can doubt that this law is binding on all human beings, to a man, and it is also clear from this that:

[ii] In the second place, this natural duty will never be abolished; for human beings cannot alter this law, because they are subject to it, and it is not the business of subjects to abrogate laws at their liking, and because God certainly would not wish to do so. For

since, according to his infinite and eternal wisdom, he has made man such that these duties of his necessarily follow from his very nature, he surely will not alter what has been made and create a new race of men, who would have another law and moral rule, seeing that natural law stands and falls together with the nature of man as it is at present. God could have created men such that they would be without eyes and not need them; but so long as they use their eyes and want to open them, and so long as the sun shines, they must of necessity come to know the alternations of day and night, be aware of the differences of colours, and see with their eyes the difference between a curved and a straight line.

Other arguments to show that the binding force of natural law is universal could be derived *a posteriori*, namely from the inconveniences that would follow on the assumption that this binding force came somewhere to an end. For there would be no religion, no fellowship among men, no fidelity, and countless other such things. But it is sufficient to mention this merely in passing. It remains now to cope briefly with some doubts about this matter.

[i] A proof that the binding force of the law of nature is not everlasting and universal can be given in this way: namely by showing that, though by general agreement it is a law of nature that every man should be allowed to keep his own property, or, if you like, that no one may take away and keep for himself what is another's property, yet at God's command the binding force of this law can lapse, for this actually happened, as we read, in the case of the Israelites when they departed from Egypt and journeyed to Palestine [Exod. 12:35]. To this we reply by denying the minor premiss; for if God should order someone not to restore something he has received on loan, the ownership of the thing itself, but not the binding force of natural law, would cease; the law is not violated, but the owner is changed, for the previous owner loses together with the possession of the thing his right to it. In fact, the goods of fortune are never so much ours that they cease to be God's: that supreme lord of all things can, without doing wrong, give of his property to anyone as he pleases by his sovereign will.

[ii] If sometimes we are, and sometimes we are not, bound to render the same obedience to parents, then this shows that the binding force of natural law is not perpetual; nay, rather, if a prince commands differently, we are not bound to obey parents. Then, in

that case we reply that we are no doubt bound to comply with the orders of parents but only in things lawful, and this obligation is never annulled; but if a king commands otherwise, a parent's orders become unlawful; for instance, an order to stay at home and show concern for the family, when the king is summoning a man for military service. Thus the binding force of natural law does not by any means cease, yet the nature of the case itself changes.

[iii] If anyone doubts whether that binding force is universal on the ground that the opinions about their duty vary so much from men to men and their habitual actions are so different, it ought to be remembered that this diversity among mortals, both in their manner of life and in their opinions, does not occur because the law of nature varies among different nations, but because men are either carried off by inveterate habit and traditional examples or led aside by their passions, thus yielding to the morality of others; also they follow the herd in the manner of brute beasts, since they do not allow themselves the use of their reason, but give way to appetite. In like manner, in fact, he who will not open his eyes, as well as he who is born blind, is liable to errors, though possibly the road is unobstructed and his eyesight is sufficiently sharp.

There is no reason that we should deal with the case of children and idiots. For although the law is binding on all those to whom it is given, it does not, however, bind those to whom it is not given, and it is not given to those who are unable to understand it.

VIII
Is Every Man's Own Interest the Basis of the Law of Nature? No

There are some who in their attack upon natural law have adopted the following argument: 'it is on a basis of utility that men have laid down for themselves legal codes varying in accordance with their manners and customs, and often changed with changing times among the same people; there is, however, no law of nature, for all men as well as other living creatures are driven by innate impulse to seek their own interests; and there is likewise no such thing as a natural law of justice, or, if it exists, it is the height of folly, inasmuch as to be mindful of the advantages of others is to do harm to oneself'. This and other such arguments Carneades once maintained in his Academy.[35] His very sharp intellect and power of speech left nothing untouched, almost nothing unshaken, and there have been a number of people ever since who have assented to this doctrine very eagerly. Since these people have lacked virtues and those gifts of the mind whereby they might prepare for themselves the way to honours and wealth, they have complained that mankind has been treated unfairly and have contended that civil affairs were not conducted without injustice, as long as they were debarred from general and natural advantages destined for the common good. They went so far as to proclaim that the yoke of authority should be shaken off, and natural liberty be vindicated, and every right and equity be determined not by an extraneous law but by each person's own self-interest. This most harmful opinion has, however, always been opposed by the more rational part of men, in whom there was some sense of a common humanity, some concern for fellowship. However, in order that we may define the matter more carefully, we must first give some explanation of the terms, namely what we mean firstly by the basis of natural law, and then, by each man's private interest.

[1] First, by the basis of natural law we mean some sort of groundwork on which all other and less evident precepts of that law are built and from which in some way they can be derived, and thus they acquire from it all their binding force in that they are in accordance with that, as it were, primary and fundamental law which is the standard and measure of all the other laws depending on it.

[2] Secondly, when we say that each man's personal interest is not the basis of natural law, we do not wish to be understood to say that the common rules of human equity and each man's private interest are opposed to one another, for the strongest protection of each man's private property is the law of nature, without the observance of which it is impossible for anybody to be master of his property and to pursue his own advantage. Hence it will be clear to anyone who candidly considers for himself the human race and the practices of men that nothing contributes so much to the general welfare of each and so effectively keeps men's possessions safe and

---

[35] Carneades: critic of Stoic moral philosophy, second century BC. Locke's summary is taken from Lactantius, *Divine Institutes*, v, 16.

secure as the observance of natural law. Nevertheless we do deny that each person is at liberty to do what he himself, according to circumstances, judges to be of advantage to him. You have certainly no reason for holding that each person's own interest is the standard of what is just and right, unless you let every single man be judge in his own case and himself determine what is in his own interest, seeing that no one can be a fair and just appraiser of another's advantages; and you deceive a man with what is only a semblance of utility, if you say he is permitted to do what is useful and yet would let another man have the power to determine what is and what is not useful. Hence the point of the question is precisely this: is it true that what each individual in the circumstances judges to be of advantage to himself and his affairs is in accordance with natural law, and on that account is not only lawful for him but also unavoidable, and that nothing in nature is binding except so far as it carries with it some immediate personal advantage? It is this we deny, for three reasons:

[i] First, it is impossible for something to be the basis of natural law or to be the principal law, which is not the ground of the binding force of other, less universal, laws of that same nature. But the binding force of other laws does not rest on the principle of utility as its foundation, for if you should run over all the dutiful actions of human life, you will find none that arises out of mere utility and is binding for the sole reason that it is advantageous. In fact a great number of virtues, and the best of them, consist only in this: that we do good to others at our own loss. By virtuous actions of this kind heroic men in former times were raised to the sky and placed among the number of gods, purchasing heaven not with a mass of riches brought together from all sides, but with toil, hazards, and generosity. They did not pursue their own advantage but the interests of the commonwealth and of all mankind. Some earned immortality by their works, some by their studies, some by their death; none achieved either greatness or excellence by being idle or covetous. Yet if it were the principal law of nature that each man should be mindful of himself and his own affairs, those noble examples of virtue which the records of history have hallowed would have to be consigned to oblivion, so that the memory of so much folly, of so much perversity, would be completely blotted out. The very same people, in fact, whom we now admire as the best and the most

eminent of men would have to be regarded not only as foolish but even as wicked and most pernicious. For they were so zealously contemptuous of themselves and of their own affairs only to purchase infamy at a higher price and, by throwing away their own property, by the same act to cast off their innocence; and they believed they were bound to exert themselves thus in order that injuries should multiply and crimes too. If we wish utility to be the standard of what is right, your labours, Hercules, deserved a felon's cross rather than a place in heaven, and you declared war on nature itself rather than on monsters. What Curtius[36] did, when for the sake of his country he leaped into the yawning chasm and plunged into the earth alive lest Rome should be engulfed in the grave of her own forebodings, was not so much virtue as madness: he bid both life and innocence farewell and he deserved his death the moment he entered his grave. To be sure, nature undoubtedly deserves to be called the most kindly mother of all, if she wishes our duties to be not only unavoidable but also pleasant and lucrative and no actions to be virtuous unless they are profitable! Well indeed is it for mankind that virtue should increase in proportion to the increase of wealth itself! Why, then, do we praise the indigence of Fabricius[37] and paint that abominable stinginess of his in bright colours? He preferred to sell his fortune and his virtue rather than his country, and he foolishly held the Roman republic in greater esteem, and loved it more dearly, than himself. How much more fitly should we praise the fine spirit of Catilina[38] who, perfectly instructed in the precepts of nature, preferred his own interest to that of the world's capital and did not fear to drive the enemy's plough over the walls of Rome itself, so long as he could hope thereby to reap a harvest! Cicero may perhaps be called a father to his country,[39] Catilina certainly was a true son of nature and, while he attacked Rome, he rather than Cicero who defended it deserved to rule the world. Surely, one feels ashamed to fasten such infamy upon nature and to impute so much evil to her ordinances. Besides

---

[36] Marcus Curtius, a mythic hero, in 362 BC.

[37] Fabricius Luscinus (third century BC) was famous for his frugality and his generous conduct towards Rome's enemy Pyrrhus.

[38] Lucius Sergius Catalina (Cataline): conspirator against Rome, exposed and foiled by Cicero.

[39] The title awarded to Cicero for saving the republic in 63 BC.

(since there is nothing so sacred that avarice has not at one time or other treated it with violence), if the ground of duty were made to rest on gain and if expediency were acknowledged as the standard of rightness, what else would this be than to open the door to every kind of villainy?

[ii] Secondly, it is impossible that the primary law of nature is such that its violation is unavoidable. Yet, if the private interest of each person is the basis of that law, the law will inevitably be broken, because it is impossible to have regard for the interests of all at one and the same time. In point of fact, the inheritance of the whole of mankind is always one and the same, and it does not grow in proportion to the number of people born. Nature has provided a certain profusion of goods for the use and convenience of men, and the things provided have been bestowed in a definite way and in a predetermined quantity; they have not been fortuitously produced nor are they increasing in proportion with what men need or covet. Clothes are not born with us, nor do men, like tortoises, possess and carry about shelters that have originated with them and are growing up together with them. Whenever either the desire or the need of property increases among men, there is no extension, then and there, of the world's limits. Victuals, clothes, adornments, riches, and all other good things of this life are provided for common use. And so, when any man snatches for himself as much as he can, he takes away from another man's heap the amount he adds to his own, and it is impossible for anyone to grow rich except at the expense of someone else. Someone here will possibly amend the statement by saying that if we make every man's self-interest the basis of natural law, this must not be understood in the sense that each person would be required to be prosperous and happy and to have everything in abundance, but that everyone is obliged, as much as he can, to have regard for himself, so that the standard of rightness is private interest and all the duties of life are founded on it. From this assumption it follows, first, that men are under an obligation to do what cannot be realised. For in such a case each person is required to procure for himself and to retain in his possession the greatest possible number of useful things; and when this happens it is inevitable that the smallest possible number is left to some other person, because surely no gain falls to you which does not involve somebody else's loss. But obviously a contrary result

follows if we lay down another foundation for moral virtue. In fact, virtuous actions themselves do not clash nor do they engage men in conflict: they kindle and cherish one another. Justice in me does not take away equity in another, nor does the liberality of a prince thwart the generosity of his subjects. The moral purity of a parent does not corrupt his children, nor can the moderation of a Cato lessen the austerity of a Cicero. The duties of life are not at variance with one another, nor do they arm men against one another – a result which, secondly, follows of necessity from the preceding assumption, for upon it men are, as they say, by the law of nature in a state of war; so all society is abolished and all trust, which is the bond of society. For what reason is there for the fulfilment of promises, what safeguard of society, what common life of man with man, when equity and justice are one and the same as utility? What else indeed can human intercourse be than fraud, violence, hatred, robbery, murder, and such like, when every man not only may, but must, snatch from another by any and every means what the other in his turn is obliged to keep safe?

[iii] Hence there arises a third argument, namely, that it is impossible for any principle to be the basis of natural law, whereby, if it is laid down as true, all justice, friendship, and generosity are taken away from life. For what justice is there where there is no personal property or right of ownership, or what personal property when a man is not only allowed to possess his own, but what he possesses is his own, merely because it is useful to him. In truth, one may observe here briefly that the upholders of this doctrine seek the principles of moral action and a rule to live by in men's appetites and natural instincts rather than in the binding force of a law, just as if that was morally best which most people desired. Hence it furthermore follows either that the law of nature is not binding (but this no one will be found to say, for then there would be no law), or that human life is so constituted that it would be unlawful for a man to renounce his own rights or to impart benefits to another without a definite hope of reward. In fact, if the rightness of a course of action be derived from expediency and men are bound to comply with that sort of rectitude, I know not in what way it would be possible for anyone, without breaking this law, to grant or give anything to a friend, incur expenses on his behalf, or in any other manner do him a favour out of pure kindness. I leave others

to judge the absurdity of this and how contrary it is to reason, to human nature, and to an honourable conduct of life. An objector, however, might say that if the observance of natural law and of every duty of life always leads to what is useful and if whatever we do according to the law of nature cannot but create, either directly or indirectly, great advantages, then the basis of natural law is each man's own interest. But (he goes on) the truth of the minor premiss is evident, for the observance of this law gives rise to peace, harmonious relations, friendship, freedom from punishment, security, possession of our property, and – to sum it all up in one word – happiness. Our answer to the objector is this: utility is not the basis of the law or the ground of obligation, but the consequence of obedience to it. Surely, it is one thing for an action of itself to yield some profit, another for it to be useful because it is in accordance with the law, so that if the law were abolished it would have in it no utility whatever: for example, to stand by one's promise, though it were to one's own hindrance. In fact we must distinguish between an action as such and obedient action, for an action itself can be inexpedient – for example, the restitution of a trust that diminishes our possessions – whereas obedient action is useful in so far as it averts the penalty due to a crime. But this penalty would not be due and hence need not be shunned, if the standard of rightness were immediate advantage. And thus the rightness of an action does not depend on its utility; on the contrary, its utility is a result of its rightness.

Thus thought J. Locke, 1664[40]

---

[40] There then follows the ninth essay, the Valedictory Address: 'Can anyone by nature be happy in this life? No.'

An Essay on Toleration

1667. There are four manuscript versions: (1) MS Locke, c. 28, fos. 21–32; (2) PRO 30/24/47/1; (3) Huntington Library, California, HM 584 (Bodleian Library, MS Film 151); (4) Adversaria 1661, pp. 106–25 (Bodleian Library, MS Film 77). MS 3 is the earliest and is in Locke's hand, but is a rough draft. The others are copies. MS 1 is probably the latest draft, and is extensively amended by Locke. MS 1 is printed in Viano 1961, pp. 81–103; Inoue 1974; Wootton 1993, pp. 186–210; extracts in Gough 1950, pp. 197–9; MS 2 is printed in Fox Bourne 1876, I, 174–94; an extract in King 1829, p. 156; 1830, I, 289–91. There is no full critical edition. MS 4 has two unique, detached paragraphs, which are printed later in this volume as 'Toleration A'. On textual matters see Milton 1993. Fox Bourne's is the most widely used version. The version printed below follows MS 1, but records significant variants. The essay is cited by Laslett, Second Treatise, §§110, 120.

The essay marks a decisive shift from the position that Locke had adopted in the *Two Tracts* and towards the tolerationist views espoused in the *Letter Concerning Toleration*. It marks the first fruit of his close association with Lord Ashley (later the Earl of Shaftesbury). The period between 1667 and 1674 saw an intensive debate about toleration, launched by Simon Patrick's inaptly named *Friendly Debate* (1666), a savage attack upon the Dissenters. The best known episode is Andrew Marvell's response to Samuel Parker's *Ecclesiastical Politie* (1669); Locke wrote notes on Parker's book, printed later in this volume.

Locke proceeds as follows. [1] He sketches the purposes of magistracy, whether construed as deriving from divine right or from a grant of the people. [II] He considers the magistrate's role in three sorts of actions and opinions: (1) speculative opinions and modes of worship; (2) practical opinions and actions in matters indifferent (including the public expression of opinion); (3) practical actions which are inherently good or evil (including the restraint of immorality). [III] He deals with two problematic cases, Roman Catholics and Protestant 'fanatics'. He next insists that compulsion never changes minds; and determines whether sects are dangerous in practice. [IV] (marked 'Part 2' in MS 2) Locke turns from theoretical considerations to the condition of England, and argues that toleration is a prudent policy. Catholics and Dissenters are again discussed. Locke reiterates the inefficacy of force, for it creates only martyrs or hypocrites.

[I] In the question of liberty of conscience, which has for some years been so much bandied amongst us, one thing that hath chiefly perplexed the question, kept up the dispute, and increased the animosity, hath been, I conceive, this, that both parties have, with equal zeal and mistake, too much enlarged their pretensions, whilst one side preach up absolute obedience, and the other claim universal liberty in matters of conscience, without assigning what those things are which have a title to liberty, or showing the boundaries of imposition and obedience.

To clear the way to this, I shall lay down this for a foundation, which I think will not be questioned or denied, viz.:

That the whole trust, power, and authority of the magistrate is vested in him for no other purpose but to be made use of for the good, preservation, and peace of men in that society over which he is set, and therefore that this alone is and ought to be the standard and measure according to which he ought to square and proportion his laws, model and frame his government. For, if men could live peaceably and quietly together, without uniting under certain laws, and entering[1] into a commonwealth, there would be no need at all of magistrates or polities, which are only made to preserve men in this world from the fraud and violence of one another; so that what was the end of erecting of government ought alone to be the measure of its proceeding.

There are some that tell us that monarchy is *jure divino* [by divine right]. I will not now dispute this opinion, but only mind the

---

[1] Other versions have 'growing'; a telling amendment.

assertors of it that if they mean by this (as certainly they must) that the sole, supreme, arbitrary power and disposal of all things is and ought to be by divine right in a single person, 'tis to be suspected they have forgot what country they are born in, under what laws they live, and certainly cannot but be obliged to declare Magna Charta to be downright heresy. If they mean by monarchy *jure divino* not an absolute but limited monarchy (which I think an absurdity, if not a contradiction) they ought to show us this charter from heaven, and let us see where God hath given the magistrate a power to do anything but barely in order to the preservation and welfare of his subjects in this life, or else leave us at liberty to believe as we please; since nobody is bound, or can allow anyone's pretensions to a power (which he himself confesses limited) further than he shows his title.

There are others who affirm that all the power and authority the magistrate hath is derived from the grant and consent of the people; and to those I say, it cannot be supposed the people should give any one or more of their fellow men an authority over them for any other purpose than their own preservation, or extend the limits of their jurisdiction beyond the limits of this life.

[II] This being premised, that the magistrate ought to do or meddle with nothing but barely in order to securing the civil peace and propriety[2] of his subjects, let us next consider the opinions and actions of men, which, in reference to toleration, divide themselves into three sorts. Either they:

First, are all such opinions and actions as in themselves concern not government or society at all, and such are all purely speculative opinions and divine worship; or

Secondly, are such as, in the[ir] own nature are neither good nor bad, but yet concern society and men's conversations one with another, and these are all practical opinions and actions in matters of indifferency; [or]

Thirdly, are such too as concern society, but are also good or bad in their own nature, and these are moral virtues and vices.

(1) I say that the first sort only, viz., speculative opinions and divine worship, are those things alone which have an absolute and universal right to toleration.

---

[2] Locke used 'propriety' and 'property' interchangeably.

First, purely speculative opinions, as the belief of the Trinity, purgatory, transubstantiation, antipodes,[3] Christ's personal reign on earth, etc.: and that in these every man hath his unlimited freedom appears, because bare speculations give no bias to my conversation with men, nor having any influence on my actions as I am a member of any society, but being such as would be still the same with all the consequences of them, though there were no other person besides myself in the world, cannot by any means either disturb the state or inconvenience my neighbour, and so come not within the magistrate's cognisance. Besides, no man can give another man power (and it would be to no purpose if God should) over that over which he has no power himself. Now that a man cannot command his own understanding, or positively determine today what opinion he will be of tomorrow, is evident from experience and the nature of the understanding, which can no more apprehend things otherwise than they appear to it, than the eye see other colours in the rainbow than it doth, whether those colours be really there or no. ⟨ I[4] must only remark before I leave this head of speculative opinions that the belief of a deity is not to be reckoned amongst purely speculative opinions, for it being the foundation of all morality, and that which influences the whole life and actions of men, without which a man is to be considered no other than one of the most dangerous sorts of wild beasts, and so incapable of all society. ⟩

The other thing that hath just claim to an unlimited toleration is the place, time, and manner of worshipping my God. Because this is a thing wholly between God and me, and of an eternal concernment, above the reach and extent of polities and government, which are but for my well-being in this world. For the magistrate is but umpire between man and man; he can right me against my neighbour, but cannot defend me against my God; whatever evil I suffer by obeying him in other things, he can make me amends in this world, but if he force me to a wrong religion, he can make me no reparation in the other world. To which let me add that, even in things of this world over which the magistrate hath an authority, he never does, and it would be injustice if he should, any further than it concerns the good of the public, enjoin men the care of their

---

[3] Locke has in mind the treatment of the Copernican system of astronomy as heretical, especially by the Catholic church in the case of Galileo.

[4] This passage added in the MS.

private civil concernments, or force them to a prosecution of their own private interests, but only protects them from being invaded and injured in them by others (which is a perfect toleration). And therefore we may well suppose he hath nothing at all to do with my private interest in another world, and that he ought not to prescribe me the way, or require my diligence, in the prosecution of that good which is of a far higher concernment to me than anything within his power, having no more certain or more infallible knowledge of the way to attain it than I myself, where we are both equally inquirers, both equally subjects, and wherein he can give me no security that I shall not, nor make me any recompense if I do, miscarry. Can it be reasonable that he that cannot compel me to buy a house should force me his way to venture the purchase of heaven? That he that cannot in justice prescribe me rules of preserving my health should enjoin me methods of saving my soul? He that cannot choose a wife for me should choose a religion? But if God (which is the point in question) would have men forced to heaven, it must not be by the outward violence of the magistrate on men's bodies, but the inward constraints of his own spirit on their minds, which are not to be wrought on by any human compulsion; the way to salvation not being any forced exterior performance, but the voluntary and secret choice of the mind; and it cannot be supposed that God would make use of any means which could not reach, but would rather cross, the attainment of the end. Nor can it be thought that men should give the magistrate a power to choose for them their way to salvation, which is too great to give away, if not impossible to part with. Since, whatsoever the magistrate enjoined in the worship of God, men must in this necessarily follow what they themselves thought best, since no consideration could be sufficient to force a man from, or to, that which he was fully persuaded was the way to infinite happiness or infinite misery. Religious worship, being that homage which I pay to that God I adore in a way I judge acceptable to him, and so being an action or commerce passing only between God and myself, hath in its own nature no reference at all to my governor, or to my neighbour, and so necessarily produces no action which disturbs the community. For kneeling or sitting in the sacrament can in itself tend no more to the disturbance of the government or injury of my neighbour than sitting or standing at my own table; wearing a cope or surplice in the church can no more in its own nature alarm or threaten the peace of the state than wearing a cloak or coat in the market; being rebaptised no more make a tempest in the commonwealth than it doth in the river, nor than barely washing myself would do in either. If I observe the Friday with the Mahomedan, or the Saturday with the Jew, or the Sunday with the Christian; whether I pray with or without a form; whether I worship God in the various and pompous ceremonies of the papist, or in the plainer way of the Calvinists; I see nothing in any of these, if they be done sincerely and out of conscience, that can of itself make me either the worse subject to my prince, or worse neighbour to my fellow-subject; unless it be that I will, out of pride or overweeningness of my own opinion, and a secret conceit of my own infallibility, taking to myself something of a godlike power, force and compel others to be of my mind, or censure or malign them if they be not. This indeed often happens, but 'tis not the fault of the worship, but the men, and is not the consequence of this or that form of devotion, but the product of depraved, ambitious human nature, which successively makes use of all sorts of religion, as Ahab did of keeping a fast, which was not the cause, but means and artifice, to take away Naboth's vineyard; which miscarriages of some professors do no more discredit any religion (for the same happens in all) than Ahab's rapine does fasting [1 Kings, ch. 21].

⟨'Twill[5] be said that if a toleration shall be allowed as due to all the parts of religious worship it will shut out the magistrate's power from making laws about those things over which it is acknowledged on all hands that he has a power, viz. things indifferent, as many things made use of in religious worship are, viz. wearing a white or a black garment, kneeling or not kneeling, etc. To which I answer, that in religious worship nothing is indifferent, for it being the using of those habits, gestures, etc., and no other, which I think acceptable to God in my worshipping of him, however they may be in their own nature perfectly indifferent, yet when I am worshipping my God in a way I think he has prescribed and will approve of, I cannot alter, omit, or add any circumstance in that which I think the true way of worship. And therefore if the magistrate permit me to be of a profession or church different from his, 'tis incongruous that he

---

[5] This paragraph added in the MS.

should prescribe any one circumstance of my worship, and 'tis strange to conceive upon what grounds of uniformity any different profession of Christians can be prohibited in a Christian country, where the Jewish religion (which is directly opposite to the principles of Christianity) is tolerated; and would it not be irrational, where the Jewish religion is permitted, that the Christian magistrate, upon pretence of his power in indifferent things, should enjoin or forbid anything, or any way interpose in their way or manner of worship?⟩

From what is premissed I think will follow: that in speculations and religious worship every man hath a perfect, uncontrollable liberty, which he may freely use, without, or contrary to, the magistrate's command, without any guilt or sin at all, provided always that it be all done sincerely and out of conscience to God, according to the best of his knowledge and persuasion. But, if there be any ambition, pride, revenge, faction, or any such alloy that mixes itself with what he calls conscience, so much there is of guilt, and so much he shall answer for at the day of judgement.

(2) I say all practical principles, or opinions, which men think themselves obliged to regulate their actions with one another; as that men may breed their children, or dispose of their estates, as they please; that men may work or rest when they think fit; that polygamy and divorce are lawful or unlawful: these opinions and the actions following from them, with all other things indifferent, have a title also to toleration; but yet only so far as they do not tend to the disturbance of the state, or do not cause greater inconveniences than advantages to the community. For all these opinions, except such of them as are apparently destructive to human society, being things either of indifferency or doubt, and neither the magistrate [n]or subject being on either side infallible, he ought no further to consider them than as the making laws and interposing his authority in such opinions may conduce to the welfare and safety of his people. But yet no such opinion hath any right to toleration on this ground, that it is a matter of conscience, and some men are persuaded that it is either a sin or a duty, because the conscience or persuasion of the subject cannot possibly be a measure by which the magistrate can or ought to frame his laws, which ought to be suited to the good of all his subjects, not the persuasions of a part, which, often happening to be contrary one to another, must produce

contrary laws; and, there being nothing so indifferent which the consciences of some or other do not choke at, a toleration of men in all that which they pretend out of conscience they cannot submit to will wholly take away all the civil laws, and all the magistrate's power; and so there will be no law, nor government, if you deny the magistrate's authority in [in]different things, over which it is acknowledged on all hands that he hath jurisdiction. And therefore the errors or scruples of anyone's conscience, which lead him to, or deter him from, the doing of anything, do not destroy the magistrate's power, nor alter the nature of the thing, which is still indifferent. For I will not doubt here to call all these practical opinions in respect of the lawmaker indifferent, though perhaps they are not so in themselves. For, however the magistrate be persuaded in himself of the reasonableness or absurdity, necessity or unlawfulness of any of them, and is possibly in the right, yet, whilst he acknowledges himself not infallible, he ought to regard them, in making of his laws, no otherwise than as things indifferent, except only as that, being enjoined, tolerated, or forbidden, they carry with them the good and welfare of the people; though at the same time he be obliged strictly to suit his personal actions to the dictates of his own conscience and persuasion in these very opinions. For, not being made infallible in reference to others by being made a governor over them, he shall hereafter be accountable to God for his actions as a man, according as they are suited to his own conscience and persuasion; but shall be accountable for his laws and administration as a magistrate, according as they are intended to the good, preservation, and quiet of all his subjects in this world, as much as is possible; which is a rule so certain and so clear than he can scarce err in it, unless he do it wilfully.

But before I proceed to show the limits of restraint and liberty in reference to those things, it will be necessary to set down the several degrees of imposition that are or may be used in matters of opinion: (i) The prohibiting to publish or vent any opinion. (ii) Forcing to renounce or abjure any opinion. (iii) Compelling to declare an assent to the contrary opinion. There are answerable to these the same degrees of toleration, from all which I conclude:

(i) That the magistrate may prohibit the publishing of any of these opinions when in themselves they tend to the disturbance of government, because they are then under his cognisance and jurisdiction.

(ii) That no man ought to be forced to renounce his opinion, or assent to the contrary, because such a compulsion cannot produce any real effect to that purpose for which it is designed. It cannot alter men's minds; it can only force them to be hypocrites; and by this way the magistrate is so far from bringing men to embrace the truth of his opinion, that he only constrains them to lie for their own. Nor does this injunction at all conduce to the peace or security of the government; but quite the contrary, because hereby the magistrate does not make anyone to be one jot the more of his mind, but to be very much more his enemy.

(iii) That any actions flowing from any of these opinions, as also in all other indifferent things, the magistrate has a power to command or forbid so far as they tend to the peace, safety, or security of his people, whereof though he be judge, yet he ought still to have a great care that no such laws be made, no such restraints established, for any other reason but because the necessity of the state and the welfare of the people called for them. And perhaps it will not be sufficient that he barely thinks such impositions and such rigour necessary or convenient, unless he hath seriously and impartially considered and debated whether they be so or no; and his opinion (if he mistake) will no more justify him in the making of such laws, than the conscience or opinion of the subject will excuse him if he disobey them, if consideration and inquiry could have better informed either of them. And I think it will easily be granted that the making of laws to any other end but only for the security of the government and protection of the people in their lives, estates, and liberties, i.e. the preservation of the whole, will meet with the severest doom at the great tribunal, not only because the abuse of that power and trust which is in the lawmaker's hands produces greater and more unavoidable mischiefs than anything else to mankind, for whose good only governments were instituted, but also because he is not accountable to any tribunal here; nor can there be a greater provocation to the supreme preserver of mankind than that the magistrate, [who] should make use of that power which was given him only for the preservation of all his subjects and every particular person amongst them as far as it is practicable, should misuse it to the service of his pleasure, vanity, or passion, and employ it to the disquieting and oppression of his fellow men, between whom and himself, in respect of the kings of kings, there is but a small and accidental difference.

(iv) That if the magistrate, in these opinions or actions by laws and impositions, endeavour to restrain or compel men contrary to the sincere persuasions of their own consciences, they ought to do what their consciences require of them, as far as without violence they can; but withal are bound at the same time quietly to submit to the penalty the law inflicts for such disobedience; for by this means they secure to themselves their grand concernment in another world, and disturb not the peace of this, offend not against their allegiance either to God or the king, but give both their due, the interest of the magistrate and their own being both safe. And certainly he is a hypocrite, and only pretends conscience, and aims at something else in this world, who will not, by obeying his conscience and submitting also to the law, purchase heaven for himself and peace for his country, though at the rate[6] of his estate, liberty, or life itself. But here also the private person, as well as the magistrate in the former case, must take great care that his conscience or opinion do not mislead him in the obstinate pursuit or flight of anything as necessary or unlawful which in truth is not so, lest by such an error or wilfulness he come to be punished for the same disobedience in this world and the other too; for, liberty of conscience being the great privilege of the subject, as the right of imposing is the great prerogative of the magistrate, they ought the more narrowly to be watched that they do not mislead either magistrate or subject, because of the fair pretences they have; those wrongs being the most dangerous, most carefully are to be avoided, and such as God will most severely punish, which are done under the specious semblances and appearances of right.

(3) I say there are besides the two former a third sort of actions which are good or bad in themselves; viz., the duties of the second table,[7] or trespasses against it, or the moral virtues and vices of the philosophers. These, though they are the vigorous, active part of religion, and that wherein men's consciences are very much concerned, yet I find that they make but a little part of the disputes of

---

[6] I.e. 'the cost of'.
[7] The second half of the Ten Commandments.

liberty of conscience. I know not whether it be that, if men were more zealous for these, they would be less contentious about the other. But this is certain, that the countenancing virtue is so necessary a prop to a state, and the allowance of some vices brings so certain a disturbance and ruin to society, that it was never found that any magistrate did, nor can be suspected that he ever will, establish vice by a law or prohibit the practice of virtue, which does by its own authority, and the advantages it brings to all governments, sufficiently deserve the countenance of the magistrate everywhere. Yet give me leave to say, however strange it may seem, that the lawmaker hath nothing to do with moral virtues and vices, nor ought to enjoin the duties of the second table any otherwise than barely as they are subservient to the good and preservation of mankind under government. For, could public societies well subsist, or men enjoy peace or safety, without the enforcing of those duties by the injunctions and penalties of laws, it is certain the lawmaker ought not to prescribe any rules about them, but leave the practice of them entirely to the discretion and consciences of his people. For, could even those moral virtues and vices be separated from the relation they have to the weal of the public, and cease to be a means to settle or disturb men's peace and properties, they would then become only the private and super-political concernment between God and a man's soul, wherein the magistrate's authority is not to interpose. God hath appointed the magistrate his vicegerent in this world, with power to command; but 'tis but like other deputies, to command only in the affairs of that place where he is vicegerent. (Whoever meddle in the concernments of the other world have no other power but to entreat and persuade.)

The magistrate as magistrate hath nothing to do with the good of men's souls or their concernments in another life, but is ordained and entrusted with his power only for the quiet and comfortable living of men in society, one with another, as hath been already sufficiently proved. And it is yet further evident that the magistrate commands not the practice of virtues, because they are virtuous and oblige the conscience, or are the duties of man to God and the way to his mercy and favour, but because they are the advantages of man with man, and most of them the strong ties and bonds of society, which cannot be loosened without shattering the whole frame; for some of them, which have not that influence on the state, and yet are vices, and acknowledged to be so as much as any, as covetousness, disobedience to parents, ingratitude, malice, revenge, and several others, the magistrate never draws his sword against; nor can it be said that those are neglected because they cannot be known, when the secretest of them, revenge and malice, put the distinction in judicature between manslaughter and murder.

⟨Yea,[8] even charity itself, which is certainly the great duty both of a man and a Christian, hath not yet, in its full latitude, a universal right to toleration; since there are some parts and instances of it which the magistrate hath absolutely forbidden, and that, for aught I could ever hear, without any offence to the tenderest consciences; for who doubts that to relieve with an alms the poor, though beggars (if one sees them in want), is, if considered absolutely, a virtue and every particular man's duty; yet this is amongst us prohibited by a law and the rigour of a penalty, and yet nobody in this case complains of the violation of his conscience or the loss of his liberty, which certainly, if it was an unlawful restraint upon the conscience, could not be overlooked by so many tender and scrupulous men. God does sometimes (so much does he take care of the preservation of government) make his law in some degrees submit and comply with man's; his laws forbids the vice, but the law of man often makes the measure of it. There have been commonwealths that have made theft lawful for such as were not caught in the fact, and perhaps 'twas as guiltless a thing to steal a horse at Sparta as to win a horse race in England. For the magistrate, having a power of making rules of transferring properties from one man to another, may establish any [laws], so they be universal, equal and without violence, and suited to the interest and welfare of that society, as this was at Sparta, who, being a warlike people, found this no ill way to teach their citizens vigilancy, boldness, and activity. This I only note by the by, to show how much the good of the commonwealth is the standard of all human laws, when it seems to limit and alter the obligation even of some of the laws of God, and change the nature of vice and virtue. Hence it is that the magistrate who could make theft innocent could not yet make perjury or breach of faith lawful, because destructive to human society.⟩

From the power, therefore, that the magistrate hath over good and bad actions, I think it will follow:

---

[8] This paragraph deleted in the MS, but extant in other versions.

(1) That he is not bound to punish all, i.e. he may tolerate some vices; for, I would fain know what government in the world doth not?

(2) That he ought not to command the practice of any vice, because such an injunction cannot be subservient to the good of the people, or preservation of the government.

⟨(3)[9] That if it can be supposed that he should command the practice of any vice, the conscientious and scandalised subject is bound to disobey his injunctions, and submit to his penalty, as in the former case.⟩

[III] These, I suppose, are the limits of imposition and liberty, and these three several sorts of things wherein men's consciences are concerned have right to such a latitude of toleration as I have set down, and no more, if they are considered separately and abstractly in themselves. But yet there is a case[10] which may still upon the same grounds vary the magistrate's usage of the men that claim this right of toleration.

(1) Since men usually take up their religion in gross, and assume to themselves the opinions of their party all at once in a bundle, it often happens that they mix with their religious worship and speculative opinions other doctrines absolutely destructive to the society wherein they live, as is evident in the Roman Catholics that are subjects of any prince but the pope. These, therefore, blending such opinions with their religion, reverencing them as fundamental truths, and submitting to them as articles of their faith, ought not to be tolerated by the magistrate in the exercise of their religion, unless he can be secured that he can allow one part without the spreading of the other, and that those opinions will not be imbibed and espoused by all those who communicate with them in their religious worship,[11] which, I suppose, is very hard to be done. ⟨And[12] that which may render them yet more incapable of toleration is when, [in addition] to these doctrines dangerous to government, they have the power of a neighbour prince of the same religion at hand to countenance and back them upon any occasion.⟩

---

[9] This paragraph deleted in the MS, but extant in other versions.

[10] Amended from 'there are two cases', the second case below being deleted.

[11] Amended from 'and that the propagation of those opinions may be separated from their religious worship'.

[12] This passage added in the MS.

⟨(2)⟩[13] Since experience vouches the practice, and men are not all saints that pretend conscience, I think I shall not injure any party if I say that most men, at least factions of men, when they have power sufficient, make use of it, right or wrong, for their own advantage and the establishment of themselves in authority, few men forbearing to grasp at dominion that have power to seize and hold it. When, therefore, men herd themselves into companies with distinctions from the public, and a stricter confederacy with those of their own denomination and party than other [of] their fellow subjects, whether the distinction be religious or ridiculous matters not, otherwise than as the ties of religion are stronger, and the pretences fairer and apter to draw partisans, and therefore the more to be suspected and the more heedfully to be watched; when, I say, any such distinct party is grown or growing so numerous as to appear dangerous to the magistrate and seem visibly to threaten the peace of the state, the magistrate may and ought to use all ways, either of policy or power, that shall be convenient, to lessen, break, and suppress the party, and so prevent the mischief. For, though their separation were really in nothing but religious worship, and he should use as the last remedy force and severity against them, who did nothing but worship God in their own way, yet did he not really persecute their religion or punish them for that, more than in a battle the conqueror kills men for wearing white ribbons in their hats, or any other badge about them, but because this was a mark they were enemies and dangerous; religion, i.e. this or that form of worship, being the cause of their union and correspondence, not of their factiousness and turbulency. For the praying to God in this or that posture does no more make men factious or at enmity one with another, nor ought otherwise to be treated, than the wearing of hats or turbans, which yet either of them may do, by being a note of distinction, and giving men an opportunity to number their forces, know their strength, be confident of one another, and readily unite upon any occasion. So that they are not restrained because of this or that opinion or worship, but because such a number, of any opinion whatsoever, who dissented would be dangerous. The same thing would happen if any fashion of clothes, distinct from that of the magistrate and those that adhere to him,

---

[13] This section deleted in the MS, but extant in other versions.

should spread itself and become the badge of a very considerable part of the people, who thereupon grow into a very strict correspondency and friendship one with another. Might not this well give the magistrate cause of jealousy, and make him with penalties forbid the fashion, not because unlawful, but because of the danger it might occasion? Thus a lay cloak may have the same effect with an ecclesiastical cowl or any other religious habit.

And perhaps the Quakers, were they numerous enough to become dangerous to the state, would deserve the magistrate's care and watchfulness to suppress them, were they no other way distinguished from the rest of his subject but by the bare keeping on their hats, as much as if they had a set form of religion separate from the state; in which case nobody would think that the not standing bare were a thing the magistrate levelled his severity against, any otherwise than as it united a great number of men, who, though they dissented from him in a very indifferent and trivial circumstance, yet might thereby endanger the government; and in such case he may endeavour to suppress and weaken or dissolve any party of men which religion or any other thing hath united, to the manifest danger of his government, by all those means that shall be most convenient for that purpose, whereof he is to be judge, nor shall he be accountable in the other world for what he does directly in order to the preservation and peace of his people, according to the best of his knowledge.

Whether force and compulsion be the right way to this end I will not here dispute; but this I dare affirm,⟩

⟨The[14] objection usually made against toleration, that the magistrate's great business being to preserve [the] peace and quiet of his government, he is obliged not to tolerate different religions in his country, since they bring distinctions wherein men unite and incorporate into bodies separate from the public, [and] they may occasion disorder, conspiracies and seditions in the commonwealth and endanger the government.

I answer: if all things that may occasion disorder or conspiracy in a commonwealth must not be endured in it, all discontented and active men must be removed, and whispering must be less tolerated than preaching, as much likelier to carry on and foment a con-

---

[14] This passage added in the MS, as an alternative to the preceding deleted passage.

spiracy. And if all numbers of men joined in a union and corporation distinct from the public be not to be suffered, all charters of towns, especially great ones, are presently to be taken away. Men united in religion have as little and perhaps less interest against the government than those united in the privileges of a corporation. This I am sure: they are less dangerous as being more scattered and not formed into that order. And the minds of men are so various in matters of religion, and so nice and scrupulous in things of an eternal concernment, that when men are indifferently tolerated, and persecution and force does not drive them together, they are apt to divide and subdivide into so many little bodies, and always with the greatest enmity to those they last parted from or stand nearest to, that they are a guard one upon another, and the public can have no apprehensions of them as long as they have their equal share of common justice and protection. And if the example of old Rome (where so many different opinions, gods, and ways of worship were promiscuously tolerated) be of any weight, we have reason to imagine that no religion can become suspected to the state of ill intention to it, till the government first by a partial usage of them, different from that of the rest of the subjects, declare its ill intentions to its professors, and so make a state business of it. And if any rational man can imagine that force and compulsion can at any time be the right way to get an opinion or religion out of the world, or to break a party of men that unite in the profession of it, this I dare affirm:⟩ that it is the worst, the last to be used, and with the greatest caution, for these reasons:

(1) Because it brings that upon a man which, that he might be freed from is the only reason why he is a member of the commonwealth, viz., violence. For, were there no fear of violence, there would be no government in the world, nor any need of it.

(2) Because the magistrate, in using of force, does in part cross what he pretends to do, which is the safety of all. For, the preservation, as much as is possible, of the property, quiet, and life of every individual being his duty, he is obliged not to disturb or destroy some for the quiet and safety of the rest, till it hath been tried whether there be not ways to save all. For, so far as he undoes or destroys the safety of any of his subjects for the security of the rest, so far as he opposes his own design, which is professed, and ought to be only for preservation, to which even the meanest have

a title. 'Twould be but an uncharitable as well as unskilful way of cure, and such as nobody would use or consent to, to cut off so much as an ulcered toe, though tending to a gangrene, till other gentler remedies had proved unsuccessful, though it be a part as low as the earth and far distant from the head. I can see but one objection that can be made to this, and that is, that by the application of gentler remedies such slow methods may make you lose the opportunity of those remedies that, if timely, would be effectual, whereas, in the faint way of proceeding, the malady increases, the faction grows strong, gathers head, and becomes your master. To this I answer, that parties and factions grow slowly and by degrees, have their time of infancy and weakness, as well as full growth and strength, and become not formidable in an instant, but give sufficient time for experimenting other kind of cures, without any danger by the delay. But if the magistrate chance to find the dissenters so numerous as to be in a condition to cope with him, I see not what he can gain by force and severity, when he thereby gives them the fairer pretence to embody and arm, and make them all united the firmer against him. But this, bordering something upon that part of the question which concerns more the interests of the magistrate than his duty, I shall refer to a fitter place [§IV, which follows].

[IV] Hitherto I have only traced out the bounds that God hath set to the power of the magistrate and the obedience of the subject, both which are subject and equally owe obedience to the king of kings, who expects from them the performance of those duties which are incumbent on them in their several stations and conditions; the sum whereof is that:

(1) There are some opinions and actions that are wholly separate from the concernment of the state, and have no direct influence upon men's lives in society, and these are all speculative opinions and religious worship, and these have a clear title to universal toleration, which the magistrate ought not to entrench on.

(2) There are some opinions and actions which are in their natural tendency absolutely destructive to human society, as, that faith may be broken with heretics, that if the magistrate doth not make public reformation in religion the subjects may, that one is bound publicly to teach and propagate any opinion he believes himself,

and such like, and, in actions, all manner of frauds and injustice, etc.; and these the magistrate ought not to tolerate at all.

(3) There is a third sort of opinions and actions which in themselves do not inconvenience or advantage human society, but only as the temper of the state, and posture of affairs, may vary their influence to good or bad; as, that polygamy is lawful or unlawful, that flesh and fish is to be eaten or abstained from at certain seasons, and such other practical opinions; and all actions conversant about matters of indifferency have a right to toleration so far only as they do not interfere with the advantages of the public or serve any way to disturb the government.

And thus far of toleration as it concerns the magistrate's duty. Having showed what he is bound in conscience to do, it will not be amiss to consider a little what he ought to do in prudence.

But because the duties of men are contained in general established rules, but their prudence is regulated by circumstances relating to themselves in particular, it will be necessary, in showing how much toleration is the magistrate's interest, to come to particulars.

To consider therefore the state of England at present, there is but this one question in the whole matter, and that is, whether toleration or imposition be the readiest way to secure the safety and peace, and promote the welfare, of this kingdom?

As to securing the peace, there is but one way, which is that your friends at home be many and vigorous, and your enemies few and contemptible, or at least that the inequality of their number make it very dangerous and difficult for malcontents to molest you.

As to promoting the welfare of the kingdom, which consists in riches and power, to this most immediately conduces the number and industry of your subjects.

What influence toleration hath on all these cannot be well seen without considering the different parties now among us, which may well be comprehended under these two, papists and fanatics.

(1) As to the papists, 'tis certain that several of their dangerous opinions, which are absolutely destructive to all governments but the pope's, ought not to be tolerated in propagating those opinions; and whosoever shall spread or publish any of them the magistrate is bound to suppress so far as may be sufficient to restrain it. And this rule reaches not only the papists, but any other sort of men

amongst us; for such restraint will something hinder the spreading of those doctrines which will always be of ill consequence, and, like serpents, never be prevailed on by kind usage to lay by their venom.

(2) Papists are not to enjoy the benefit of toleration, because, where they have power, they think themselves bound to deny it to others. For it is unreasonable that any should have a free liberty of their religion who do not acknowledge it as a principle of theirs that nobody ought to persecute or molest another because he dissents from him in religion. For, toleration being settled by the magistrate as a foundation whereon to establish the peace and quiet of his people, by tolerating any who enjoy the benefit of this indulgence, which at the same time they condemn as unlawful, he only cherishes those who profess themselves obliged to disturb his government as soon as they shall be able.

(3) It being impossible, either by indulgence or severity, to make papists, whilst papists, friends to your government, being enemies to it both in their principles and interest, and therefore considering them as irreconcilable enemies, of whose fidelity you can never be secured whilst they owe a blind obedience to any infallible pope, who hath the keys of their consciences tied to his girdle, and can, upon occasion, dispense with all their oaths, promises, and the obligations they have to their prince, especially being (in their sense) a heretic, and arm them to the disturbance of the government, [I] think they ought not to enjoy the benefit of toleration, because toleration can never, but restraint may, lessen their number, or at least not increase it, as it does usually all other opinions, which grow and spread by persecution, and recommend themselves to bystanders by the hardships they undergo; men being forward to have compassion for sufferers, and esteem for that religion as pure, and the professors of it as sincere, which can stand the test of persecution. But I think it is far otherwise with Catholics, who are less apt to be pitied than others, because they receive no other usage than what the cruelty of their own principles and practices are known to deserve; most men judging those severities they complain of [to be] just punishments due to them as enemies to the state, rather than persecutions of conscientious men for the religion, which indeed it is not; nor can they be thought to be punished merely for their consciences who own themselves at the same time subjects of a foreign enemy prince. Besides, the principles and doctrines of that religion are less

apt to take inquisitive heads and unstable minds. Men commonly, in their voluntary changes, do pursue liberty and enthusiasm, wherein they are still free and at their own disposal, rather than give themselves up to the authority and imposition of others. This is certain, that toleration cannot make them divide amongst themselves, nor a severe hand over them (as in other dissenting parties) make them cement with the fanatics (whose principles and worship and tempers are so utterly inconsistent), and, by that means increasing the numbers of the united malcontents, make the danger greater. Add to this, that popery, having been brought in upon the ignorant and zealous world by the art and industry of their clergy, and kept up by the same artifice, backed by power and force, it is the most likely of any religion to decay where the secular power handles them severely, or at least takes from them those encouragements and supports they received by their own clergy.

But, if restraint of the papists do not lessen the number of our enemies in bringing any of them over to us, yet it increases the number, and it strengthens the hands of our friends, and knits all the Protestant party firmer to our assistance and defence. For the interest of the king of England, as head of the Protestants, will be much improved by the discountenancing of popery amongst us. The differing parties will sooner unite in a common friendship with us, when they find we really separate from and set ourselves against the common enemy, both to our church and all Protestant professions; and this will be a hostage of our friendship to them, and a security that they shall not be deceived in the confidence they have of us, and the sincerity of the accord we make with them.

All the rest of the dissenters come under the opprobrious name of fanatics; which (by the way) I think might with more prudence be laid aside and forgotten than made use of. For, what understanding man, in a disordered state, would find out and fix notes of distinction, a thing to be coveted only by those that are factious, or, by giving one common name to different parties, teach those to unite whom he is concerned to divide and keep at a distance one among another?

But to come to what is more material. I think it is agreed on all hands that it is necessary the fanatics should be made useful and assisting, and as much as possible firm to the government as it now stands, both to secure it from disturbance at home, and defend it against invasions from abroad, which nothing can possibly bring to pass but what is able to alter their minds and bring them over to our profession, or else, if they do not part with their opinions, yet may persuade them to lay by their animosities, and become friends to the state, though they are not sons of the church.

What efficacy force and severity hath to alter the opinions of mankind – though history be full of examples, and there is scarce an instance to be found of any opinion driven out of the world by persecution, but where the violence of it at once swept away all the professors too – I desire nobody to go further than his own bosom for an experiment whether ever violence gained anything upon his opinion; whether even arguments managed with heat do not lose something of their efficacy, and have not made him the more obstinate in his opinion; so chary is human nature to preserve the liberty of that part wherein lies the dignity of a man, which could it be imposed on, would make him but little different from a beast. I ask those who in the late times so firmly stood the ineffectual force of persecution themselves, and found how little it obtained on their opinions, and yet are now so forward to try it upon others, whether all the severity in the world could have drawn them one step nearer to a hearty and sincere embracing the opinions that were then uppermost. Let them not say it was because they knew they were in the right, for every man in what he believes has so far this persuasion that he is in the right. But how little this obstinacy or constancy depends upon knowledge may appear in those galley slaves who return from Turkey, who, though they have endured all manner of miseries rather than part with their religion, yet one would guess by the lives and principles of most of them that they had no knowledge of the doctrine and practice of Christianity at all. Who thinks not that those poor captives who, for renouncing a religion they were not over-instructed in, nor during the enjoyment of their freedom at home were over-zealous for, might have regained their liberty for changing their opinions, would not (had their chains given them leave) have cut the throats of those cruel patrons who used them so severely, to whom they would yet have done no violence, had they been treated civilly, like fair prisoners of war? Whereby we may see it would be an hazardous attempt, if any should design it, to bring this island to the condition of a galley, where the greater part shall be reduced to the condition of slaves, be forced with blows to row the vessel, but share in none of the lading [cargo], nor have any privilege or protection, unless they will make chains for all those who are to be used like Turks, and persuade them to stand still whilst they put them on. For, let divines preach duty as long as they will, 'twas never known that men lay down quietly under the oppression and submitted their backs to the blows of others, when they thought they had strength enough to defend themselves.

I say not this to justify such proceedings, which in the former part of this discourse I think I have sufficiently condemned; but to show what the nature and practice of mankind is, and what has usually been the consequence of persecution. Besides, the forcible introducing of opinions keeps people off from closing with them, by giving men unavoidable jealousies that it is not truth that is thus carried on, but interest, and dominion that is sought in making proselytes by compulsion. Who takes this course to convince anyone of the certain truths of mathematics? 'Tis likely, it will be said, that those are truths on which depend not my happiness. I grant it, and am much indebted to the man that takes care I should be happy; but 'tis hard to think that that comes from charity to my soul which brings such ill usage to my body, or that he is much concerned I should be happy in another world who is pleased to see me miserable in this. I wonder that those who have such a zealous regard to the good of others do not a little more look after the relief of the poor, or think themselves concerned to guard the estates of the rich, which certainly are good things too, and make a part of one's happiness, if we may believe the lives of those who tell us the joys of heaven, but endeavour as much as others for large possessions on earth.

But, after all this, could persecution not only now and then conquer a tender, faint-hearted fanatic (which yet it rarely does, and that usually by the loss of two or three orthodox); could it, I say, at once drive all dissenters within the pale of the church, it would not thereby secure, but more threaten, the government, and make the danger as much greater as it is to have a false, secret, but exasperated enemy, rather than a fair, open adversary. For punishment and fear may make men dissemble; but, not convincing anybody's reason, cannot possibly make them assent to the opinion, but will certainly make them hate the person of their persecutor and give them the greater aversion to both. Such compliers only prefer impunity to the declaring of their opinion, but do not thereby approve of ours. Fear of the power, not love of the government, is that which restrains them, and if that be the chain that ties them to you, it would certainly hold them surer were they open dissenters than secret malcontents, because it would not only be something easier to be worn, but hard to be knocked off. At least, this is certain, that compelling men to your opinion, any other way than by convincing them of the truth of it, makes them no more your friends than forcing the poor Indians by droves into the rivers to be baptised made them Christians.

Though force cannot master the opinions men have, nor plant new ones in their breasts, yet courtesy, friendship, and soft usage may. For several men whose business or laziness keeps them from examining, take many of their opinions upon trust, even in things of religion, but never take them from any man of whose knowledge, friendship, and sincerity they are not well assured; which it's impossible they should be of one that persecutes them.

But inquisitive men, though they are not of another's mind, because of his kindness, yet they are the more willing to be convinced, and will be apter to search after reasons that may persuade them to be of his opinion whom they are obliged to love.

Since force is a wrong way to bring dissenters off from their persuasions (and by drawing them to your opinion you cement them fast to the state), it will certainly prevail much less with those to be your friends who steadfastly retain their persuasion and continue in an opinion different from you. He that differs in an opinion is only so far at a distance from you; but if you use him ill for that which he believes to be right, he is then at perfect enmity. The one is barely a separation, but the other a quarrel. Nor is that all the mischief which severity will do among us as the state of things is at present, for force and harsh usage will not only increase the animosity but number of enemies. For the fanatics, taken all together, being numerous, and possibly more than the hearty friends to the state religion, are yet crumbled into different parties amongst themselves, and are at as much distance from one another as from you, if you drive them not further off by the ill treatment they receive from you; for their bare opinions are as inconsistent one with another as with the Church of England. People, therefore, that are so shattered into different factions are best secured by toleration; since, being in as good a condition under you as they can hope for under any, 'tis not like[ly] they should join to set up another, whom they cannot be certain will use them so well. But, if you persecute them, you make them all of one party and interest against you, tempt them to shake off your yoke, and venture for a new government, wherein everyone has hopes to get the dominion themselves, or better usage under others; who cannot but see that the same severity of the government which helped them to power and partisans to get up, will give others the same desire and same strength to pull them down; and therefore may it be expected they will be cautious how they exercise it. But, if you think the different parties are already grown to a consistency, and formed into one body and interest against you, whether it were the hardships they suffered under you make them unite or no, when they are so many as to equal or exceed you in number, as, perhaps, they do in England, force will be but an ill and hazardous way to bring them to submission. If uniformity in England be so necessary as many pretend, and compulsion be the way to it, I demand of those who are so zealous for it, whether they really intend by force to have it or no. If they do not, it is not only imprudent, but malicious, under that pretence, by ineffectual punishments to disquiet and torment their brethren. For to show how little persecution, if not in the extremest degree, has been able to establish uniformity, I shall ask but this one plain question: was there ever a free toleration in this kingdom? If there were not, I desire to know of any of the clergy who were once sequestered, how they came to be turned out of their livings, and whether impositions and severity were able to preserve the Church of England, and hinder the growth of puritans, even before the war. If, therefore, violence be to settle uniformity, 'tis in vain to mince the matter. That severity which must produce it cannot stop short of the total destruction and extirpation of all dissenters at once. And how well this will agree with the doctrine of Christianity, the principles our church, and reformation from popery, I leave them to judge who can think the massacre of France[15] worthy their imitation, and desire them to consider, if death (for nothing less can make uniformity) were the penalty of not coming to common

---

[15] The St Bartholomew's Day Massacre of the Huguenots, 1572.

prayer and joining in all our church worship, how much such a law would settle the quiet and secure the government of the kingdom.

The Romish religion, that had been but a little while planted and taken but small root in Japan (for the poor converts had but a little of the efficacious truths and light of Christianity conveyed to them by those teachers who make ignorance the mother of devotion, and knew very little beyond an Ave Maria or Paternoster), could not be extirpated but by the death of many thousands;[16] which, too, prevailed not at all to lessen their numbers, till they extended the severity beyond the delinquents, and made it death, not only to the family that entertained a priest, but also to all of both the families that were next neighbours on either hand, though they were strangers or enemies to the new religion, and invented exquisite, lingering torments, worse than a thousand deaths, which, though some had strength enough to endure fourteen days together, many renounced their religion, whose names were all registered, with a design that, when the professors of Christianity were all destroyed, these too should be butchered all on a day, never thinking the opinion rooted out beyond possibility of spreading again, as long as there were any alive who were the least acquainted with it, or had almost heard anything of Christianity more than the name. Nor are the Christians that trade there to this day suffered to discourse, fold their hands, or use any gesture that may show the difference of their religion. If anyone thinks uniformity in our church ought to be restored, though by such a method as this, he will do well to consider how many subjects the king will have left by that time it is done. There is this one thing more observable in the case, which is, that it was not to set up uniformity in religion (for they tolerate seven or eight sects, and some so different as is the belief of the mortality or immortality of the soul; nor is the magistrate at all curious or inquisitive what sect his subjects are of, or does in the least force them to his religion), nor any aversion to Christianity, which they suffered a good while quietly to grow up among them, till the doctrine of popish priests gave them jealousy that religion was but their pretence, but empire their design, and made them fear the subversion of their state; which suspicion their own priests improved all they could to the extirpation of this growing religion.

[16] The bloody suppression of the Shimabara Revolt, 1638.

But to show the danger of establishing uniformity.

To give a full prospect of this subject there remain yet these following particulars to be handled:

(1) To show what influence toleration is like to have upon the number and industry of your people, on which depends the power and riches of the kingdom.

(2) That if force must compel all to a uniformity in England, to consider what party alone, or what parties, are likeliest to unite to make a force able to compel the rest.

(3) To show that all that speak against toleration seem to suppose that severity and force are the only arts of government and way to suppress any faction, which is a mistake.

(4) That for the most part the matters of controversy and distinction between sects are no parts, or very inconsiderable ones and appendices, of true religion.

(5) To consider how it comes to pass that Christian religion hath made more factions, wars, and disturbances in civil societies than any other, and whether toleration and latitudinism[17] would prevent those evils.

(6) That toleration conduces no otherwise to the settlement of a government than as it makes the majority of one mind, and encourages virtue in all, which is done by making and executing strict laws concerning virtue and vice, but making the terms of church communion as large as may be, i.e., that your articles in speculative opinions be few and large, and ceremonies in worship few and easy, which is latitudinism.

(7) That the defining and undertaking to prove several doctrines which are confessed to be incomprehensible, and to be no otherwise known but by revelation, and requiring men to assent to them in the terms proposed by the doctors of your several churches, must needs make a great many atheists.

But of these when I have more leisure.

---

[17] A recent coinage. The cognate term was given vogue in [Simon Patrick?], *A Brief Account of the New Sect of Latitude-Men* (1662). See Spurr 1988; Marshall 1992.

The Fundamental Constitutions of Carolina

1669. PRO 30/24/47/3. This MS is dated 21 July 1669; the main text is in an unknown hand, but the first two paragraphs and the first sentence of the third, and most of the large number of amendments, are in Locke's hand; some amendments are in a third hand. This version, as amended, is printed here. A later version, embodying further amendments, and known only from printed copies, is dated 1 March 1670. The 1669 version is printed in Sainsbury 1872, pp. 258–69; the 1670 version in Locke 1720; *Works* 1801, X, 175–99; Wootton 1993, pp. 210–32; both versions in Parker 1963, pp. 132–85. There were yet further versions printed in 1682 and 1698. The amendments made in 1669 and 1670 were mainly clarificatory and cosmetic. I have indicated in square brackets the new numeration of articles in the 1670 version. The most important substantive addition in 1670 was an article specifying an Anglican Establishment – which Desmaizeaux said Locke opposed (Locke 1720, p. 42).

The subject matter of the Constitutions is as follows. Articles 1–26: the proprietors, nobility, offices of state, and division of land; 27–54: the courts and grand council; 55–64: the administration of justice; 65–73: parliament; 74–85: registration and town corporations; 86–100: religion; 101–11: miscellaneous. For discussion see Haley 1968, pp. 242–8; Farr 1986; Glausser 1990; McGuinness 1990; Milton 1990; Tully 1994. Cited by Laslett, First Treatise, §144; Second Treatise, §§12, 24, 119.

The extent of Locke's contribution to the authorship is a vexed matter. Several scholars have mistakenly claimed that the 1669 manuscript is wholly in Locke's hand. Others have held that Locke could not have articulated the Constitution's 'antiquated feudalism', but that is not an accurate description of its regime. The Constitution is very unlikely to have originated with Locke: he was acting as secretary to the lords proprietors of Carolina. Some suggest he was no more than a copyist. What probably happened was that Locke was handed a draft and asked to comment and amend. However, for the rest of his life he closely associated himself with Carolina and its Constitutions. He was made a landgrave (nobleman) of Carolina, and Locke Island (today Edisto Island) was named after him. Important evidence is a remark in 1673 by Sir Peter Colleton, one of the lords proprietors: 'that excellent form of government in the composure of which you had so great a hand' (Letter 279). Locke often lent copies to friends. MS Locke, c. 30, fo. 4 refers to the purchase of one hundred copies of the Constitutions (1673). In letters to Nicolas Toinard Locke playfully proposed to flee a wicked Europe for Carolina (Letters 475, 600, 633); Toinard and Henri Justel refer to 'vos constitutions', 'vos lois' (Letters 481, 504, but cf. 490). There are further references to Carolina in Letters 354, 355, 849, 878, 888, 924, 1403, 3483, 3488. See Milton 1990. Locke's interest in constitution making is also evinced in his fragmentary critique of William Penn's 'Frame of Government for Pennsylvania' (1686): Cranston 1957, pp. 261–2. MS Locke, c. 39, fo. 3, is a further scrap on Carolina, which contains a stipulation that voting shall be by ballot and not by voice.

Carolina had begun to be settled in the 1650s; it received a royal charter in 1663. The eight proprietors comprised five peers: Albermarle, Ashley (later earl of Shaftesbury), Berkeley, Clarendon (his son by 1669), and Craven; and three commoners: Sir William Berkeley, Sir George Carteret, and Sir John Colleton (Sir Peter by 1669). The Constitutions never made much impact on the actual government of Carolina.

(1) Our sovereign lord the king having, out of his royal grace and bounty, granted unto us the province of Carolina, with all the royalties, proprieties, jurisdictions, and privileges of a county palatine, as large and ample as the county palatine of Durham, with other great privileges; for the better settlement of the government of the said place, and establishing the interest of the lords proprietors with equality, and without confusion; and that the government of this province may be made most agreeable unto the monarchy under which we live, and of which this province is a part; and that we

may avoid erecting a numerous democracy: we, the true and absolute lords and proprietors of the province aforesaid, have agreed to this following form of government, to be perpetually established amongst us, unto which we do oblige ourselves, our heirs and successors, in the most binding ways that can be devised.

(2) [1] The eldest of the lords proprietors shall be palatine; and upon the decease of the palatine, the eldest of the seven surviving proprietors shall always succeed him.[1]

(3) [2] There shall be seven other chief offices erected, viz., the chief justice's, chancellor's, constable's, high steward's, treasurer's, chamberlain's, admiral's; which places shall be enjoyed by none but the lords proprietors, to be assigned at first by lot; and upon the vacancy of any one of the seven great offices by death, or otherwise, the eldest proprietor shall have his choice of the said place.

(4) [3] Each [i.e. the whole] province shall be divided into counties; each county shall consist of eight seigniories, eight baronies, and four precincts; each precinct shall consist of six colonies.

(5) [4] Each colony, seigniory, and barony shall consist of twelve thousand acres, the eight seigniories being the share of the eight proprietors, and the eight baronies of the nobility; both which shares, being each of them a fifth part of the whole, are to be perpetually annexed, the one to the proprietors, the other to the hereditary nobility, leaving the colonies, being three-fifths, amongst the people; that so, in the setting out and planting the lands, the balance of government may be preserved.

(6) [5] At any time before the year 1701, any of the lords proprietors shall have power to relinquish, alienate, and dispose, to any other person, his proprietorship, and all the seigniories, powers, and interest thereunto belonging, wholly and entirely together, and not otherwise. But after the year 1700, those who are then lords proprietors shall not have power to alienate, make over, or let their proprietorship, with the seigniories and privileges thereunto belonging, or any part thereof, to any person whatsoever, otherwise than as in article 18, but it shall descend unto their heirs male; and for want of heirs male, it shall descend on that landgrave or cacique[2] of

---

[1] Before amendment this article closed with: 'to prevent the making of the office in this little government hereditary and to avoid the mischief of faction in elections'.

[2] The nomenclature for the Carolina nobility is borrowed from Germany (landgrave: a count) and Spanish America (cacique: a chief).

Carolina who is descended of the next heir female of the said proprietor; and for want of such heirs, it shall descend on the next heir general; and for want of such heirs, the remaining seven proprietors shall, upon the vacancy, choose a landgrave to succeed the deceased proprietor, who being chosen by the majority of the seven surviving proprietors, he and his heirs successively shall be proprietors as fully, to all intents and purposes, as any of the rest.

(7) [6] And that the number of eight proprietors may be constantly kept, if, upon the vacancy of any proprietorship, the surviving seven proprietors shall not choose a landgrave as a proprietor before the second biennial parliament after the vacancy, then the next biennial parliament but one after such vacancy shall have power to choose any landgrave to be proprietor; but [7] whosoever after the year 1700, either by inheritance or choice, shall succeed any proprietor in his proprietorship, and seigniories thereunto belonging, shall be obliged to take the name and arms of that proprietor whom he succeeds, which from thenceforth shall be the name and arms of his family and their posterity.

(8) Whatsoever landgrave or cacique shall [in] any way come to be a proprietor shall take the seigniories annexed to the said proprietorship, but his former dignity, with the baronies annexed, shall devolve into the hands of the lords proprietors.

(9) To every county there shall be three as the hereditary nobility of this palatinate, who shall be called the one a landgrave and the other two caciques, and shall have place in the parliament there; the landgrave shall have four baronies, and the two caciques, each of them, two apiece, hereditarily and unalterably annexed to and settled upon the said dignity.

(10) The first landgrave and caciques of every county shall be nominated, not by the joint election of the proprietors all together, but the eight proprietors shall, each of them separately, nominate and choose one landgrave and two caciques to be the eight landgraves and the sixteen caciques for the eight first counties to be planted; and when the said eight counties shall be planted, the proprietors shall, in the same manner, nominate and choose eight more landgraves and sixteen caciques for the eight next counties to be planted; and so proceed, in the same manner, till the whole province of Carolina be set out and planted according to the proportions in these fundamental constitutions.

(11) Any landgrave or cacique, at any time before the year 1701, shall have power to alienate, sell, or make over, to any other person, his dignity, with the baronies thereunto belonging, all entirely together; but after the year 1700, no landgrave or cacique shall have power to alienate, sell, make over, or let the hereditary baronies of his dignity, or any part thereof, otherwise than as in article 18; but they shall all entirely, with the dignity thereunto belonging, descend unto his heirs male; and for want of such heirs male, all entirely and undivided, to the next heir general; and for want of such heirs, shall devolve into the hands of the proprietors.

(12) That the due number of landgraves and caciques may be always kept up, if, upon the devolution of any landgraveship or caciqueship, the palatine's court shall not settle the devolved dignity, with the baronies thereunto annexed, before the second biennial parliament after such devolution, the next biennial parliament but one after such devolution shall have power to make anyone landgrave or cacique in the room of him, who, dying without heirs, his dignity and baronies devolved.

(13) No one person shall have more than one dignity, with the seigniories or baronies thereunto belonging; but whensoever it shall happen that anyone who is already [a] proprietor, landgrave, or cacique shall have any of those dignities descend to him by inheritance, it shall be at his choice to keep which of the two dignities, with the lands annexed, he shall like best, but shall leave the other, with the lands annexed, to be enjoyed by him who, not being his heir apparent, and certain successor to his present dignity, is next of blood, unless when a landgrave or cacique comes to be proprietor, and then his former dignity and baronies shall devolve as in article 8.

(14) Whosoever, by right of inheritance, shall come to be landgrave or cacique shall take the name and arms of his predecessor in that dignity, to be from thenceforth the name and arms of his family and their posterity.

(15) Since the dignity of proprietor, landgrave, or cacique cannot be divided, and the seigniories or baronies thereunto annexed must for ever, all entirely, descend with and accompany that dignity, whenever, for want of heirs male, it shall descend upon the issue female, the eldest daughter and her heirs shall be preferred; and in the inheritance of those dignities, and in the seigniories or baronies annexed, there shall be no coheirs.

(16)[3] After the year 1700, whatsoever landgrave or cacique shall, without leave from the palatine's court, be out of Carolina during two successive biennial parliaments shall, at the end of the second biennial parliament after such his absence, be summoned by proclamation; and if he come not into Carolina before the next biennial parliament after such summons, then the grand council shall have power thenceforward to receive all the rents and profits arising out of his baronies until his return or death, and to dispose of the said profits as they shall think fit.

(17) [16] In every seigniory, barony, and manor, the respective lord shall have power, in his own name, to hold court there, for trying of all causes, both civil and criminal; but where it shall concern any person being no inhabitant, vassal, or leet man[4] of the said barony, seigniory, or manor, he, upon paying down of forty shillings to the lords proprietors' use, shall have an appeal from the seigniory or barony court to the county court, and from the manor court to the precinct court.

(18) The lords of seigniories and baronies shall have power only of granting estates, not exceeding three lives or one and thirty years, in two-thirds of the said seigniories or baronies; and the remaining third shall be always demesne.

(19) [17] Every manor shall consist of not less than three thousand acres and not above twelve thousand acres in one entire piece; but any three thousand acres or more in one piece and the possession of one man shall not be a manor unless it be constituted a manor by the grant of the palatine's court.

(20) [21] Every lord of a manor, within his manor, shall have all the powers, jurisdictions, and privileges which a landgrave or cacique has in his baronies.

(21) [19] Any lord of a manor may alienate, sell, or dispose, to any other person, and his heirs, for ever, his manor, all entirely together, with all the privileges and leet men thereunto belonging, so far forth as any other colony lands; but no grant of any part thereof, either in fee or for any longer term than three lives or twenty-one years, shall be good against the next heir; [20] neither shall a manor, for want of issue male, be divided amongst coheirs;

---

[3] This article omitted in 1670 version.
[4] Leet man: inhabitant within the manor's jurisdiction. Court-leet: a manorial court.

but the manor, if there be but one, shall all entirely descend to the eldest daughter and her heirs; if there be more manors than one in the possession of the deceased, the eldest sister shall have her choice, the second next, and so on, beginning again at the eldest, till all the manors be taken up; that so, the privileges which belong to manors being indivisible, the lands of the manor to which they are annexed may be kept entire, and the manor not lose those privileges, which upon parcelling out to several owners must necessarily cease.

(22) In every seigniory, barony, and manor, all the leet men shall be under the jurisdiction of the respective lord of the said seigniory, barony, or manor, without appeal from him; nor shall any leet man or leet woman have liberty to go off from the land of his particular lord and live anywhere else without licences obtained from his said lord, under hand and seal.

(23) All the children of leet men shall be leet men, and so to all generations.

(24) No man shall be capable of having a court-leet or leet men but a proprietor, landgrave, or cacique, or lord of a manor. Nor shall any man be a leet man who has not voluntarily entered himself a leet man in the registry of the county court.

(25) [26][5] Whoever is lord of leet men shall, upon the marriage of a leet man or leet woman of his, give them ten acres of land for their lives, they paying to him therefore not more than one-eighth of all yearly produce and growth of the said ten acres.

(26) [27] No landgrave or cacique shall be tried for any criminal cause in any but in the chief justice court, and that by a jury of his peers.[6]

(27) [28] There shall be eight supreme courts, the first, called the palatine's court, consisting of the palatine and the other seven proprietors. The other seven courts of the other seven great officers shall consist, each of them, of a proprietor and six councillors added to him; under each of these latter seven courts shall be a college of twelve assistants. The twelve assistants of the several colleges shall be chosen: two out of the landgraves, by the landgraves' chamber; two out of the caciques, by the caciques' chamber; two out of the

---

[5] Additional article 25 in 1670 version: anyone may register himself a leet man.

[6] Before amendment, this article provided that contracts between lords and tenants be adjudicated in the county court.

landgraves, caciques, or eldest sons of the proprietors, by the palatine's court; four more of the twelve shall be chosen by the commons' chamber out of such as have been or are members of parliament, sheriffs, or justices of the county court; the other two shall be chosen by the palatine's court out of the aforesaid members of parliament, or sheriffs, or justices of the county court, or the eldest sons of landgraves or caciques, or younger sons of proprietors.

(28) [29] Out of these colleges shall be chosen six councillors to be joined with each proprietor in his court; of which six, one shall be of those who were chosen into any of the colleges by the palatine's court out of the landgraves, caciques, or eldest sons of proprietors; one out of those who were chosen by the landgrave's chamber; and one out of those who were chosen by the caciques' chamber; two out of those who were chosen by the commons' chamber; and one out of those who were chosen by the palatine's court out of the proprietors' younger sons, or eldest sons of landgraves or caciques, or commons qualified as aforesaid.

(29) [30] When it shall happen that any councillor dies, and thereby there is a vacancy, the grand council shall have power to remove any councillor that is willing to be removed out of any other of the proprietors' courts to fill up this vacancy, provided they take a man of the same degree and choice the other was of whose vacant place is to be filled; but if no councillor consent to be removed, or upon such remove, the last remaining vacant place in any of the proprietors' courts shall be filled up by the choice of the grand council, who shall have power to remove out of any of the colleges any assistant who is of the same degree and choice that councillor was of into whose vacant place he is to succeed; the grand council, also, shall have power to remove any assistant that is willing out of one college into another, provided he be of the same degree and choice; but the last remaining vacant place in any college shall be filled up by the same choice and out of the same degree of persons the assistant was of who is dead or removed. No place shall be vacant in any proprietor's court above six months; no place shall be vacant in any college longer than the next session of parliament.

(30) [31] No man being a member of the grand council or any of the seven colleges shall be turned out but for misdemeanour, of which the grand council shall be judge; and the vacancy of the person so put out shall be filled, not by the election of the grand

council, but by those who first chose him, and out of the same degree he was of who is expelled. But[7] it is not hereby to be understood that the grand council has any power to turn out any one of the lords proprietors, or their deputies, the lords proprietors having in themselves an inherent original right.

(31) [32] All elections in the parliament, in the several chambers of the parliaments, and in the grand council shall be passed by balloting.

(32) [33] The palatine's court shall consist of the palatine and seven proprietors, wherein nothing shall be acted without the presence and consent of the palatine, or his deputy, and three others of the proprietors, or their deputies. This court shall have power to call parliaments, to pardon all offences, to make elections of all officers in the proprietors' dispose, to nominate and appoint port towns; and also, shall have power, by their order to the treasurer, to dispose of all public treasure, excepting money granted by the parliament and by them directed to some particular public use; and also, shall have a negative upon all acts, orders, votes, and judgements of the grand council and the parliament, except only as in articles 7 and 12; and also, shall have a negative upon all acts and orders of the constable's court and admiral's court relating to wars; and shall have all the powers granted to the proprietors by their patent from our sovereign lord the king, except in such things as are limited by these fundamental constitutions.

(33) [34] The palatine himself, when he in person shall be either in the army or in any of the proprietors' courts, shall then have the power of general or of that proprietor in whose court he is then present; and the proprietor in whose court the palatine then presides shall, during his presence there, be but as one of the council.

(34) [35] The chancellor's court, consisting of one of the proprietors and his six councillors, who shall be called vice-chancellors, shall have the custody of the seal of the palatinate, under which all charters, of lands or otherwise, commissions, and grants of the palatine's court shall pass, etc. And it shall not be lawful to put the seal of the palatinate to any writing which is not signed by the palatine, or his deputy, and three other proprietors, or their depu-

---

[7] This sentence occurs among the amendments.

ties. To this court, also, belongs all state matters, dispatches, and treaties, with the neighbour Indians or any other, so far forth as is permitted by our charter from our sovereign lord the king. To this court, also, belongs all invasions of the law of liberty of conscience, and all disturbances of the public peace upon pretence of religion, as also, the licence of printing. The twelve assistants belonging to this court shall be called recorders.

(35) [37][8] The chancellor, or his deputy, shall be always speaker in parliament and president of the grand council, and in his and his deputy's absence, one of his vice-chancellors. [38] The chief justice's court, consisting of one of the proprietors and his six councillors, who shall be called justices of the bench, shall judge all appeals, both in cases civil and criminal, except all such cases as shall be under the jurisdiction and cognisance of any other of the proprietors' courts, which shall be tried in those courts respectively. The government and regulations of the registries of writings and contracts shall belong to the jurisdiction of this court. The twelve assistants of this court shall be called masters.

(36) [39] The high constable's court, consisting of one of the proprietors and his six councillors, who shall be called marshals, shall order and determine of all military affairs by land, and all land forces, arms, ammunition, artillery, garrisons, and forts, etc., and whatever belongs unto war. His twelve assistants shall be called lieutenant generals. [40] In time of actual war, the high constable, whilst he is in the army, shall be general of the army, and the six councillors, or such of them as the palatine's court shall for that time and service appoint, shall be the immediate great officers under him, and the lieutenant generals next to them.

(37) [41] The admiral's court, consisting of one of the proprietors and his six councillors, called consuls, shall have the care and inspection over all ports, moles, and navigable rivers so far as the tide flows; and also, all the public shipping of Carolina, and stores thereunto belonging, and all maritime affairs. This court, also, shall have the power of the court of admiralty, and also, to hear and try by law-merchant all cases in matters of trade between the merchants of Carolina amongst themselves,

---

[8] New article 36 in 1670 version: what passes the palatine's seal is to be registered.

arising without the limits of Carolina; as also, all controversies in merchandising that shall happen between denizens of Carolina and foreigners. The twelve assistants belonging to this court shall be called proconsuls. [42] In time of actual war, the high admiral, whilst he is at sea, shall command in chief, and his six councillors, or such of them as the palatine's court shall for that time and service appoint, shall be the immediate great officers under him, and the proconsuls next to them.

(38) [43] The treasurer's court, consisting of one proprietor and his six councillors, called under-treasurers, shall take care of all matters that concern the public revenue and treasury. The twelve assistants shall be called auditors.

(39) [44] The high steward's court, consisting of a proprietor and his six councillors, who shall be called comptrollers, shall have the care of all foreign and domestic trade, manufactures, public buildings and workhouses, highways, passages by water above the flood of the tide, drains, sewers, and banks against inundations, bridges, posts, carriers, fairs, markets, corruptions or infections of the common air and water, and all things in order to public commerce and health; and also, the setting out and surveying of lands; and also, the setting out and appointing places for towns to be built on in the precincts, and the prescribing and determining the figure and bigness of the said towns according to such models as the said court shall order, contrary or differing from which models it shall not be lawful for anyone to build in any town.

(40) [44 contd] The court shall have power, also, to make any public building or any new highway, or enlarge any old highway, upon any man's land whatsoever; as also, to make cuts, channels, banks, locks, and bridges, for making rivers navigable, for draining of fens, or any other public uses; the damage the owner of such land, on or through which any such public thing shall be made, shall receive thereby shall be valued, and satisfaction made, by such ways as the grand council shall appoint. The twelve assistants belonging to this court shall be called surveyors.

(41) [45] The chamberlain's court, consisting of a proprietor and his six councillors, called vice-chamberlains, shall have the power to convocate the grand council; shall have the care of all ceremonies, precedency, heraldry, reception of public messengers, and pedigrees; the registries of all births, burials, and marriages; legitimation

and all cases concerning matrimony or arising from it; and shall, also, have power to regulate all fashions, habits, badges, games, and sports. The twelve assistants belonging to this court shall be called provosts.

(42) [46] All causes belonging to, or under the jurisdiction of, any of the proprietors' courts shall in them respectively be tried and ultimately determined, without any further appeal.

(43) [47] The proprietors' courts shall have a power to mitigate all fines and suspend all executions, either before or after sentence, in any of the other respective inferior courts.

(44) [48] In all debates, hearings, or trials in any of the proprietors' courts, the twelve assistants belonging to the said court respectively shall have liberty to be present, but shall not interpose unless their opinions be required, nor have any vote at all; but their business shall be, by direction of the respective courts, to prepare such business as shall be committed to them; as also, to bear such offices and dispatch such affairs, either where the court is kept or elsewhere, as the court shall think fit.

(45) [49] In all the proprietors' courts, the proprietor and any three of his councillors shall make a quorum, provided always, that, for the better dispatch of business, it shall be in the power of the palatine's court to direct what sort of causes shall be heard and determined by a quorum of any three.

(46) [50] The grand council shall consist of the palatine, and seven proprietors, and the forty-two councillors of the several proprietors' courts; who shall have power to determine any controversies that may arise between any of the proprietors' court about their respective jurisdictions, or between the members of one and the same court about their manner and methods of proceeding; to make peace and war, leagues, treaties, etc., with any of the neighbour Indians; to issue out their general orders to the constable's and admiral's court for the raising, disposing, or disbanding the forces, by land or by sea; [51] to prepare all matters to be proposed in parliament; nor shall any matter whatsoever be proposed in parliament but what has first passed the grand council, which, after having been read three several days in the parliament, shall be passed or rejected.

(47) [52] The grand council shall always be judges of all causes and appeals that concern the palatine, or any of the proprietors, or any councillor of any proprietors' court in any case which otherwise

should have been tried in that court in which the said councillor is judge himself.

(48) [53] The grand council, by their warrants to the treasurer's court, shall dispose of all the money given by the parliament and by them directed to any particular public use.

(49) [54] The quorum of the grand council shall be thirteen, whereof a proprietor, or his deputy, shall be always one.

(50) [56][9] The palatine, or any of the proprietors, shall have power, under hand and seal, to be registered in the grand council, to make a deputy; who shall have the same power, to all intents and purposes, that he himself who deputes him, except in confirming acts of parliament, as in article 70; all such deputation shall cease and determine of themselves at the end of four years, and at any time shall be revocable at the pleasure of the deputator.

(51) [57] No deputy of any proprietor shall have any power whilst the deputator is in any part of Carolina, except the proprietor whose deputy he is be a minor.

(52) [58] During the minority of any proprietor, his guardian shall have power to constitute and appoint his deputy.

(53) [59] The eldest of the proprietors who shall be personally in Carolina shall of course be the palatine's deputy; and if no proprietor be in Carolina, he shall choose his deputy out of the heirs apparent of any of the proprietors, if any such be there; and if there be no heir apparent of any of the proprietors, above twenty-one years old, in Carolina, then he shall choose for deputy any one of the landgraves of the grand council; and till he have, by deputation, under hand and seal, chosen any one of the forementioned heirs apparent or landgrave to be his deputy, the eldest man of the landgraves, and for want of landgraves, the eldest man of the caciques, who shall be personally in Carolina shall of course be his deputy.

(54) [60] Each proprietor's deputy shall be always one of their own six councillors respectively; and in case any of the proprietors has not, in his absence out of Carolina, a deputy in Carolina, commissioned under his hand and seal, the eldest nobleman of his court shall of course be his deputy.

(55) [61] In every county there shall be a court, consisting of a sheriff and four justices of the county court, for every precinct one.

---

[9] New article 55 in 1670 version: the grand council to meet monthly, or oftener.

The sheriff shall be an inhabitant of this county and have at least five hundred acres of freehold within the said county; and the justices shall be inhabitants and have, each of them, five hundred acres apiece in the precinct for which they serve respectively. These five shall be chosen, commissioned from time to time by the palatine's court.

(56) [62] For any personal causes exceeding the value of two hundred pounds, or in title of lands, or in any criminal cause, either party, upon paying twenty pounds to the proprietors' use, shall have liberty of appeal from the county court unto the respective proprietors' court.

(57) [63] In every precinct there shall be a court, consisting of a steward and four justices of the precinct, being inhabitants and having three hundred acres of freehold within the said precinct; who shall judge all criminal causes, except for treason, murder, and any other offences punished with death, and all criminal causes of the nobility; and all civil causes whatsoever, and in all personal actions not exceeding fifty pounds without appeal; but where the cause shall exceed that value, or concern a title of land, and in all criminal causes, there, either party, upon paying five pounds to the proprietors' use, shall have liberty of appeal unto the county court.

(58) [64] No cause shall be twice tried in any one court, upon any reason or pretence whatsoever.

(59) [65] For treason, murder, and all other offences punishable with death, there shall be a commission, twice a year at least, granted unto one or more members of the grand council or colleges, who shall come as itinerant judges to the several counties, and, with the sheriff and four justices, shall hold assizes, and judge all such causes. But upon paying of fifty pounds to the proprietors' use, there shall be liberty of appeal to the respective proprietors' court.

(60) [66] The grand juries at the several assizes shall, upon their oaths, and, under their hands and seals, deliver in to the itinerant judges a presentment of such grievances, misdemeanours, exigencies, or defects which they shall think necessary for the public good of the country; which presentment shall, by the itinerant judges, at the end of their circuit, be delivered in to the grand council at their next sitting; and whatsoever therein concerns the execution of laws already made, the several proprietors' courts, in the matters

belonging to each of them respectively, shall take cognisance of it, and give such order about it as shall be effectual for the due execution of the laws; but whatever concerns the making of any new laws shall be referred to the several respective courts to which that matter belongs, and by them prepared and brought to the grand council.

(61) [67] For terms, there shall be quarterly such a certain number of days, not exceeding twenty-one at any one time, as the several respective courts shall appoint; the time for the beginning of the term in the precinct court shall be the first Monday in January, April, July, and October; and in the county court, the first Monday of February, May, August, November; and in the proprietors' courts, the first Monday of March, June, September, and December.

(62) [68] In the precinct court, no man shall be a jury man under fifty acres of freehold. In the county court, or at the assizes, no man shall be a jury man under two hundred acres of freehold. No man shall be a grand jury man under three hundred acres of freehold; and in the proprietors' courts, no man shall be a jury man under five hundred acres of freehold.

(63) [69] Every jury shall consist of twelve men; and it shall not be necessary they should all agree, but the verdict shall be according to the consent of the majority.

(64) [70] It shall be a base and vile thing to plead for money or reward; nor shall anyone, except he be a near kinsman, not further off than cousin german to the party concerned, be admitted to plead another man's cause till, before the judge in open court, he has taken an oath that he does not plead for money or reward, nor has nor will receive, nor directly nor indirectly bargained with a party, whose cause he is going to plead, for any money or other reward for pleading his cause.

(65) [71] There shall be a parliament, consisting of the proprietors, or their deputies, the landgraves and caciques, and one freeholder out of every precinct, to be chosen by the freeholders of the said precinct respectively. They shall sit all together in one room, and have every member one vote.

(66) [72] No man shall be chosen a member of parliament who has less than five hundred acres of freehold within the precinct for which he is chosen; nor shall any have a vote in choosing the said

member that has less than fifty acres of freehold within the said precinct.

(67) [73] A new parliament shall be assembled the first Monday of the month of November every second year, and shall meet and sit in the town they last sat in, without any summons, unless by the palatine's court they be summoned to meet at any other place; and if there shall be any occasion of a parliament in these intervals, it shall be in the power of the palatine's court to assemble them on forty days' notice, at such time and place as the said court shall think fit; and the palatine's court shall have power to dissolve the said parliament when they shall think fit.

(68) [74] At the opening of every parliament, the first thing that shall be done shall be the reading of these fundamental constitutions, which the palatine, and proprietors, and the rest of the members then present shall subscribe. Nor shall any person whatsoever sit or vote in the parliament till he has, that sessions, subscribed these fundamental constitutions in a book kept for that purpose by the clerk of the parliament.

(69) [75] In order to the due election of members for this biennial parliament, it shall be lawful for the freeholders of the respective precincts to meet the first Tuesday in September every two years, in the same town or place that they last met in, to choose parliament men, and there choose those members that are to sit the next November following, unless the steward of the precinct shall, by sufficient notice thirty days before, appoint some other place for their meeting in order to the election.

(70) [76] No act or order of parliament shall be of any force unless it be ratified in open parliament, during the same session, by the palatine, or his deputy, and three more of the proprietors, or their deputies; and then not to continue longer in force but until the end of the next biennial parliament, unless in the mean time it be ratified under the hand and seal of the palatine himself and three more of the proprietors themselves, and, by their order, published at the next biennial parliament.

(71) [77] Any proprietor, or his deputy, may enter his protestation against any act of the parliament, before the palatine or his deputy's consent be given as aforesaid, if he shall conceive the said act to be contrary to this establishment or any of these fundamental

constitutions of the government; and in such case, after a full and free debate, the several estates shall retire into four several chambers, the palatine and proprietors into one, the landgraves into another, and the caciques into another, and those chosen by the precincts into a fourth; and if the major part of any of these four estates shall vote that the law is not agreeable to this establishment and these fundamental constitutions of the government, then it shall pass no further, but be as if it had never been proposed. [78] The quorum of the parliament shall be one half of those who are members and capable of sitting in the house that present session of parliament. The quorum of each of the chambers of parliament shall be one half of the members of that chamber.

(72) [79] To avoid multiplicity of laws, which by degrees always change the right foundations of the original government, all acts of parliament whatsoever, in what form soever passed or enacted, shall, at the end of sixty years after their enacting, respectively cease and determine of themselves, and, without any repeal, become null and void, as if no such acts or laws had ever been made.

(73) [80] Since multiplicity of comments, as well as of laws, have great inconveniences, and serve only to obscure and perplex, all manner of comments and expositions on any part of these fundamental constitutions, or on any part of the common or statute law of Carolina, are absolutely prohibited.

(74) [81] There shall be a registry in every precinct, wherein shall be enrolled all deeds, judgements, mortgages, or other conveyances which may concern any of the land within the said precinct; and all such conveyances not so entered or registered shall not be of force against any person not privy to the said contract or conveyance.

(75) [82] No man shall be register [registrar] of any precinct who has not at least three hundred acres of freehold within the said precinct.

(76) [83] The freeholders of every precinct shall nominate three men, out of which three the chief justice court shall choose and commission one to be register of the said precinct, whilst he shall well behave himself.

(77) [84] There shall be a registry in every seigniory, barony, and colony, wherein shall be recorded all the births, marriages, and deaths that shall happen within the said colony.

(78) [85] No man shall be register of a colony that has not above fifty acres of freehold within the said colony.

(79) [86] The time of everyone's age that is born in Carolina shall be reckoned from the day that his birth is entered in the registry, and not before.

(80) [87] No marriage shall be lawful, whatever contract or ceremonies they have used, till both the parties mutually own it before the register where they were married, and he enter it, with the names of the father and mother of each party.

(81) [88] No man shall administer to the goods, or have right to them, or enter upon the estate, of any person deceased till his death be registered in the respective registry.

(82) [89] He that does not enter in the respective registry the death or birth of any person that dies or is born in his house or ground shall pay to the said register one shilling per week for each such neglect, reckoning from the time of each death or birth respectively to the time of registering it.

(83) [90] In like manner, the births, marriages, and deaths of the lords proprietors, landgraves, and caciques shall be registered in the chamberlain's court.

(84) [91] There shall be in every colony one constable, to be chosen annually by the freeholders of the colony, his estate to be above one hundred acres of freehold within the said colony; and such subordinate officers appointed for his assistance as the county court shall find requisite, and shall be established by the said county court; the election of the subordinate annual officers shall be also in the freeholders of the colony.

(85) [92] All towns incorporate shall be governed by a mayor, twelve aldermen, and twenty-four of the common council; the said common council to be chosen by the present householders of the said town; and the aldermen to be chosen out of the common council, and the mayor out of the aldermen, by the palatine's court.

(86) [95][10] No man shall be permitted to be a freeman of Carolina, or to have any estate or habitation within it, that does not acknowledge a God, and that God is publicly and solemnly to be worshipped.

---

[10] New articles 93 and 94 in the 1670 version concern port towns.

(87) [97]¹¹ But since the natives of that place, who will be concerned in our plantations, are utterly strangers to Christianity, whose idolatry, ignorance, or mistake gives us no right to expel or use them ill; and those who remove from other parts to plant there will unavoidably be of different opinions concerning matters of religion, the liberty whereof they will expect to have allowed them, and it will not be reasonable for us, on this account, to keep them out; that civil peace may be maintained amidst the diversity of opinions, and our agreement and compact with all men may be duly and faithfully observed, the violation whereof, upon what pretence soever, cannot be without great offence to Almighty God, and great scandal to the true religion that we profess; and also, that heathens, Jews, and other dissenters from the purity of Christian religion may not be scared and kept at a distance from it, but, by having an opportunity of acquainting themselves with the truth and reasonableness of its doctrines, and the peaceableness and inoffensiveness of its professors, may, by good usage and persuasion, and all those convincing methods of gentleness and meekness suitable to the rules and design of the Gospel, be won over to embrace and unfeignedly receive the truth: therefore, any seven or more persons agreeing in any religion shall constitute a church or profession, to which they shall give some name to distinguish it from others.

(88) [98] The terms of admittance and communion with any church or profession shall be written in a book and therein be subscribed by all the members of the said church or profession.

(89) [99] The time of everyone's subscription and admittance shall be dated in the same book, or record.

(90) [100] In the terms of communion of every church or profession, these following shall be three, without which no agreement or assembly of men upon pretence of religion shall be accounted a church or profession within these rules: (i) that there is a God; (ii) that God is publicly to be worshipped; (iii) that it is lawful, and the duty of every man, being thereunto called by those that govern, to

---

¹¹ New article 96 in 1670 version: 'As the country comes to be sufficiently planted and distributed into fit divisions, it shall belong to the parliament to take care for the building of churches and the public maintenance of divines, to be employed in the exercise of religion according to the Church of England, which, being the only true and orthodox, and the national religion of all the king's dominions, is so also of Carolina, and therefore, it alone shall be allowed to receive public maintenance by grant of parliament.'

bear witness to truth; and that every church or profession shall, in their terms of communion, set down the external way whereby they witness a truth as in the presence of God, whether it be by laying hands on and kissing the Bible, as in the Protestant and Papist churches, or by holding up the hand, or any other sensible way.

(91) [101] No person above seventeen years of age shall have any benefit or protection of the law, or be capable of any place of profit or honour, who is not a member of some church or profession, having his name recorded in some one, and but one religion record at once.

(92) [added to 98] The religious record of every church or profession shall be kept by the public register of the precinct where they reside.

(93) [102] No man[12] of any other church or profession shall disturb or molest any religious assembly.

(94) [103] No person whatsoever shall speak anything in their religious assembly irreverently or seditiously of the government or governors or state matters.

(95) [104] Any person subscribing the terms of communion of any church or profession in the record of the said church before the precinct register and any five members of the church or profession shall be thereby made a member of the said church or profession.

(96) [105] Any person striking out his own name out of any religious record, or his name being struck out by any officer thereunto authorised by each church of profession respectively, shall cease to be a member of that church or profession.

(97) [106] No person shall use any reproachful, reviling, or abusive language against the religion of any church or profession, that being the certain way of disturbing the public peace, and of hindering the conversion of any to the truth, by engaging them in quarrels and animosities, to the hatred of the professors and that profession, which otherwise they might be brought to assent to.

(98) [107] Since charity obliges us to wish well to the souls of all men, and religion ought to alter nothing in any man's civil estate or right, it shall be lawful for slaves, as all others, to enter themselves and be of what church any of them shall think best, and thereof be as fully members as any freemen. But yet, no slave shall

---

[12] Changed to 'person' in 1670 version.

hereby be exempted from that civil dominion his master has over him, but be in all other things in the same state and condition he was in before.

(99) [108] Assemblies, upon what pretence soever of religion, not observing and performing the abovesaid rules shall not be esteemed as churches, but unlawful assemblies, and be punished as other riots.

(100) [109] No person whatsoever shall disturb, molest, or persecute another for his speculative opinions in religion or his way of worship.

(101) [110] Every freeman of Carolina shall have absolute power and authority over his negro slaves, of what opinion or religion soever.

(102) [112][13] No person whatsoever shall hold or claim any land in Carolina by purchase or gift or otherwise, from the natives or any other person whatsoever, but merely from and under the lords proprietors, upon pain of forfeiture of all his estate, moveable or unmoveable, and perpetual banishment.

(103) [113] Whoever shall possess any freehold in Carolina, upon what title or grant soever, shall, at the furthest, from and after the year 1689, pay yearly unto the proprietors for each acre of land, English measure, as much fine silver as is at this present in one English penny, or the value thereof, to be as a chief rent and acknowledgement to the proprietors, their heirs and successors, for ever; and it shall be lawful for the proprietors, by their officers, at any time, to take a new survey of any man's land, not to out him of any part of his possession, but that, by such a survey, the just number of acres he possesses may be known, and the rent thereupon due may be paid by him.

(104) [114] All wrecks, mines, minerals, quarries of gems and precious stones, with whale fishing, pearl fishing, and one half of all ambergris, by whomsoever found, shall wholly belong to the proprietors.

(105) [115] All revenues and profits arising out of anything but their distinct particular lands and possessions shall be divided into ten parts, whereof the palatine shall have three, and each proprietor

---

[13] New article 111 in 1670 version: no freeman's cause to be tried without a jury of his peers.

one; but if the palatine shall govern by a deputy, his deputy shall have one of those three tenths, and the palatine the other two tenths.

(106) [116] All inhabitants and freemen of Carolina above seventeen years of age and under sixty shall be bound to bear arms and serve as soldiers whenever the grand council shall find it necessary.

(108)[14] [117] A true copy of these fundamental constitutions shall be kept in a great book by the register of every precinct, to be subscribed before the said register. Nor shall any person, of what condition or degree soever, above seventeen years old, have any estate or possession in Carolina, or protection or benefit of the law there, who has not subscribed these fundamental constitutions in this form: 'I, A.B. [name], do promise to bear faith and true allegiance to our sovereign lord King Charles the Second; and will be true and faithful to the palatine and lords proprietors of Carolina; and, with my utmost power, will defend them and maintain the government, according to this establishment in these fundamental constitutions.'

(109) [118] Whatsoever alien shall, in this form, before any precinct register, subscribe these fundamental constitutions shall be thereby naturalised.

(110) [119] In the same manner shall every person at his admittance into any office subscribe these fundamental constitutions.

(111) [120] These fundamental constitutions in number 111, and every part thereof, shall be, and remain as, the sacred unalterable form and rule of government of Carolina for ever. Witness our hands and seals, this twenty-first day [of] July, in the year of our Lord 1669.

---

[14] There is no article 107 in the 1669 version.

An Essay on the Poor Law

September–October 1697. 'Draft of a Representation, Containing [a] Scheme of Methods for the Employment of the Poor'. PRO, co/388/5/86–95, fos. 232–49. Printed in *An Account of the Origin, Proceedings, and Intentions of the Society for the Promotion of Industry* (Louth, Lincolnshire, 1789), pp. 101–49 (from which the text below is taken); Fox Bourne 1876, II, 377–90. There is a draft of part of the text in MS Locke, c. 30, fos. 87–8, 94–5, 111, which includes significant differences, some of which are recorded below. The essay is discussed in Mason 1962; Hundert 1972; Sheasgreen 1986; Beier 1988. It is sometimes referred to as an essay on working schools.

The memorandum was written by Locke in his capacity as a Commissioner on the Board of Trade: in Letter 2398 he refers to it as 'my project about the better relief and employment of the poor'. He continues, 'It is a matter that requires every Englishman's best thoughts; for there is not any one thing that I know upon the right regulation whereof the prosperity of his country more depends.' It was presented to the Board in October 1697, and in due course rejected. A minor enactment ensued: 8 and 9 W. III, c. 30. See also Letter 2084.

Locke's plan was to reinvigorate and amend the Elizabethan Poor Law (39 Eliz., c. 4; 43 Eliz., c. 2), under which each parish was obliged to provide work for able-bodied men and subsistence for the poor, and could levy a poor rate. He proposed to replace the authority of individual parishes by that of groups of parishes ('hundreds' in the countryside and corporations of the poor in the towns). These bodies would punish vagrants and set up 'working schools' – wool spinning factories. Fifteen cities secured Acts of

Parliament to establish corporations of the poor between 1696 and 1715; they were, in part, Whig devices for circumventing Tory parish control. In London the leading lights were Sir Robert Clayton and Locke's friend Thomas Firmin. See Macfarlane 1982. Similar schemes to Locke's were mooted in Firmin's *Some Proposals for the Employing of the Poor* (1678), Sir Matthew Hale's *Discourse Touching Provision for the Poor* (1683), and John Bellers's *Proposals for Raising a Colledge of Industry* (1695) (see Clarke 1987). Locke refers to Firmin in his draft (c. 30, fo. 87).

I have added numeration to mark the clauses of Locke's proposals. Clauses 1–8 concern the punishment of vagabonds; 9–10 the provision of work, 11–16 the provision of working schools for children; 17–22 the schools' manufactures and their oversight; 23–6 the powers of guardians of the poor; 27–37 the establishment of corporations of the poor in cities and towns; 38–40 are miscellaneous.

Locke refers to several traditional aspects of local government. The least familiar are the 'hundred': a group of parishes, a subdivision of a county; the 'vestry', a parish committee; the 'quarter-sessions': a court held quarterly by justices of the peace; the 'tithingman', a chief officer or constable of a tithing, a district containing a few households (nominally ten). In Locke's time one pound (£) was made up of twenty shillings (s), and a shilling of twelve pence (d).

May it please your excellencies –

His majesty having been pleased, by his commission, to require us particularly to consider of some proper methods for setting on work and employing the poor of this kingdom, and making them useful to the public, and thereby easing others of that burden, and by what ways and means such design may be made most effectual, we humbly beg leave to lay before your excellencies a scheme of such methods as seem unto us most proper for the attainment of those ends.

The multiplying of the poor, and the increase of the tax for their maintenance, is so general an observation and complaint that it cannot be doubted of. Nor has it been only since the last war[1] that this evil has come upon us. It has been a growing burden on the kingdom these many years, and the two last reigns felt the increase of it, as well as the present.

[1] War against France was waged from 1689 to 1697.

If the cause of this evil be well looked into, we humbly conceive it will be found to have proceeded neither from scarcity of provisions, nor from want of employment for the poor, since the goodness of God has blessed these times with plenty, no less than the former, and a long peace during those reigns gave us as plentiful a trade as ever. The growth of the poor must therefore have some other cause, and it can be nothing else but the relaxation of discipline and corruption of manners; virtue and industry being as constant companions on the one side as vice and idleness are on the other.

The first step, therefore, towards the setting of the poor on work, we humbly conceive, ought to be a restraint of their debauchery by a strict execution of the laws provided against it, more particularly by the suppressing of superfluous brandy shops and unnecessary alehouses, especially in country parishes not lying upon great roads.

Could all the able hands in England be brought to work, the greatest part of the burden that lies upon the industrious for maintaining the poor would immediately cease. For, upon a very moderate computation, it may be concluded that above one half of those who receive relief from the parishes are able to get their livelihood. And all of those who receive such relief from the parishes, we conceive, may be divided into these three sorts.

First, those who can do nothing at all towards their own support.

Secondly, those who, though they cannot maintain themselves wholly, yet are able to do something towards it.

Thirdly, those who are able to maintain themselves by their own labour. And these last may be again subdivided into two sorts: viz., either those who have numerous families of children whom they cannot, or pretend they cannot, support by their labour, or those who pretend they cannot get work, and so live only by begging, or worse.

For[2] the suppression of this last sort of begging drones, who live unnecessarily upon other people's labour, there are already good

---

[2] Locke's draft begins here: 'The poor that cannot work, these must be maintained. The poor that can work but will not, these are only wandering beggars which therefore instead of being relieved should be carefully punished. The laws against these I think are such as would suppress that sort of drones. But laws without execution being but waste paper, and the officers being fallen into a general neglect of their duty, it would be convenient that a proclamation . . .'

and wholesome laws, sufficient for the purpose, if duly executed. We therefore humbly propose that the execution thereof may be at present revived by proclamation, till other remedies can be provided; as also that order be taken every year, at the choosing of churchwardens and overseers of the poor, that the statutes of the 39th Eliz. Cap. IV and the 43rd Eliz. Cap. II be read and considered, paragraph by paragraph, and the observation of them, in all their parts, pressed on those who are to be overseers; for we have reason to think that the greatest part of the overseers of the poor, everywhere, are wholly ignorant, and never so much as think that it is the greatest part, or so much as any part, of their duty to set people to work.

But for the more effectual restraining of idle vagabonds, we further humbly propose that a new law may be obtained, by which it be enacted:

[1] That all men sound of limb and mind, above 14 and under 50 years of age, begging in maritime counties out of their own parish without a pass, shall be seized on, either by any officer of the parish where they so beg (which officers, by virtue of their offices, shall be authorised, and under a penalty required to do it), or by the inhabitants of the house themselves where they beg; and be by them, or any of them, brought before the next justice of the peace or guardian of the poor (to be chosen as hereafter mentioned [§23]), who in this case shall have the power of a justice of the peace, and, by such justice of the peace or guardian of the poor (after the due and usual correction in the case), be by a pass sent, not to the house of correction (since those houses are now in most counties complained of to be rather places of ease and preferment to the masters thereof than of correction and reformation to those who are sent thither), nor to their places of habitation (since such idle vagabonds usually name some very remote part, whereby the country is put to great charge; and they usually make their escape from the negligent officers before they come thither and so are at liberty for a new ramble). But, if it be in a maritime county, as aforesaid, that they be sent to the next seaport town, there to be kept at hard labour,[3] till some of his majesty's ships, coming in or near there,

---

[3] Locke's draft makes clear that hard labour means 'lump breaking', the breaking of stones for road building.

give an opportunity of putting them on board, where they shall serve three years under strict discipline, at soldier's pay (subsistence money being deducted for their victuals on board),[4] and be punished as deserters if they go on shore without leave, or, when sent on shore, if they either go further or stay longer than they have leave.

[2] That all men begging in maritime counties without passes, that are maimed, or above 50 years of age, and all of any age so begging without passes in inland counties nowhere bordering on the sea, shall be sent to the next house of correction, there to be kept at hard labour for three years.

[3] And, to the end that the true use of the houses of correction may not be prevented, as of late it has for the most part been, that the master of each such house shall be obliged to allow unto everyone committed to his charge 4d per diem for their maintenance in and about London. But, in remoter counties, where wages and provisions are much cheaper, there the rate to be settled by the grand jury and judge at the assizes; for which the said master shall have no other consideration nor allowance but what their labour shall produce; whom, therefore, he shall have power to employ according to his discretion, consideration being had of their age and strength.

[4] That the justices of the peace shall, each quarter-sessions, make a narrow inquiry into the state and management of the houses of correction within their district, and take a strict account of the carriage of all who are there, and, if they find that anyone is stubborn, and not at all mended by the discipline of the place, that they order him a longer stay there and severer discipline, that so nobody may be dismissed till he has given manifest proof of amendment, the end for which he was sent thither.

[5] That whoever shall counterfeit a pass shall lose his ears for the forgery the first time that he is found guilty thereof, and the second time, that he shall be transported to the plantations, as in the case of felony.

[6] That whatever female above 14 years old shall be found begging out of her own parish without a pass (if she be an inhabitant

---

[4] Locke's draft proposes three-quarters pay, one-third deducted for subsistence, payable at the end of three years.

of a parish within five miles distance of that she is found begging in) shall be conducted home to her parish by the constable, tithingman, overseer of the poor, churchwarden, or other sworn officer of the parish wherein she was found begging, who, by his place and office, shall be required to do it, and to deliver her to the overseer of the poor of the parish to which she belongs, from whom he shall receive 12d for his pains; which 12d, if she be one that receives public relief, shall be deducted out of her parish allowance; or, if she be not relieved by the parish, shall be levied on her, or her parents' or her master's goods.

[7] That, whenever any such female above 14 years old, within the same distance, commits the same fault a second time, and whenever the same or any such other female is found begging without a lawful pass, the first time, at a greater distance than five miles from the place of her abode, it shall be lawful for any justice of the peace or guardian of the poor, upon complaint made, to send her to the house of correction, there to be employed in hard work three months, and so much longer as shall be to the next quarter-sessions after the determination of the said three months, and that then, after due correction, she have a pass made her by the sessions to carry her home to the place of her abode.

[8] That, if any boy or girl, under 14 years of age, shall be found begging out of the parish where they dwell (if within five miles distance of the said parish), they shall be sent to the next working school, there to be soundly whipped, and kept at work till evening, so that they may be dismissed time enough to get to their place of abode that night. Or, if they live further than five miles off from the place where they are taken begging, that they be sent to the next house of correction, there to remain at work six weeks, and so much longer as till the next sessions after the end of the said six weeks.

These idle vagabonds being thus suppressed, there will not, we suppose, in most country parishes, be many men who will have the pretence that they want work. However, in order to the taking away of that pretence, whenever it happens, we humbly propose that it may be further enacted:

[9] That the guardian of the poor of the parish where any such pretence is made, shall, the next Sunday after complaint made to him, acquaint the parish that such a person complains he wants

work, and shall then ask whether anyone is willing to employ him at a lower rate than is usually given, which rate it shall then be in the power of the said guardian to set; for it is not to be supposed that anyone should be refused to be employed by his neighbours, whilst others are set to work, but for some defect in his ability or honesty, for which it is reasonable he should suffer; and he that cannot be set on work for 12d per diem, must be content with 9d or 10d rather than live idly. But, if nobody in the parish voluntarily accepts such a person at the rate proposed by the guardians of the poor, that then it shall be in the power of the said guardian, with the rest of the parish, to make a list of days, according to the proportion of everyone's tax in the parish to the poor, and that, according to such list, every inhabitant in the same parish shall be obliged, in their turn, to set such unemployed poor men of the same parish on work, at such under-rates as the guardians of the poor shall appoint; and, if any person refuse to set the poor at work in his turn as thus directed, that such person shall be bound to pay them their appointed wages, whether he employ them or no.

[10] That, if any poor man, otherwise unemployed, refuse to work according to such order (if it be in a maritime county), he shall be sent to the next port, and there put on board some of his majesty's ships, to serve there three years as before proposed; and that what pay shall accrue to him for his service there, above his diet and clothes, be paid to the overseers of the poor of the parish to which he belongs, for the maintenance of his wife and children, if he have any, or else towards the relief of other poor of the same parish; but, if it be not in a maritime county, that every poor man, thus refusing to work, shall be sent to the house of correction.

These methods we humbly propose as proper to be enacted, in order to the employing of the poor who are able, but will not work; which sort, by the punctual execution of such a law, we humbly conceive, may be quickly reduced to a very small number, or quite extirpated.

But the greatest part of the poor maintained by parish rates are not absolutely unable, nor wholly unwilling, to do anything towards the getting of their livelihoods; yet even those, either through want of fit work provided for them, or their unskilfulness in working in what might be a public advantage, do little that turns to any account, but live idly upon the parish allowance, or begging, if not worse. Their labour, therefore, as far as they are able to work, should be saved to the public, and what their earnings come short of a full maintenance should be supplied out of the labour of others, that is, out of the parish allowance.

These are of two sorts:

(i) Grown people, who, being decayed from their full strength, could yet do something for their living, though, under pretence that they cannot get work, they generally do nothing. In the same case with these are most of the wives of day labourers, when they come to have two or three or more children. The looking after their children gives them not liberty to go abroad to seek for work, and so, having no work at home, in the broken intervals of their time they earn nothing; but the aid of the parish is fain to come in to their support, and their labour is wholly lost; which is much loss to the public.[5]

Everyone must have meat, drink, clothing, and firing. So much goes out of the stock of the kingdom, whether they work or no. Supposing, then, there be 100,000 poor in England, that live upon the parish, that is, who are maintained by other people's labour (for so is everyone who lives upon alms without working), if care were taken that every one of those, by some labour in the woollen or other manufacture, should earn but 1d per diem (which, one with another, they might well do, and more), this would gain to England £130,000 per annum,[6] which, in eight years, would make England above a million of pounds richer.

This, rightly considered, shows us what is the true and proper relief of the poor. It consists in finding work for them, and taking care they do not live like drones upon the labour of others. And, in order to this end, we find the laws made for the relief of the poor were intended; however, by an ignorance of their intention or a neglect of their due execution, they are turned only to the mainten-

---

[5] The draft adds: 'Now no part of any poor body's labour that can work should be lost. Things should be so ordered that everyone should work as much as they can, and what that comes short of maintaining them that the parish should make up.'

[6] The draft adds: ''Tis therefore worth everybody's care that the poor should have employment, for I may confidently say that of those who are now maintained by parish rates and begging there is not one of ten, I might I think make the number a great deal less, who could not well earn above 2d a day. Nay, take them all together one with another they might earn 3d a day, which would be above £400,000 a year got to England.'

ance of people in idleness, without at all examining into the lives, abilities, or industry, of those who seek for relief.

In order to the suppression of these idle beggars, the corporations in England have beadles authorised and paid to prevent the breach of the law in that particular; yet, nevertheless, the streets everywhere swarm with beggars, to the increase of idleness, poverty, and villainy, and to the shame of Christianity. And, if it should be asked in any town in England, how many of these visible trespassers have been taken up and brought to punishment by those officers this last year, we have reason to think the number would be found to have been very small, because that [number] of beggars swarming in the street is manifestly very great.

But the remedy of this disorder is so well provided by the laws now in force that we can impute the continuance and increase of it to nothing but a general neglect of their execution.

(ii) Besides the grown people above mentioned, the children of labouring people are an ordinary burden to the parish, and are usually maintained in idleness, so that their labour also is generally lost to the public till they are 12 or 14 years old.

[11] The most effectual remedy for this that we are able to conceive, and which we therefore humbly propose, is that in the forementioned new law to be enacted, it be further provided that working schools be set up in each parish, to which the children of all such as demand relief of the parish, above 3 and under 14 years of age, whilst they live at home with their parents, and are not otherwise employed for their livelihood by the allowance of the overseers of the poor, shall be obliged to come.

By this means the mother will be eased of a great part of her trouble in looking after and providing for them at home, and so be at more liberty to work; the children will be kept in much better order, be better provided for, and from infancy be inured to work, which is of no small consequence to the making of them sober and industrious all their lives after; and the parish will be either eased of this burden, or at least of the misuse in the present management of it. For, a great number of children giving a poor man a title to an allowance from the parish, this allowance is given once a week, or once a month, to the father in money, which he not seldom spends on himself at the alehouse, whilst his children, for whose sake he had it, are left to suffer or perish under the want of necessaries, unless the charity of neighbours relieve them.

We humbly conceive that a man and his wife, in health, may be able by their ordinary labour to maintain themselves and two children. More than two children at one time, under the age of 3 years, will seldom happen in one family. If, therefore, all the children above 3 years old be taken off their hands, those who have never so many, whilst they remain themselves in health, will not need any allowance for them.

We do not suppose that children of 3 years old will be able at that age to get their livelihoods at the working school, but we are sure that what is necessary for their relief will more effectually have that use, if it be distributed to them in bread at that school than if it be given to their fathers in money. What they have at home from their parents is seldom more than bread and water, and that, many of them, very scantily too. If, therefore, care be taken that they have each of them their bellyfull of bread daily at school, they will be in no danger of famishing, but, on the contrary, they will be healthier and stronger than those who are bred otherwise. Nor will this practice cost the overseers any trouble; for a baker may be agreed with to furnish and bring into the schoolhouse every day the allowance of bread necessary for all the scholars that are there. And to this may be added, without any trouble, in cold weather, if it be thought needful, a little warm water-gruel; for the same fire that warms the room may be made use of to boil a pot of it.

From this method the children will not only reap the forementioned advantages with far less charge to the parish than what is now done for them, but they will be also thereby the more obliged to come to school and apply themselves to work, because otherwise they will have no victuals, and also the benefit thereby both to themselves and the parish will daily increase; for, the earnings of their labour at school every day increasing, it may reasonably be concluded that, computing all the earnings of a child from 3 to 14 years of age, the nourishment and teaching of such a child during that whole time will cost the parish nothing; whereas there is no child now which from its birth is maintained by the parish, but, before the age of 14, costs the parish £50 or £60.

Another advantage also of bringing poor children thus to a working school is that by this means they may be obliged to come constantly to church every Sunday, along with their schoolmasters or dames, whereby they may be brought into some sense of religion; whereas ordinarily now, in their idle and loose way of breeding up, they are as utter strangers both to religion and morality as they are to industry.[7]

[12] In order, therefore, to the more effectual carrying on of this work to the advantage of this kingdom, we further humbly propose that these schools be generally for spinning or knitting, or some other part of the woollen manufacture, unless in countries [districts] where the place shall furnish some other materials fitter for the employment of such poor children; in which places the choice of those materials for their employment may be left to the prudence and direction of the guardians of the poor of that hundred; and that the teachers in these schools be paid out of the poor's rate, as can be agreed.[8]

This, though at first setting up it may cost the parish a little, yet we humbly conceive that (the earnings of the children abating the charge of their maintenance, and as much work being required of each of them as they are reasonably able to perform) it will quickly pay its own charges, with an overplus.

[13] That, where the number of poor children of any parish is greater than for them all to be employed in one school they be there divided into two, and the boys and girls, if thought convenient, taught and kept to work separately.

[14] That the handicraftsmen in each hundred be bound to take every other of their respective apprentices from amongst the boys in some one of the schools in the said hundred, without any money; which boys they may so take at what age they please, to be bound to them till the age of 23 years, that so the length of time may more than make amends for the usual sums that are given to handicraftsmen with such apprentices.

[15] That those also in the hundred who keep in their hands land of their own to the value of £25 per annum or upwards, or who rent £50 per annum or upwards, may choose out of the schools of

---

[7] The draft has: 'utter strangers to industry, morality and religion'.

[8] The draft has: 'All children at 5 years old or sooner of parents that receive alms or pay no taxes to be sent to the spinning school there to learn to spin (on the double-handed wheel if practicable) woollen or worsted, and to be continued there from sun rising to sunset only allowing them an hour for dinner, till they are 14, the boys to go prentices, and the girls to service, and no longer.'

the said hundred what boy each of them pleases, to be his apprentice in husbandry upon the same condition.

[16] That whatever boys are not by this means bound out apprentices before they are full 14 shall, at the Easter meeting of the guardians of each hundred every year, be bound to such gentlemen, yeomen, or farmers within the said hundred as have the greatest number of acres of land in their hands, who shall be obliged to take them for their apprentices till the age of 23, or bind them out at their own cost to some handicraftsmen; provided always that no such gentleman, yeoman, or farmer shall be bound to have two such apprentices at a time.

[17] That grown people also (to take away their pretence of want of work) may come to the said working schools to learn, where work shall accordingly be provided for them.

[18] That the materials to be employed in these schools, and among other the poor people of the parish, be provided by a common stock in each hundred, to be raised out of a certain portion of the poor's rate of each parish as requisite; which stock, we humbly conceive, need be raised but once; for, if rightly managed, it will increase.

[19] That some person, experienced and well skilled in the particular manufacture which shall be judged fittest to set the poor of each hundred on work, be appointed storekeeper for that hundred, who shall, accordingly, buy in the wool or other materials necessary; that this storekeeper be chosen by the guardians of the poor of each hundred, and be under their direction, and have such salary as they shall appoint to be paid pro rata upon the pound, out of the poor's tax of every parish; and, over and above which salary, that he also have 2s in the pound yearly for every 20s that shall be lessened in the poor's tax of any parish, from the first year of his management.

[20] That to this storekeeper one of the overseers of the poor of every parish shall repair, as often as there shall be occasion, to fetch from him the materials for the employment of the poor of each parish; which materials the said overseer shall distribute to the teachers of the children of each school, and also to other poor who demand relief of the said parish, to be wrought by them at home in such quantity as he or the guardian of the parish shall judge reasonable for each of them respectively to dispatch in one week, allowing unto each such poor person, for his or her work, what he and the

storekeeper shall agree it to be worth; but, if the said overseer and storekeeper do not agree about the price of any such work, that then any three or more of the guardians of that hundred (whereof the guardian of the same parish in which the contest arises is to be always one) do determine it.

[21] That the sale of the materials thus manufactured be made by the storekeeper in the presence of one or more of the guardians of each hundred, and not otherwise, and that an exact account be kept by the said storekeeper of all that he buys in and sells out, as also of the several quantities of unwrought materials that he delivers to the respective overseers, and of the manufactured returns that he receives back again from them.

[22] That, if any person to whom wool, or any other materials are delivered to be wrought, shall spoil or embezzle the same, if it be one who receives alms from the parish, the overseers of the poor of that parish shall pay into the storekeeper what it cost, and deduct the sum out of the parish allowance to the person who has so spoiled or embezzled any such materials, or, if it be one that receives no allowance from the parish, then the said overseers shall demand it in money of the person that spoiled or embezzled it, and if the person so offending refuse to pay it, the guardian of the poor of that parish, upon oath made to him by any of the said overseers that he delivered such materials to such person, and that he paid for them such a sum to the storekeeper (which oath every guardian may be empowered to administer), shall grant unto the said overseer a warrant to distrain upon the goods of the person so offending, and sell the goods so distrained, rendering the overplus.

[23] That the guardian of the poor of every parish, to be chosen by those who pay to the relief of the poor of the said parish, shall be chosen, the first time, within three months of the passing of the act now proposed; that the guardians thus chosen by the respective parishes of each hundred shall have the inspection of all things relating to the employment and relief of the poor of the said hundred; that one third part of the whole number of the guardians of every hundred thus chosen shall go out every year, the first year by lot out of the whole number, the second year by lot out of the remaining two-thirds, and for ever afterwards in their turns, so that, after the first two years, everyone shall continue in three years successively and no longer; and that, for the supply of any vacancy as

it shall happen, a new guardian be chosen as aforesaid in any respective parish, at the same time that the overseers of the poor are usually chosen there, or at any other time within one month after any such vacancy.

[24] That the guardians of the poor of each respective hundred shall meet every year in Easter week, in the place where the stores of that hundred are kept, to take an account of the stock; and as often, also, at other times as shall be necessary to inspect the management of it and to give directions therein, and in all other things relating to the poor of the hundred.

[25] That no person in any parish shall be admitted to an allowance from the parish but by the joint consent of the guardian of the said parish and the vestry.

[26] That the said guardian also, each of them, within the hundred whereof he is guardian, have the power of a justice of the peace over vagabonds and beggars, to make them passes, to send them to the seaport towns, or houses of correction, as before proposed.

These foregoing rules and methods being what we humbly conceive most proper to be put in practice for the employment and relief of the poor generally throughout the country, we now further humbly propose for the better and more easy attainment of the same end in cities and towns corporate, that it may be enacted:[9]

[27] That in all cities and towns corporate the poor's tax be not levied by distinct parishes, but by one equal tax throughout the whole corporation.[10]

[28] That in each corporation there be twelve guardians of the poor, chosen by the said corporation, whereof four to go out by lot at the end of the first year, [an]other four of the remaining number to go out also by lot the next year, and the remaining four the third year, and a new four chosen every year in the rooms of those that go out, to keep up the number of twelve full, and that no one continue in above three years successively.

[29] That these guardians have the power of setting up and ordering working schools as they see convenient, within each corporation respectively, to which schools the children of all that are

---

[9] Draft: for every town 'except such as have already Acts'.

[10] The draft specifies a 'general court to consist of the inhabitants that pay at least 2d per week to the poor'.

relieved by the said corporation, from 3 to 14 years of age, shall be bound to come, as long as they continue unemployed in some other settled service, to be approved of by the overseers of the poor of that parish to which they belong.

[30] That these guardians also have the sole power of ordering and disposing of the money raised in each corporation for the use of the poor, whether for the providing of materials to set them on work, or for the relieving of those whom they judge not able to earn their own livelihoods; and that they be the sole judges who are, or are not, fit to receive public relief, and in what proportion.

[31] That the said guardians have also the power to send any persons begging without a lawful pass to the next seaport town or house of correction, as before propounded.

[32] That they have likewise power to appoint a treasurer to receive all money raised for the relief of the poor; which treasurer shall issue all such money only by their order, and shall once a year pass his accounts before them; and that they also appoint one or more storekeepers, as they shall see occasion, with such rewards or salaries as they think fit; which storekeepers shall in like manner be accountable unto them, provided always that the mayor or bailiff, or other chief officer of each corporation, have notice given them that he may be present (which we humbly propose may be enjoined on all such officers respectively) at the passing of the accounts both of the treasurer and storekeepers of the poor within each respective corporation.

[33] That the teachers in each school, or some other person thereunto appointed, shall fetch from the respective storekeepers the materials they are appointed to work upon in that school, and in such quantities as they are ordered, which materials shall be manufactured accordingly, and then returned to the storekeeper, and by him be either given out to be further manufactured, or else disposed of to the best advantage, as the guardians shall direct.

[34] That the overseers of the poor shall in like manner take from the storekeeper, and distribute unto those who are under the public relief, such materials, and in such proportions, as shall be ordered each of them for a week's work, and not pay unto any of the poor so employed the allowance appointed them till they bring back their respective tasks well performed.

[35] That the overseers of the poor of each parish shall be chosen as they are now, and have the same power to collect the poor's rates

of their respective parishes as now; but that they issue out the money so collected for the relief and maintenance of the poor according to such orders and directions as they shall receive from the guardians. And that the accounts of the overseers of the poor of each parish, at the end of their year, shall be laid before such persons as the parish shall appoint to inspect them, that they may make such reservations on the said accounts, or exceptions against them, as they may be liable to, and that then the said accounts, with those observations and exceptions, be examined by the treasurer and two of the guardians (whereof one to be nominated by the guardians themselves and the other by the parish), and that the said accounts be passed by the allowance of those three.

[36] That the said guardians shall have power to appoint one or more beadles of beggars, which beadles shall be authorised and required to seize upon any stranger begging in the streets, or anyone of the said corporation begging either without the badge appointed to be worn or at hours not allowed by the said guardians to beg in, and bring all such persons before any one of the said guardians. And that, if any of the said beadles neglect their said duty, so that strangers or other beggars not having the badge appointed, or at hours not allowed, be found frequenting the streets, the said guardians, upon complaint thereof made to them, shall have power and be required to punish the beadle so offending, for the first fault, according to their own discretion; but, upon a second complaint proved before them, that they send the said beadle to the house of correction, or (if it be in a maritime county, and the beadle offending be a lusty [able-bodied] man, and under 50 years of age), to the next seaport town, in order to the putting him aboard some of his majesty's ships, to serve there three years as before proposed.

[37] That those who are not able to work at all, in corporations where there are no hospitals to receive them, be lodged three or four or more in one room, and yet more in one house, where one fire may serve, and one attendant may provide for many of them, with less charge than when they live at their own choice scatteringly.

[38] And, since the behaviour and wants of the poor are best known amongst their neighbours, and that they may have liberty to declare their wants, and receive broken bread and meat, or other charity, from well-disposed people, that it be therefore permitted to those whose names are entered in the poor's book, and who wear

the badges required, to ask and receive alms in their respective parishes at certain hours of the day to be appointed by the guardians; but, if any of these are taken begging at any other hour than those allowed, or out of their respective parishes, though within the same corporation, they shall be sent immediately, if they are under 14 years of age, to the working school to be whipped, and, if they are above 14, to the house of correction, to remain there six weeks and so much longer as till the next quarter-sessions after the said six weeks are expired.

[39] That, if any person die for want of due relief in any parish in which he ought to be relieved, the said parish be fined according to the circumstances of the fact and the heinousness of the crime.

[40] That every master of the king's ships shall be bound to receive without money, once every year (if offered him by the magistrate or other officer of any place within the bounds of the port where his ship shall be), one boy, sound of limb, above 13 years of age, who shall be his apprentice for nine years.

Minor Essays

Verses on Cromwell and the Dutch War

1654. Untitled. Printed in *Musarum Oxoniensium Helaiophoria* (Oxford, 1654), pp. 45, 94–5. The first poem appeared in Latin: printed here in translation ('Englished by Locke') from *Biographia Brittanica* (1760), V, 2993; it was also printed in *State Poems* (1697). The second appeared in English. Both printed in Fox Bourne 1876, I, pp. 50–2. The publishing of collections of congratulatory poems by the universities on state occasions was a regular practice; this collection was organised by the Vice-Chancellor, John Owen. Locke's poems, his first publication, appeared among dozens offered by Oxford scholars. The first follows the convention of likening great princes to the Emperor Augustus. The second was occasioned by the conclusion of the first Anglo-Dutch war at the Treaty of Westminster in April 1654; there had been no clear victory.

Verses on Oliver Cromwell

A peaceful sway the great Augustus bore,
O'er what great Julius gain'd by arms before:[1]
Julius was all with martial trophies crown'd,
Augustus for his peaceful arts renown'd.
Rome calls them great, and makes them Deities,
This for his valour, that his policies.
You, mighty Prince! than both are greater far;
You rule in peace that world, you gain'd by war.
You, Sir, from Heav'n a finish'd hero fell,
Who thus alone two Pagan Gods excel.

Verses upon peace with the Dutch

If Greece with so much mirth did entertain
Her Argo,[2] coming laden home again,
With what loud mirth and triumph shall we greet
The wish'd approaches of our welcome fleet,

---

[1] The Roman Emperor Augustus (63 BC–AD 14) succeeded the martial Julius Caesar and was praised by Virgil for encouraging the flourishing of the arts and sciences under a peaceful reign.

[2] In Greek mythology Jason and the Argonauts sailed in the ship Argo in search of the Golden Fleece.

When of that prize our ships do us possess
Whereof their fleece was but an emblem – Peace,
Whose welcome voice sounds sweeter in our ears
Than the loud music of the warbling spheres,
And, ravishing more than those, doth plainly show
That sweetest harmony we do discord owe?
Each seaman's voice, pronouncing peace, doth charm,
And seems a siren's, but that 't has less harm
And danger in't, and yet like theirs doth please
Above all other, and make us love the seas.
We've heaven in this peace: like souls above,
We've nought to do now but admire and love.
    Glory of war is victory. But here
Both glorious be, 'cause neither's conqueror.
'T had been less honour, if it might be said
They fought with those that could be conquered.
    Our re-united seas, like streams that flow
Into one river, do the smoother flow
Where ships no longer grapple, but, like those,
The loving seamen in embraces close.
We need no fire-ships now: a nobler flame
Of love doth us protect, whereby our name
Shall shine more glorious, a flame as pure
As those of heaven, and shall as long endure.
This shall direct our ships, and he that steers
Shall not consult heaven's fires, but those he bears
In his own breast. Let Lilly[3] threaten wars,
Whilst this conjunction lasts, we'll fear no stars.
    Our ships are now most beneficial grown,
Since they bring home no spoils but what's their own.
Unto these branchless pines[4] our forward spring
Owes better fruit than autumn's wont to bring;
Which gives not only gems and Indian ore,
But adds at once whole nations to the store:
Nay, if to make a world's but to compose
The difference of things, and make them close
In mutual amity, and cause peace to creep
Out of the jarring chaos of the deep,

---

[3] William Lilly (1602–81), famous astrologer and publisher of almanacs and prophecies.
[4] Ships' masts were made from pine.

Our ships do this; so that, whilst others' take
Their course about the world, ours a world make.

Verses on King Charles II's Restoration

1660. Untitled. Published in *Britannia Rediviva* (Oxford, 1660),
sig. Ff 2v–3r, one among 158 poems by Locke's Oxford colleagues.
See Letter 134. The poem uses Aristotelian conceits about the
imposition of ordered form upon primal matter or chaos. It dwells
upon the anarchy of recent times: compare Letters 59, 81, 82.

Our prayers are heard! nor have the Fates in store
An equall blisse, for which we can implore,
Their bounty, For in you, Great SIR's, the summe
Of all our present joys, of all to come:
Joys that have spoke so loud, as if to heaven
They'd rise, from whence they, and their cause were given:
Kings always are the gifts of Heaven, but you
Are not its gift alone, but transcript too;
Your vertues match its stars, which you disclose
To th' world, as bright, and numberless as those.
Your motions all as regular, which dispence
A warmth to all, and quickning influence.
How shall we prize your bounty!, whilst you thus
Approaching to our Earth, bring Heaven to us.
 Your fortunes oft have varied, but your minde
Like your religion still the same wee find.
When he that rul'd the world, the mighty Jove,
Would make a present worth One mortall's love,
To gain admittance chang'd himself, though he
From Heaven came, and brought a Deity;
More liberall, but less chang'd, yourself alone
Can enter, and enrich a Nation.
Thus when they'd be most bright, and tempting shewn,
Great Jove must change his shape, CHARLES keep his own.
 As in the world's Creation, when this frame
Had neither parts, distinction, nor a name,
But all confus'd did in the Chaos jarre,
Th'embleme, and product of intestine warre,
Light first appears (Light that n'ere since could shew

A thing more welcome than its self, but You)
Beauty, and Order follow, and display
This stately Fabrick, guided by that ray.
So now in this our new creation, when
This Isle begins to be a world agen,
You first dawn on our Chaos, with designe
To give us order, and then on us shine.
Till you upon us rose, and made it day,
We in disorder all, and darkness lay;
Only some *Ignes fatui* [5] did rise,
To scare us into errors, cheat our eyes,
Off-springs of Earth! which nought could render bright
Or visible, but darkness, and the night.
A night not meant for rest, but full of pain,
And to be felt, scarce hope of day again:
Aegyptian darkness with 'ts many Gods to sway
As many plagues, and prodigies as they;
Where each thing claim'd our worship, and would be
Ador'd, forceing obeysance, and a knee,
Upstart and unknown Gods! to whom with shame
We first gave Adoration, then a Name,
Worshipp'd those Crocadiles that always had
Tears to bestow, on ruins that they made.
      But these sad shades doe vanish with their fears,
As soon as our Apollo now appears.
At whose returne the Muses too would sing
Their joys aloud, and welcome home their King
Accept these poore endeavours, till your rays
Have given new growth to our late witherd bays,[6]
Wit too must be your Donative, 'tis You
Who give AUGUSTUS, must give MARO's[7] too.

Infallibility

1661 or early 1662. 'An necesse sit dari in ecclesia infallibilem sacro sanctae scripturae interpretem? Negatur.' ('Is it necessary that an infallible interpreter of Holy Scripture be granted in the church? No.') PRO 30/24/47/33. Printed in Biddle 1977; extract in Fox

---

[5] Delusive illuminations.
[6] Laurels, and by implication literary renown.
[7] Maro is Virgil.

Bourne 1876, I, 161–2. In Latin: the translation is Biddle's. The format is similar to that of the *Essays on the Law of Nature* and the content is closely related to the *Two Tracts on Government*. See also Letter 75. Locke addresses the topic of Scriptural hermeneutics and evinces a conventional Protestant hostility to Catholicism. He may have borrowed from William Chillingworth's *The Religion of Protestants* (1638) and Jeremy Taylor's *Liberty of Prophesying* (1647). He affirms the principle of *sola scriptura* (the self-sufficiency of Scripture alone), in opposition to the Catholic claim that Scripture is often obscure and must be understood in the light of the church's tradition of authoritative teaching. Catholics believed that the church's authority to interpret the Bible was infallible, but did not necessarily place that infallibility in the pope. Locke warns against clogging the mysteries of faith with vain philosophy. He stresses the amplitude of 'things indifferent' (as opposed to 'things necessary') for salvation, a sphere within which human authority may intervene to establish religious order. He concedes that there is no easy path between individual conscience and church authority, and between reason and 'enthusiasm'.

While in any state [*civitate*] and society of men the right of making laws is the highest and greatest power, certainly next and almost equal to this is the authority of interpreting these laws. For what is the point of drawing up dumb, silent statements of laws, if anybody may attach a new meaning to the words to suit his own taste, find some remote interpretation, and twist the words to fit the situation and his own opinion? Observing this, sharp-sighted priests have violated both these powers in their efforts to establish in every way that control over the conduct and consciences of men which they so strongly claim. On the one hand these persons force upon the church their own traditions which grow up continually as the occasion demands, and they contend that these possess the force of laws and oblige men's consciences. On the other hand the priests insist that the Roman pontiff is the sole and infallible interpreter of the Holy Bible. Nor does it matter very much what God himself dictated to his people on Mount Sinai, or what our lawgiver, Christ, declared on the Mount of Olives,[8] as long as, loftier than either, the seven hills of Rome dominate both. Blindness is certainly inevitable,

---

[8] The Ten Commandments were delivered on Mount Sinai and the Sermon on the Mount at the Mount of Olives.

where Heaven itself does not have enough light to guide our steps. Or does that same God, who made the tongue and organs of speech and who gave the use of language to mankind, address men in such a way that he cannot be understood without an interpreter? Who will explain the mind of God better than God himself? Or perhaps the words of God are obscure and ambiguous, while those of men are clear and certain? Is he who first made the souls of men unable to instruct them? Or does Christ so address the waves and storms that they do understand and speak to men alone so that they do not [Matt. 8:23–7]? Or, indeed, will the eyes of the blind heed his words which open ears are unable to grasp? Does he instruct ignorant and wretched mankind in such a way that the diseases understand his commands better than the diseased? The prophets, the apostles, even his own Son clothed in human form and not unaware of our weakness and ignorance – all of these God sent so that he might teach men what he wanted to be done, that mankind might know what the worship and reverence of the deity should be and what unity and fellowship should exist among themselves. After so many emissaries there is by now no need for an interpreter. So it is agreed that it is not necessary that an infallible interpreter of Holy Scripture be granted in the church.

Firstly, because an infallible interpreter of this sort has not existed since the time of the apostles; for here the argument from fact to necessity is valid. It cannot be doubted that God, who promised to preserve his church continuously until the end of time [Matt. 16:18–22], will provide that nothing necessary to it should be lacking. That there has been no infallible interpreter is sufficiently shown by the disagreements of Christians among themselves about divine matters; and the dissension of opinions (and these notions are not only various but contradictory) troubled the diverse members of the church dispersed in various regions of the world and divided them into factions. All this, perhaps the priests will say, is only the quarrel and battle of the true church – that is to say their own – with the ignorant and heretical. Yet, it is obvious enough to anyone, however slightly acquainted with ecclesiastical history, that even in the Church of Rome and its infallible interpreter opinions about faith and morals and interpretations of Holy Scripture differ enormously.

Secondly, that is not necessary which would be utterly useless to both the faith and peace of the church. Even granting that some infallible interpreter of Holy Scripture be given, he will still not be able, however . . .[9] he may be, to contribute anything to the solution of problems of faith or to the establishment of peace among Christians, unless he can infallibly show that he is infallible. Since he cannot prove this about himself, for nobody's testimony about himself is acceptable, and since the Scripture is silent, I cannot easily discover how he can be recognised. So we cannot expect any remedy from this quarter for so great a disagreement and so many errors; for there is no difference between everyone's being subject to error and someone's being infallible but unknown and uncertain. What help is it to be certain about something when you are uncertain about the person? How anxiously you must anticipate a cure for vice and ignorance from someone, when you do not know whether the man to whose trust you commit yourself is a doctor or a charlatan.

As to the Scripture whose interpreter we seek – since it was written at different times and not in the same style, embraces within itself various arguments, and contains the history of past events, rules of conduct, and the articles of faith, it can be considered in many ways.

(1) Thus, there are many things contrived for arrogance and the display of learning, which are frivolous and empty quibbles that have not arisen from Holy Scripture, but are violently expressed by the hollow talents of madmen. Of such a kind are the questions, 'What was the forbidden fruit of Paradise?', 'Where was that lovely garden?', and others of that sort, which neither need an interpreter nor deserve a reader. Problems of this sort can perhaps exercise petty minds but scarcely detain a sober and pious man. Although these are difficult matters to know, they can safely be ignored. Moreover, they hardly seem to concern the Scripture, which is the standard of faith and conduct.

(2) The Holy Scripture also contains within it the profound mysteries of divine matters which utterly transcend the human intellect. These, although they are obscure, nevertheless cannot have an

---

[9] An illegible word in the manuscript.

interpreter. For, since to interpret is nothing else than to bring out the meaning of obscure words and to express unfamiliar language clearly in words of everyday speech, here such interpretation is clearly impossible, because God has proclaimed in the clearest and most unambiguous terms what he wanted men to know and believe. Whoever attempts to explain the trinity of persons in the divine nature in words other than those in which God has revealed it brings not so much light to the Scripture as darkness. We can add to this the union of divine and human nature in the person of the mediator, the infinity and eternity of God, and several other matters, the truth of which is certain and is to be believed, but the way in which they are true cannot be expressed in discourse nor grasped by the mind. Whatever it is that impedes us in these matters, it is certainly not the obscurity of the words but the magnitude of the matters themselves and the weakness of our minds. Whoever wants to interpret these things ought to bring to them not an extensive vocabulary and a facility of expression but a power and an intellect new to human souls.

(3) There are other things in Holy Writ, things most necessary to salvation, so clear and unambiguous that virtually nobody can doubt them, for to hear is to understand them. Such are the principal duties of a Christian man – justice, chastity, charity, and benevolence – which certainly have little need of an interpreter, since they are so clearly transmitted that if any interpretation were added, it would in turn inevitably require another interpretation.

(4) There are some precepts and instructions in Holy Writ of a more general nature. For example, there is that passage to the Corinthians: 'Doth not even nature itself (i.e. custom) teach you that, if a man has long hair, it is a shame to him?' [1 Cor. 11:14]. Scripture does not state what length of hair is too long, and so it is to be determined by the church. Similarly, it is stated in chapter 14: 'Let all things be done decently and in order' [1 Cor. 14:40]. Since these precepts relate to matters which are in themselves and by their nature indifferent and can neither be applied to everyday life nor govern human behaviour without an interpreter, in these and other similar cases I agree that an infallible interpreter is given, possible, and needed. Such interpreters are the fathers and leaders of every church, who in these matters can be called infallible, but as I see it, their infallibility is directive not definitive. To be sure,

the shepherds of the church can perhaps err while they are leading, but the sheep certainly cannot err while they are following. The path of obedience is safe and secure. For, since obedience is a certain and undeniable duty of Christian people, even if the interpretation of a text of Scripture is perhaps uncertain, the man who errs least is he who follows what is sure and applies himself to both obedience and the peace of the church. Interpreters of such divine laws can be called 'infallible', since even if they can perhaps be deceived themselves, they cannot mislead others.

In the interpretation of Scripture, however, how much is to be granted to each individual and how much to the authority of the church, and then what is achieved by reason and what by the illumination of the Holy Spirit, is not so easy and straightforward to state. Great caution must be exercised, however, lest by relying too heavily on our reason we disregard our faith, or by neglecting the mysteries of the gospel embrace philosophy instead of religion. On the other hand, enthusiasm must be carefully avoided, lest, while we await the inspiration of the Holy Spirit, we honour and worship our own dreams. It is certainly true that much is contributed to the interpretation of the Holy Bible by learning, much by reason, and finally much by the Holy Spirit's enlightening the minds of men. However, the most certain interpreter of Scripture is Scripture itself, and it alone is infallible.

Verses on Queen Catherine

1662. *Domiduca Oxoniensis* (Oxford, 1662), sig. B 2v–3v. Locke's poem is among 126 in this volume. See Letter 134. In this year King Charles II married Catherine of Braganza. The poem displays some of the characteristic sentiments of Restoration royalism, exhibited also in the *Tracts on Government*.

> Crowns, Scepters, Thrones, and the whole state of Kings
> With all the Pompe and Majesty it brings,
> May give a luster to each outward part,
> But cannot reach the soule, and warme the heart;
> Such flames have no abode beneath the skies,
> But in those little Heavens, a Princesse eyes.
> Kings are Gods here, but yet as 'tis above,
> There is no heaven where there is no Love.

When the first man without a rivall stood
Possest of all, and all like him was good:
Heaven thought that All imperfect, till beside
'T had made another self, and given a Bride:
Empire, and Innocence were there, but yet
'Twas Eve made Man, and Paradise compleat.
So what e're fruit our Eden can afford
Of Peace, or Glory to its mighty Lord,
Though Loyall hearts labour to make his state,
As are their wishes, or his Virtues great;
And the unruly brutish herd doth pay
Due homage, and again learn to obey:
Yet all our best endeavours for his blisse
Doe perfect our own happinesse, not his.
  That work is Yours (Great Queen) and that to You
We leave which three whole Kingdomes could not doe,
'Tis you must Crown, and fill that heart, the Fates
Meant the Controuler of the Western states:
A heart so fram'd as if 'twere made, and fit
Only for you, and all the world for it;
Whereof you could at distance make a prize,
Without the common method of the eyes.
So rules great Jove with flames, whose influence
Workes without aid or notice of the sence.
  When on your Charles from home, and throne exil'd
Fortune still frown'd, and all the Ladies smild:[10]
Unmov'd with both a direct path he knew
To tread, to hidden happinesse and You.
So the skild Pilot, when the waves engage
To sinke the ship that plays upon their rage,
If darke, and threatning clouds his Pole-star hide,
Regards not all that shine in Heaven beside,
A steddy course by that star safely stears,
Which nowhere, whilst the tempest lasts, appears.
  He saw, and sleighted all the rest, but You
Were th'undiscovered world, His rich Peru,
Stor'd with those Mines of worth, which yet retain
The Golden age, or bring it back again.

---

[10] Charles was in exile in France, Germany and the Spanish Netherlands between 1646 and 1660. Among his mistresses was Lucy Walter, who bore him the Duke of Monmouth, later favoured by some Whigs as the Protestant claimant to succeed Charles.

'Tis want of worth calls for a cautious eye
To scan each part, and blemishes discry.
He's fondly nice, that would be loth to come,
Unlesse h'had seen it, to Elyzium.
He search'd the world, and view'd it every part,
But found all these too little for his heart:
Two things alone remain'd hid from his view,
Could make him fully happy, Heaven and you:
Like heaven you come with ravishments of blisse,
Desir'd unknown, at once seen, and made his.

On Samuel Parker

1669 or early 1670. Endorsed: 'Qs on S.P.'s discourse of toleration 69'. MS Locke, c. 39, pp. 7–9. Incompletely printed in Cranston 1957, pp. 131–3. A commentary upon Samuel Parker's *Discourse of Ecclesiastical Polity: wherein the authority of the civil magistrate over the consciences of subjects in matters of religion is asserted; the mischiefs and inconveniences of toleration are represented, and all pretences pleaded on behalf of liberty of conscience are fully answered* ('1670', in fact 1669). This book was one of the most influential and virulent attacks on the Protestant Nonconformists or Dissenters. It was encouraged by Archbishop Gilbert Sheldon and was part of the inaptly styled 'friendly debate' between Churchmen and Dissenters, which spanned the years 1666 to 1674, and was launched by Simon Patrick. John Owen, 'Cromwell's pope', and Andrew Marvell took part on the Nonconformist side. Locke's master, Lord Ashley, hoped to persuade the king to grant toleration, while Sheldon and Parker worked with the Anglican gentry in Parliament to implement further coercive legislation against Dissenters. Extracts from Parker are supplied in order to make sense of Locke's comments. Locke purchased a copy of Parker in October 1669 (BL, Add. MS 46,470, p. 27).

SP: The peace and tranquillity of the commonwealth, the prime and most important end of government, can never be sufficiently secured, unless religion be subject to the authority of the supreme power, in that it has the strongest influence upon human affairs. [p. 11]

JL: Whether [this] proves anything but that the magistrate's business being only to preserve peace, those wrong opinions are to be restrained that have a tendency to disturb it (and this is by every sober man to be allowed)?

SP: As true piety secures the public weal by taming and civilising the passions of men, and inuring them to a mild, gentle and governable spirit: so superstition and wrong notions of God and his worship are the most powerful engines to overturn its settlement. And therefore unless princes have power to bind their subjects to that religion that they apprehend most advantageous to public peace and tranquillity, and restrain those religious mistakes that tend to its subversion, they are no better than statues and images of authority. [p. 12]

JL: Whether assigning these ill effects that follow to 'wrong notions of God and his worship' he does not suppose the magistrate's power to proceed from [his] being in the right? Whether by 'bind the subject to his religion' he means that whether the magistrate's opinion be right or wrong he has power to force the subject to renounce his own opinions however quiet and peaceable, and declare assent and consent to those of the magistrate? And if so why Christ and the apostles directed not their discourses and addressed their miracles to the princes and magistrates of the world to persuade them, whereas by preaching to and converting the people, they according to this doctrine [lay] under a necessity of being either seditious or martyrs.

SP: If conscience be ever able to break down the restraints of government, and all men have licence to follow their own persuasions, the mischief is infinite ... There never yet was any commonwealth that gave a real liberty to men's imaginations, that was not suddenly overrun with numberless divisions and subdivisions of sects. [pp. 21–2]

JL: Whether subdivision of opinions into small sects be of such danger to the government?

SP: Because the Church of Rome, by her unreasonable impositions, has invaded the fundamental liberties of mankind they presently conclude [i.e. the Dissenters now include] all restraints upon licentious practices and persuasions about religion under the hated name of popery. [p. 24]

JL: What fundamental liberties of mankind were invaded by the Church of Rome that will not be in the same condition under the civil magistrate according to his doctrine, since the power of the Church of Rome was allowed and their decrees enforced by the civil magistrate?

SP: If the prince's jurisdiction be limited to civil affairs, and the concerns of religion be subject to another government, then may subjects be obliged to (what is impossible) contradictory commands. Seeing no man can be subject to contradictory obligations, 'tis by consequence utterly impossible he should be subject to two supreme powers. [p. 26]

JL: The end of government being public peace 'tis no question the supreme power must have an uncontrollable right to judge and ordain all things that may conduce to it, but yet the question will be whether uniformity established by law be (as is here supposed) a necessary means to it, i.e. whether it be at all dangerous to the magistrate that, he believing free will, some of his subjects shall believe predestination, or whether it be more necessary for his government to make laws for wearing surplices than it is for wearing vests?

SP: The wisdom of providence ... so ordered affairs, that no man could be born into the world without being subject to some superior: every father being by nature vested with a right to govern his children. And the first governments in the world were established purely upon the natural rights of paternal authority, which afterward grew up to a kingly power by the increase of posterity. [p. 29]

JL: Whether, allowing the paternal right of governments (which is asserted not proved), that paternal monarchy descended upon [the] death of the father it descended wholly to the eldest son, or else that the brothers had an equal power over their respective affairs. If the first, then monarchy is certainly *jure naturali* [by natural right], but there can be but one rightful monarch over the whole world, i.e. the right heir of Adam; if the second, all government, whether monarchical or other, is only from the consent of the people.

SP: Nothing more concerns the interest of the civil magistrate than to take care what particular doctrines of religion are taught within his dominions, because some are peculiarly advantageous to the ends of government, and others as naturally tending to its disturbance. [p. 144]

JL: Whether hence it will follow that the magistrate ought to force men by severity of laws and penalties to be of the same mind with him in the speculative opinions in religion, or worship God with the same ceremonies? That the magistrate should restrain seditious doctrines who denies, but because he may, then has he power over all other doctrines to forbid or impose? If he has not your argument is short, if he hath, how far is this short of Mr Hobbes's doctrine?[11]

SP: Fanaticism is both the greatest and the easiest vice that is incident to religion; 'tis a weed that thrives in all soils, and there is the same fanatic spirit that mixes itself with all the religions in the world. [p. 153]

JL: Whether this fanatic spirit be not the same passion, fired with religious zeal, whose fanatic heats he in that same paragraph accuses of having committed such dire outrages, massacres, and butchery, and done such mischiefs among men, and if it be, mixes itself with all religions? I desire him to examine those that be of the Church of England what spirit that is which sets him so zealously to stir up the magistrate to persecute all those who

---

[11] Locke occasionally mentions Hobbes elsewhere: *Two Treatises*, Preface; I, 14; II, 98; *Mr Locke's Reply to the Bishop of Worcester's Answer to his Second Letter* – 'I am not so well read in Hobbes or Spinoza . . . those justly decried names' (*Works*, IV, 477); *A Second Vindication of the Reasonableness of Christianity* – denies he has borrowed from *Leviathan* (*Works*, VII, 420–1); *Remarks upon Norris and Malebranche* – 'the religion of Hobbes and Spinoza . . . resolving all . . . into an irresistible fatal necessity' (*Works*, X, 255–56); *ECHU*, bk I, ch. 3: 'If a Christian . . . be asked why a man must keep his word, he will give this as a reason: because God, who has the power of eternal life and death, requires it of us. But if an Hobbist be asked why; he will answer: because the public requires it, and the Leviathan will punish you, if you do not'; MS Locke, c. 33, pp. 29, 35; f. 4, pp. 16, 71 (notebook entries); the essay 'Study' (see Appendix); 'Critical Notes on Stillingfleet' (MS Locke, c. 34, p. 40). See Cox 1960, ch. 1.

dissent from him in those opinions and ways of worship the public support whereof is to give him preferment?

Adversaria A

c. 1670? Adversaria 1661, fos. 1–3. Untitled. Partially printed in Abrams 1967, pp. 245–6 (who dates it to 1661). Translated from the Latin; Locke's tabular arrangement is not reproduced; the second part, concerning the natural world (*Physica sive Corporum Scientia*), is omitted. There is a similar table in MS Locke, c. 28, fo. 41 ('Sapientia [16]72'). Locke made several attempts at a typology of knowledge, sometimes by way of advice about note-taking ('commonplacing' or 'adversaria'). Compare 'Adversaria B' and 'C' and 'Knowledge A' and 'B'. There are further examples at: MS Locke, f. 15, pp. 110, 119–20, 122–3; and c. 42B, p. 22. Locke published 'A New Method of a Common-Place-Book' in 1686 (*Works*, III, 305–23). *ECHU*, bk IV, ch. 21 is called 'Of the Division of the Sciences', where the compass of human understanding is divided into three parts: knowledge of things (*physica*), knowledge of what is 'good and useful', especially ethics (*practica*), and knowledge of signs (words and ideas).

THEOLOGY. Historical or rational. God. Spirit: angels. Immortality: the separated soul; resurrection. Worship: rites, ceremonies, invocation of the saints, priests. Ethics: law of nature; virtues and vices. Revelation: miracles, predictions, dreams, visions, inspirations, prophecies, oracles. Judaica (creation); Christiana.

POLITY. Fundamentals: paternal right; popular consent. Forms: monarchy; aristocracy; democracy; mixed; fundamental constitutions. Administration: civil laws.

PRUDENCE. The end is: happiness (heavenly, which pertains to theology); tranquillity; health (which pertains to physic); wealth (which pertains to economy), power (which pertains to politics), reputation, favour, etc. The means to these ends: self-knowledge; mastery of one's passions. Knowledge of intellectual capacities; search for counsel; directing of minds (rhetoric); economy: selling and accounting (history, trades, etc.); military arts.[12]

---

[12] There are problematic translations here. For example, I have used 'physic' and 'economy' rather than the modern terms 'medicine' and 'economics'.

Civil and Ecclesiastical Power

1674. 'Of the difference between civil and ecclesiastical power';
endorsed 'excommunication'. MS Locke, c. 27, fo. 29. Partly in
Locke's hand. Incompletely printed in King 1829, 297–304; 1830,
II, 108–19. Locke is emphatic that the civil magistrate has no business to enforce religious conformity. He allows that churches have
the right to discipline their members by excommunication, but
without civil penalties attached. In the manuscript the numbered
paragraphs occur in two parallel columns, headed 'Civil society, or
the state' and 'Religious society, or the church'; these columns
are not reproduced here; instead, 'State' and 'Church' are inserted
against these paragraphs.

There is a twofold society, of which almost all men in the world
are members, and that from the twofold concernment they have to
attain a twofold happiness; viz. that of this world and that of the
other: and hence there arises these two following societies, viz.
religious and civil.

STATE (1) The end of civil society is civil peace and prosperity, or
the preservation of the society and every member thereof in a
free and peaceable enjoyment of all the good things of this life
that belong to each of them; but beyond the concernments of this
life, this society hath nothing to do at all.

CHURCH (1) The end of religious society is the attaining happiness
after this life in another world.

STATE (2) The terms of communion with, or being a part of this
society, is promise of obedience to the laws of it.

CHURCH (2) The terms of communion or conditions of being members of this society, is promise of obedience to the laws of it.

STATE (3) The proper matter, *circa quam*, of the laws of this society,
are all things conducing to the end above-mentioned, i.e. civil
happiness; and are in effect almost all moral and indifferent
things, which yet are not the proper matter of the laws of the

society, till the doing or omitting of any of them come to have a tendency to the end above-mentioned.

CHURCH (3) The proper matter of the laws of this society are all things tending to the attainment of future bliss, which are of three sorts: (i) *Credenda*, or matters of faith and opinion, which terminate in the understanding. (ii) *Cultus religiosus*, which contains in it both the ways of expressing our honour and adoration of the deity, and of address to him for the obtaining any good from him. (iii) *Moralia*, or the right management of our actions in respect of ourselves and others.

STATE (4) The means to procure obedience to the laws of this society, and thereby preserve it, is force or punishment; i.e. the abridgement of anyone's share of the good things of the world within the reach of the society, and sometimes a total deprivation, as in capital punishments. And this, I think, is the whole end, latitude, and extent of civil power and society.

CHURCH (4) The means to preserve obedience to the laws of this society are the hopes and fears of happiness and misery in another world. But though the laws of this society be in order to happiness in another world, and so the penalties annexed to them are also of another world; yet the society being in this world and to be continued here, there are some means necessary for the preservation of the society here, which is the expulsion of such members as obey not the laws of it, or disturb its order. And this, I think, is the whole end, latitude, and extent of ecclesiastical power and religious society.

This being, as I suppose, the distinct bounds of church and state, let us a little compare them together. The parallel:

STATE (1) The end of civil society is present enjoyment of what this world affords.

CHURCH (1) The end of church communion, future expectation of what is to be had in the other world.

STATE (2) Another end of civil society is the preservation of the society or government itself for its own sake.

CHURCH (2) The preservation of the society in religious communion is only in order to the conveying and propagating those laws and truths which concern our well-being in another world.

STATE AND CHURCH (3) The terms of communion must be the same in all societies.

STATE (4) The laws of a commonwealth are mutable, being made within the society by an authority not distinct from it, nor exterior to it.

CHURCH (4) The laws of religious society, bating [excepting] those which are only subservient to the order necessary to their execution, are immutable, not subject to any authority of the society, and only proposed by and within the society, but made by a lawgiver without the society, and paramount to it.

STATE (5) The proper means to procure obedience to the law of the civil society, and thereby attain the end, civil happiness, is force or punishment. (i) It is [the] effectual and adequate way for the preservation of the society, and of civil happiness, [which] is the immediate and natural consequence of the execution of the law. (ii) It is just, for the breach of laws being mostly the prejudice and diminution of another man's right, and always tending to the dissolution of the society, in the continuance whereof every man's particular right is comprehended, it is just that he who has impaired another man's good, should suffer the diminution of his own. (iii) It is within the power of the society, which can exert its own strength against offenders, the sword being put in the magistrate's hands to that purpose. But civil society has nothing to do without [outside] its own limits, which is civil happiness.

CHURCH (5) The proper enforcement of obedience to the laws of religion, is the rewards and punishments of the other world; but civil punishment is not so. (i) Because it is ineffectual to that purpose; for punishment is never sufficient to keep men to the obedience of any law, where the evil it brings is not certainly greater than the good which is obtained or expected from the disobedience. And therefore no temporal worldly punishment can be sufficient to persuade a man to that, or from that way which he believes leads to everlasting happiness or misery. (ii) Because it is unjust in reference both to *credenda* [matters of faith] and *cultus* [forms of worship], that I should be despoiled of my good things of this world, where I disturb not in the least the enjoyment of others; for my faith or religious worship hurts not another man in any concernment of his; and in moral transgressions, the third and real part of religion, the religious society cannot punish, because it then invades the civil society, and wrests the magistrate's sword out of his hand. In civil society one man's good is involved and complicated with another's, but in religious societies every man's concerns are separate, and one man's transgressions hurt not another any further than he imitates him, and if he err, he errs at his own private cost. Therefore I think no external punishment, i.e. deprivation or diminution of the goods of this life, belongs to the church. Only because for the propagation of the truth (which every society believes to be its own religion) it is equity it should remove those two evils which will hinder its propagation, (i) disturbance within, which is contradiction or disobedience of any of its members to its doctrines and discipline; (ii) infamy without, which is the scandalous lives or disallowed profession of any of its members; and the proper way to do this, which is in its power, is to exclude and disown such vicious members.

STATE AND CHURCH (6) Church membership is perfectly voluntary, and may end whenever anyone pleases without any prejudice to him, but in civil society it is not so.

But because religious societies are of two sorts, wherein their circumstances very much differ, the exercise of their power is also much different. It is to be considered that all mankind (very few or none excepted) are combined into civil societies in various forms, as force, chance, agreement, or other accidents have happened to constrain them: there are very few also that have not some religion. And hence it comes to pass, that very few men but are members both of some church and of some commonwealth; and hence it comes to pass –

(1) That in some places the civil and religious societies are co-extended, i.e. both the magistrate and every subject of the same commonwealth is also member of the same church; and thus it is in Muscovy, whereby they have all the same civil laws, and the same opinions and religious worship.

(2) In some places the commonwealth, though all of one religion, is but a part of the church or religious society which acts and is acknowledged to be one entire society; and so it is in Spain and the principalities of Italy.

(3) In some places the religion of the commonwealth, i.e. the public established religion, is not received by all the subjects of the commonwealth; and thus the Protestant religion in England, the Reformed in Brandenburg, the Lutheran in Sweden.

(4) In some places the religion of part of the people is different from the governing part of the civil society; and thus the Presbyterian, Independent, Anabaptists, Quakers and Jewish in England, the Lutheran and Popish in Cleve,[13] etc.; and in these two last the religious society is part of the civil.

There are also three things to be considered in each religion as the matter of their communion: (i) Opinions or speculations or *credenda*. (ii) *Cultus religiosus* [religious ceremonial]. (iii) *Mores* [morals]. Which are all to be considered in the exercise of church power, which I conceive does properly extend no further than excommunication, which is to remove a scandalous or turbulent member.

(1) In the first case there is no need of excommunication for immorality, because the civil law hath provided, or may sufficiently, against that by penal laws, enough to suppress it; for the civil magistrate hath moral actions under the dominion of his sword, and therefore 'tis not like[ly] he will turn away a subject out of his country for a fault which he can compel him to reform. But if anyone differ from the church in *fide aut cultu* [faith or worship], I think first the civil magistrate may punish him for it where he is fully persuaded that it is likely to disturb the civil peace, otherwise not. But the religious society may certainly excommunicate him,

---

[13] Locke had visited the city of Cleves in 1665–6 and had been deeply impressed that civil peace and religious pluralism could subsist together. See Letters 175–84.

the peace whereof may by this means be preserved; but no other evil ought to follow him upon that excommunication as such, but only upon the consideration of the public peace, for if he will silently conceal his opinion or carry away his opinion or differing worship out of the sight of that government, I know not why he can be hindered.

(2) In the second case I think the church may excommunicate for faults in faith and worship, but not those faults in manners which the magistrate has annexed penalties to, for the preservation of civil society and happiness.

(3) The same also I think ought to be the rule in the third case.

(4) In the fourth case, I think the church has power to excommunicate for matters of faith, worship, or manners, though the magistrate punish the same immorality with his sword, because the church cannot otherwise remove the scandal which is necessary for its preservation and the propagation of its doctrines. And this power of being judges who are fit to be of their society, the magistrate cannot deny to any religious society which is permitted within his dominions. This was the state of the church till Constantine.[14] But in none of the former cases is excommunication capable to be denounced by any church upon anyone but the members of that church, it being absurd to cut off that which is no part. Neither ought the civil magistrate to inflict any punishment upon the score of excommunication, but to punish the fact or forbear, just as he finds it convenient for the preservation of the civil peace and prosperity of the commonwealth (within which his power is confined), without any regard to the excommunication at all.

Trade

1674. Endorsed 'TAEI / Trade / Essay 1674'. MS Locke, c. 30, fo. 18. Printed in Thirsk and Cooper 1972, p. 96; Kelly 1991, II, 485–6. Locke's remarks draw upon Carew Reynell's *The True English Interest* (1674). The tabular form of Locke's two final paragraphs is not reproduced here; most items in these lists are mentioned by Reynell.

The chief end of trade is riches and power which beget each other. Riches consist in plenty of movables, that will yield a price to [a]

---

[14] The first Christian emperor, converted *c.* 313.

foreigner, and are not like to be consumed at home, but especially in plenty of gold and silver. Power consists in numbers of men, and ability to maintain them. Trade conduces to both these by increasing your stock and your people, and they each other.

Trade is twofold. (1) Domestic manufacture, whereby is to be understood all labour employed by your people in preparing commodities for the consumption, either of your own people (where it will exclude foreign importation) or of foreigners. (2) Carriage, i.e. navigation and merchandise.

People also are twofold. (1) Those that contribute [in] any way to your trade, especially in commodities for exportation, the chief whereof are men employed in husbandry, drapery, mines, and navigation. (2) Such as are either idle and so do not help, as retainers to gentry and beggars or, which is worse, hinder trade, as retailers in some degree, multitudes of lawyers, but above all soldiers in pay.

Promoters of trade: freedom of trade; naturalisation easy; freedom of religion; register or certainty of property; small customs; public workhouses; coin good, certain, hard to be counterfeited; transferring of bills; increase and encouragement of seamen in an island, no seamen nor navigation in a continent that wants not supply but can subsist of itself; cheap labour; fashions suited to your own manufacture; suitable manufactures to the markets whose commodities we want; low customs on exportation;[15] new manufactures at home.

Hindrances of trade: intricacy of law; arrests; imprisonments;[16] arbitrary power; vices tending to prodigality.

The Particular Test for Priests

c. 1674. 'The particular test for priests'. Endorsed 'Papists Test' and 'Te[st] Walsh'. MS Locke, c. 27, fo. 30. Not hitherto printed. Not in Locke's hand, and of uncertain authorship. It is the draft of an oath containing doctrines which Catholic priests must renounce, and illustrates the doctrines that Catholics were widely held to believe. Peter Walsh was an Irish Franciscan priest who

---

[15] At this time customs duties were charged on exports as well as imports; they were abolished in 1722.

[16] I.e. for debt. The severity of the laws of debt was a constant complaint from the seventeenth to the nineteenth centuries.

drew up a 'Loyal Formulary or Irish Remonstrance' in 1661, an oath of allegiance which he hoped Irish Catholics would take, and thereby achieve toleration in return. The Irish Catholic Church rejected it and Walsh was excommunicated in 1670. The 'Particular Test for Priests' goes much further than Walsh's oath. It was probably prompted by Walsh's *Some Few Questions Concerning the Oath of Allegiance* (1674), a copy of which Locke had in his library. See Brennan 1957.

I A.B. [name] do from my heart utterly renounce and abjure all these following positions or doctrines.

(1) That the pope is infallible in defining questions or controversies of faith.

(2) That councils[17] being called and confirmed by the pope, by virtue of such confirmation, obliges all Christians to observe their decrees, without the consent and approbation of particular churches and kingdoms.

(3) That the pope has authority, at least in some special cases, to depose princes from their sovereignty and that it is rendered lawful for any person whatsoever, on account of such deposition, to make any attempt on their lives or estates.

(4) That the duty of allegiance, whether by oath, or without it, to a sovereign prince, may either be nulled, or dispensed with, or the breach of it pardoned by the pope's authority; or that the pope, by virtue of any plenitude of power, challenged [claimed] by him, can take away the force of any laws of the land.

(5) That although the pope do not dispense with the oath of allegiance, it may be sufficient satisfaction to any man's conscience, to break that oath, if he have the opinion of several divines and casuists for the nullity, and invalidity of it.

(6) That notwithstanding any laws of the land to the contrary, any man is bound to obey or publish the Bulls of the pope: or that upon summons or citations from Rome, the persons concerned are bound to appear, and give answer there.

(7) That it is lawful in taking oaths, or giving answer before persons, authorised by the king, to make use of equivocations, or mental reservations.

---

[17] I.e. general councils of the church.

(8) That it is lawful not to keep faith with heretical princes, or subjects in case either pope or councils absolve men from the faith given or promised, or declare that they had no power to require or give it.

(9) The seal of confession not only extends to all sins past, and truly repented of, but even to future treasons and conspiracies not reported of, but still intended to be put in execution.

(10) That any having received the order of priesthood in the Roman Church, or entered into religious orders, with vows of obedience to their superiors, are thereby, and without and against the consent of the civil power, exempt from subjection and obedience to civil authority, and not accountable for their disobedience and other criminal actions, as other subjects are.

(11) That the oath prescribed in the Roman pontifical, to be taken by every bishop at his consecration, is a lawful oath, so as to bind in conscience, notwithstanding any duty of allegiance, or any oath the same person hath taken, or may take to his natural prince, if the pope judge the one to contradict the other.

Advertisements.

(1) That since the king, not the pope, is our only true supreme lord on earth, peradventure it were also advisable to make it treason for any of the king's subjects to take the said oath, or obey any that hitherto at any time has taken it, or shall hereafter take it.

(2) And if so, why should it not in like manner be advisable to make it treason for any of the said subjects, deliberately to assert, maintain, or defend by word, writing, or otherwise, any kind of authority in the pope for deposing the king, or raising his subjects in arms against him.[18]

(3) Whatever be thought of either of these advertisements, it must be always supposed, that the above Test was never intended for all English priests universally without exception; because not for those English priests who are withal Jesuits, i.e. of that special regular order, institute, or society, called by themselves the Society of Jesus.

---

[18] A note in the margin reads: 'The Third Estate of France voted for such an act in their kingdom, and had carried it, if Cardinal Perron had not interposed by his elegant but ill-grounded speech.'

Philanthropy

1675. 'Philanthropoy or The Christian Philosopher's' [sic]; endorsed 'Phil 75'. MS Locke, c. 27, fo. 30. Printed in Sina 1972, pp. 59–61; Milton 1993, pp. 65–6; Wootton 1993, pp. 232–4. This paper may be a statement of intent for a philosophical society, though only the title and one sentence near the end explicitly indicate this. It is a reflection on the things which distort the pursuit of truth: compare *ECHU*, bk iv.

Mankind is supported in the ways of virtue or vice by the society he is of, and the conversation he keeps, example and fashion being the great governors of this world. The first question every man ought to ask in all things he doth, or undertakes, is, how is this acceptable to God? But the first question most men ask, is, how will this render me to my company, and those, whose esteem I value? He that asks neither of these questions is a melancholy rogue, and always of the most dangerous, and worst of men. This is the foundation of all the sects and orders, either of religion or philosophy, that have been in the world. Men are supported, and delighted, with the friendship, and protection, they enjoy, from all the rest of the same way; and as these are more or less really performed amongst them, so the party increaseth or diminisheth. The Protestant religion whilst it was a sect and a party, cherished and favoured each other; [and] increased strangely against all the power and persecution of the Church of Rome. But since the warmth of that is over, and 'tis embraced only as a truer doctrine, this last forty years hath hardly produced as many converts from the Romish fopperies; the greater clergy plainly inclining to go back to their interest, which is highest exalted in that religion; but the greater part of the laity, having an abhorrence to their cruelty and ambition, as well as their interests contrary, have divided themselves into sects and churches, of new and different names and ways; that they may keep up some warmth, and heat, in opposition to the common enemy, who otherwise was like to find us all asleep. The Quakers are a great instance, how little truth and reason operates upon mankind, and how great force society and conversation hath amongst those that maintain an inviolable friendship and concern, for all of their way. 'Tis a true proverb, what is every man's business, is no man's. This befalls truth, she hath no sect, no corporation, 'tis made no man's interest to own her: there is no body of men, no council sitting that should take care of him that suffers for her; the clergy have pretended to that care, for many hundreds of years past; but how well they have performed it the world knows; they have found a mistress, called the present[19] power, that pays them much better than truth can. Whatever she enjoins, they offer us to be worshipped as this great goddess; and their impudence hath been so great that though they vary it as often as the present power itself changeth, yet they affirm it still to be the same goddess, truth. Neither is it possible that the greatest part of that sort of men should not either flatter the magistrate, or the people: in both truth suffers. Learning is a trade that most men apply themselves to with pains and charge, that they may hereafter live, and make advantage by it: 'tis natural for trade, to go to the best market: truth and money, truth and hire, did never yet long agree. These thoughts moved us [to] endeavour to associate ourselves with such as are lovers of truth, and virtue, that we may encourage, assist, and support each other, in the ways of them; and may possibly become some help in the preserving truth, religion and virtue amongst us; whatever deluge of misery and mischief may overrun this part of the world. We intermeddle not with anything that concerns the just and legal power of the civil magistrate; the government and laws of our country cannot be injured by such as love truth, virtue, and justice; we think ourselves obliged to lay down our lives and fortunes in the defence of it. No man can say he loves God that loves not his neighbour; no man can love his neighbour that loves not his country. 'Tis the greatest charity to preserve the laws, and rights of the nation, whereof we are. A good man, and a charitable man, is to give to every man his due. From the king upon the throne, to the beggar in the street.

Catholic Infallibility

1675. Headed 'Queries'; endorsed 'Queries Popery 75'. MS Locke, c. 27, fos. 32–3. Not in Locke's hand; authorship not definite. Printed in Sina 1972, pp. 62–4. These notes show Locke's distaste

---

[19] The MS has 'praes', which Sina transcribes as 'priest'.

for the Catholic doctrine of infallibility. Note that before the nineteenth century many Catholics believed that infallibility lay in the general council of the church, rather than in the pope personally.

(1) Whether there be any infallible judge on earth.

(2) Whether any church be that judge.

(3) Whether the Roman church be that church.

(4) If it be, what capacity, whether the infallibility be in the pope as the head, or in the body of the church, and then whether in the whole body diffusive or in the collective in a council, and if a council be infallible, then whether it be so only with the pope's confirmation, or without it.

(5) How shall we certainly know who must be members of it, clergy and laics, or only clergy, or only bishops, presbyters too and deacons, or chorepiscopy[20] at least, for we find all these usually subscribing.

(6) Or let the council be as they would have it; how shall I be sure they are infallible, for are they so absolutely infallible as they cannot determine falsely *in rebus fidei* [in matters of faith], do what they will.

(7) How shall I know when they determine aright, and what is required to a synodical constitution; must all concur in the votes, or will the major part serve the turn.

(8) What makes a council general; must all the bishops of the Christian world be called.

(9) When they are all called must they all come, or else it is no general council.

(10) Who must call the general council, the pope or the Christian king, and emperors, and how shall I be assured which of them must.

(11) How far are those determinations infallible, whether in matters of fact as well as faith.

(12) And if in matters of faith then whether in fundamentals only or in superstructures.

(13) How shall I infallibly know which points are fundamental, which not.

(14) But admit all these were determined, and our infallible judge were a general council with the pope, yet in a time of schism where

---

[20] A country bishop in the early church, a suffragan bishop serving the hinterland of a city.

there are two or three popes at once: Clement III, Gregory VII; Gelasius II, Gregory VIII; Celestine II, Honorius II; Anacletus II, Innocent II; Victor IV, Alexander III; Clement VII, Urban VI; Eugene IV, Felix V:[21] you may see [in] Gautior the Jesuit's book[22] a large catalogue more, and these warring one against another for forty or fifty years together: so that the learnedest clergymen alive know not which was St Peter's true successor, and thus saith reason there may be again, then I ask how I shall know which is the infallible judge or by what rule a Romanist may tell when a truth is defined and when not, since Sixtus V defined one Bible to be true *anno* 1590, and Clement V another two years after and each of them prohibited and condemned all but his own; and these two Bibles contain many contradictions each to other and certainly contradictory propositions cannot both be Gospel and if not then either one of these two was not really (whence inconveniency enough will follow) or they were both true popes, and so both these definitions true, and so no true papist hath any true Bible.

(15) But suppose there be no schism and all agreed on the pope and a general council met, how shall I be sure that he that is reputed pope is so indeed, seeing by their own principles secret simony makes him none, so [says] the Bull of Pope Julius II *Super simoniaca Papae Electione si contigerit . . .* [*Concerning the Simoniacal Election of the Pope . . .*], and that he was not simoniacal it is impossible for me to know;[23] the election of Sixtus V was notoriously simoniacal, for Cardinal D'Essy, whom he bribed and promised to obey and defend against any opposite faction etc., sent all these obligations subscribed by Sixtus V [in] his own hand to Philip then king of Spain, who in the year 1599 sent to Rome to bid the cardinals who had been elected before Sixtus V come to the see, to come to a council at Seville in Spain where the original writing was produced and the crime was evidently proved, and if so all the cardinals which

---

[21] One of each of these pairs is deemed by the Catholic Church an antipope; the first five pairs date from the late eleventh to mid-twelfth centuries, the final two pairs from the late fourteenth and mid-fifteenth centuries. Locke does not mention the popes of the early fifteenth century when three simultaneously claimed the title. I have anglicised papal names.

[22] I am unable to identify this.

[23] The Bull is dated 1505; it is generally acknowledged that Julius's own election was simoniacal.

were made by this Sixtus were in reality no cardinals, and then all the popes which have been really are no popes.

(16) But admit it the pope were certainly known to be such, that neither he nor any of his predecessor came in by simony, yet how shall I know whether those bishops, who with him make up a council, are bishops. Indeed, for if they be no bishops then it is no council. And that they are true bishops it is for ever impossible for any papist certainly to know, for if he that did ordain them did not intend it when he gave orders.[24] And whether he did or no, God only knows, then by their own principles, they are no bishops and by consequence no council.

(17) How shall I know that the pope and bishops so met (at Trent for example)[25] are Christians, for, if not, then they are no legislative council or church representative, and that they are Christians it is impossible for any Catholic to know with any infallible certainty, for if they be not baptised then I am sure with them they are no Christians, and if the priest that baptised them did not intend to do it then by the canon of the Trent Council's they are not baptised. Now what the priest intended when he administered that sacrament 'tis impossible that any (save God that knows the heart) should certainly know without immediate revelation which they pretend not to, and consequently 'tis impossible that any of them should certainly know that ever there was a pope or a bishop or a priest since our saviour's days. Nay impossible that they should know whether there be now one Christian in their church and therefore much less that there is or hath been a lawful council.

(18) But admit all these doubts were clearly resolved and a council (in their own sense lawful) sitting and determining matters in controversy, yet how shall we know certainly that these are their determinations, specially since the Greek Church near 300 years since accused the Roman for forcing a canon into the Nicene Councils[26] in behalf of the popes being head of the universal church,

---

[24] In this and the following paragraph Locke refers to the Roman Catholic principle of 'defect of intention', whereby an action may be deemed null and void if the agent did not intend what was outwardly done. (Annulments of marriage today are often made on this ground.)

[25] The Council of Trent (1545–63) was the great council which launched the Counter-Reformation.

[26] Early general councils of the church, held in AD 325 and 787.

which could never be found in the authentic copies, though the African bishops sent to Constantinople, Alexandria, and Antioch to search for them, Codex Can. Eccles. afri. Iustel p. 39, 40.[27] We must rely on the honesty of the amanuensis or of those persons that convey them to us, and those are certainly not infallible, and we know there are Indices Expurgatory, [and] foisting in and blotting out of manuscripts.

(19) But admit all this cleared, yet when I have indeed the genuine canons and am sure of it, how shall I be assured of the true meaning of them for we know that Voga and Soto[28] (two famous and learned men in the Council of Trent) writ and defended contradictory opinions, yet each thinketh the canon of the council to determine on his side, now of necessity one of them must mistake the doctrine of the council, unless you will say the council determined contradictions and then the council is not infallible itself, and if either of them mistook the council, then it was not an infallible guide to him; now if learned men who were members of the council (such as disputed much in it) could not infallibly know the meaning of it, how can I who am neither?

(20) What necessity of an infallible judge at all; the Christian world had no such judge for 325 years, for the Nicene Council was the first general [council] and if they understood Scripture and were saved then, when they had no such thing, why may not we now? and if they were not saved, the Church of Rome must blot our many hundreds and thousands of saints and martyrs out of her martyrology.

Till these twenty questions be infallibly resolved it seems impossible that any man should have any infallible knowledge of the Church of Rome's infallibility.

Toleration A

c. 1675. Adversaria 1661, pp. 125, 270–1. The first of these passages is untitled; the second has a marginal keyword, 'Toleration'. Mostly printed in King 1829, pp. 287–91; 1830, II, 82–92; extract

[27] Probably Henri Justel, *Bibliotheca Juris Canonici Veteris* (Paris, 1661). The 'Indices Expurgatory', below: the Papal Index of Banned Books. Locke's *Essay* and *Reasonableness of Christianity* were placed on the Index in the 1730s.

[28] Francisco Vargas and Domingo de Soto.

in Fox Bourne 1876, I, 156–60. King and Fox Bourne mistakenly
conflated this text with 'Sacerdos' (1698); they also omitted the
first paragraph, which has not hitherto been printed. The text is
an addition to the 1667 *Essay concerning Toleration*: the first passage
immediately follows the *Essay* and was copied into the Adversaria
1661 notebook no earlier than 1671. Locke sketches the corruption
of Christianity by the ambition of priests, and the rise of the persecution of heresy and dissent. He suggests that there has often
been an unholy alliance between priests and princes, the former
preaching the divine right of kings, the latter persecuting the
churchmen's enemies. Locke notes the propensity of priesthoods to domineer over princes, exemplified not only by the
papacy but also by the Presbyterians. There are similarities with
the themes of the 'Letter from a Person of Quality' (1675): see
Appendix below.

Methinks the clergy should, like ambassadors, endeavour to entreat,
convince, and persuade men to the truth rather than thus solicit the
magistrate to force them into their fold. This was the way that
gained admittance for Christianity and spread the religion they profess so far into the world: whereas whilst they once a week uncharit-
ably preach against, and the rest of the week as impudently rail at
their dissenting brethren, and do not endeavour by the meekness
and tender methods of the Gospel, and by the soft cords of love, to
draw men to them, but would have [illegible word] those compelled
under their jurisdiction whom they now take care to instruct in
their opinions, for I think I may say that preaching a sermon once
a week at most[?] perhaps [illegible word] doth very little towards
instructing men in the knowledge of faith, which after many years
hearing one may be still ignorant of, and is seldom effectual to
persuade them to good lives. This makes some men suspect that
'tis not the feeding of the sheep but the benefit of the fleece that
makes these men endeavour by such methods to enlarge their fold.
This I am sure is quite contrary to the first way which nursed up
Christianity.

Though the magistrate have a power of commanding or forbidding things indifferent which have a relation to religion, yet this
can only be within that church whereof he himself is a member,
who being a lawgiver in matters indifferent in the commonwealth
under his jurisdiction, as it is purely a civil society, for their peace,

is fittest also to be lawgiver in the religious society (which yet must be understood to be only a voluntary society and during every member's pleasure), in matters indifferent, for decency and order, for the peace of that too. But I do not see how hereby he hath any power to order and direct even matters indifferent in the circumstances of a worship, or within a church whereof he is not professor or member. 'Tis true he may forbid such things as may tend to the disturbance of the peace of the commonwealth to be done by any of his people, whether they esteem them civil or religious. This is his proper business; but to command or direct any circumstances of a worship as part of the religious worship which he himself does not profess nor approve, is altogether without his authority, and absurd to suppose. Can anyone think it reasonable, yea, or practicable, that a Christian prince should direct the form of Mahomedan worship, the whole religion being thought by him false and profane? and vice versa; and yet it is not impossible that a Christian prince should have Mahomedan subjects who may deserve all civil freedom; and *de facto* the Turk hath Christian subjects. As absurd would it be that a magistrate, either Popish, Protestant, Lutheran, Presbyterian, Quaker, etc. should prescribe a form to any or all of the different churches in their ways of worship. The reason whereof is because religious worship being that homage which every man pays his God, he cannot do it in any other way, nor use any other rites, ceremonies, nor forms, even of indifferent things, than he himself is persuaded are acceptable and pleasing to the God he worships; which depending upon his opinion of his God, and what will best please him, it is impossible for one man to prescribe or direct any one circumstance of it to another: and this being a thing different and independent wholly from every man's concerns in the civil society, which hath nothing to do with a man's affairs in the other world, the magistrate hath here no more right to intermeddle than any private man, and has less right to direct the form of it, than he has to prescribe to a subject of his in what manner he shall do his homage to another prince to whom he is feudatory, for something which he holds immediately from him, which, whether it be standing, kneeling, or prostrate, bareheaded or barefooted, whether in this or that habit, etc. concerns not his allegiance to him at all, nor his well government of his people. For though the things in themselves are perfectly indifferent, and it may be trivial, yet as to the worshipper, when he considers them as required by his God, or forbidden, pleasing or displeasing to the invisible power he addresses, they are by no means so, and till you have altered his opinion (which persuasion can only do) you can by no means, nor without the greatest tyranny, prescribe him a way of worship; which was so unreasonable to do, that we find little bustle about and scarce any attempts towards it by the magistrates in the several societies of mankind till Christianity was well grown up in the world, and was become a national religion; and since that [time] it hath been the cause of more disorders, tumults, and bloodshed, than all other causes put together.

But far be it from anyone to think Christ the author of those disorders, or that such fatal mischiefs are the consequence of his doctrine, though they have grown up with it. Antichrist hath sown those tares in the field of the church; the rise whereof hath been only hence, that the clergy, by degrees, as Christianity spread, affecting dominion, laid claim to a priesthood, derived by succession from Christ, and so independent from the civil power, receiving (as they pretend) by the imposition of hands, and some other ceremonies agreed on (but variously) by the priesthoods of the several factions, an indelible character, particular sanctity, and a power immediately from heaven to do several things which are not lawful to be done by other men. The chief whereof are – (1) To teach opinions concerning God, a future state, and ways of worship. (2) To do and perform themselves certain rites exclusive of others. (3) To punish dissenters from their doctrines and rules. Whereas [1] it is evident from Scripture, that all priesthood terminated in the great high priest, Jesus Christ, who was the last priest. (2) There are no footsteps in Scriptures of any so set apart, with such powers as they pretend to, after the apostles' time; nor that had any indelible character. (3) That it is to be made out, that there is nothing which a priest can do, which another man without any such ordination (if other circumstances of fitness, and an appointment to it, not disturbing peace and order, concur), may not lawfully perform and do, and the church and worship of God be preserved, as the peace of the state may be by justices of the peace, and other officers, who had no ordination, or laying on of hands, to fit them to be justices, and by taking away their commissions may cease to be so; so ministers, as well as justices, are necessary, one for the administration of religious public worship, the other of civil justice; but an indelible character, peculiar sanctity of the function, or a power immediately derived from heaven, is not necessary, or as much as convenient, for either.

But the clergy (as they call themselves, of the Christian religion, in imitation of the Jewish priesthood) having, almost ever since the first ages of the church, laid claim to this power, separate from civil government, as received from God himself, have, wherever the civil magistrate hath been Christian and of their opinion, and superior in power to the clergy, and they not able to cope with him, pretended this power only to be spiritual, and to extend no further; but yet still pressed, as a duty on the magistrate, to punish and persecute those whom they disliked and declared against. And so when they excommunicated, their under officer, the magistrate, was to execute; and to reward princes for this doing their drudgery, they have (whenever princes have been serviceable to their ends) been careful to preach up monarchy *jure divino* [by divine right]; for commonwealths have hitherto been less favourable to their power. But notwithstanding the *jus divinum* [divine right] of monarchy, when any prince hath dared to dissent from their doctrines or forms, or been less apt to execute the decrees of the hierarchy, they have been the first and forwardest in giving check to his authority, and disturbance to his government. And princes, on the other side, being apt to hearken to such as serve to advance their authority, and bring in religion to the assistance of their absolute power, have been generally very ready to worry those sheep who have ever so little straggled out of those shepherds' folds, where they were kept in order to be shorn by them both, and to be howled on, both upon subjects and neighbours at their pleasure: and hence have come most of those calamities which have so long disturbed and wasted Christendom. Whilst the magistrate, being persuaded it is his duty to punish those the clergy please to call heretics, schismatics, or fanatics, or else taught to apprehend danger from dissension in religion, thinks it his interest to suppress them; [and] persecutes all who observe not the same forms in the religious worship which is set up in his country. The people, on the other side, finding the mischiefs that fall on them for worshipping God according to their own persuasions, enter into confederacies and combinations to secure themselves as well as they can; so that oppression and vexation on one side, self-defence and desire of religious liberty on the other, create dislikes, jealousies, apprehensions, and factions, which seldom fail to break out into downright persecution, or open war.

But notwithstanding the liberality of the clergy to princes, when they have not strength enough to deal with them, be very large; yet when they are once in a condition to strive with them for the mastery, then is it seen how far their spiritual power extends, and how, *in ordine ad spiritualia* [into the spiritual order], absolute temporal power comes in. So that ordination, that begins in priesthood, if it be let alone, will certainly grow up to absolute empire; and though Christ declares himself to have no kingdom of this world, his successors have (whenever they can but grasp the power) a large commission to execute, and that a rigorously civil dominion. The popedom hath been a large and lasting instance of this. And what Presbytery could do, even in its infancy when it had a little humbled the magistrate, let Scotland show.

Obligation of Penal Laws

25 February 1676. Marginal keywords: 'Obligation of Penal Laws', 'Lex Humana'. MS Locke, f. 1, pp. 123–6. Printed in King 1829, pp. 57–9; 1830, I, 114–17; Wootton 1993, pp. 234–6. This paper is an important measure of Locke's political opinions at this time. It is conservative in tone, showing no hint of a right of resistance, and suggesting that the transition to the *Two Treatises of Government* was abrupt. Locke does, however, stress that most human laws are purely regulatory, and that divine authority cannot be invoked beyond the general duty of obeying governments which uphold civil peace and mutual preservation. Similarly, no particular form of government has divine sanction.

There are virtues and vices antecedent to, and abstract from, society, e.g. love of God, unnatural lust: other virtues and vices there are that suppose society and laws, as obedience to magistrates, or dispossessing a man of his heritage. In both these the rule and obligation is antecedent to human laws, though the matter about which that rule is, may be consequent to them, as property in land, distinction and power of persons, etc.

All things not commanded or forbidden by the law of God are indifferent, nor is it in the power of man to alter their nature; and so no human law can lay any new obligation on the conscience, and therefore all human laws are purely penal, i.e. have no other obligation but to make the transgressors liable to punishment in this life. All divine laws oblige the conscience, i.e. render the transgressors liable to answer at God's tribunal, and receive punishment at his hands. But because very frequently both these obligations concur, and the same action comes to be commanded or forbidden by both laws together, and so in these cases men's consciences are obliged, men have thought that civil laws oblige their consciences to entire obedience; whereas, in things in their own nature indifferent, the conscience is obliged only to active or passive obedience, and that not by virtue of that human law which the man either practises or is punished by, but by that law of God which forbids disturbance or dissolution of governments. The Gospel alters not in the least civil affairs, but leaves husband and wife, master and servant, magistrate and subject, every one of them, with the very same power and privileges that it found them, neither more nor less. And therefore when the New Testament says, obey your superiors in all things, etc. [Col. 3:18–22], it cannot be thought that it laid any new obligation upon the Christians after their conversion, other than what they were under before; nor that the magistrate had any other extent of jurisdiction over them than over his heathen subjects: so that the magistrate has the same power still over his Christian as he had [over] his heathen subjects; so that, when he had power to command, they had still, notwithstanding the liberty and privileges of the Gospel, obligation to obey.

Now, to heathen politics (which cannot be supposed to be instituted by God for the preservation and propagation of true religion) there can be no other end assigned but the preservation of the members of that society in peace and safety together. This being found to be the end will give us the rule of civil obedience. For if the end of civil societies be civil peace, the immediate obligation of every subject must be to preserve that society or government which was ordained to produce it; and no member of any society can possibly have any obligation of conscience beyond this. So that he that obeys the magistrate to that degree as not to endanger or disturb the government, under what form of government soever he lives, fulfils all the law of God concerning government, i.e. obeys to the utmost [all] that the magistrate or society can oblige his conscience, which can be supposed to have no other rule set it by God in this matter but this. The end of the institution being always the measure of operation.

The obligation of conscience then upon every subject being to preserve the government, 'tis plain that where any law is made with a penalty, is submitted to, i.e. the penalty is quietly undergone without other obedience, the government cannot be disturbed or endangered. For whilst the magistrate has power to increase the penalty, even to loss of life, and the subject submits patiently to the penalty, which he in conscience is obliged to do, the government can never be in danger, nor can the public want active obedience in any case where it hath power to require it under pain of death. For no man can be supposed to refuse his active obedience in a lawful or indifferent thing, when the refusal will cost him his life, and lose all his civil rights at once, for want of performing one civil action; for civil laws have only to do with civil actions.

This, thus stated, clears a man from that infinite number of sins that otherwise he must unavoidably be guilty of, if all penal laws oblige the conscience further than this.

One thing further is to be considered, that all human laws are penal, for where the penalty is not expressed, it is by the judge to be proportioned to the consequence and circumstances of the fault. See the practice of the King's Bench. Penalties are so necessary to civil laws, that God found it necessary to annex them even to the civil laws he gave the Jews.[29]

Pleasure, Pain, the Passions

16 July 1676. MS Locke, f. 1, pp. 325–47. Mostly in shorthand. Printed in Von Leyden 1954, pp. 265–72; the title and transcription are Von Leyden's. Lough 1953 records it as 'Passions'. Locke has several marginal keywords: 'Passions, Love, Desire, Hope, Hatred, Pain, Pleasure, Weariness, Vexation, Sorrow, Grief, Torment, Melancholy, Anxiety, Anguish, Misery, Mirth, Delight, Joy, Comfort, Happiness, Misery, Bonum, Pleasure, Desire, Power, Will'. This is a preparatory paper for the *ECHU*, as its final phrase

---

[29] Locke adds a reference which I cannot identify: 'vide Att: plea for ye Mag. p. 101'.

indicates. See *ECHU*, bk II, chs. 20–1. Its theme occurs in the fourth of the *Essays on the Law of Nature*, but is not developed in 'Draft B' of *ECHU*. It marks a turn in Locke's thinking towards an hedonic account of the psychological groundwork of ethics.

In *voluptas* and *dolor*, pleasure and pain, I mean principally that of the mind, there are two roots out of which all passions spring and a centre on which they all turn. Where they are removed, the passions would all cease, having nothing left to wind them up or set them going. To know our passions, then, and to have right ideas of them, we ought to consider pleasure and pain and the things that produce them in us, and how they operate and move us.

God has [so] framed the constitutions of our minds and bodies that several things are apt to produce in both of them pleasure and pain, delight and trouble, by ways that we know not, but for ends suitable to his goodness and wisdom. Thus the smell of roses and the tasting of wine, light and liberty, the possession of power and the acquisition of knowledge please most men, and there are some things whose very being and existence delights others, as children and grandchildren. So that where anything offers itself to the understanding as capable to produce pleasure, there it constantly and immediately produces love, which seems to be nothing but the consideration or having in the mind the idea of some thing that is able in some way of application to produce delight or pleasure in us. It is true there accompanies this thought as well as all other passions a particular motion of the blood and spirits, but that being such as is not always observed nor a necessary ingredient of the idea of any passion, it is not necessary here, where we are only seeking the ideas of the passions, to inquire into it. To love, then, is nothing but to have in our mind the idea of something which we consider as capable to produce satisfaction or delight in us, for when a man says he loves roses, wine, or knowledge, what does he mean else but that the smells of roses, the taste of wine, and knowledge delight him or produce pleasure in him, and so of all other things? Indeed, because man considers that that particular thing that delights him cannot be had without the preservation of several others that are annexed to it or go to the producing of it, he is said to love them when he wishes and endeavours to preserve them. Thus men are said to love the trees that produce the fruit they are delighted with, and thus they often love their friends with whose good offices or conversation they are delighted, endeavouring and wishing their good, thereby to preserve to themselves those things they have pleasure in; which though we call love of their friends is not truly love of their persons but a care to preserve with their persons and friendship those good things which they do love and which they cannot have without them. For we often see that, when the good offices cease, love to the person often dies and sometimes turns into hatred, which does not so in our love to our children, because nature for wise ends of her own has made us so that we are delighted with the very being of our children. Some wise minds are of a nobler constitution, having pleasure in the very being and the happiness of their friends, and some yet of a more excellent make [are] delighted with the existence and happiness of all good men, some with that of all mankind in general, and this last may be said properly to love. Others with their *amor concupiscentiae* [sexual appetite] are only provident, so that in this and, I believe, in all other instances love will be found to take its rise and extent only from objects of pleasure and to be nothing else but having in our minds the idea of something that is so suited to our particular make and temper as to be fit to produce pleasure in us. This gives us the reason why love, the principal and first [of] all passions, is the most untractable of all the rest and to be represented as blind. Desire and hope, though their proper and ultimate objects be the same with that of love, yet they may be prevailed on by reason and consider ation to fix upon painful and troublesome things when they may be a means to another end; but talk, reason, and consider as much as you will, love is not moved till you propose something that in itself is delightful. Many have desired to take off a limb and in some cases have desired and hoped for pains, as in childbirth, but I think nobody was ever in love with them. Love fixes only upon an end and never embraces any object purely as serviceable to some other purpose, nor could it be otherwise, since it is a sympathy of the soul and is nothing but the union of the mind with the idea of something that has a secret faculty to delight it, and whenever such an idea is in the mind and considered there as such, then it is that we properly exercise the passion of love.

Hatred is placed directly opposite to love, and so there needs not much ado to find that it is nothing but the presence of an idea in the mind considered as naturally disposed to disease and vex us and has the same effect that love [has], for when that that troubles us cannot be separated from the thing it is in, hatred often carries us to desire and endeavour the destruction of the thing, as love for the same reason carries us to desire and endeavour its preservation. But this passion of hatred usually carries us further and with more violence than that of love, because the sense of evil or pain works more upon us than that of good or pleasure; we bear the absence of a great pleasure more easily than the presence of a little pain. Ἀναισθησία[30] is not in the middle between pleasure and pain; insensibility that is not perpetual is reckoned on the better side: sleep, that always robs us of the sense of our enjoyments, is never complained of, but when it gives a cessation from any of our pains we take it for a pleasure.

The pleasure and pain I spoke so much of here is principally that of the mind, for impressions made on the body, if they reach not the mind, produce neither pain nor pleasure. As the mind is delighted or disturbed, so have we pain or pleasure. Whatever motions may be produced in the body from some degree of heat that causes pleasure by its application to one hand moderately cold [and] causes great pain being applied at the same time to the other hand very much chilled with snow, and at the same time a sudden occasion of great joy or sorrow supervening, neither of them is felt. That pleasure or pain coming from the body is quite lost and perishes as soon as the mind ceases to be affected by them or to take notice of them.

This pleasure and pain, *dolor* and *voluptas animi*, distinguished by several degrees and other circumstances, i.e. made into several complex ideas, come to have several names; some, whereby to show these two simple ideas a little more clearly, it cannot be amiss to mention. For instance, a pain of the mind, when it arises from the long continuance of anything, is called weariness; when from some small cause, whereof the mind is very sensible, vexation; when from a thing that is past, sorrow; when from the loss of a friend, grief; when from a violent pain of the body, torment; when it hinders discourse and conversation, melancholy; when accompanied with a great feebleness, anxiety; when very violent, anguish; when it is the

---

[30] Lack of sensation, insensibility.

utmost we can conceive without any mixture of comfort, misery. There are several other differences of this idea that is disagreeable to the mind and more names to distinguish it than there are of the pleasures, because we are more sensible of, and in this world more accustomed to, pain than to pleasure. On the other side, this pleasure of the mind, when it arises from light causes, especially in conversation, is called mirth; when from the presence of agreeable sensible objects, delight; when from the consideration of some great and solid good, joy; when [from] some precedent sorrow which it removes, comfort; and when perfect and free from all trouble, happiness. So that happiness and misery seem to me wholly to consist in this pleasure and pain of the mind, of which every little trouble or satisfaction is a degree; and the completion of either is when the mind to the highest degree and utmost capacity is filled and possessed by the ideas of either kind.

Thus we see from the simple ideas of pain and pleasure which we find in our minds, when extended and enlarged, we get the ideas of happiness and misery, for whatsoever makes any part of our happiness or misery, that which produces in us any pleasure or pain, that is so far properly and in its own nature good, and whatsoever serves anyway to procure anything of happiness to us that is also good, though the first is that which is called *bonum jucundum* [the pleasurable good], which ought not to be understood only in reference to the body, but, as we have used the name pleasure, as belonging principally to the mind. And under the latter are comprehended two other sorts of good which are called *utile* [useful] and *honestum* [honest], which, were they not ordained by God to procure the *jucundum* [pleasure] and be a means to help us to happiness, at least in some degrees of it, I do not see how they would be reckoned good at all. What good were there more in diamonds than pebbles, if they cannot procure us more of those things that are pleasant and agreeable than pebbles will? What makes temperance a good and gluttony an evil but that the one serves to procure us health and ease in this world and happiness in the other, when gluttony does quite the contrary? And repentance and sorrow for some would have but very little good in it, if it were not a means and way to our happiness.

If it were not beside our present purpose, we might here observe that we have no clear and distinct ideas of pleasure but such as we have felt in ourselves. The imagination of fuller and greater is but by way of similitude and resemblance to those we have experimented, and so are confused and obscure, not being able clearly to conceive the pleasure which unknown objects can produce in us (the pleasure that is in tasting of pineapple or in having children to those that are not experimented being very hard to be fancied); and how much more inconceivable are the pleasures of spiritual objects (which certainly as more proportioned to the nature of the mind are more capable to touch and move it with lovely and ravishing delights) to us [who], being immersed in the body and beset with material objects, when they are continually importuning us, have very little sense or perception of spiritual things, which are as it were at a distance and affect us but seldom; and therefore it is that I believe that our idea of happiness, such as the blessed enjoy and such as we are capable of, is very imperfect in this world; yet such as it is leaves us inexcusable and under the brand and condemnation of the greatest folly, if we use not our greatest care and endeavours to obtain it. But this *in transitu* [in passing].

To return to our ideas of the passions. The mind finding in itself the ideas of several objects which, if enjoyed, would produce pleasure, i.e. the ideas of the several things it loves, contemplating the satisfaction which would arise to itself in the actual enjoyment or application of some one of those things it loves and the possibility or feasibleness of the present enjoyment, or doing something toward the procuring the enjoyment, of that good, observes in itself some uneasiness or trouble or displeasure till it be done, and this is that we call desire, so that desire seems to me to be a pain the mind is in till some good, whether *jucundum* or *utile*, which it judges possible and seasonable, be obtained.

To have the clearer idea of this passion, it cannot be amiss to consider that desire is of far less extent than love, for love, being but the looking on anything as delightful or capable to produce pleasure in us, embraces at once whatever appears to be so, whether near or remote, attainable or not. But desire, terminating in enjoyment, is moved with nothing further than as it is capable of present enjoyment or may present a means towards it.

Desire also, which, as I have said, is nothing but a pain the mind suffers in the absence of some good, is increased and varied by divers considerations; for instance, when it is in pursuit of a positive good, the first consideration that sets it on work or at least quickens it is the possibility, for we have little desire for what we once conceive impossible. It is true, men sometimes wish for roses in winter and that their daughters were sons, which is no more but saying or thinking that such things, if they were possible, might please them, but when they consider them as impossible, not having them leaves but little trouble upon their mind, and so little desire. But in the desire of the removal of some present evil it is quite otherwise, for there, the evil causing a constant pain, there is a constant desire to be eased of it, whether it be considered as possible or no. Whereby we might see how much desire consists in pain.

If possibility excite our desire, easiness of attainment is certainly a further incentive to it, which we very much judge of by the season wherein such things used to be had and the enjoyments of others of the same good. Thus men, that wish but for health and strength to their children when infants, desire obedience and docility in them in their youth, and skill or knowledge and preferment when they are grown up.

Another thing that governs and regulates our desire is the greatness or smallness of the good, which is not estimated barely as it is in itself or as it has naturally a fitness to produce pleasure in us or is a fit means in itself to procure it, but as it is consistent with other enjoyments that we have. Love, indeed, extends itself universally to all that has the appearance of being able to do us good, i.e. produce pleasure in us, because it lies barely in the contemplation and so may extend itself to things incompatible and inconsistent: it being as easy to have the ideas of the pleasures of company and conversation and play with those of retirement and study and contemplation, and consequently to love them both at once, as it is to have at once the ideas of white and black, which never yet exist and not together in the same subject. But desire employing itself only about the actual enjoyment of some good which consists in actual existence and application, which bears not with contrarieties, it very much is regulated by the agreement or contrariety it is conceived to have with other good things we either enjoy or desire.

The simple ideas we have from the mind are thinking, power, pleasure, and pain. Of thinking we have spoken already,[31] and to

---

[31] In a journal entry, 13 July 1676: Aaron and Gibb 1936, pp. 80–1. There Locke's 'simple ideas' are perception (or thinking), willing, pleasure, and pain.

understand what the idea of power is and how we come by it, it will be convenient to consider action a little, which is always a product of power. There seems, then, to me to be but two sorts of actions in the world, viz. that which belongs and is peculiar to matter or body and that is motion, and thought which is proper only to the soul. Motion though it be a property of body, yet body in itself is indifferent to it, so that it can indifferently be in motion or in rest but cannot move itself, and, on the other side, though thinking be a property of the soul, yet the soul is indifferent to think or not to think. This, I say, I imagine, speaking of the soul and finite spirits, that, thinking being their action, it is not necessary to conceive that they would be always in action, i.e. think, any more than that a body would be always in motion. But be that as it will, this is certain, that the inherent inseparable property of the soul is a power to act, i.e. a power to produce some motions in the body and some thoughts in the mind. Thus a man finds that he can rise out of a seat where he sat still and walk, and so produce a motion that is not before, and can also at pleasure, being in France, think of England or Italy, of respiration, playing at cards, the sun, Julius Caesar, anger, etc., and so produce in his mind thoughts that are not there before; and so by this means and this experience within itself the mind comes by the idea of power. I grant the mind, in a waking man, is never without thought, but whether sleep without dreaming be not an affection of mind as well as body may be thought worth an inquiry by one who considers that it is hard to imagine that the soul should think and not be conscious of it, and that it will be difficult to give a reason why the soul out of the body cannot be in a state without perceiving any ideas and wholly insensible of any pleasure or pain, as well as in the body. But to put by this speculation and that other whether the primary and inseparable affection of spirit be not power as that of matter is extension, I say one of the simple ideas that a man gets from the observation of what passes within himself is that of power, which when it exerts itself in consequence of any thought is called the will; which happens not always, for the several notions in our sleep and the first thoughts we have when we wake, being without choice or deliberation and not consequent to any precedent thought, cannot be ascribed to the will or be counted voluntary. By these steps and by such observations of its own internal operations it is that the mind comes to have the ideas of pain, pleasure, thinking, power, and will (memo., all this about these ideas should come in before the discourse of the passions).

Atheism

29 July 1676. The passage has four marginal headings: 'Essay Morall', 'A Deity', 'God', 'Atheisme'. Listed by Lough 1953 as 'A Deity'. MS Locke, f. 1, pp. 367–70. Incompletely printed in Aaron and Gibb 1936, pp. 81–2. Locke's subject is the unreasonableness of atheism; he offers a version of Pascal's wager. The author upon whom Locke is commenting is Pierre Nicole, whose *Essais de Morale* he translated at this time.

I shall only add that if perhaps the proofs of our author, which I think are very clear and cogent, are not yet perfect demonstrations, and that after all there will remain some doubts and difficulties unresolved, it is not reasonable for anyone to reject the doctrine of a deity, and the immortality of the soul, [which] if he will be true to himself he cannot part with, because he can raise some objections against it, till he hath established some other hypothesis upon surer foundations made out by clearer evidence and deduction of reason, and wherein there are not to be found any such difficulties as he pretends frights him from the embracing of this. If he doth otherwise 'tis to be suspected that there is some secret and strong bias that inclines him the other way, and it must needs be some great irregularity that must force a man against his reason, ⟨there is nothing but a wilful prejudice and shameless imposing on himself can make a man⟩ ⟨which always follows the more probable side, and makes him⟩[32] in the great concernment of religion and happiness take a course quite contrary and proceed by other measures than he doth in all his other persuasions and the ordinary affairs of his life, wherein no one thinks himself at liberty to reject any doctrine or excused from acting suitable to it because he cannot clear some doubts he has about it, so long as the contrary opinion involves gross absurdities and manifest contradictions. There are difficulties about matter and motion so great that I believe the wit of man will

---

[32] Locke inserted the first bracketed passage but did not delete the second; the sentence should be read using one or other.

of man will never be able to resolve and yet, for all that, men are unshaken in their persuasions that they have bodies, and sit not still till all the doubts are removed that may arise even concerning their own motions. And after all this, if anyone should so far be prevailed on by prejudice or corruption as to fancy [that] he found in the wild inconsistent thoughts of atheism less contrariety to reason and experience than in the belief of a deity, which I think is impossible, yet even then the great venture he runs in that way will always stick with a considerate [reflective] man. For suppose the seeming probability lay on the atheist's side, yet when annihilation or, which is nothing better, eternal insensibility, the best estate the atheist can hope for if he be in the right, shall be put in the balance with everlasting happiness, the reward of the religious if his persuasion deceive him not, and, on the other side, annihilation (which is the worst [that] can happen to the believer if he be mistaken) be compared with infinite misery which will certainly overtake the atheist if his opinion should happen to prove false, it would make a man very wary how he embraces an opinion where there is such unequal odds and where the consequences are of such moment and so infinitely different. This consideration, this advantage, will always be, on the side of morality and religion, necessary consequences of the belief of a god, and will never suffer anyone (who would pass for a rational creature, anyone who hath the least care or kindness for himself) in the choice he is to make of two contrary opinions to betake himself to that wherein the best he can hope is the worst [that] can follow from the other, unless compelled by plain undeniable demonstration and that one would think too should be scarce enough to persuade one to venture the loss of infinite happiness and put himself in danger of infinite eternal misery and that in exchange for and expectation of just nothing. JL

Toleration B

23 August 1676. Marginal keywords: 'Toleration', 'Peace'. MS Locke, f. 1, pp. 412–15. Printed in Von Leyden 1954, pp. 274–5. In shorthand: Von Leyden's transcription. Von Leyden aggregates this and the next two items (together with another, 'Transubstantiation') under the title 'Faith and Reason'. Locke answers objections to religious toleration and distinguishes between

civil and ecclesiastical government. Remarks which Locke attributes to an imagined opponent are placed in inverted commas.

Penal laws, made about matters of religion in a country where there is already a diversity of opinions, can hardly avoid that common injustice which is condemned in all laws whatsoever, viz. in retrospect. It would be thought a hard case, if by a law, now made, all would have to be fined that should wear French hats for the future, and those also who had worn them at any time in the year past. It is the same case to forbid a man to be a Quaker, Anabaptist, Presbyterian, for it is as easy for me not to have had on the hat yesterday, which I then wore, as it is in many cases not to have the same opinions, the same thought, in my head as I had yesterday – both being impossible. The great dispute in all this diversity of opinions is where the truth is. But let us suppose at present that it is wholly and certainly on the state's side, though it will be pretty hard to suppose it so in England, in France, Sweden, and Denmark at the same time; and yet in all these places they have an equal power to make laws about religion. But let us suppose yet that all dissenters are in error, are out of their wits, *esto*; but your law found them in this delirium, and will you make a law that will hang all that are beside themselves? 'But we fear their rage and violence.' If you fear them only because they are capable of a raging fit, you may as well fear all other men, who are liable to the same distemper. If you fear it because you treat them ill, and that produces some symptom of it, you ought to change your method, and not punish them for what you fear because you go the way to produce it. If a distemper itself has a tendency to rage, it must be watched and fit remedies applied. If they are perfect innocents, only a little crazed, why cannot they be let alone, since, though perhaps their brains are a little out of order, their hands work well enough? 'But they will infect others.' If those others are infected but by their own consent, and that to cure another disease that they think they have, why should they be hindered any more than a man is that might make an issue to cure palsy, or might willingly have haemorrhoids to prevent an apoplexy? 'But then all people will run into this error.' This supposes either that it is true and so prevails, or that the teachers of truth are very negligent and let it, and that they are to blame; or that people are more inclined to error than truth: if so, then, error being manifold, they will be as distant one from another as from you, and so no fear of their uniting, unless you force them by making yourself an enemy to all by ill-treatment.

To settle the peace of places where there are different opinions in religion, two things are to be perfectly distinguished: religion and government, and their two sorts of officers, magistrates and ministers, and their provinces, to be kept well distinct (the not doing whereof was perhaps a great cause of distraction); a magistrate only to look at the peace and security of a city, ministers only concerned with the saving of the soul, and if they were forbidden meddling with making or executing laws in their preaching, we should be perhaps much more quiet.

Faith and Reason

24–6 August 1676. Marginal keywords: 'Faith & Reason', 'Ignorance', 'Faith & Reason' (again). MS Locke, f. 1, pp. 415–21, interspersed with extracts from Gabriel Naudé. Printed in Von Leyden 1954, pp. 275–7; his transcription from shorthand. Locke discusses the relationship between reason and revelation. Compare *ECHU*, bk IV, chs. 17–18, to which it is very close.

In matters of religion it would be well, if anyone would tell how far we are to be guided by reason, and how far by faith. The want of this is one of the causes that keep up in the world so many different opinions, for every sect, as far as reason will help them, makes use of it gladly, and where it fails them, they cry out that it is [a] matter of faith and above reason. And I do not see how they can ever be convinced by any who makes use of the same plea, without setting down a strict boundary between faith and reason, which ought to be the first point established in all disputes of religion.

Q. Whether our ignorance comes from anything but the want, imperfection, or confusion of ideas? For our reason seems not to fail us but in the second case. (1) The fallacy of words in a long train of consequences, and this is our fault, not the fault of our reason; (2) the imperfection of our ideas, and there we are involved in difficulties and contradictions. Thus, not having a perfect idea of the least extension of matter, nor of infinity, we are at a loss about the divisibility of matter; but having perfect as well as clear and distinct ideas of number, our reason makes no mistakes or meets with no contradictions in numbers. Thus we, having but imperfect ideas of the first motions of our own wills or minds, and much imperfecter yet of the operations of God, run into great difficulties about 'free will', which reason cannot resolve. This perhaps may give us the measure where to appeal to faith and quit reason, which is only where, for want of clear and perfect ideas, we find ourselves involved in inextricable difficulties and contradictions of our notions, and nowhere else decided. I say of such doubts faith and revelation take the place, as they do also in the discovery of truths which reason, acting upon our natural ideas, cannot reach; for if we had but such a clear and perfect idea of the operations of God as to know whether that power would make a 'free agent', wherein, I think, lies the bottom of the question about predestination and free will, the dispute about it would quickly be determined by human reason, and faith would have little to do in the case. For in a proposition, built upon clear and perfect ideas, we need not the assistance of faith as absolutely necessary to gain our assent and introduce them to our minds; because through knowledge I have settled them there already, or am able to do it; which is the greatest assurance we can possibly have of anything, unless it be where God immediately reveals it to us: and there, too, our assurance can be no greater than our knowledge is that it is the revelation from God. And in propositions that are contrary to our clear and perfect ideas, faith will in vain endeavour to establish them or move our assent. For faith can never convince us of anything that contradicts our knowledge. Because, though faith be founded on the testimony of God (which cannot lie), yet we cannot have an assurance of the truth of it greater than our own knowledge. Since the whole strength of that certainty depends upon our knowledge that God revealed it, which, in this case, where revelation is pretended to contradict our knowledge or reason, will always have this objection hanging to it, that we cannot tell how to conceive that to come from God, the bountiful author of our being, which, if believed for true, must overturn all our principles and foundations of knowledge, render all our faculties useless, and wholly destroy the most excellent part of his workmanship, our understanding, and put a man in a condition wherein he will have less light, less conduct than the beasts that perish. Indeed, in matters above our reason, which what they are I have said, we ought not only to admit, but we stand in need of, revelation, and there faith is to govern us wholly. But this takes not away the landmarks of knowledge; this shakes not the foundations of reason, but leaves us the full use of our faculties.

And if the distinct provinces of faith and reason are not to be set out by these boundaries, I believe, in matters of religion, that there will be no use, no room, for reason at all; and those extravagant opinions and ceremonies that are to be found in the several religions of the world will not deserve to be blamed. For [to] this crying up of faith in opposition to reason, we may, I think in good measure ascribe those absurdities that fill almost all the religions which possess and divide mankind. For men having been principled with an opinion that they must not consult reason in the things of God, which were above or contrary to it, have let loose their fancies and natural superstitions, and have been by them led into so strange opinions, and extravagant practices in religion, that a considerate [reflective] man cannot but stand amazed at their follies, and judge them so far from being acceptable to God that he cannot avoid thinking them ridiculous and offensive to sober men. So that, in effect, in that wherein we should show ourselves most to be rational creatures, that which most properly should distinguish us from beasts, we appear most irrational, and more senseless than beasts themselves. *Credo, quia impossible est*[33] might, in a good man, pass for a mark of zeal, but would prove the very last rule for men to choose their opinions by.

Knowledge A

1 September 1676. Marginal keyword: 'Knowledge'. MS Locke, f. 1, pp. 430–2. Printed in Von Leyden 1954, p. 281; his transcription from shorthand. Locke considers the knowledge of God and of morality by the light of nature. Compare *ECHU*, bk IV, ch. 17, §24.

Men, by the common light of reason that is in them, know that God is the most excellent of all beings, and therefore deserves most

---

[33] 'I believe, because it is impossible', a famous remark by the Church Father Tertullian.

to be honoured and beloved, because he is good to all his creatures and all the good we receive comes from him. By the same light of nature we know also that we ought to do good to other men, because it is good for ourselves so to do. Men are capable of it, it is the only tribute we can pay to God for all the good we receive from him, and it cannot but be acceptable to God, being done for his sake, and to men whom we cannot but know that he has the same kindness for as for us. They, then, that consider that they ought to love God and be charitable to men, and do to that purpose seek to know more of him and his mysteries, that they may better perform their duty of love to him and charity to their neighbours, shall no doubt find all that God requires of them to know, and shall run into no damnable errors, but will find God and his truth. The same cannot be said of those who begin at the other end, who, giving way to their lusts, and taking their swing in the prosecution of their own desires, making themselves their own god and their own end, will not hearken to any of the truths of natural or revealed religion, till they can have all objections answered, all scruples removed, and will, if there remains but a little doubt in the whole system, reject the whole, because some one part has some difficulty. It is not, I say, likely that these men should find truth, because both they seek it unreasonably, i.e. otherwise than rational men and they themselves too do in other cases, and also they seek it not for that end for which God designed it, which is not as an improvement of our parts and speculations, but of our love of him and charity to our neighbour, and that increase of our knowledge should make our lives better.

Happiness A

26 September 1676. 'Happynesse'. MS Locke, f. 1, pp. 445-7. Imperfectly printed in Driscoll 1972, pp. 101-2.

There is not that thing in the world which men hunt after and place great value on which hath not been exposed by the pen of some writer or other. The vanity of honour, the emptiness of riches, and the sordidness, shame and dissatisfaction of sensual pleasures have been sufficiently discoursed of and made evident, not only by Christian writers but even heathen philosophers. This proceeds not from the omnipotent wit of man which can turn everything into ridicule that it pleases, and by the dress and light it bestows on things make them appear handsome or ugly as it pleases, but from this, that in all those things there is really a deficiency or dark side which whoever has the skill to show cannot fail to produce contempt or dislike of it. We are so remote from true and satisfying happiness in this world that we know not wherein it consists, but yet so much we apprehend it that we are sure it is beyond what all those imperfect things can afford us. Since it is such that nobody yet hath attempted to write against it, to discredit it, or give mankind any disgust of it, everyone being by the strong impressions he finds in his own mind convinced that happiness is a state that hath no imperfection, nor [is] liable to any exception.

Politica

14 October 1676. Marginal keyword: 'Politica'. MS Locke, f. 1, p. 469. Transcribed from shorthand by J.R. Milton.

Beware of excise or any other indetermined tax because upon [the] people's charge it maintains [an] army of enemies to [the] people's liberty. Let therefore every parish know it[s] tax precisely and let [the] inhabitants be collectors of it.

Atlantis

1676–9. There are several notes headed 'Atlantis' scattered through Locke's journals: MS Locke, f. 1, pp. 280 (12 June 1676), 319 (14 July 1676); f. 2, pp. 289 (4 October 1677), 296–8 (14 October 1677); f. 3, pp. 92 (31 March 1678), 95 (2 April 1678), 142–3 (26 May 1678), 198–201 (15 July 1678); BL, Add. MS 15,642, pp. 13–14 (14 February 1679), 18–22 (20–1 February 1679); MS Locke, c. 42B, p. 36 (1679). Locke deleted a number of passages: these are included below in angle brackets. Two entries are brief notes on Locke's anthropological reading and are not printed here: f. 3, pp. 92 and 95 are drawn from François Pyrard's *Voyage aux Indes Orientales* (1679) – in the Maldives those who do not obey the magistrate's summons are ostracised; in 'Calecut' the king is sole judge, and 'where there are no lawyers there are very few law suits'. The 1676–7 and the 1679 (MS c. 42B) notes have not hitherto been printed; the

26 May 1678 note is in Fox Bourne 1876, I, 387 (described as
a note on sumptuary); there is an unreliable version of the 1679
(MS 15,642) entries in Bastide 1907, pp. 377–9. Discussed in
De Marchi 1955. MS Locke, f. 3, p. 199 is cited by Laslett,
Second Treatise, §81. For the transcription of Locke's shorthand
I am indebted to J.R. Milton.

Some scholars have speculated whether Locke intended to
write a utopia. In fact, Locke's remarks are closely related to
ideas expressed in the *Fundamental Constitutions of Carolina* and
in his essays on naturalisation and the Poor Law. He explicitly
refers to the colonies and to Carolina. In MS f. 2, p. 289 he
urges, in a sentence marked 'Atlantis', that public records
should, when naming individuals, indicate the place where they
are registered, 'viz. T. Mathews of Charlestown' – the capital
of Carolina. The Atlantis entries are arresting for the extent to
which Locke argues for intrusions into people's lives. He displays
a strong sense of the community's and the magistrate's duty to
exert moral discipline. He seeks to limit vagrancy by controlling
mobility. He also reveals a preoccupation with population
growth, proposing marriage laws to encourage progenitiveness.
Compare *First Treatise*, §§33, 41, 59; 'Marriage' (1679); Aristotle, *Politics*, bk II, 1270. Utopian these notes are not, but for
discussion of More's *Utopia* see Letters 60 and 66.

MS Locke, f. 1, p. 280: 12 June 1676

He that pleads more than once [a] term in one court let him be
uncapable of office.

MS Locke, f. 1, p. 319: 14 July 1676

In Eutopia every one to be of some handicraft and to be bound,
when well and at home, to work at it at l[east] one hour every day
or six hours every week.

MS Locke, f. 2, pp. 296–8: 14 October 1677

Every ten neighbouring houses shall have a tithingman[34] who
shall inform the judge of the colony in writing of the faults or

---

[34] The office of tithingman still continued. Locke paid, on behalf of his Somerset
tenants, taxes to cover the tithingmen, the poor rate and church rate (BL, Add.
MS 46,470, p. 15).

suspected course of life of anyone living in his tithing, who shall thereupon record the information, ⟨and according as he finds it more or less⟩ convene and examine the accused thereupon, and if he finds him guilty of any fault punish him accordingly. If his manner of life be such as he finds suspicious, he shall make him find sureties who shall be answerable for his future life or else commit him to some public workhouse. If afterwards he commit any fault that is criminal he shall not only be punished proportionably to the crime but his sureties shall make reparation for it, viz. if he has robbed he shall be hanged and his sureties make good to the robbed both their loss and the charge of prosecution. If he has committed murder they shall pay proportionably to the dignity of the person or the loss that anyone sustains by his death, and [al]so in perjury. If anyone of the tithing deliver in an information to the tithingman signed, and he delivered it not in to the judge of the colony, the tithingman shall be looked on as surety. If the tithingman deliver it into the judge and he makes not the accused find sureties he shall be looked on as surety. If there be no information at all the tithing shall be surety, which shall be answerable as the sureties above for all the faults of the tithing. Thus, every man being a watch upon his neighbour, faults will be prevented, which is better than that they should be punished.

No man shall inhabit anywhere seven days without entering his name in the tithingman's book together with the colony where he was first registered and the tithing where he was last inhabitant. By this means wandering and suspicious vagabonds and men of ill courses will be found out and prevented. If he does not within seven days it shall be looked on as a breach of good behaviour and if the master of the house where he is lodged or who sells or lets him the house do not give notice of him to the tithingman the eighth day, he having not done it for himself before, he shall be looked on as his surety.

It is well to be considered how far knowledge and learning is to be extended in a country for the well government of it, ignorance making men brutes and learning proud, especially those of the lower sort.

MS Locke, f. 3, pp. 142–3: 26 May 1678

Since sumptuary laws where the age inclines to luxury and excess do not restrain but rather increase the evil, as we may observe in Tacitus, *Annals*, bk III, p. 87,[35] perhaps the best way to set bounds to people's expenses and hinder them from spending beyond their income would be to enact that no landed men should be obliged to pay any book-debts to retailing tradesmen, whereby the interest of tradesmen would make them [the tradesmen] very cautious of trusting those who usually are the leaders in fashion and thereby a great restraint would be brought on the usual excess, and on the other side the credit of poor labouring people would be preserved as before for the supply of their necessities. JL

MS Locke, f. 3, pp. 198–201: 15 July 1678

Multitude of strong and healthy people bring the riches of every country and that which makes it flourish.

That the children may be strong, care is to be taken that copulation be not too young.

That they may be many, marriage is to be encouraged *nam vaga vinea debilitat sine prole*,[36] fornication therefore to be hindered.

No man shall be contracted before 17 years old, nor woman before 15. No man shall be married before 18 years old, nor woman before 16. Whosoever marries, himself not being 18 years old, or a woman that is not 16, shall enjoy no privileges by virtue of the matrimony and the children born before the respective age and six months more of either parent shall not be legitimate.

He that has neither wife nor child shall be a minor till 40 years old. He that is married or has a child shall be a major at 21. He that is above 40 and has neither wife nor child shall be incapable of inheritance or legacy from anyone but his father. He that lives to 40 years old unmarried, and having a younger brother married, shall lose his birthright. He that is married or has a child shall not be pressed to the wars. He that is 70 years old shall not be obliged to bear any public office but what he himself thinks fit. And for any

[35] Cornelius Tacitus (AD *c.* 55–115): Roman historian and critic of imperial corruption.
[36] 'For the rambling vineyard weakens without offspring.'

child that he has living in 5 years shall be abated of that. Those children who have died actually in arms for their country shall be accounted to their parents as living. And those who are settled in other countries shall be accounted as dead. For adultery a man may put away his wife and [also] any time after seven years matrimony, i.e. marry again, if he never had a child by her. In the case of adultery he shall not be obliged to give her anything; in the case of barrenness he shall pay her back her dowry. For a woman to converse in private i.e. out of the sight of witnesses, with a man, whose company has been forbidden her by her husband solemnly before two witnesses, shall be accounted adultery.

⟨He that is already married may marry another woman with his left hand. The children of the left hand marriage shall be legitimate, but not capable to inherit but as younger to all those of the right hand marriage, though elder in years, i.e. shall have in succession the place of the next brother's children. The ties, duration, and conditions of the left hand marriage shall be no other than what are expressed in the contract of marriage between the parties. Bastards shall be incapable of inheritance or legacy by will.⟩

BL, Add. MS 15,642, pp. 13–14: 14 February 1679

Whoever marries a woman more than five years older than himself ⟨or more than ten years younger⟩ shall forfeit one half of all she brings him in marriage ⟨to the public⟩.

A marriage wherein the man is not [yet] 14, nor the woman 13, shall be *ipso facto* [thereby] null, i.e. *ante pubertatem* [before puberty].

He that marries ⟨a woman⟩, not being himself 18, or a woman not 16, shall forfeit one half her portion and shall lose the benefit of her privilege of children.

A bachelor after 40 years old during his celibate [celibacy] shall be incapable of being heir or legataire [legatee] to anybody but his father or mother unless he has been maimed in the wars for his country. The will and testament of him that dies a bachelor past 50 shall be null unless he be killed in the wars of his country [or] unless maimed.[37]

---

[37] By an Act of 1694 (6 & 7 W. & M., c. 6) bachelors over the age of 25 had to pay an extra tax. See Letter 1847.

He that is 70 years old shall be at liberty to refuse any public employment or office whatsoever.

He that has five children living, at 65 years old, six at 60, seven at 55, eight at 50, nine at 45, shall have the privilege of one of 70 years.

He or she that has ten children living shall be exempted and free from all public taxes and burdens. ⟨Grandchildren and great grandchildren shall in regard of these foregoing privileges be counted as children.⟩ And those [children] that have been killed in the wars for their country shall be reckoned as alive in this respect.

Loss of the use of a hand or foot or eye, or a hurt penetrating into the hollow of the head or body, shall be counted for a maim. JL

BL, Add. MS 15,642, pp. 18–22: 20 February 1679

Every ten houses nearest adjoining shall have a tithingman and so [up] to nineteen, but when they come to be twenty they shall be divided into two tithings.

Nobody shall stay two days in a place, unless it be a fair, without going and acquainting the tithing man with it and showing him the testimonial of the last tithingman where his abode was, wherein shall be set down his name, age, description and manner of living in the last tithing where he lived and how long he dwelt there. To prevent vagabonds and other dangerous and wandering persons.

The tithingman shall once a month at least visit the houses of all his tithing, or oftener if he see occasion, to see what lives they lead. To inform the judge of the colony if he find any [who are] debauched, disorderly, suspicious, or that cannot give a good account how they maintain themselves. That the judge may take order therein. And also to inform the judge if any person or family through sickness, age, charge of children, or otherwise, be not able to maintain himself that also order may be taken. And if the tithing-man neglect his duty herein he shall be punished according [to] the mischief that hath or probably might have followed thereby.

If anyone, through age, sickness, charge of children, or otherwise, thinks fit to demand assistance, he shall speak to the tithingman, and the tithingman to the judge of the colony, who shall take care to provide for them in the public almshouse of the colony, where they shall be employed for, and nourished by, the public the rest of their days.

All beggars shall *ipso facto* [automatically] be taken and sent to the public workhouse and there remain the rest of their lives.

All travellers with a certificate from the judge of a colony and a tithingman of the same colony shall be relieved and lodged one night in any of the almshouses that lie in the way to the place whither by his certificate he ought to go.

All laws commanding or forbidding anything without a penalty shall be enforced by such penalties as the judge and jury shall judge in the particular occasions either to be sufficient punishment for the evil that hath already accrued by the past disobedience, or may be sufficient to secure the obedience for the future; but to be content with the gentlest that will be effectual, and to increase it till the evil be amended. But this arbitrary power is never to extend to life.[38]

If anyone shall relieve a beggar without giving notice of his begging within twenty-four hours after to the tithingman, he shall be liable to pay double his tax in the said tithing a whole year following of what sort soever, the abatement whereof shall be equally made to his neighbours of the same tithing. But nothing herein shall be construed to hinder the charity of well disposed people to bestow their charity in money, clothes, foot[wear], or any other way on poor people in their own houses and nowhere else, that do not go about begging. JL

BL, Add MS 15,642, pp. 18–22: 21 February 1679

The Athenians and Germans were not to marry before 20, the Lacedaemonians before 25 and the Egyptians not before 30. Methinks men should not be of age to marry before they were of age for other things, i.e. 21 years.

He that marries before 21 years shall not be able to sell, mortgage, or alienate, or lease, for any longer term than seven years any land he has any time during his life, but it shall be all looked on as the freehold of his children amongst whom it shall be equally divided after his death. The same shall be also of lands and tenements held

---

[38] I.e. the death penalty.

by lease. Only if there be but one manor, because indivisible, it shall go to the son that is first born after 21 years, the second manor, if more than one, to his next younger brother, etc.

In the privilege granted to the number of children, three grand-children shall be counted for one child.

Children born before the father be 21 years old shall not be counted to this privilege.

Children also not registered according to law (i.e. with the names of father and mother and the names of their respective places of registry) shall not be counted.

A man in the year from the day of his marriage shall not be bound to pay any tax, go to the wars, nor bear any office but what he himself desires.

No man that has a wife [and] children shall be bound to serve in arms without the bounds of his country, and in this sense here his country shall be supposed to end where it is no further inhabited by people under the same government. JL

MS Locke, c. 42B, p. 36: 1679.

In this country [Atlantis], those who have married their daughters well and who have brought up their sons to any good calling or provided well for them are plentifully maintained by them in their old age. JL

The son that is not nursed by the mother inherits not the estate of the father. Unless, upon testimony of a physician and the mid-wife that it could not be done without evident danger to the mother or the child, the magistrate gave leave and the leave be recorded.

They [are to] have no masters nor tutors for their children [who are] under 40 years old.

Those that have lost their children in the war adopt young children that are taken prisoners, and the affection on both sides is as great as amongst the natural, vide Sagard, [*Histoire du Canada*], p. 954.

More things for the good of the public are to be introduced by custom and fashion than by law and punishment. JL

Nobody bears a burdensome office that has a child living under five years old. JL

Understanding

8 February 1677. Marginal keywords: 'Understanding', 'Knowledge its extent and measure', 'End of knowledge', 'Knowledge'. MS Locke, f. 2, pp. 42–55. Printed in King 1829, pp. 84–90; 1830, I, 161–71; Aaron and Gibb 1936, pp. 84–90. King entitles it 'Knowledge, its extent and measure'. This is not a technical epistemological enquiry, but a disquisition on the proper sphere of man's use of his understanding. In the spirit of Francis Bacon and Robert Boyle, Locke appeals to people to avoid abstract metaphysical speculations, and to seek instead the acquisition of useful, 'experimental' knowledge. He touches on invention and economic improvement. He turns to the other offices of reason, which are to understand God's purposes and to search after moral rules.

Quod volumus facile credimus.[39] Q. how far and by what means the will works upon the understanding and assent.

Our minds are not made as large as truth nor suited to the whole extent of things amongst those that come within its ken; it meets with a great many too big for its grasp, and there are not a few that it is fain [wont] to give up as incomprehensible. It finds itself lost in the vast extent of space, and the least particle of matter puzzles it with an inconceivable divisibility, and they who out of a great care not to admit unintelligible things deny or question an eternal omniscient spirit run themselves into a greater difficulty by making an eternal and intelligent matter, nay our minds whilst they think and move our bodies find it past their capacity to conceive how they do the one or the other. This state of our minds however remote from that perfection whereof we ourselves have an idea, ought not however to discourage our endeavours in the search of truth or make us think we are incapable of knowing anything because we cannot fully understand all things. We shall find that we are set out into the world furnished with those faculties that are fit to obtain knowledge, and knowledge sufficient if we will but confine it within those purposes and direct it to those ends which the constitution of our nature and the circumstances of our being point out to us. If we consider ourselves in the condition we are in this world we cannot but observe that we are in an estate the necessities whereof

---

[39] 'We find it easy to believe what we want to.' The phrase (from Caesar and Bacon) recurs in *ECHU*, bk IV, ch. 20.

call for a constant supply of meat, drink, clothing, and defence from the weather, and very often physic; and our conveniences demand yet a great deal more. To provide these things nature furnish[es] us only with the materials for the most part rough and unfitted to our uses; it requires labour, art, and thought to suit them to our occasions, and if the knowledge of men had not found out ways to shorten the labour and improve several things which seem not at first sight to be of any use to us we should spend all our time to make a scanty provision for a poor and miserable life, a sufficient instance whereof we have in the inhabitants of that large and fertile part of the world the West Indies, who lived a poor uncomfortable laborious life [and] with all their industry [were] scarce able to sub- sist and that perhaps only for want of knowing the use of that stone out of which the inhabitants of the old world had the skill to draw iron and thereof make themselves utensils necessary for the carrying on and improvement of all other arts, no one of which can subsist well, if at all, without that one metal. Here then is a large field for knowledge proper for the use and advantage of men in this world, viz., to find out new inventions of dispatch to shorten or ease our labours, or applying sagaciously together several agents and patients[40] to procure new and beneficial productions whereby our stock of riches (i.e. things useful for the conveniences of our life) may be increased or better preserved. And for such discoveries as these the mind of man is well fitted, though perhaps the essence of things, their first original, their secret way of working, and the whole extent of corporal beings, be as far beyond our capacity as it is besides our use, and we have no reason to complain that we do not know the nature of the sun or stars, that the consideration of light itself leaves us in the dark, and a thousand other speculations in nature, since if we knew them they would be of no solid advan- tage to us nor help to make our lives the happier, they being but the useless employments of idle or over curious brains which amuse themselves about things out of which they can by no means draw any real benefit. So that if we will consider man as in this world, and that his mind and faculties were given him for any use, we must necessarily conclude it must be to procure him the happiness

---

[40] One meaning of 'patient' is a thing that passively undergoes some action or receives impressions from external agents.

which this world is capable of, which certainly is nothing else but plenty of all sorts of those things which can with most ease, pleasure and variety preserve him longest in it, so that had mankind no concernments but in this world, no apprehension of any being after this life, they need trouble their heads with nothing but the history of nature and an enquiry into the qualities of the things in this mansion of the universe which hath fallen to their lot, and, being well skilled in the knowledge of material causes and effects of things in their power, directing their thoughts to the improvement of such arts and inventions, engines and utensils as might best contribute to their continuation in it with conveniency and delight. They might well spare themselves the trouble of looking any further, they need not concern or perplex themselves about the original, frame or constitution of the universe, drawing this great machine into systems of their own contrivance and building hypotheses obscure, perplexed, and of no other use but to raise disputes and continue wrangling. For what need have we to complain of our ignorance in the more general and foreign parts of nature when all our business lies at hand; why should we bemoan our want of knowledge in the particular apartments of the universe when our portion lies only here in this little spot of earth, where we and all our concernments are shut up. Why should we think ourselves hardly dealt with that we are not furnished with compass nor plummet [plumbline] to sail and fathom that restless and innavigable ocean of the universal matter, motion and space since if there be shores to bound our voyage and travel, there are at least no commodities to be brought from thence serviceable to our uses now that will better our condition, and we need not be displeased that we have not knowledge enough to discover whether we have any neighbours or no in those large bulks of matter we see floating in that abyss, and of what kind they are since we can never have any communication with them nor entertain a commerce that might turn to our advantage, so that considering [that] man, barely as an animal of three or four score years duration and then to end his condition and state, requires no other knowledge than what may furnish him with these things which may help him to pass out to the end of that time with ease, safety and delight, which is all the happiness he is capable of, and for the attainment of a competent measure of this knowledge mankind is sufficiently provided, he hath faculties and organs well adapted to these discoveries if he think fit to employ and use them. Another use of his knowledge is to live in peace with his fellow men and this also he is capable of.

Besides a plenty of the good things of this world and with life, health and peace to enjoy them we can think of no other concernment mankind hath that leads him not out of it, and places him not beyond the confines of this earth and it seems probable that there should be some better state somewhere else to which men might arrive since when he hath all that this world can afford or he with himself in it, he is still unsatisfied, uneasy, and far from happiness. 'Tis certain, and that which all men must consent to, that there is a possibility of another state when this scene is over, and that the happiness and misery of that depends on the ordering of ourselves in our actions in this time of our probationership here. The acknowledgement of a God will easily lead anyone to this and he hath left so many footsteps of himself, so many proofs of his being, in every creature as are sufficient to convince any who will but make use of their faculties that way, and I dare say nobody [e]scapes this conviction for want of light but if any be so blind 'tis only because they will not open their eyes and see, and those only doubt of a supreme ruler, and an universal law who would willingly be under no law, accountable to no judge, those only question another life hereafter who intend to lead such a one here as they fear to have examined and would be loath to answer for when it is over. This opinion I shall always be of till I see that those who would cast off all thoughts of God, heaven and hell lead such lives as would become rational creatures or observe but that one unquestionable moral rule, do as you would be done to. It being then possible and at least probable that there is another life wherein we shall give an account for our past actions in this, to the great God of heaven and earth, here comes in another, and that the main, concernment of mankind and that is to know what those actions are that he is to do, what those are he is to avoid, what the law is he is to live by here and shall be judged by hereafter, and in this part too he is not left so in the dark but that he is furnished with principles of knowledge and faculties able to discover light enough to guide him; his understanding seldom fails him in this part unless where his will would have it so. If he takes a wrong course 'tis most commonly because he wilfully goes out of the way or at least chooses to be bewildered, and there are few if any that dreadfully mistake who are willing to be in the right and I think one may safely say that amidst the great ignorance that is so justly complained of amongst mankind, where anyone endeavoured to know his duty sincerely with a design to do it scarce ever anyone miscarried for want of knowledge.

The business of men being to be happy in this world by the enjoyment of the things of nature subservient to life, health, ease, and pleasure and by the comfortable hopes of another life when this is ended: and in the other world by an accumulation of higher degrees of bliss in an everlasting security, we need no other knowledge for the attainment of those ends but of the history and observation of the effects and operations of natural bodies within our power, and of our duties in the management of our own actions as far as they depend on our wills, i.e. as far also as they are in our power. One of those is the proper enjoyment of our bodies and the highest perfection of that, and the other of our souls, and to attain both those we are fitted with faculties both of body and soul. Whilst then we have abilities to improve our knowledge in experimental natural philosophy, whilst we want not principles whereon to establish moral rules,[41] nor light (if we please to make use of it) to distinguish good from bad actions, we have no reason to complain if we meet with difficulties in other things which put our reasons to a non plus, confound our understandings, and leave us perfectly in the dark under the sense of our weakness, for those relating not to our happiness [in] any way are no part of our business and therefore 'tis not to be wondered if we have not abilities given us to deal with things that are not to our purpose, nor conformable to our state or end.

God having made this great machine of the universe suitable to his infinite power and wisdom why should we think so proudly of ourselves whom he hath put into a small canton and perhaps the most inconsiderable part of it, that he hath made us the surveyors of it, and that it is not as it should be unless we can thoroughly comprehend it in all the parts of it. It is agreeable to his goodness and our condition that we should be able to understand so far some parts of that we have to do with as to be able to apply them to our

---

[41] Locke originally wrote, 'whilst we want not light to discover moral philosophy'.

uses and make them subservient to the conveniencies of our life, as proper to fill our hearts and mouths with praises of his bounty. But 'tis also agreeable to his greatness that it should exceed our capacities and the highest flights of our imagination the better to fill us with admiration of his power and wisdom besides its serving to other ends and being suited probably to the uses of other more intelligent creatures which we know not of. And if it be not reasonable to expect that we should be able to penetrate into all the depths of nature and understand the whole fabric of the universe 'tis yet an higher insolence to doubt of the existence of a God because he is above our narrow understandings, or to think there is not an infinite being because we are not so, i.e. because our minds are not large enough to comprehend it. If all things must stand or fall by the measure of our understandings, and that denied to be wherein we find inextricable difficulties, there will very little remain in the world, and we shall scarce leave ourselves so much as understandings, souls, or bodies. It will become us better to consider well our own weakness and exigencies, what we are made for and what we are capable of, and to apply the powers of our bodies and faculties of our souls, which are well suited to our condition, in the search of that natural and moral knowledge which as it is not beyond our strength so is not besides our purpose but may be attained by moderate industry and improved to our infinite advantage.

Adversaria B

4 September 1677. Marginal keyword: 'Adversaria'. MS Locke, f. 2, pp. 247–52. Printed in King 1829, pp. 116–18; 1830, 1, 218–22 (misdated); Aaron and Gibb 1936, pp. 92–4. Some of Locke's tabulations have been rendered here in continuous prose. This is one of Locke's several remarks on note-taking and on the 'division of the sciences'. There is a very similar version in c. 28, fos. 50–1 (12 November 1677). Compare 'Adversaria A' and 'C', and 'Knowledge B'.

In the reading of books and making Adversaria, methinks these are the principal parts or heads of things to be taken notice of. The first of which is the knowledge of things, their essence and nature, properties, causes and consequences of each species, which I call *philosophica* and must be divided according to the several orders and species of things. And of these so far as we have the true notions of things as really they are in their distinct beings, so far we advance in real and true knowledge. And this improvement of our understandings is to be got more by meditation than reading, though that also be not to be neglected. And the faculty chiefly exercised about this, the judgement.

The second head is History wherein it being both impossible in itself, and useless also to us to remember every particular, I think [it is] the most useful to observe the opinions we find amongst mankind concerning God, religion and morality and the rules they have made to themselves, or practice has established in any of these matters. And here the memory is principally employed.

The third head is that which is of most use and that is what things we find amongst other people fit for our imitation whether politic or private wisdom; any arts conducing to the convenience of life.

The fourth is any natural productions that may be transplanted into our country, or commodities which may be an advantageous commerce. And these concern practice or action.

The first then I call *Adversaria Philosophica*, which must be divided into the several species of things as they come in one's way.

The second I call *Adversaria Historica*, comprehending, (1) the opinions or traditions to be found amongst men concerning God, creation, revelation, prophecies, miracles. (2) Their rules or institutes concerning things that are duties, sins, or indifferent in matters of religion, or things that are commanded, forbidden, or permitted by their municipal laws in order to civil society, which I call *Instituta*, which contain: (i) [matters] by divine law and for divine worship (religious duties, sins, 'things indifferent'); (ii) [matters] by civil law (civil duties, crimes, permissible actions).[42]

The ways they use to obtain blessings from the divinity or atone for their sins, which I call *Petitoria* [petition], *Expiatoria* [expiation]. And, last of all, any supernatural things that are to be observed amongst them, as any magical arts or real predictions.

The third I call *Adversaria Immitanda*.[43] That is, whatsoever wise practices are to be found either for governing of polities or a man's

---

[42] These categories translated from the Latin.
[43] Things to be imitated, actions to be emulated.

private self or any beneficial arts employed on natural bodies for their improvement to our use, which contain these heads: Politics or civil wisdom; prudence or private wisdom; physic, or arts concerning: drink, food, medicine, human motions, sensory organs.[44]

The fourth I call *Adversaria Acquirenda*, which are the natural products of the country fit to be transplanted into ours and there propagated, or else brought thither for some very useful quality they have. Or else to mark the commodities of the country whether natural or artificial which they send out and are the proper business of merchandise to get by their commerce and these are the following: *Acquirenda* and *Merces* [commodities and merchandise].

There is yet one more, which is the history of natural causes and effects, wherein it may be convenient in our reading to observe those several properties of bodies and the several effects that several bodies or their qualities have one upon another, and principally to remark those that may contribute either to the improvement of arts or give light into the nature of things which is that which I called above *philosophica*, which I conceive to consist in having a true, clear and distinct idea of the nature of anything which in natural things or real beings, because we are ignorant of their essence, takes in their causes, properties and effects or as much of them as we can know, and in moral beings their essence and consequences. This natural history I call *Historica Physica, referenda secundum species* [to be referred to according to species].

Morality

c. 1677–8. 'Morality'. MS Locke, c. 28, fos. 139–40. Printed in Sargentich 1974, pp. 26–8 (who dates it to the 1690s). The opening restates Locke's hedonic principles; he then comments on the origin of property and justice.

Morality is the rule of man's actions for the attaining happiness.

For the end and aim of all men being happiness alone, nothing could be a rule or a law to them whose observation did not lead to happiness and whose breach did [not] draw misery after it.

---

[44] These categories translated from the Latin.

Definition: Happiness and misery consist in pleasure and pain. Good is what gives or increases pleasure or takes away or diminishes pain, and evil is the contrary.

Axiom 1. All men desire the enjoyment of happiness and the absence of misery, and that only and always.

Axiom 2. Men act only for what they desire.

Happiness therefore being their end the means of attaining it can be alone the rule of action. Everyone knows that man is capable of some degrees of happiness and great degrees of misery in this life.

It is also evident that that power that made a man exist here in a state capable of pleasure and pain[45] can as well make him exist again after he has lost all sense and perception by death as he that first made him exist can bring him back again to a state of sensibility and continue in it capable of pleasure or pain as long as he pleases.

This therefore is evident that there is pleasure and pain to be had in this life and[46] that it is possible there may be a state after this life wherein men may be capable of enjoyments or sufferings.

As to this life then let us see what is the way of attainment of pleasure and avoiding of pain for that must needs be the rule of action to all sorts of beings who have no prospect beyond this life.

Man made not himself nor any other man.

Man made not the world which he found made at his birth.

Therefore[47] man at his birth can have no right to anything in the world more than another. Men therefore must either enjoy all things in common or by compact determine their rights. If all things be left in common, want, rapine and force will unavoidably follow in which state, as is evident, happiness cannot be had which cannot consist without plenty and security.

To avoid this estate, compact must determine people's rights.

These compacts are to be kept or broken. If to be broken their making signifies nothing; if to be kept then justice is established as a duty and will be the first and general rule of our happiness.

But it may be objected, it may be sometimes a man's advantage to break his word and then I may do it as contributing to my happiness. Response: All men being equally under one and the same rule,

---

[45] There follows a deleted phrase: 'could make him continue in such an estate longer than is the ordinary life of man'.

[46] The MS has 'life and all': 'all' deleted for sense.

[47] The MS has 'Therefore no man': 'no' deleted for sense.

if it be permitted to me to break my word for my advantage it is also permitted everyone else, and then whatever I possess will be subjected to the force or deceit of all the rest of the men in the world, in which state it is impossible for any man to be happy unless he were both stronger and wiser than all the rest of mankind, for in such a state of rapine and force it is impossible any one man should be master of those things whose possession is necessary to his well being.

Justice, the greatest and difficultest duty, being thus established, the rest will not be hard.

The next sort of virtues are those which relate to society and so border on justice, but yet are not comprised under direct articles of contract such as are civility, charity, liberality.

Civility is nothing but outward expressing of goodwill and esteem or at least of no contempt or hatred.

Toleration C

19 April 1678. Marginal keyword: 'Toleration'. MS Locke, f. 3, p. 107. Not hitherto printed.

However people imagine that the Jews had a strict church discipline without any toleration yet it is to be observed besides that it was a law immediately given by God Almighty;   (1) That there were no articles of faith that they were required to subscribe to, or at least that there was but one God and that Jehovah [was] their God;

(2) That there were several laws given for excluding people [such] as bastards and eunuchs [and] Ammonites,[48] etc. out of their congregation but none for forcing anybody in.

Law

21 April 1678. Marginal keyword: 'Law'. MS Locke, f. 3, pp. 111–12. Printed in King 1829, p. 116; 1830, I, 217 (misdated); Wootton 1993, p. 236.

A civil law is nothing but the agreement of a society of men either by themselves, or one or more authorised by them, determining the

---

[48] An ancient Semitic people in constant conflict with the Israelites.

rights, and appointing rewards and punishments to certain actions of all within that society.

Law of Nature

15 July 1678. Marginal keyword: 'Lex nat[urae]'. MS Locke, f. 3, pp. 201–2. Printed in Von Leyden 1956, pp. 34–5; and partially in Dunn 1967, pp. 155–6.

God having given man above other creatures of this habitable part of the universe a knowledge of himself which the beasts have not, he is thereby under obligations which the beasts are not, for knowing God to be a wise agent he cannot but conclude that he has that knowledge and those faculties which he finds in himself above the other creatures given him for some use and end. If therefore he comprehend the relation between father and son and find it reasonable that his son whom he hath begot (only in pursuance of his pleasure without thinking of his son) and nourished should obey, love, and reverence him, and be grateful to him, he cannot but find it much more reasonable that he and every other man should obey and revere, love and thank the author of their being to whom they owe all that they are. If he find it reasonable to punish one of his children that injures another, he cannot but expect the same from God, the father of all men, when anyone injures another; if he finds it reasonable that his children should assist and help one another and expects it from them as their duty, will he not also by the same reason conclude that God expects the same of all men one to another. If he finds that God has made him and all other men in a state wherein they cannot subsist without society and has given them judgement to discern what is capable of preserving that society, can he but conclude that he is obliged and that God requires him to follow those rules which conduce to the preserving of society?

Virtue A

26 August 1678. Marginal keyword: 'Vertue'. MS Locke, f. 3, pp. 266–7. Not hitherto printed. Locke comments on a quotation from Jean de Lery, *Histoire d'un voiage fait en la terre de Brasil* (1594).

That virtue is but the name of such actions as are most conducing to the good of the society and are therefore by the society recommended by all means to the practice of the people seems to me very plain.

Happiness B

1 October 1678. Marginal keyword: 'Happynesse'. MS Locke, f. 3, pp. 304–5. Printed in King 1829, p. 115; 1830, I, 216; Fox Bourne 1876, I, 124–5; Driscoll 1972, p. 100, who notes a similarity to François Bernier's *Abrégé de la Philosophie de Gassendi* (1678).

That the happiness of man consists in pleasure whether of body or mind, according to everyone's relish, and *summum malum* [ultimate evil] is pain, or dolour of body and mind; that this is so, I appeal not only to the experience of all mankind, and the thoughts of every man's breast, but to the best rule of this, the Scripture, which tells that at the right hand of God, the place of bliss, are pleasures for ever more; and that which men are condemned for is not for seeking pleasure, but for preferring the momentary pleasures of this life to those joys which shall have no end.

Reputation

12 December 1678. Marginal keywords: 'Credit, Disgrace'. MS Locke, f. 3, pp. 381–2. Printed in King 1829, pp. 108–9; 1830, I, 203–4; Fox Bourne 1876, I, 403–4; Wootton 1993, pp. 236–7. Locke added references to Gabriel Sagard, *Le Grand Voyage du Pays des Hurons* (1632) and Pierre Boucher, *Histoire du Canada* (1664). For Locke's anthropological reading see Batz 1974, Bonno 1955.

The principal spring from which the actions of men take their rise, the rule they conduct them by, and the end to which they direct them, seems to be credit and reputation, and that which at any rate they avoid, is in the greatest part shame and disgrace. This makes the Hurons and other people of Canada with such constancy endure inexpressible torments. This makes merchants in one country, and soldiers in another. This puts men upon school divinity in one country, and physic or mathematics in another. This cuts out the dresses for the women, and makes the fashions for the men; and makes them endure the inconveniences of all. This makes men drunkards and sober, thieves and honest, and robbers themselves true to one another. Religions are upheld by this and factions maintained, and the shame of being disesteemed by those with whom one hath lived, and to whom one would recommend oneself, is the great source and director of most of the actions of men. Where riches are in credit, knavery and injustice that produce them are not out of countenance, because, the state being got, esteem follows it, as it is said in some countries the crown ennobles the blood. Where power, and not the good exercise of it, gives reputation, all the injustice, falsehood, violence, and oppression that attains that, goes for wisdom and ability. Where love of one's country is the thing in credit, there we shall see a race of brave Romans; and when being a favourite at court was the only thing in fashion, one may observe the same race of Romans all turned flatterers and informers. He therefore that would govern the world well, had need consider rather what fashions he makes, than what laws; and to bring anything into use he need only give it reputation. JL

Carolina

20 February 1679. 'Carolina'. BL, Add. MS 15,642, p. 18. Not hitherto printed. Locke draws on Gabriel Sagard, *Histoire du Canada* (1636).

In dealing with the Indians one should never pardon on any consideration the murder of any of our people when we are in a condition to do it. Vide hist. in Sagard, p. 236. But in all other injuries received it may be convenient to forgive and be reconciled upon other considerations, reparation being made. But in [the] case of murder life still for life, and not to take notice of it if you are not in a condition to demand that and stand upon it.[49] JL

---

[49] Locke's meaning seems to be that a blind eye is to be turned if one is not in a position to exact the full penalty.

Marriage

22 February 1679. Untitled. BL, Add. MS 15,642, p. 22. Not hitherto printed. Locke is again concerned to promote population growth.

There are several things to be introduced by custom and fashion which are of great use and yet cannot be well established by laws.

Viz., for the encouragement of marrying, especially of poor people. Those of their friends and acquaintance to invite themselves to the houses of new married people after the marriage day, send in their provisions to make merry there, and everyone that goes there make them presents of household stuff or money, as is most suitable to the condition of the persons. This to be taken for a mark of esteem and friendship, and the leave for it to last during the first year. JL.

Pietas

25 March 1679. 'Pietas'. MS Locke, c. 33, fo. 10. Not hitherto printed. Cited by Laslett, Second Treatise, §58. Locke again draws on Sagard. Janissaries were Turkish foot soldiers, drawn originally from renegade prisoners and tributes of Christian children.

Education not generation gives the obligation and the affection for the children taken prisoners when men make war against their parents and country as heartily as any, [Sagard, p.] 454. We see the same in the Janissaries. JL

Justitia

25 March 1679. 'Iustitia'. MS Locke, c. 33, fo. 11; also in c. 42B, fo. 60. Not hitherto printed.

Since most of the wrong judgements that are given in the world are rather the faults of the will than the understanding, to have justice well administered care should be taken to choose rather upright than learned men. JL

Politia

25 March 1679. 'Politia'. MS Locke, c. 33, fo. 11; also in c. 42B, fo. 6. Cited by Laslett, *Second Treatise*, §106. Not hitherto printed. Locke on Sagard again.

The kings of Canada are elective, but the sons never fail to succeed their fathers when they are heirs to their virtues, otherwise not, and their kings are rather obeyed by consent and persuasion, than by force and compulsion, the public good being the measure of their authority. Sagard, p. 418. And this seems to be the state of regal authority in its original at least in all this part of the world. JL

Opinion

17 June 1679. 'Opinion'. BL, Add. MS 15,642, p. 101. Printed in Aaron and Gibb 1936, p. 112; King 1829, p. 136; 1830, I, 252–3.

Though a thinking considerate [reflective] man cannot believe anything with a firmer assent than is due to the evidence and validity of those reasons on which it is founded yet the greatest part of men not examining the probability of things in their own nature, nor the testimony of those who are their vouchers, take the common belief or opinion of those of their country, neighbourhood or party to be proof enough, and so believe as well as live by fashion and example, and thus men are zealous Turks as well as Christians. JL

Love of Country

1679. 'Patriae Amor' and 'Amor Patriae'. MS Locke, d. 1, pp. 53, 57. Printed in King 1829, pp. 291–2; 1830, II, 92–4. Cited by Laslett, *Second Treatise*, §58.

Patriae Amor: is from the idea of settlement there, and not leaving it again, the mind not being satisfied with anything that suggests often to it the thoughts of leaving it, which naturally attends a man in a strange country. For though, in general, we think of dying, and so leaving the place where we have set up our rest in this world, yet, in particular, deferring and putting it off from time to time, we make our stay there eternal, because we never set precise bounds to our abode there, and never think of leaving it in good earnest. JL

Amor Patriae. The remembrance of pleasures and conveniences we have had there; the love of our friends whose conversation and assistance may be pleasant and useful to us; and the thoughts of recommending ourselves to our old acquaintance, by the improvements we shall bring home, either of our fortunes or abilities, or the increase of esteem we expect for having travelled and seen more than others of this world, and the strange things in it; all these preserve in us, in long absence, a constant affection to our country, and a desire to return to it. But yet I think this is not all, nor the chief cause, that keeps in us a longing after our country. Whilst we are abroad we look on ourselves as strangers there, and are always thinking of departing; we set not up our rest, but often see or think of the end of our being there; and the mind is not easily satisfied with anything it can reach to the end of. But when we are returned to our country, where we think of a lasting abode, wherein to set up our rest, an everlasting abode, for we seldom think of anything beyond it, we do not propose to ourselves another country whither we think to remove and establish ourselves afterwards. This is that, I imagine, that sets mankind so constantly upon desires of returning to their country, because they think no more of leaving it again; and, therefore, men married and settled in any place are much more cold in these desires. And, I believe, when anyone thinks often of this world, as of a place wherein he is not to make any long abode, where he can have no lasting fixed settlement, but that he sees the bounds of his stay here, and often reflects upon his departure, he will presently upon it put on the thoughts of a stranger, be much more indifferent to the particular place of his nativity, and [be] no more fond of it than a traveller is of any foreign country, when he thinks he must leave them all indifferently to return and settle in his native soil. JL

Love

1679. 'Amor'. MS Locke, d. 1, p. 57. Not hitherto printed.

All men have a stock of love laid up in them by nature which they cannot forbear to bestow on something or other. We should therefore take care to choose fit and worthy objects of our love, lest like women that want children, the proper objects of their affection, we grow fond of little dogs and monkeys. JL.

Toleration D

1679. 'Toleratio'. MS Locke, d. 1, pp. 125–6. Printed in Inoue 1974, p. 47.

No man has power to prescribe to another what he should believe or do in order to the saving of his own soul, because it is only his own private interest, and concerns not another man. God has nowhere given such power to any man or society, nor can man possibly be supposed to give it [to] another over him absolutely.

(1) Because man in all states being liable to error, as well governors as those under them, doctors or scholars, it would be unreasonable to be put under the absolute direction of those who may err in a matter of that concernment, eternal concernment, wherein if they misguide us they can make us no reparation.

(2) Because such a power can by no means serve to the end for which only it can be supposed to be given, viz. to keep men in the right way to salvation. For supposing all the different pretenders to this power were nearer agreed in the matters they prescribe, or could consent to resign all their pretensions to this power to one certain guide, neither of which is ever like[ly] to happen, yet the power of using force to bring men to believe in faith and opinions and uniformity in worship could not serve to secure men's salvation, even though that power were in itself infallible, because no compulsion can make a man believe against his present light and persuasion, be it what it will, though it may make him profess indeed. But profession without sincerity will little set a man forwards in his way to any place but that where he is to have his share with hypocrites, and to do anything in the worship of God which a man judges in his own conscience not to be that worship he requires and will accept, is so far from serving or pleasing God in it, that such a worshipper affronts God only to please men. For even the circumstances of the worship of God cannot be indifferent to him that thinks them not so, nor can the time, habit, posture, etc., be at

pleasure used or omitted by one who thinks either acceptable or displeasing to the God he worships.

But though nobody can have a right to force men to receive such doctrines or to practise such ways of worship, yet this will not hinder the power of every society or profession of religion to establish within themselves confessions of faith, and rules of decency and order, which yet are not to be imposed on anyone with constraint. It only forbids that men should be compelled into that communion or anyone be hindered from withdrawing from it whenever anything comes to be established in it which he judges contrary to the end for which he enters into such a communion or religious society, i.e. the believing and owning certain truths which are taught and professed there, and the worshipping of God in a way acceptable to him.[50]

Of God's Justice

1 August 1680. Untitled. MS Locke, f. 4, pp. 145–51. Printed in King 1829, pp. 122–3; 1830, I, 228–30; Wootton 1993, pp. 237–8 (entitled 'The Idea we have of God'). Locke argues that goodness as well as power is a necessary component of God's justice for humankind.

Whatsoever carries any excellency with it, and includes not imperfection, it must needs make a part of the idea we have of God. So that with being, and the continuation of it, or perpetual duration, power and wisdom and goodness must be ingredients of that perfect or super-excellent being which we call God, and that in the utmost or infinite degree. But yet that unlimited power cannot be an excellency without it be regulated by wisdom and goodness. For since God is eternal and perfect in his own being, he cannot make use of that power to change his own being into a better or another state; and therefore all the exercise of that power must be in and upon his creatures, which cannot but be employed for their good and benefit, as much as the order and perfection of the whole can allow each individual in its particular rank and station; and therefore looking on God as a being infinite in goodness as well as power, we

---

[50] The passage closes with a Latin phrase which appears to indicate a cross-reference.

cannot imagine he hath made anything with a design that it should be miserable, but that he hath afforded it all the means of being happy that its nature and estate is capable of, and though justice be also a perfection which we must necessarily ascribe to the supreme being, yet we cannot suppose the exercise of it should extend further than his goodness has need of it for the preservation of his creatures in the order and beauty of the state that he has placed each of them in. For since our actions cannot reach unto him, or bring him any profit or damage, the punishments he inflicts on any of his creatures, i.e. the misery or destruction he brings upon them, can be nothing else but to preserve the greater or more considerable part, and so being only for preservation, his justice is nothing but a branch of his goodness, which is fain by severity to restrain the irregular and destructive parts from doing harm; for to imagine God under a necessity of punishing for any other reason but this, is to make his justice a great imperfection, and to suppose a power over him that necessitates him to operate contrary to the rules of his wisdom and goodness, which cannot be supposed to make anything so idly as that it should be purposely destroyed or be put in a worse state than destruction (misery being as much a worse state than annihilation, as pain is than insensibility, or the torments of a rack less eligible than quiet sound sleeping). The justice then of God can be supposed to extend itself no further than infinite goodness shall find it necessary for the preservation of his works.

Religion

3 April 1681. Untitled. MS Locke, f. 5, pp. 33–8. Printed in King 1829, pp. 123–5; 1830, I, 230–34; Fox Bourne 1876, I, 462–4 (misdated); Aaron and Gibb 1936, pp. 114–16; Wootton 1993, pp. 238–40 (entitled 'Inspiration'). Locke discusses the role of reason in religion; inspiration or imagined revelation; and miracles. See *ECHU*, bk IV, ch. 16, §13; and chs. 18–19; *The Reasonableness of Christianity*; and the *Discourse on Miracles* (*Works*, IX, 256–65).

Religion being that homage and obedience which man pays immediately to God, it supposes that man is capable of knowing that there is a God, and what is required by and will be acceptable to him thereby to avoid his anger and procure his favour. That there is a

God and what that God is nothing can discover to us nor judge in us but natural reason. For whatever discoveries we receive any other way must come originally from inspiration, which is an opinion in, or persuasion of, the mind whereof a man knows not the rise nor reason, but is received there as a truth coming from an unknown and therefore a supernatural cause, and not founded upon those principles nor observations nor the way of reasoning which makes the understanding admit other things for truths. But no such inspiration concerning God or his worship can be admitted for truth by him that thinks himself thus inspired, much less by any other whom he would persuade to believe him inspired any further than it is conformable to his reason. Not only because where reason is not judge it is impossible for a man himself to distinguish betwixt inspiration and fancy, truth and error. But also it is impossible to have such a notion of God as to believe that he should make a creature to whom the knowledge of himself was necessary and yet not to be discovered by that way which discovers everything else that concerns us, but was to come into the minds of men only by such a way by which all manner of errors come in and is more likely to let in falsehoods than truths, since nobody can doubt from the contradiction and strangeness of opinions concerning God and religion in the world that men are likely to have more fancies than inspirations.

Inspiration then barely in itself cannot be a ground to receive any doctrine not conformable to reason.

In the next place let us see how far inspiration can enforce on the mind any opinion concerning God or his worship when accompanied with a power to do a miracle and here too I say the last determination must be that of reason.

(1) Because reason must be the judge what is a miracle and what not, which not knowing how far the power of natural causes do extend themselves and what strange effects they may produce is very hard to determine.

(2) 'Twill always be as great a miracle that God should alter the course of natural things to overturn the principles of knowledge and understanding in a man, by setting up anything to be received by him as a truth which his reason cannot assent to, as the miracle itself, and so at best it will be but one miracle against another, and the greater still on reason's side, it being harder to believe that God

should alter and put out of its ordinary course some phenomenon of the great world for once, and make things out contrary to their ordinary rule, purposely that the mind of man might do so always afterwards, than that this is some fallacy or natural effect of which he knows not the cause let it look never so strange.

(3) Because man does not know whether there be not several sorts of creatures above him and between him and the supreme, amongst which there may be some that have the power to produce in nature such extraordinary effects as we call miracles and may have the will to do it for other reasons than the confirmation of truth. For 'tis certain the magicians of Egypt turned their rods into serpents as well as Moses [Exod. 7:11–12] and since so great a miracle as that was done in opposition to the true God and the revelation sent by him, what miracle can have certainty and assurance greater than that of man's reason?

And if inspiration have so much the disadvantage of reason in the man himself who is inspired, it has much more so in him who receives this revelation only from another and that too very remote in time and place.

I do not hereby deny in the least that God can or hath done miracles for the confirmation of truths but I only say that we cannot think he should do them to enforce doctrines or notions of himself or any worship of him not conformable to reason, or that we can receive such for truths for the miracle's sake and even in those books which have the greatest proof of revelation from God and the attestation of miracles to confirm their being so. The miracles were to be judged by the doctrine and not the doctrine by the miracles, vide Deuteronomy 13:1[-3], Matthew 14:24[-33], and St Paul says if an angel from heaven should teach any other doctrine [Gal. 1:8].

Reason, Passion, Superstition

16 May 1681. Untitled. MS Locke, f. 5, p. 59. Printed in King 1829, p. 119; 1830, I, 223–4; Cox 1960, p. 33.

The three great things that govern mankind are reason, passion, and superstition. The first governs a few, the two last share the bulk of mankind, and possess them in their turns; but superstition most powerfully and produces the greatest mischiefs. JL

Knowledge B

26 June 1681. Marginal keyword: 'Knowledge'. MS Locke, f. 5, pp. 77–83. Printed in Aaron and Gibb 1936, pp. 116–18; Wootton 1993, pp. 259–61 (entitled 'Two sorts of knowledge'). A paper preparatory to *ECHU*, bk IV, ch. 21, on the nature and kinds of knowledge. Locke suggests that moral principles can have 'demonstrative certainty', but distinguishes such truths from those about 'polity and prudence' which depend upon experience and probable knowledge.

There are two sorts of knowledge in the world, general and particular, founded upon two different principles, i.e. true ideas and matter of fact or history. All general knowledge is founded only upon true ideas and so far as we have these we are capable of demonstration or certain knowledge, for he that has the true idea of a triangle or circle is capable of knowing any demonstration concerning these figures, but if he have not the true idea of a scalenon [triangle] he cannot know anything concerning a scalenon though he may have some confused or imperfect opinion concerning a scalenon upon a confused or imperfect idea of it or he may have some uncertain opinion concerning its properties, but this is belief and not knowledge. Upon the same reason he that has a true idea of God, of himself as his creature, or the relation he stands in to God and his fellow creatures, and of justice, goodness, law, happiness, etc., is capable of knowing moral things, or having a demonstrative certainty in them, but though I say a man that hath such ideas is capable of certain knowledge in them yet I do not say that presently he hath thereby that certain knowledge no more than that he that hath a true idea of a triangle and a right angle doth presently thereby know that the three angles of a triangle are equal to two right ones; he may believe others that tell him so but know it not till he himself hath employed his thoughts on it and seen the connection and agreement of those ideas and so made to himself the demonstration i.e. upon examination seen it to be so. The first and great step therefore to knowledge is to get the mind furnished with true ideas, which the mind being capable of having of moral things as well as figure[s] I cannot but think morality as well as mathematics capable of demonstration if men would employ their understanding to think more about it and not give themselves up to the lazy traditional way of talking one after another. By the knowledge of natural bodies and their operations reaching little further than bare matter of fact without having perfect ideas of the ways and manners [in which] they are produced nor the concurrent causes they depend on. And also the well management of public or private affairs depending upon the various and unknown humours, interests, and capacities of men we have to do with in the world and not upon any settled ideas of things physic, polity and prudence are not capable of demonstration but a man is principally helped in them by the history of matter of fact and a sagacity of enquiring into probable causes and finding out an analogy in their operations and effects. Knowledge then depends upon right and true ideas, opinion upon history and matter of fact, and hence it comes to pass that our knowledge of general things are *eternae veritates* [eternal truths] and depend not upon the existence or accidents of things, for the truths of mathematics and morality are certain whether men make true mathematical figures, or suit their actions to the rules of morality or no. For that the three angles of a triangle are equal to two right ones is infallibly true whether there be any such figure as a triangle existing in the world or no, and it is true that it is every man's duty to be just whether there be any such thing as a just man in the world or no. But whether this course in public or private affairs will succeed well, whether rhubarb will purge, or quinquina [quinine] cure an ague, is only known by experience and there is but probability grounded upon experience or analogical reasoning, but no certain knowledge or demonstration. JL

Laws

28 June 1681. Untitled. MS Locke, f. 5, pp. 86–7. Printed in Von Leyden 1954, pp. 67–8. Occasioned by Locke's reading of Hooker's *Laws of Ecclesiastical Polity*. He distinguishes between the law of nature, civil law, and the law of reputation. He also does so in a Latin note headed 'lex triplex' (f. 3, p. 201; 15 July 1678).

The observation of the laws of one country *officium civile*, the breach of a penal law, *crimen* or *delictum*; the observation of what in any country is thought enjoined by the law of nature *virtus*, the contrary *vitium*; the observation or omission of what is in credit and esteem anywhere *laus* and *vituperium*; *licitum* is what is not forbidden or commanded by the laws of the society. *Indifferens* what is so by all the other laws. JL[51]

Selecting the Grand Jury

c. July–August 1681. Untitled; written in Locke's hand. PRO 30/ 24/47/30, fos. 32–5. Printed in Milton and Milton 1997, which provides a full treatment of the context. This document shows Locke's involvement in the Earl of Shaftesbury's legal defence, and evinces his support for the civil liberties of religious Dissenters. It must have been written between Shaftesbury's arrest on 2 July and the throwing out of the treason charge against him by the Grand Jury on 24 November. Shaftesbury could not be tried until indicted by a Grand Jury, whose members were selected by the sheriffs, who were Whigs. The Tory justices sought to weed the packed Whig panel of jurors by disqualifying Dissenters. The law allowed the justices discretion to overrule the sheriffs' nominations. Locke denied that their discretion extended so far. He went on to deny that justices in *oyer* and *terminer*, as opposed to justices of the peace, or of gaol delivery, had any discretion in this case: Shaftesbury, a peer, could only be indicted for treason before justices of *oyer* and *terminer*. In practice, however, the same jurors presented indictments before all three bodies of justices. In a complex manoeuvre, Locke argued that, notwithstanding, they constituted three distinct panels. In writing this memorandum Locke had in front of him the opinion of William Thomson (a Whig lawyer), Sir Edward Coke's *Institutes* (a lawyers' bible), and a tract which shared Locke's view and to which he twice refers: *None but the Sheriffs Ought to Name and Return Jurors to Serve in Inquests before Commissioners of Oyer and Terminer*. J.R. Milton's and P. Milton's recent discovery of this tract adds to our knowledge of Locke's involvement in the politics of the Exclusion Crisis. See also Haley 1968, pp. 667n and 670. For other new evidence see Knights 1993.

Whatever power some would pretend to be in the Justices of the Peace or Justices of Gaol Delivery to reform panels returned by the sheriffs, yet it is evident by the statute itself of the 3 H. VIII [c. 12

---

[51] The Latin terms respectively connote: civil duty; crime, delict; virtue, vice; praiseworthiness, blameworthiness; that which is licit; that which is permitted ('things indifferent').

(1512)] that unless it does appear to the court upon reasonable evidence that the present sheriffs are guilty of the same or such like misdemeanours as are mentioned in the preamble of the statute, or that the persons impanelled are such sort of persons as therein are set forth, they have no power by that statute to reform the panel. The preamble of a statute being always accounted an excellent key to open the meaning of the purview. And therefore though the body or purview of the statute may seem very large, referring all to the discretion of the court, yet 'tis very well known that discretion according to interpretation of law is not an extravagant liberty or licence to do what they please; but their proceedings are to be limited and bounded within the rule of law and reason. Discretion being a faculty of discerning *per legem quid sit justum*, and not to be guided by will or private affection because *talis discretio discretionem confundit.*[52] And there can be no better guide to their discretion in this case than the preamble of the statute.

If therefore it appears that the sheriffs for extorsive or oppressive designs to draw profits or rewards to themselves have impanelled these juries, or that the persons impanelled are men of ill fame and such as probably make no conscience of an oath, there may be reason to reform the panel. But every breach of law, or repeated breaches of law, especially of some penal laws, the observation of which is not rigorously exacted, will not render a man suspected of being guilty of wilful perjury which the statute takes notice of. For at this rate everyone that eats flesh on Fridays or that doth not exactly keep Lent or observe all the holy days will be made incapable.

And as to the Dissenters from the rites and ceremonies of the Church of England (which hath been objected) they cannot be brought within the meaning of that Act. Because the dissent is in such things wherein wise and good men have heretofore differed and do and will always herein more or less differ. And the dissent being so much against the profit and secular interest of the Dissenters, it cannot be presumed to proceed from anything but impulse of conscience, wherein although they may err and therefore be or be thought weak, yet there can be no reason to conclude them

---

[52] This definition, and the Latin tags, follow Coke's *Institutes* (Part II) and his *Reports*. 'What would be just according to law'; 'Such discretion confounds discretion.'

wicked, but rather that they fear and therefore will keep their oaths, lawfully administered and taken. Besides that the Dissenters cease not thereby to be freemen of England, but are equally with others capable of the same privileges and liable to the same burdens and services, and the law makes no such distinction nor is there any reason for it.

From all which it follows that if the court should command the sheriffs to reform the panel where there is no fault which this statute of 3 H. VIII takes notice of the sheriffs may refuse to obey and stand to their own panel without any forfeiture of £20.

But if the sheriffs should yield themselves guilty of having returned such persons in their panels as 'for the singular advantage, benefit and gain of the said sheriffs or their ministers [they] will be wilfully forsworn and perjured by the sinister labour of the said sheriffs and their ministers',[53] which is the only cause wherein the law provides and allows the reformation of the panel by the command of the bench. If (I say) the sheriffs should be prevailed on by the court to lay so deep an infamy and so lasting a disparagement on themselves and those citizens whose names they strike out of the panel, yet they are further to consider, that this power of reforming panels is given only to the Justices of the Peace (who in the precept which they send forth are styled *justiciarii Domini Regis ad pacem in dicta civitate conservand.*) and to the Commissioners or Justices of Gaol Delivery (who in the precept they send forth are styled *Justic. Domini Regis ad Gaolem de Newgate de prisonar. in eadem existent deliberand. assignat*), but the Commissioners or Justices of Oyer and Terminer have no power at all to reform the panel returned upon and annexed to their precept, wherein they are styled *Justic. Domini Regis ad inquirend. pro dicto Domino Rege de quibuscunque prodiconibus*, etc.

To understand this aright we must know that in the City of London, though it be the practice that the same men who are returned and sworn of the Grand Jury at the sessions of the peace at Guildhall be also the Grand Jury of Gaol Delivery and of Oyer and Terminer at the Old Bailey yet their being the same persons hinders not but that they are three distinct juries returned upon

---

[53] Locke adds a marginal note: 'Vide preamble of the statute 3 H. VIII in the printed paper.'

three distinct panels in obedience to three distinct precepts and pursuant of three distinct commissions, viz. the Commission of the Peace (which in London is held by charter, and the sessions thereupon begin at Guildhall and adjourn to the Old Bailey), the Commission of Gaol Delivery, and the Commission of Oyer and Terminer which are begun and held at the Old Bailey. And the sheriffs might, if they pleased, return upon each distinct panel different men, did not the ease of the people (when the business can as well or better be dispatched by the same men serving in these different juries) recommend and warrant this practice both in London and at the County Assizes where the same persons who are of the Grand Jury are returned upon three several panels as matters do happen.

One thing further must be observed to avoid confusion, viz. that the Justices of Gaol Delivery and the Justices of Oyer and Terminer being the same persons, when the same jurors' names are returned upon the two distinct panels of Gaol Delivery and of Oyer and Terminer, the said jurors are usually sworn but once, because the commissioners or justices sit there in both capacities. But yet this hinders not but that they are still two distinct juries.

These therefore being distinct panels with the same names in them, if the Justices of Gaol Delivery, who are the same with those of Oyer and Terminer, should by virtue of the statute 3 H. VIII find reason to command the panel upon the precept of Gaol Delivery to be reformed, and the sheriffs find reason to submit to it, yet this will not concern nor affect the panel upon the precept of Oyer and Terminer, which must and ought to stand immutable as returned by the sheriffs, as appears by the Stat. 11 H. IV [c. 9 (1410)],[54] whereby it is absolutely enjoined that nobody shall be returned upon any nomination to the sheriff by any person of the names which by him should be impanelled. And if anyone will look into the preamble of that statute he shall find that that law was particularly made to hinder the justices from making any such alterations in panels, or nominating anyone to be put into them, which is so absolutely provided against that, if it should happen at any time to be done, all proceedings thereupon are made void as appears by the same law. So that whatever may happen to the panel of Gaol Delivery, the court has no power to alter or reform anything in the panel

---

[54] Marginal note: 'vide printed paper'.

of Oyer and Terminer, but the law is directly against it, and therefore that panel as once returned by the sheriffs must stand. Besides, if commissioners to enquire should have such power over panels, great part of the miseries practised by Empson and Dudley, Inst. 4,[55] may be practised again.

Virtue B

1681 (initially dated by King 1829 and Schankula 1973 to *c.* 1660–3). 'Virtus'. Adversaria 1661, pp. 10–11. Printed in King 1829, pp. 292–3; 1830, II, 94–6; Fox Bourne 1876, I, 162–4; Wootton 1993, pp. 240–2. Locke discusses the ways in which virtue and vice, as derived from benefit and harm, differ between natural and developed societies; he uses the example of polygamy and female modesty.

Virtue, as in its obligation it is the will of God, discovered by natural reason, and thus has the force of a law; so in the matter of it, it is nothing else but doing of good, either to oneself or others; and the contrary hereunto, vice, is nothing else but doing of harm. Thus the bounds of temperance are prescribed by the health, estates, and the use of our time; justice, truth, and mercy, by the good or evil they are like[ly] to produce; since everybody allows one may with justice deny another the possession of his own sword, when there is reason to believe he would make use of it to his own harm. But since men in society are in a far different estate than when considered single and alone, the instances and measures of virtue and vice are very different under these two considerations; for though, as I said before, the measures of temperance, to a solitary man, be none but those above mentioned; yet if he be a member of a society, it may, according to the station he has in it, receive measures from reputation and example; so that what would be no vicious excess in a retired obscurity, may be a very great one amongst people who think ill of such excess, because, by lessening his esteem amongst them, it makes a man incapable of having the authority, and doing the good which otherwise he might. For esteem and reputation being a sort of moral strength, whereby a man is enabled to do, as

---

[55] Richard Empson and Edmund Dudley were ministers of Henry VII executed for treason in 1510; Coke in the *Fourth Institute* execrates them.

it were, by an augmented force, that which others, of equal natural parts and natural power, cannot do without it; he that by an intemperance weakens this his moral strength, does himself as much harm as if by intemperance he weakened the natural strength either of his mind or body, and so is equally vicious by doing harm to himself. This, if well considered, will give us better boundaries of virtue and vice, than curious questions stated with the nicest distinctions; that being always the greatest vice whose consequences draw after it the greatest harm; and therefore the injury and mischiefs done to society are much more culpable than those done to private men, though with greater personal aggravations. And so many things naturally become vices amongst men in society, which without that would be innocent actions: thus for a man to cohabit and have children by one or more women, who are at their own disposal, and when they think fit to part again, I see not how it can be condemned as a vice since nobody is harmed, supposing it done amongst persons considered as separate from the rest of mankind; but yet this hinders not but it is a vice of deep dye when the same thing is done in a society, wherein modesty, the great virtue of the weaker sex, has often other rules and bounds set by custom and reputation, than what it has by direct instances of the law of nature in a solitude or an estate separate from the opinion of this or that society. For if a woman, by transgressing those bounds which the received opinion of her country or religion, and not nature or reason, have set to modesty, has drawn any blemish on her reputation, she may run the risk of being exposed to infamy, and other mischiefs, amongst which the least is not the danger of losing the comforts of a conjugal settlement, and therewith the chief end of her being, the propagation of mankind. JL

Adversaria C

c. 1681? Untitled. MS Locke, c. 28, fos. 157–8. Hard to date, but an almost identical tabulation is in Adversaria 1661, pp. 290–1, dated 1681; compare 'Adversaria A' and 'B'. Not hitherto printed. Translated from the Latin. Locke's tabular form is not reproduced; numeration is added. Three of his categories are printed here; the four remaining, Metaphysica, Theologia, Physica, and Semiotica, are omitted.

[I] Polity: [1] Fundamentals: paternal right; popular consent; arms. [2] Forms: monarchy, aristocracy, democracy, mixed. [3] Administration: civil laws (civil duty, crime, permissible action); magistracy.

[II] History: [1] Ecclesiastical, of religion or clergy. [2] Civil: of states or peoples; of men, biographically. [3] Chronological, of epochs.

[III] Prudence: [1] Ends: [i] Eternal and heavenly felicity (theology); [ii] Earthly: tranquillity; health (physic); wealth (economy [political economy, economics]); power (politics); favour; reputation. [2] Means: [i] self-knowledge; [ii] mastery of the passions; [iii] moral rectitude (virtue praised; vice blamed; things indifferent); [iv] intellectual discretion; [v] discrimination of parts; [vi] search for counsel; [vii] directing of minds (rhetoric, logic); [viii] the household (wife, freemen, servants); [ix] agriculture; [x] trade; [xi] military arts.

Enthusiasm

19 February 1682. Untitled. MS Locke, f. 6, pp. 20–5. Printed in King 1829, pp. 125–7; 1830, I, 234–7; Aaron and Gibb 1936, pp. 119–21, 123–5. Locke comments on the first of John Smith's *Select Discourses* (1660), concerning 'The true way or method of attaining to divine knowledge'. Locke wrote three commentaries: the first is printed here, the second (on the immortality of the soul) and the third (on knowledge) are omitted: they are printed in Aaron and Gibb 1936, pp. 121–5. The first paragraph of 'Enthusiasm' is the same as Letter 696; the third commentary is Letter 687; both were addressed to Damaris Masham. See also Letters 684, 688, 699; and *ECHU*, bk IV, ch. 19.

A strong and firm persuasion of any proposition relating to religion for which a man hath either no or not sufficient proofs from reason but receives them as truths wrought in the mind extraordinarily by God himself and influences coming immediately from him, seems to me to be enthusiasm, which can be no evidence or ground of assurance at all nor can by any means be taken for knowledge.[56] For

---

[56] Added in the margin: 'If such groundless thoughts as those concern ordinary matters and not religion possess the mind strongly we call it raving and everyone thinks it a degree of madness, but in religion men accustomed to the thoughts of revelation make a greater allowance to it, though indeed it be a more dangerous

I find that Christians, Mahomedans, and Brahmins all pretend to it (and I am told the Chinese too). But 'tis certain that contradictions and falsehoods cannot come from God, nor can anyone that is of the true religion be assured of anything by a way whereby those of a false religion may be and are equally confirmed in theirs.[57] For the Turkish Dervishes pretend to revelations, ecstasies, vision rapture to be swallowed up and transported with illuminations of God, discoursing with God, seeing the face of God, v[ide] Ricaut 216 (i.e. Of the Ottoman Empire, fol. London 70, l. 2 c. 13, etc.)[58] and the Jaugis [Yogis] amongst the Hindoos talk of being illuminated and entirely united to God, Bernier 173 (i.e. Memoires, Tome III, 8vo, London 72) p. 36,[59] as well as the most spiritualised Christians.

It is to be observed concerning these illuminations that how clear soever they may seem they carry no knowledge nor certainty any further than there are proofs of the truth of those things that are discovered by them and so far they are parts of reason and have the same foundation with other persuasions in a man's mind and whereof his reason judges, and if there be no proofs of them they can pass for nothing but mere imaginations of the fancy, how clearly soever they appear to or acceptable they may be to the mind for 'tis not the clearness of the fancy, but the evidence of the truth of the thing which makes the certainty. He that should pretend to have a clear sight of a Turkish paradise and of an angel sent to direct him thither might perhaps have a very lively imagination of all this, but it altogether no more proved that either there were such a place or that an angel had the conduct of him thither than if he saw all this in colours well drawn by a painter, these two pictures being no more different (as to the assurance of anything resembled by them) than that one is a fleeting draught in the imagination [and] the other a lasting one on a sensible [sentient] body.

That which makes all these pretences to supernatural illumination further to be suspected to be merely the effect and operation of the fancy is that all the preparation and ways used to dispose the

---

madness, but men are apt to think that in religion they may and ought to quit their reason.'

[57] Added in the margin: 'Enthusiasm is a fault in the mind opposite to brutish sensuality as far in the other extreme exceeding the just measures of reason as thoughts grovelling only in matter and things of sense come short of it.'

[58] Sir Paul Rycaut, *Present State of the Ottoman Empire* (1667; 3rd edn, 1670).

[59] François Bernier, *A Continuation of the Memoirs*, vols. III–IV (1672).

mind to these illuminations and make it capable of them are such as are apt to disturb and depress the rational power of the mind, but to advance and set on work the fancy such are fasting, solitude, intense and long meditation on the same thing, opium, intoxicating liquors, long and vehement turning round, etc., all which are used by some or other of those who would attain to those extraordinary discoveries as fit preparations of the mind to receive them, all which do naturally weaken or disturb the rational faculty and thereby let loose the imagination and thereby make the mind less steady in distinguishing betwixt truth and fancy but [rather] mistake [them], as crazy, weak, drunken or mad men do, one for the other.

I do not remember that I have read of any enthusiasts amongst the Americans or any who have not pretended to a revealed religion, as all those before mentioned do; which if so it naturally suggests this inquiry: whether those that found their religion upon revelation do not from thence take occasion to imagine that since God has been pleased by revelation to discover to them the general precepts of their religion, they that have a particular interest in his favour have reason to expect that he will reveal himself to them if they take the right way to seek it, in those things that concern them in particular in reference to their conduct, state, or comfort. But of this I shall conclude nothing till I shall be more fully assured in matter of fact.

Ecclesia

c. 1682. 'Ecclesia'. MS Locke, d. 10, pp. 43–4. A commentary on Hooker's *Ecclesiastical Polity* (see Hooker 1989, pp. 117–18). Printed in King 1830, II, 99–101. Locke bought a copy of Hooker in June 1681 and took extensive notes (MS Locke, f. 5, pp. 67–77).

Hooker's description of the church, bk I, ch. 15, amounts to this: that it is a supernatural but voluntary society, wherein a man associates himself to God, angels, and holy men. The original of it, he says, is the same as of other societies, viz. an inclination unto sociable life, and a consent to the bond of association, which is the law and order they are associated in. That which makes it supernatural is, that part of the bond of their association which is a law revealed concerning what worship God would have done unto him, which natural reason could not have discovered. So that the worship of God so far forth as it has anything in it more than the law of reason doth teach, may not be invented of men. From whence I think it will follow:

(1) That the church being a supernatural society, and a society by consent, the secular power, which is purely natural, nor any other power, can compel one to be of any particular church society, there being many such to be found.

(2) That the end of entering into such society being only to obtain the favour of God, by offering him an acceptable worship, nobody can impose any ceremonies unless positively and clearly by revelation enjoined, any further than everyone who joins in the use of them is persuaded in his conscience they are acceptable to God; for if his conscience condemns any part of unrevealed worship, he cannot by any sanction of men be obliged to it.

(3) That since a part only of the bond of this association is a revealed law, this part only is unalterable, and the other, which is human, depends wholly upon consent, and so is alterable, and a man is held by such laws, or to such a particular society, no longer than he himself doth consent.

(4) I imagine that the original of this society is not from our inclination, as he says, to a sociable life, for that may be fully satisfied in other societies, but from the obligation man, by the light of reason, finds himself under, to own and worship God publicly in the world. JL

Superstition

c. 1682. 'Superstitio'. MS Locke, d. 10, p. 161. Printed in King 1830, II, 101. Locke draws upon remarks by the Cambridge Platonist John Smith in his *Select Discourses* (1660, 2nd edn, 1673).

The true cause and rise of superstition is indeed nothing else but a false opinion of the deity, that renders him dreadful and terrible, as being rigorous and imperious; that which represents him as austere and apt to be angry, but yet impotent and easy to be appeased again by some flattering devotions, especially if performed with sanctimonious shows and a solemn sadness of mind. Smith, p. 25. This root of superstition diversely branched forth itself sometimes into magic and exorcisms, oftentimes into pedantical rites and idle observations of things and times, as Theophrastus hath largely set forth in his tract.[60]

Superstition is made up of apprehension of evil from God, and hopes, by formal and outward addresses to him, to appease him without real amendment of life. JL

Tradition

c. 1682. 'Traditio'. MS Locke, d. 10, p. 163. Printed in King 1830, II, 101–2. Locke here addresses the 'rule of faith' controversy: the question whether Scripture is a sufficient guide to truth, without the interpretative authority of church traditions.

The Jews, the Romanists, and the Turks, who all three pretend to guide themselves by a law revealed from heaven, which shows them the way to happiness, do yet all of them have recourse very frequently to tradition, as a rule of no less authority than their written law, whereby they seem to allow that the divine law (however God be willing to reveal it) is not capable to be conveyed by writings to mankind, distant in place, time, languages and customs; and so, through the defect of language no positive law of righteousness can be that way conveyed sufficiently and with exactness to all the inhabitants of the earth in remote generations; and so must resolve all into natural religion and that light which every man has born with him. Or else they give occasion to enquiring men to suspect the integrity of their priests and teachers, who, unwilling that the people should have a standing known rule of faith and manners, have, for the maintenance of their own authority, foisted in another of tradition, which will always be in their power, to be varied and suited to their own interest and occasions. JL

The Labadists

22 August 1684. Untitled. MS Locke, f. 8, pp. 114–21. Not hitherto printed. The Labadists were similar to the early Quakers, relying upon the 'inner light' and professing an austere simplicity of

---

[60] Theophrastus: Greek philosopher, pupil of Aristotle.

manners. They were founded by a French Jesuit, Jean de Labadie, who defected to Protestantism in 1650, moved to Holland, and died in 1674. Labadie had helped Edmund Ludlow and other English regicides find asylum in Switzerland in 1662. His followers, now led by Pierre Yvon, settled at Wieuwerd in North Holland, on the estate of Cornelis van Sommelsdyck, the governor of Surinam, whose sisters were Labadists. The sect did not survive into the next generation. Locke made a special journey to see them (as William Penn had done in 1677); his remarks reveal his opinion of sectarian cults. See Saxby 1987.

Here in Mr Somerdike's [Sommelsdyck's] house is the church of the Labadists, now under the charge of Mr Yvon. They receive all ages, sexes and degrees upon approbation after trial. They live all in common and whoever is admitted is to give with himself all that he has to the Lord, i.e. to the church, which is managed by officers appointed by the church. For it is a fundamental miscarriage, and such as will deserve cutting off, to possess anything in property. Those who are obliged by any reason to go abroad, or for their health should be obliged to live abroad, have allowance made them by the church out of their common stock. Their rule is the word of God and mutual brotherly love one to another. The discipline whereby they prevent or correct offences are, first, brotherly reprehension; if that suffices not, the next is suspension from the sacrament and also from their common table; if this makes not an amendment they cut him off from their body.

They meet every morning about five of the clock when some discourse is made to them upon some place of Scripture, before and after which they pray, and then they go every one about their private occupations, for they have amongst them of almost all trades. Nobody is compelled to work by any set rule but they do it out of an instinct of charity and duty. At dinner there is read to them some parcel of Scripture which is commonly the subject of their discourse during the meal. At supper they sing a psalm. Though they hold not any obligation on them to observe the Sunday by the law either of Moses or the Gospel, yet not to scandalise others they work not that day, but in cases of necessity, and therefore they assemble and preach twice that day. They say that a Christian's whole life ought to be a Sabbath from sin. Baptism they administer not but to grown people who show themselves to be Christians by their lives as well as professions. This is all they differ in from the reformed churches of this country, and in their interpretation of the old and new covenant, that [traditional practice of the Sabbath] being, as they understand it, the law of Moses, consisting in exterior services, and [not] typical of the new covenant, which is the Gospel, consisting in a spiritual worship.

Their clothes are plain and modest, their mien and behaviour demure and a little affected, if I mistake not. They are very civil one to another as well as to strangers, carefully saluting one another with their hats as often as they meet.

They have been here these nine years and, as they tell me, increase daily, but yet I could not learn their number, though I asked both Mr Yvon and Mr van der Meulen, which were those I had most conversation with, the latter telling me about a hundred and the former about eighty. They are very shy to give an account particularly about their manner and rule of living and discipline, and 'twas with much difficulty I got so much of them, for they seemed to expect that a man should come there disposed to desire and court admittance into their society without enquiring particularly into their ways, and if the Lord, as they say, dispose him to it, and they see the signs of grace in him, they will proceed to give him further instructions and further trial, and if at last they judge him right admit him, which signs of grace seem to me to be at last a perfect submission to the will and rules of their pastor Mr Yvon, who, if I mistake not, has established to himself a perfect empire over them. For though both officers, censures, and all their administration be in appearance in their church, yet it is easy to perceive how at last it determines in him and his *dominus factotum*. And though I believe they are much separated from the world and are generally speaking people of very good and exemplary lives, yet the tone of the voice, mien, and fashion of those I conversed with seemed to make some suspect a little of Tartuffe[61] amongst them. Besides that, all their discourse carries with it a supposition of more purity in them than ordinary and as if nobody were in the way to heaven but they, [and is] not without a mixture of canting in referring things immediately to the Lord even on those occasions and instances when one enquires after the rational means and measures

---

[61] A hypocritical pretender to religion, after Molière's play of 1664.

of proceeding, as if they did all things by revelation. It was above two hours after I came before I could receive audience of Mr Yvon, though recommended by a friend, and had a letter for him. There was no assembly this morning, Mr Yvon being, as I was told, sick, and I saw him not when I came away. And how many offers soever I made towards it, I could not be admitted to see their place of exercise or eating or any of their chambers in the house but was kept all the while I was there in *atrio gentium* [the public entrance], a little house without the gate, for, as I said before, they seemed very shy of discovering the *secreta domus* [secrets of the house] which seemed to me not altogether so suitable to the pattern of Christianity.

Thus I Think

c. 1686–8? 'Thus I thinke'. MS Locke, c. 28, fos. 143–4. Printed in King 1829, pp. 304–5; 1830, II, 120–2; Fox Bourne 1876, I, 164–5; Cranston 1957, pp. 123–4. On happiness, pleasure, and conduct.

'Tis a man's proper business to seek happiness and avoid misery. Happiness consists in what delights and contents the mind, misery is what disturbs, discomposes or torments it. I will therefore make it my business to seek satisfaction and delight and avoid uneasiness and disquiet and to have as much of the one and as little of the other as may be. But here I must have a care I mistake not, for if I prefer a short pleasure to a lasting one, 'tis plain I cross my own happiness.

Let me then see wherein consists the most lasting pleasures of this life and that as far as I can observe is in these things:

(1) Health, without which no sensual pleasure can have any relish.

(2) Reputation, for that I find everybody is pleased with and the want of it is a constant torment.

(3) Knowledge, for the little knowledge I have, I find I would not sell at any rate, nor part with for any other pleasure.

(4) Doing good. For I find the well-cooked meat I eat today does now no more delight me, nay, I am diseased after a full meal. The perfumes I smelt yesterday now no more affect me with any pleasure. But the good turn I did yesterday, a year, seven years since, continues still to please and delight me as often as I reflect on it.

(5) The expectation of eternal and incomprehensible happiness in another world is that also which carries a constant pleasure with it.

If, then, I will faithfully pursue that happiness I propose to myself, whatever pleasure offers itself to me, I must carefully look that it cross not any of these five great and constant pleasures above mentioned. For example, the fruit I see tempts me with the taste of it that I love, but if I endanger my health, I part with a constant and lasting for a very short and transient pleasure, and so foolishly make myself unhappy, and am not true to my own interest. Hunting,[62] plays and other innocent diversions delight me. If I make use of them to refresh myself after study and business, they preserve my health, restore the vigour of my mind, and increase my pleasure. But if I spend all, or the greatest part of my time in them, they hinder my improvement in knowledge and useful arts, they blast my credit, and give me up to the uneasy state of shame, ignorance and contempt, in which I cannot but be very unhappy. Drinking, gaming and vicious delights will do me this mischief, not only by wasting my time, but by a positive efficacy endanger my health, impair my parts, imprint ill habits, lessen my esteem, and leave a constant lasting torment on my conscience.

Therefore all vicious and unlawful pleasures I will always avoid, because such a mastery of my passions will afford me a constant pleasure greater than any such enjoyments, and also deliver me from the certain evil of several kinds, that by indulging myself in a present temptation I shall certainly afterwards suffer. All innocent diversions and delights, as far as they will contribute to my health, and consist with my improvement, condition, and my other more solid pleasures of knowledge and reputation, I will enjoy, but no further, and this I will carefully watch and examine, that I may not be deceived by the flattery of a present pleasure to lose a greater.

Of Ethic in General

c. 1686–8? 'Of Ethick in General'. MS Locke, c. 28, fos. 146–52. Printed incompletely in King 1829, pp. 306–12; 1830, II, 122–33. It was intended for *ECHU*, bk IV, ch. 21; it is close to bk II, ch.

---

[62] Locke deleted 'drinking, gaming'. An earlier deletion listed 'eating, drinking, hearing music, seeing fine shows'.

28. It is one of the most frequently discussed of Locke's essays. He expounds his hedonic principle. He discusses the universal principles of morality and the law of nature, and their relationship to conventional languages of morality, to punishment and reward, and to the lawgiver. J.R. Milton has pointed out that one passage replicates a section from 'Draft B' of *ECHU* (1671). Locke made several important revisions to his text.

(1) Happiness and misery are the two great springs of human actions, and through the different ways we find men so busy in the world, they all aim at happiness, and desire to avoid misery, as it appears to them in different places and shapes.

(2) I do not remember that I have heard of any nation of men who have not acknowledged that there has been right and wrong in men's actions, as well as truth and falsehood in their sayings; some measures there have been everywhere owned, though very different; some rules and boundaries to men's actions, by which they were judged to be good or bad; nor is there, I think, any people amongst whom there is no distinction between virtue and vice; some kind of morality is to be found everywhere received; I will not say perfect and exact, but yet enough to let us know that the notion of it is more or less everywhere, and that men think that even where politic societies and magistrates are silent, men yet are under some laws to which they owe obedience.

(3) But however morality be the great business and concernment of mankind, and so deserves our most attentive application and study; yet in the very entrance this occurs very strange and worthy of our consideration,[63] that morality hath been generally in the world treated as a science distinct from theology, religion, and law; and that it hath been the proper province of philosophers, a sort of men different both from divines, priests, and lawyers, whose profession it has been to explain and teach this knowledge to the world; a plain argument to me of some discovery still amongst men, of the law of nature, and a secret apprehension of another rule of action which rational creatures had a concernment to conform to, besides

---

[63] Locke deleted an alternative opening to this paragraph: 'Having had occasion to speak here of virtue and vice it will be convenient to consider morality a little further, it being that knowledge which mankind is most concerned to be acquainted with. 'Tis pretty strange to consider . . .'

what either the priests pretended was the immediate command of
their God (for all the heathen ceremonies of worship pretended to
revelation, reason failing in the support of them), or the lawyer told
them was the command of the government.

(4) But yet these philosophers seldom deriving these rules up to
their original, nor urging them as the commands of the great God
of heaven and earth, and such as according to which he would retri-
bute to men after this life, the utmost enforcements they could add
to them were reputation and disgrace, by those names of virtue and
vice, which they endeavoured by their authority to make names of
weight to their scholars and the rest of the people. Were there no
human law, nor punishment, nor obligation of civil or divine sanctions, there would yet still be such species of actions in the world
as justice, temperance, and fortitude, drunkenness and theft, which
would also be thought some of them good, some bad; there would
be distinct notions of virtues and vices; for to each of these names
there would belong a complex idea, or otherwise all these and the
like words which express moral things in all languages would be
empty insignificant sounds, and all moral discourses would be perfect jargon. But all the knowledge of virtues and vices which a man
attained to this way would amount to no more than taking the definitions or significations of the words of any language, either from
the men skilled in that language, or the common usage of the
country, to know how to apply them, and call particular actions in
that country by their right names; and so in effect would be no
more but the skill how to speak properly, or at most to know what
actions in the country he lives in are thought laudable or disgraceful;
i.e. are called virtues and vices: the general rule whereof, and the
most constant that I can find is, that those actions are esteemed
virtuous which are thought absolutely necessary to the preservation
of society, and those that disturb or dissolve the bonds of community, are everywhere esteemed ill and vicious.

(5) This would necessarily fall out, for were there no obligation
or superior law at all, besides that of society, since it cannot be
supposed that any men should associate together and unite in the
same community, and at the same time allow that for commendable,
i.e. count it a virtue, nay not discountenance and treat such actions
as blameable, i.e. count them vices, which tend to the dissolution
of that society in which they were united; but all other actions that

are not thought to have such an immediate influence on society I find not (as far as I have been conversant in histories), but that in some countries or societies they are virtues, in others vices, and in others indifferent, according as the authority of some esteemed wise men in some places, or as inclination or fashion of people in other places, have happened to establish them virtues or vices; so that the idea of virtues taken up this way teach us no more than to speak properly according to the fashion of the country we are in, without any very great improvement of our knowledge, more than what men meant by such words; and this is the knowledge contained in the common ethics of the schools; and this is no more but to know the right names of certain complex modes, and the skill of speaking properly.

(6) The ethics of the schools, built upon the authority of Aristotle, but perplexed a great deal more with hard words and useless distinctions, telling us what he or they are pleased to call virtues and vices, teach us nothing of morality, but only to understand their names, or call actions as they or Aristotle does; which is, in effect, but to speak their language properly. The end and use of morality being to direct our lives, and by showing us what actions are good, and what bad, prepare us to do the one and avoid the other; those that pretend to teach morals mistake their business, and become only language masters where they do not do this; when they teach us only to talk and dispute, [and] call actions by the names they prescribe, when they do not show the inferments that may draw us to virtue and deter us from vice.

(7) Moral actions are only those that depend upon the choice of an understanding and free agent. And an understanding free agent naturally follows that which causes pleasure to it and flies [from] that which causes pain; i.e. naturally seeks happiness and shuns misery. That, then, which causes to anyone pleasure, that is good to him; and that which causes him pain, is bad to him: and that which causes the greater pleasure is the greater good, and that which causes the greater pain, the greater evil. For happiness and misery consisting only in pleasure and pain, either of mind or body, or both, according to the interpretation I have given above of those words [*ECHU*, bk II, ch. 28], nothing can be good or bad to anyone but as it tends to their happiness or misery, as it serves to produce in them pleasure or pain. For good and bad, being relative terms,

do not denote anything in the nature of the thing, but only the relation it bears to another, in its aptness and tendency to produce in it pleasure or pain. And thus we see and say, that which is good for one man is bad for another.

(8) Now, though it be not so apprehended generally, yet it is from this tendency to produce to us pleasure or pain, that moral good or evil has its name, as well as natural. Yet perhaps it will not be found so erroneous as perhaps at first sight it will seem strange, if one should affirm, that there is nothing morally good which does not produce pleasure to a man, nor nothing morally evil that does not bring pain to him.[64] The difference between moral and natural good and evil is only this; that we call that natural good and evil, which, by the natural efficiency of the thing, produces pleasure or pain in us; and that is morally good or evil which, by the intervention of the will of an intelligent free agent,[65] draws pleasure or pain after it, not by any natural consequence, but by the intervention of that power. Thus, drinking to excess, when it produces the headache or sickness, is a natural evil; but as it is a transgression of law, by which a punishment is annexed to it, it is a moral evil. For rewards and punishments are the good and evil whereby superiors enforce the observance of their laws; it being impossible to set any other motive or restraint to the actions of a free understanding agent but the consideration of good or evil; that is, pleasure or pain that will follow from it.

(9) Whoever treats of morality so as to give us only the definitions of justice and temperance, theft and incontinency, and tells us which are virtues, which are vices, does only settle certain complex

---

[64] Locke deleted the following passage: 'Why does a man pay another a debt he owes him when he wants the money to supply his own conveniences or necessities? Or why does another forbear his neighbour's wife? It will perhaps be answered, because there is moral rectitude and goodness in the one, and moral turpitude or illness in the other. Good words. The moral rectitude, which when considered is but conformity to the natural law of God, would signify nothing, and moral goodness be no reason to direct my action, were there not really pleasure that would follow from the doing of it and pain avoided greater than is to be found in the action itself. Were there no loss of pleasure, no pain to follow for a man's satisfying his appetite as he could, would he not be a fool to endure the pain of hunger, when his neighbour's barn or stall could furnish him, if no evil would follow from his taking what was not his but the danger of a surfeit?'

[65] The phrase 'intervention of the will of an intelligent free agent' is inserted by Locke to replace his original phrase, 'appointment of an intelligent being that has power', but he failed to delete the original phrase.

ideas of modes with their names to them, whereby we may learn to understand others well, when they talk by their rules, and speak intelligibly and properly to others who have been informed in their doctrine. But whilst they discourse never so acutely of temperance or justice, but show no law of a superior that prescribes temperance, to the observation or breach of which law there are rewards and punishments annexed, the force of morality is lost, and evaporates only into words and disputes and niceties. And, however Aristotle or Anacharsis,[66] Confucius, or any amongst us, shall name this or that action a virtue or a vice, their authorities are all of them alike, and they exercise but what power everyone has, which is to show what complex ideas their words shall stand for. For without showing a law that commands or forbids them, moral goodness will be but an empty sound, and those actions which the schools here call virtues or vices, may by the same authority be called by contrary names in another country; and if there be nothing more than their decisions and determinations in the case, they will be still nevertheless indifferent as to any man's practice, which will by such kind of determinations be under no obligation to observe them.

(10)[67] But there is another sort of morality or rules of our actions, which though they may in many parts be coincident and agreeable with the former, yet have a different foundation, and we come to the knowledge of them a different way; these notions or standards of our actions not being ideas of our own making, to which we give names, but depend upon something without us, and so not made by us, but for us, and these are the rules set to our actions by the declared will or laws of another, who hath power to punish our aberrations. These are properly and truly the rules of good and evil, because the conformity or disagreement of our actions with these, bring upon us good or evil; these influence our lives as the other do our words, and there is as much difference between these two, as between living well and attaining happiness on the one hand, compared with speaking properly and understanding of words on the other. The notion of one, men have by making to themselves a collection of simple ideas, called by those names which they take to

---

[66] Anacharsis: a Scythian prince, contemporary of Solon, reckoned a great sage.

[67] The first four-fifths of this paragraph (down to 'collection of simple ideas,') replicate almost exactly §160 of Draft B (1671): Nidditch and Rogers 1990, pp. 269–70.

be the names of virtues and vices; the notion of the other, we come by from the rules set us by a superior power.

(11) But because we cannot come to the knowledge of those rules without, first, making known a lawgiver to all mankind, with power and will to reward and punish; and, secondly, without showing how he hath declared his will and law, I must only at present suppose this rule, till a fit place to speak to these, viz. God and the law of nature; and only at present mention what is immediately to the purpose in hand, first, that this rule of our actions set us by our lawmaker is conversant about, and ultimately terminates in, those simple ideas before mentioned; viz. thou shalt love thy neighbour as thyself. Secondly, that the law being known, or supposed known by us, the relation of our actions to it, i.e. the agreement or disagreement of anything we do to that rule, is as easy and clearly known as any other relation. Thirdly, that we have moral ideas as well as others, that we come by them the same way, and that they are nothing but collections of simple ideas.

Only we are carefully to retain that distinction of moral actions, that they have a double consideration; first, as they have their proper denominations, as liberality, modesty, frugality, . . .[68] etc., and thus they are but modes, i.e. actions made up of such a precise collection of simple ideas; but it is not thereby determined that they are either good or bad, virtues or vices. Secondly, as they refer to a law with which they agree or disagree, so are they good or bad, virtues or vices. Εντραπελια[69] was a name amongst the Greeks, of such a peculiar sort of actions; i.e. of such a collection of simple ideas concurring to make them up; but whether this collection of simple ideas called Εντραπελια, be a virtue or vice, is known only by comparing it to that rule which determines virtue or vice, and this is that consideration that properly belongs to actions, i.e. their agreement with a rule. In one, any action is only a collection of simple ideas, and so is a positive complex idea; in the other it stands in relation to a law or rule, and according as it agrees or disagrees, is virtue or vice. So education and piety, feasting and gluttony, are modes alike, being but certain complex ideas called by one name, but when they are considered as virtues and vices, and rules of life

---

[68] There is a further, indecipherable item.
[69] Roughly: those things that are appraised or evaluated.

carrying an obligation with them, they relate to a law, and so come under the consideration of relation.

(12)[70] To establish morality, therefore, upon its proper basis, and such foundations as may carry an obligation with them, we must first prove a law, which always supposes a lawmaker: one that has a superiority and right to ordain, and also a power to reward and punish according to the tenor of the law established by him. This sovereign lawmaker who has set rules and bounds to the actions of men is God, their maker, whose existence we have already proved. The next thing then to show is, that there are certain rules, certain dictates, which it is his will all men should conform their actions to, and that this will of his is sufficiently promulgated and made known to all mankind.

Pacific Christians

1688. 'Pacifick Christians'. MS Locke, c. 27, fo. 80. Printed in King 1829, pp. 273–5; 1830, II, 63–7; Fox Bourne, II, 185–6; Sina 1972, pp. 73–5. Apparently a set of guiding principles for a religious society. Compare 'Rules of the Dry Club' (*c.* 1692), whose members must declare that they believe 'no person ought to be harmed in his body, name, or goods, for mere speculative opinions, or his external way of worship' (*Works* 1801, X, 312–14).

(1) We think nothing necessary to be known or believed for salvation but what God hath revealed.

(2) We therefore embrace all those who in sincerity receive the word of truth revealed in the Scripture and obey the light which enlightens every man that comes into the world.

(3) We judge no man in meats, or drinks, or habits, or days, or any other outward observances, but leave everyone to his freedom in the use of those outward things which he thinks can most contribute to build up the inward man in righteousness, holiness, and the true love of God and his neighbour in Christ Jesus.

(4) If anyone find any doctrinal part of Scripture difficult to be understood, we recommend him: (i) The study of the Scripture in humility and singleness of heart. (ii) Prayer to the Father of lights

---

[70] Locke deleted: 'That which appears to the mind the greater good at that time determines its choice.'

to enlighten him. (iii) Obedience to what is already revealed to him, remembering that the practice of what we do know is the surest way to more knowledge, our infallible guide having told us, if any man will do the will of him that sent me, he shall know of the doctrine (John 7:17). (iv) We leave him to the advice and assistance of those whom he thinks best able to instruct him. No men, or society of men, having any authority to impose their opinions or interpretations on any other, [even] the meanest Christian; since in matters of religion everyone must know and believe, and give an account for himself.

(5) We hold it to be an indispensable duty for all Christians to maintain love and charity in the diversity of contrary opinions. By which charity we do not mean an empty sound, but an effectual forbearance and good will, carrying men to communion, friendship and mutual assistance one of another, in outward as well as spiritual things. And by dehorting [dissuading] all magistrates from making use of their authority, much less their sword (which was put into their hands only against evil doers) in matters of faith or worship.

(6) Since the Christian religion we profess is not a notional science, to furnish speculation to the brain or discourse to the tongue, but a rule of righteousness to influence our lives, Christ having given himself to redeem us from all iniquity and purify unto himself a people zealous of good works (Titus 2:14), we profess the only business of our public assemblies to be to exhort, thereunto, and laying aside all controversy and speculative questions, instruct and encourage one another in the duty of a good life, which is acknowledged to be the great business of true religion, and to pray God for the assistance of his spirit for the enlightening of our understanding and subduing our corruptions, that so we may perform unto him a reasonable and acceptable service and show our faith by our works. Proposing to ourselves and others the example of our Lord and Saviour Jesus Christ, as the great pattern for our imitation.

(7) One alone being our master, even Christ, we acknowledge no masters of our assembly; but if any man in the spirit of love, peace, and meekness, has a word of exhortation we hear him.

(8) Nothing being so opposite, or having proved so fatal to unity, love and charity, the first and great characteristical duties of Christianity, as men's fondness of their own opinions, and their endeavours to set them up and have them followed, instead of the Gospel

of peace; to prevent these seeds of dissention and division, and maintain unity in the difference of opinions which we know cannot be avoided, if anyone appear contentious, abounding in his own sense rather than in love, and desirous to draw followers after himself, with destruction or opposition to others, we judge him not to have learned Christ as he ought, and therefore not fit to be a teacher of others.

(9) Decency and order in our assemblies being directed, as they ought, only to edification, can need but very few and plain rules. Time and place of meeting being settled, if anything else, need regulation; the assembly itself, or four of the ancientest, soberest and discreetest of the brethren, chosen for that occasion, shall regulate it.

(10) From every brother that after admonition walketh disorderly, we withdraw ourselves.

(11) We each of us think it our duty to propagate the doctrine and practice of universal charity, good will, and obedience in all places, and on all occasions, as God shall give us opportunity.

On Allegiance and the Revolution

c. April 1690. Untitled. MS Locke, e. 18. Printed in Farr and Roberts 1985, pp. 395–8. Cited by Laslett, *Two Treatises*, Preface (under the title 'A Call to the Nation for Unity'). Discussed in Hartogh 1990, and see Dunn 1969, ch. 10; Goldie 1980. This paper, written at a time when King William III's new regime seemed in peril, was sent to Edward Clarke, who became an MP in March 1690, and who marked it 'papers useful in Parliament'. The paper relates to a Whig attempt to pass bills which would recognise King William and Queen Mary as 'rightful and lawful' monarchs (a phrase omitted from the 1689 oath of allegiance), and would require office holders to abjure King James II. Locke defends the Revolution and warns against popery, France and Jacobitism. He notes the popularity of the distinction between *de facto* and *de jure* power among those with conscientious doubts about the Revolution. He argues that those who uphold the hereditary principle *jure divino* [by divine right] are public enemies, since they must regard William as a usurper; he calls for them to make a public renunciation of their doctrine. His targets were Tory politicians like the Earls of Nottingham and Danby, and the Tory pamphleteers who were debating allegiance to the new regime. Compare Locke's insistence upon express consent in the Second Treatise, §§119, 122. The 'rightful and lawful' clause was reinstated in the Association Oath of 1696, following a Jacobite assassination plot (see Letters 2004, 2006), while a formal renunciation of the House of Stuart was embodied in the Abjuration Oath of 1702. Locke himself swore the oath of allegiance in 1695 (and no doubt earlier), and both the Association and Abjuration oaths (MS Locke, c. 25, fos. 12, 61; Letters 2045, 2074, 3131, 3135, 3161, 3163). See Locke's critique of William Sherlock, below.

Complaints are everywhere so loud and the apprehensions that people droop under are so visible,[71] that they cannot but be taken notice of. 'Tis not the want of courage in the nation nor the distrust of our force that makes anybody despair. They are our divisions which throw a dread amongst us, and everyone sees and says unless we are better united we cannot stand. Pardon then a lover of his king and country, a lover of peace and the Protestant interest, if he humbly offer his thoughts at a time when good and honest men think they are all in danger.

England united, 'tis agreed, cannot easily be shaken; let us then put it out of danger.

(1) I shall not propose union of opinions. 'Tis not to be hoped that all men's consciences should be equally enlightened. Reason and experience show them that they are out of the way who aim at it by compulsion; constraint is known to widen the breaches. All here to be wished is that mutual charity would supply consent of thought, till by true methods all men were brought to be of the same mind, if that can ever be expected.

(2) I shall not propose a union of consent concerning persons and methods in public affairs, points unfit for private hands to meddle with. Submission to those whose business it is to take care of the public will secure that as it ought. All that I shall offer shall be what everyone must confess is absolutely necessary to the very being and subsistence of our government and without which our peace and religion cannot possibly be [in] any way secured.

Everyone, and that with reason, begins our delivery from popery and slavery from the arrival of the Prince of Orange and the com-

---

[71] Locke deleted 'of all who wish well to England', and replaced it with the phrase 'that ... visible'.

pleting of it is, by all that wish well to him and it, dated from King William's settlement in the throne. This is the fence set up against popery and France, for King James's name, however made use of, can be but a stale [decoy, pretext] to these two. If ever he return, under what pretences soever, Jesuits must govern and France be our master. He is too much wedded to the one and relies too much on the other ever to part with either. He that has ventured and lost three crowns for his blind obedience to those guides of his conscience and for his following the counsels and pattern of the French king cannot be hoped, after the provocations he has had to heighten his natural aversion, should ever return with calm thoughts and good intentions to Englishmen, their liberties, and religion. And then I desire the boldest or most negligent amongst us, who cannot resolve to be a contemned [despised] popish convert and a miserable French peasant, to consider with himself what security, what help, what hopes he can have, if by the ambition and artifice of any great man he depends on and is led by, he be once brought to this market, a poor, innocent sheep to this shambles;[72] for whatever advantageous bargains the leaders may make for themselves, 'tis eternally true that the dull herd of followers are always bought and sold.

They, then, who would not have the alliance for the security of Christendom broken, must support our present government in which it centres and on which it depends. They who would not betray England and expose it to popish rage and revenge, who have any regard to their country, their religion, their consciences, and their estates, must maintain the bulwark we have set up against it, and which alone preserves us against a more violent inundation of all sorts of misery than that we were so lately delivered from. We must all join in a sincere loyalty to his present majesty and a support of his government.

(1) The first step to this union I think 'tis plain is a general Act of Oblivion.[73] 'Twere to be wished all marks of distinction were laid aside. But since the artifice of our enemies and our own passionate heats and follies keep up names which true Englishmen might spare one to another, yet let the wisdom of our senators blot out the guilt

---

[72] I.e. lamb to the slaughter.
[73] I.e. an act of indemnity, preventing prosecutions for old offences. Such an act was passed in May 1690. Some Whigs were anxious to avenge themselves on Tories for past misdeeds.

which grew from and increased those distinctions, and restore us to as much innocency as the law can do. Let not the imputation of crimes or fear of punishments drive men to seek for security in the disorder of affairs; make men easy and safe under the government, and then they will have no reason but to desire it should go easily and steadily on. Men who love their country well yet love themselves better, and those who would be quiet if they were safe, will at any rate, even [at] the cost of the public, avoid shame or ruin.

(2) There has been a doctrine industriously propagated of late years in England as if the succession of the crown were established *jure divino* and there is ground to imagine it still possesses some men's minds. This as far as it reaches carries an irreconcilable opposition to our quiet and [the] establishment of our present constitution. Whoever holds that another has by the law and appointment of God a title to the throne of England must be an avowed enemy to King William and the present government, and that by the highest obligation, viz. that of divine right, which admits of no control, no dispensation. It cannot therefore but be fit and necessary that all who profess themselves subjects to King William should join in a solemn and public renunciation of a doctrine that annuls his title. Those who call and believe him their king cannot be unwilling to give themselves or receive from others that testimony which may convince rational men that they are in earnest and be a security to that throne on which our peace and religion depends. Who ever scruples this in himself shows evidently that under a pretended loyalty to King William he believes himself still King James's subject, and which of the two duty and conscience will carry him to favour, and assist too whenever he can find an occasion, is not hard to foresee. And whoever would not have this tenet renounced by others, whatever he may pretend, has a very little care of the public peace and security, being unwilling to have the true friends distinguished from the secret enemies of the government till it were too late, a sort of politics never yet known to princes who have always thought the discovery of persons ill affected to their government could never cost them too dear. And I desire anyone to show how a divine right of succession to the crown of England can do less than overturn our present settlement. Reconcile this to the reign of King William, and to an obedience to his rule and I shall pass it by as a scholastic speculation. But if it concern the life and crown of

his majesty, as 'tis plain it does, if it concern the quiet of his reign and welfare of his subjects, let us not think we are sufficiently united for the support of him and his government whilst 'tis uncertain who amongst us retain so dangerous a doctrine and harbour so active a principle against it.

(3) The miscarriages of the former reigns gave a rise and right to King William's coming and ushered him into the throne. His own declaration and [the] public acts of the nation put this past doubt. But yet this can be truly allowed by none as a sufficient cause of the change we have seen and the deliverance we have received who do not think fit to disown and condemn those miscarriages. If there were none, our complaints were mutiny and our redemption rebellion and we ought to return as fast as we can to our old obedience. They who think so cannot do otherwise, and they who think there were miscarriages, such miscarriages as could have no other end but an abdication,[74] have a very little care of his present majesty if they will not join in a public condemnation and abhorrence of them, since without that they can never justify his ascent to the throne nor their maintenance of him there.

(4) The Prince of Orange with an armed force, when nothing less could do, ventured himself to recover our oppressed and sinking laws, liberties, and religion. This everyone must acknowledge him to have done of right who would not have him gone again, and they who will not join in an acknowledgement of the justice, as well as generosity, of this glorious undertaking can have no other reason for their reserved squeamishness but because they look on it as the unjust invasion of an enemy whom they are uneasy under and would willingly get rid of. At least it must be confessed they keep a reserve for another change. Such men as these who would enjoy the benefit of King William's venture, without owning his cause, King James may rely on as such whose silence has sufficiently declared for him, but King William can never trust unless he be willing that his crown should be the price of their preferment. Many who have owned the justice of a cause have betrayed it, but common prudence never played so badly against itself as to expect support from those who refused to acknowledge right on that side.

---

[74] Tories liked to speak of James II as having 'abdicated' his throne, but Locke uses 'abdication' to entail 'deposition'. See Slaughter 1981.

(5) I have of late often met both in discourse and in print with the distinction of a king *de facto* and a king *de jure*, that is, a king in possession and a king by right. If the present government were our redemption a year since and be our security still, let us not trifle with it, let us own King William to be our king by right. Whoever refuse this, what do they in effect [do] but plainly call him [a] usurper! For what is a usurper but a king actually in a throne to which he has no right. I wonder not to hear that the French king calls him so, as the most pernicious opinion [which] can be fixed on him, and I should as little wonder that those who will not own his right to the crown should join with the French king or anybody else to dispossess him they judge a usurper. That which makes this yet more necessary is that there are several amongst us who with great earnestness and obstinacy denied the vacancy of the throne and would have had King William only an officer under King James, with the title of Regent, the right of the crown and allegiance of the people being still fixed and reserved to King James.[75] I do not hear that these men have ever disowned or recanted what they were then so publicly for, but 'tis evident it concerns those who look after the safety and settlement of the government to take care they should. If their judgements are now rectified in these points, they will find no difficulty to profess what they are persuaded of, especially when it will conduce so much to the quieting of men's minds and the strengthening of the government they seem to own, and if they are still of their old opinion 'tis fit that too should be known and they thereby distinguished from those who heartily unite in the support of the present government, which the union, the safety of the nation, and the preservation of our religion stands in need of.

I appeal now to every true Englishman whether the preservation of our peace, the safety of the King's person, and the security of the kingdom do not all centre in the points I have here mentioned. Those who refuse to unite in these, do they not declare they are separate from the government and will be no friends to its continuance? If they divide the kingdom against itself, how do they hope,

---

[75] In the Convention in February 1689 the Tories, having abandoned hope of James II returning to England, turned next to a proposal that William be regent during James's life. Some among these Tory grandees were now, to the anger of many Whigs, taken into government by King William.

how can they be thought to intend, it should stand? Divisions in opinions and smaller matters amongst those who hold the fundamentals shake not the frame. Governments have always subsisted and often flourished with such factions as these, but 'tis impossible to be expected that those should support any constitution who will not so much as declare for it and own the right of the prince they are to obey. This is that which all constitutions which outlasted their birth have constantly taken care of in the first place; the right of their governors and the declaration and owning of that right they never left loose and uncertain. For how can it be expected the people should be firm to a government that is not so to itself and does not assert its own right? If their legislators leave it uncertain, if the great men at court who have place and pay declare not openly and zealously for it, what shall fix the rest of the nation in a steady resolution of fidelity and obedience, when their consciences are left to doubts and the difference of pretended titles is not cleared up by public acts, nor so much as the open and decisive profession of those who have employments in and therefore should know and own the rights of the government? The public silence is of itself enough to raise scruples amongst the people and there will never want private casuists to improve them. But in our case I think it goes further. The press openly scatters doubts and everyone finds a great many questioning without knowing any that are in heart and persuasion for the government. We have a war upon our hands of no small weight. We have a potent and vigilant enemy at our doors, who has emissaries and zealous partisans enough to blow up any doubts or distrusts amongst us into disorder and confusion. The least breach amongst us (and whilst we are not publicly and declaredly united we are not far from a breach) lets in him and his dragoons inevitably upon us. I ask any the warmest Whig or Tory amongst us (except he be of the first rank and can make a bargain for himself by the sale of others) what he proposes to himself when by his heat and animosity he has let in a foreign force, enemy to our religion and nation, and thereby made his country the scene of blood, slaughter, and devastation? Will the zeal for his party make him amends for the ruin of his estate and family? Will he [be] satisfied with what he has done when he sees his children stripped and his wife ravished? For the insolence and rapine of foreigners with swords in their hands make no distinction, especially amongst those of a contrary religion. Will a French or an Irish master[76] that turns him out of all and forces even his conscience to a compliance be more tolerable than an English neighbour that would live quietly with him, though with some little difference in opinion? I desire every Protestant, every Englishman amongst us to lay his hand upon his heart and seriously consider with himself what mortal quarrel he has to any of his countrymen to that degree that rather than live on any tolerable terms with them he would venture the religion, liberty, safety of himself and his country, for all these are at stake and will be lost if we hold not now together.

On William Sherlock

Late 1690 or early 1691. MS Locke, c. 28, pp. 83–96. A commentary on Sherlock's *The Case of the Allegiance due to Soveraign Powers* (1691). Not hitherto printed. Some two hundred tracts published between 1689 and 1693 debated the legitimacy of the Glorious Revolution and the new oath of allegiance (Goldie 1980). William Sherlock, an Anglican clergyman and prominent Tory publicist for the doctrine of non-resistance, at first abjured the Revolution. Then he changed his mind, and argued his case on the grounds that the Revolution was a divine intervention, that the sovereign's protection and the subject's allegiance were correlative, and that fealty could be sworn to a *de facto* prince in possession of the government. Sherlock was promoted to the deanery of St Paul's. His tract, published on 3 November 1690, reached a sixth edition by mid-January 1691, and provoked fifty responses. He was charged with Hobbism, and his arguments are indeed close to the *de facto* defences of the Revolution of 1649. In Germany Leibniz wrote a commentary upon Sherlock (see Riley 1988, pp. 199–217; Jolley 1975). Locke's fragmentary notes are chiefly quotations and paraphrases of claims by Sherlock which he found obnoxious, self-contradictory, or self-defeating: they capture this characteristic attempt to reconcile the Revolution with Tory principles. The page references to Sherlock are Locke's own. He occasionally adds his own queries or objections. Locke's tabular format is replaced by continuous prose. Some extracts from Sherlock are also reprinted here. Compare Locke's remarks on submission, consent and usurp-

---

[76] James II was now master of Catholic Ireland, until his defeat by William at the Battle of the Boyne in July 1690.

ation in Second Treatise, esp. §§122, 186, 192, 198; and 'On Samuel Parker', 1669–70; see also Letters 1344, 1348.

Sherlock. That which has perplexed this controversy is the inter-mixing the dispute of right with the duty of obedience, or making the legal right of princes to their thrones the only reason and foundation of the allegiance due to subjects: . . . allegiance is due only to right, not to government, though it can be paid only to government. . . . It seems to me to be unfit to dispute the right of princes. . . [p. 1]. Every prince, who is settled in the throne, is to be obeyed and reverenced as God's minister, and not to be resisted [p. 4]. There is no duty subjects, as such, owe to the most legal and rightful kings, but . . . [what is] . . . due to all kings, whom God hath placed in the throne [p. 7]. A prince, who is thoroughly settled in his throne, has God's authority and must be obeyed [p. 9]. [Legal right] bars all other human claims . . . but not against God's disposal of crowns [p. 15]. There are different degrees of settlement, and must necessarily be in such new governments, which seem to me to require different degrees of submission . . . till it increases to such a full and plenary and settled possession, as requires our allegiance [p. 17]. [It is not] necessary for subjects . . . to be able to judge between a pretended and real right [p. 19]. Whether some private men, it may be but a little handful, are still bound by their oath, to make some weak and dangerous attempts, and to fight for their king against their country; certainly this was not the intention of the oath, for it is a national, not a private defence, we swear; and therefore a general revolt of a nation, though it should be wicked and unjustifiable, yet it seems to excuse those, who had neither hand nor heart in it, from their sworn defence of the king's person . . . for an oath to fight for the king, does not oblige us to fight against our country [p. 32]. Though I have as great a reverence for princes as any man, I do not think the right and interest of any prince so considerable, as the safety and preservation of a nation [p. 33]. Human societies must not dissolve into a mob, or Mr Hobbes's state of nature, because the legal prince has lost his thorne, and can no longer govern. Bishop Sanderson tells us, that the end of civil government, and of that obedience which is due to it, is the safety and tranquillity of human societies [p. 38]. If human societies must be preserved, then the necessities of government give authority to the prince, and lay an obligation of duty on the subject; if God will preserve human societies, we must conclude, that when he removes one king out of the throne, he gives his authority to him whom he places there; . . . [with] . . . the bands and ligaments of duty and conscience [p. 39]. The government of Antiochus was not settled among them, either by submission or continuance; that is, though people were forced to submit to power, his government was not owned by any public, national submission [whereas the] governing part of the nation [speedily submitted to Jaddus[77]] [p. 48]. What then shall subjects do, when the king is gone, and the government dissolved, the people left in the hands of another prince, without any reason, or any authority, or any formed power, to oppose him? The government must be administered by somebody, unless we can be contented, that the rabble should govern [p. 50].

Locke. Case of Allegiance due to sovereign powers. Terms. Allegiance. Terms. Mistakes. Allegiance is due only to right not to government though it can be paid only to government, 1. Dispute: unfit to dispute the right of princes, 1. Allegiance is neither due nor paid to right or to government which are abstract notions but only to persons having right or government. Self contradictions. Dispute: 'tis unfit to dispute the right of princes, a thing which no government can permit to be a question among their subjects, 1. Positions disadvantageous. Few men are capable of making so plain and certain a judgement of th [sic]. Terms. Jargon, p. 1.

Authority carries with it duty and conscience, 39, 43. Legal right, 2. What, 2, is a real right in opposition to a pretended: 19. Contradistinguished to invested with God's authority. Settlement, 2, what. p. 4. Different degrees of settlement, vide: 17, and different duties accordingly if by submission or continuance, 48. God's authority, p. 4, 5. God has placed in the throne, 7. Thoroughly settled, 9. Allegiance is all the duty which subjects owe to their king, 15. King signifies the person who has the supreme government in the nation, 56. King *de facto* is he that actually has the government. King *de*

---

[77] Sanderson: probably a reference to Robert Sanderson, *De Obligatione Conscientiae* (1660). Antiochus, Jaddus: refers to the oppressive rule of the Syrian king Antiochus IV, overthrown by the Jewish guerilla leader Judas Maccabeus (d. 160 BC), as recorded in the first and second books of Maccabees.

jure as opposed to it is he who of right should have the government: but has it not, 56.

Positions. Usurped powers when thoroughly settled have God's authority and must be obeyed. God sets up kings by the events of providence, 12, 13. By what means soever any prince ascends the throne he is placed there by God, 13. All kings are equally rightful kings with respect to God, they have all God's authority and who-ever has God's authority is a true and rightful king, 14. We must pay our allegiance to him who is king without legal right; not to him who is our king though it be his right to be so, 15. A legal right bars all other human claim, and the subjects are bound to maintain the right of such a prince as far as they can, 15, i.e. against all mankind. Q. Does not God's authority which the actual king has bar all other claims and are not the subjects bound to maintain the right of such a prince as far as they can?

An oath of allegiance binds not to the man but to the king and no longer than he is king, 16. We swear to defend the king's right and the right of his heirs: but we do not swear to keep them in the throne, 16. Q. What is it to defend their right and not to keep them in the throne? Natural, which is paternal authority, no man has authority to give away or usurp, 23. Submission gives no right, 24. Choice, conquest, submission can give possession of a throne which is a good title against all human claims, 24. The distinction of a king *de jure* and a king *de facto* relates only to human laws which bind subjects but are not the necessary rules and measures of divine providence, 14.

Positions. God gives the authority by placing the prince in the throne and by whatever means he does it, it is the same thing, 25. Submission is only owing to God's authority, 26. Q. Does not the dethroned prince owe submission to God's authority as well as others? An oath to fight for our king does not oblige us to fight against our country, 32. I.e. If rebels be the minority they may be fought against, if the majority they are our country and must not be fought against. No man must swear away subjection to God's authority, 32. *Ergo* [therefore] the former king who is but a man must be subject to God's authority. Worthy and gallant men, 33, were resisters and plotters against God's authority. The people are to be preferred to the prince, 33. Q. How non-resistance, p. 36, can consist with bounds of sovereign power and liberties of the subjects.

p. 30. Do princes receive a legal right from human laws and yet not their authority from human laws, 36? The end of government is the preservation of human society, 38. Providence alters not the legal right, 26.

Propositions. The preservation of human societies does of necessity force us to own the authority even of usurped powers, 41. Self-preservation is as much a law to subjects as to the prince, 42. And does God's authority which the usurper has as much oblige the deposed prince as the people? vide: his marks of a true principle, 44. The right of any prince is not so sacred as to stand in competition with the safety and preservation of all his subjects, 45. Mankind is not made for princes but princes for the government of men, 45. Rights and liberties of a country are as sacred as the rights of kings, 47. The king gone and the government dissolved, 50. In some cases it is hard to determine when the government is so settled as to make allegiance due, 51. The divine law commands us to pay all the obedience and duty of subjects to a prince in the actual possession of the throne, 52. No authority can take cognisance of the titles and claims of princes and the disposal of the crown but the estates of the realm, 52. The law does not refer the cognisance of the rights to crowns to private subjects, 52. In moral and natural duties every man may and must understand for himself, 53.

Positions. Whoever has possession of the crown has an hereditary crown, 56. Q: How then has the legal king, whose right bars all other claim? vide p. 15.

Terms. Settlement. The government was not settled amongst them either by submission or continuance, i.e. the people were forced to submit to power, his government was not owned by any public national submission and in such cases a long continuance is required to settle a government; whereas a national submission settles a government in a short time. Jaddus the high priest and the governing part of the nation submitting; this settled the government in a few days, 48.

How long a month, a year, seven or a hundred years, and by what rule, what law of God? Long and short in such cases unless defined have no meaning. People submit where they do not resist for that where there is no resistance there is a general submission. But there may be a general submission without a general consent, which is another thing.

Ethica A

1692. 'Ethica'. MS Locke, c. 42B, p. 224. Printed in Driscoll 1972, pp. 102–3; Sargentich 1974, pp. 29–31.

Nothing can attract a rational agent nor be a cause to it of action but good. That good is only pleasure or greater pleasure or the means to it. Pleasures are all of the mind, none of the body, but some consist in motions of the body, some in contemplations and satisfactions of the mind separate, abstract and independent from any motions or affections of the body. And these latter are both the greatest and more lasting. The former of these we will for shortness sake [call] pleasures of the senses, the other, pleasures of the soul, or rather, material and immaterial pleasures. Material pleasures last not beyond the present application of the object to the sense and make but a small part of the life of the most voluptuous man. Those of taste cease as soon as the stomach is full and a satiated appetite loathes the most exquisite dishes. Perfumes make men weary in a little time or, which is the same, are not smelt. Few are so delighted with music that when it is grown familiar to them either mind it not or at least do not prefer the discourse of a friend to it, as anyone may observe in himself and others. And [as] for seeing, though it be the most capacious and most employed of all our senses, yet the pleasure of it lies not so much in the delight the eyes have in the objects before it, but in other things annexed to them as the knowledge and choice of things serviceable to the other parts of our lives, and in the power of seeing so useful to us in all the parts of our lives. So that all the pleasures of the senses taken together, even that too which modesty speaks not openly of, I think one may say that the most voluptuous man has not his senses affected by them, and so has not pleasure from them, one quarter part of his time; perhaps when examined it will be found much less; the rest the body lies fallow or unaffected with pleasure. Perhaps it will be that though the bodily sensation be so short yet the enjoyment and pleasure is longer, as of a splendid entertainment: the satisfaction lasts longer than the meal; it began before it and ends not with it. Let it be so, which shows that even in those material sensual pleasures, contemplation makes up the greatest part, and when the senses have done, the mind by thought continues a pleasure wherein the senses have no share. The use I make of this is that even in voluptuous men the mind without the body makes the greatest part of their happiness or else the greatest part of their lives they are destitute of happiness.

If then happiness be our interest, end, and business 'tis evident the way to it is to love our neighbour as ourself, for by that means we enlarge and secure our pleasures, since then all the good we do to them redoubles upon ourselves and gives us an undecaying and uninterrupted pleasure. Whoever spared a meal to save the life of a starving man, much more a friend, which all men are to us whom we love, but had more and much more lasting pleasure in it than he that eat it. The other's pleasure died as he eat and ended with his meal. But to him that gave it him 'tis a feast as often as he reflects on it.

Next, pleasures of the mind are the greatest as well as most lasting. Whoever was so brutish as would not quit the greatest sensual pleasure to save a child's life whom he loved? What is this but pleasure of thought remote from any sensual delight? Love all the world as you do your child or self and make this universal, and how much short will it make the earth of heaven?

Happiness therefore is annexed to our loving others and to our doing our duty, to acts of love and charity, or he that will deny it be so here because everyone observes not this rule of universal love and charity, he brings in a necessity of another life (wherein God may put a distinction between those that did good and suffered and those who did evil and enjoyed by their different treatment there) and so enforces morality the stronger, laying a necessity on God's justice by his rewards and punishments, to make the good the gainers, the wicked losers.

Ethica B

1693. 'Ethica'. MS Locke, c. 28, fo. 113. Printed in Dunn 1969, p. 192.

There be two parts of ethics, the one is the rule which men are generally in the right in, though perhaps they have not deduced them as they should from their true principles. The other is the true motives to practise them and the ways to bring men to observe them, and these are generally either not well known or not rightly applied. Without this latter, moral discourses are such as men hear with pleasure and approve of, the mind being generally delighted with truth, especially if handsomely expressed. But all this is but the delight of speculation. Something else is required to practise, which will never be till men are made alive to virtue and can taste it. To do this, one must consider what is each man's particular disease, what is the pleasure that possesses him. Over that, general discourses will never get a mastery. But by all the prevalencies of friendship, all the arts of persuasion, he is to be brought to live the contrary course. You must bring him to practise in particular instances and so by habits establish a contrary pleasure, and then when conscience, reason and pleasure go together they are sure to prevail. Which is the way to do this in particular cases will be easier for a prudent man to find when the case offers them for anyone to foresee and determine before the case happens and the person be known. JL

Homo ante et post Lapsum

1693. 'Homo ante et post lapsum' (Man before and after the Fall). MS Locke, c. 28, fo. 113. Not hitherto printed. Locke suggests that property and social distinctions are the product of the Fall.

Man was made mortal, [and] put into a possession of the whole world, where, in the full use of the creatures, there was scarce room for any irregular desires, but instinct and reason carried him the same way, and being neither capable of covetousness or ambition, when he had already the free use of all things, he could scarce sin. God therefore gave him a probationary law whereby he was restrained from one only fruit, good, wholesome and tempting in itself. The punishment annexed to this law was a natural death. For though he was made mortal, yet the tree of life should, after [his] having observed this probationary law, to a sufficient testimony of his obedience, have clothed him with immortality without dying. But he sinned, and the sentence of death was immediately executed, for he was thrust out from the tree of life (Gen. 3:22). And so being excluded from that which could cure any distemper [which] could come from too free a use of the creatures, and renew his age, he began to die from that time, being separated from this source of life. So that now he, and in him all his posterity, were under a necessity of dying, and thus sin entered into the world and death by sin. But here again God puts him under a new covenant of grace and thereby into a state of eternal life, but not without dying. This was the punishment of that first sin to Adam and Eve, viz. death and the consequence, but not punishment of it to all their posterity, for they, never having any hopes or expectations given them of immortality, to be born mortal, as man now [is] made, cannot be called a punishment. By this sin Adam and Eve came to know good and evil, i.e. the difference between good and evil, for without sin man should not have known evil. Upon their offence they were afraid of God: this gave them frightful ideas and apprehensions of him and that lessened their love, which turned their minds to that nature, for this root of all evil in them made impressions and so infected their children, and when private possessions and labour, which now the curse on the earth made necessary, by degrees made a distinction of conditions, it gave room for covetousness, pride, and ambition, which by fashion and example spread the corruption which has so prevailed over mankind. JL

Voluntas

1693. 'Voluntas'. MS Locke, c. 28, fo. 114. Printed in Von Leyden 1954, pp. 72–3.

That which has very much confounded men about the will and its determination has been the confounding of the notion of moral rectitude and giving it the name of moral good. The pleasure that a man takes in any action or expects as a consequence of it is indeed a good in itself able and proper to move the will. But the moral rectitude of it considered barely in itself is not good or evil nor [in] any way moves the will, but as pleasure and pain either accompanies the action itself or is looked on to be a consequence of it. Which is evident from the punishments and rewards which God has annexed to moral rectitude or pravity as proper motives to the will, which would be needless if moral rectitude were in itself good and moral pravity evil. JL

For a General Naturalisation

1693. Harvard University: Houghton MS Eng. 818, pp. 1–5. Printed in Kelly 1991, II, 487–92. The paper lacks a title, which is supplied by Locke's endorsement. A 'general naturalisation' refers to the naturalisation of whole groups of immigrants, as opposed to individuals, who could seek private Acts of Parliament. Many thousands of French Huguenots settled in England after the Revocation of the Edict of Nantes in 1685. Bills for general naturalisation failed several times during the Restoration, and again in 1689, 1690, and December 1693. The last may be the occasion of Locke's paper. A further Bill was introduced in 1697, prompting an anonymous correspondent to ask Locke to publish in its favour (Letter 2206). All such Bills met with opposition from vested economic interests, xenophobic sentiment, and Anglican dislike of non-Anglican Protestants. The issue became a major point of controversy in Queen Anne's reign. Compare with Locke's economic papers, his *Essay on the Poor Law*, and 'Atlantis'. See also Letters 1745 and 1764; Resnick 1987; Statt 1995.

Naturalisation is the shortest and easiest way of increasing your people, which all wise governments have encouraged by privileges granted to the fathers of children as the *ius trium liberorum* amongst the Romans.[78] And that because

(1) People are the strength of any country or government; this is too visible to need proof.

(2) 'Tis the number of people that make the riches of any country.

This is evident in examples of all sorts: I need mention but one and that is the comparison of Holland and Spain. The latter having all the advantages of situation and the yearly afflux of wealth out of its own dominions[79] yet is for want of hands the poorest country in Europe. The other [is] ill situate[d] but being crammed with people [is] abounding in riches. For so it is to be esteemed however [much] it may now be exhausted by a long and heavy war, the support of which shows their great strength and riches.[80] And I ask whether

---

[78] A privileged status granted under the Lex Papia Poppaea, AD 9, to fathers of three children.

[79] The massive bullion imports from Spanish America.

[80] The Netherlands had been to war with France in 1667–8, 1672–7, and now during the Nine Years War from 1689.

England if half its people should be taken away would not proportionably decay in its strength and riches notwithstanding the
advantages it has in its situation, ports and the temper of its people?

If we look into the reason of this we shall not think it strange.
The riches of the world do not lie now as formerly in having large
tracts of good land which supplied abundantly the native conveniencies of eating and drinking [such] as plenty of corn and large
flocks and herds. But in trade, which brings in money and with that
all things.

Trade consists in two parts, and plenty of hands is what contributes most to both.

(1) In manufacture. (2) Next in carriage and navigation.

[1] In manufacture that which is to be endeavoured is to make as
much as you can and to vent [sell] as much abroad as you can and
for both these plenty of people are necessary.

That most can be made where are most hands needs no proof.
But that most should be vented where are most hands to make it is
not perhaps at first sight so obvious and therefore I shall a little
more explain it.

In all manufactures the greatest part of the value lies in the
labour. Where therefore labour is cheapest there 'tis plain commodities may be afforded [at] the cheapest rates and here I demand
whether plenty of hands do not everywhere make work cheaper.
And what soever at market can be afforded cheapest shall of course
be first sold and beat out others of the same sort.

[2] There have been severe laws made against the transportation
of wool, the matter of our greatest manufacture, and great complaints before this present war with France (and I wish there be no
reason for them still) that notwithstanding those laws much
unwrought wool was carried out of the King's dominions into
France. The severities of those laws could not keep it in. But yet I
think I may say that if we had hands enough employed in the woollen manufacture here to work up all our wool at a cheap rate, and
our woollen manufacture [had] a free and unrestrained vent as it
ought to have, one pound of that wool could not be carried out, for
what could be bought and employed with advantage at home cannot
be bought at dearer rates to be wrought by dearer or as dear labourers abroad. And then I ask whether if all those French men who
are employed in France in the manufacturing of that wool were

323

transported hither and settled here in England it would not be an advantage and gain to England? and that it is plain it would just as much as that raw wool, and the cloth made of it are of different values. If not why do we endeavour to keep the woollen manufacture amongst us here in England but [why not instead] sell all our wool raw to our neighbours?

We have much rapeseed transported yearly out of England into Holland, made into oil there and brought back again and sold to us, which could not be done unless labour were cheaper there whereof they make the profit. For so much of every man's manufacture as is vented abroad, so much is by his labour gained to your country though he lay not up a farthing of it, for his labour having produced so much from the foreign market he has in effect so much sent him from abroad to pay the farmer and grazier here for the bread and flesh and other consumable commodity he spends of your growth, and is so far all one as if he were a foreigner spending his rents here for the enriching your country.

But perhaps it will be objected we shall not have artisans come over to be naturalised but idle people.

To which I answer, numbers of men, nay nobody, can transport himself into another country with hopes to live upon other men's labour, and though perhaps we have very inconvenient laws for maintaining the poor which may encourage them as it does to expect it, yet these not being made in favour of foreigners or at least they may be excepted from a parish rate maintenance. For 'tis a shame any should be permitted, much less by such a law be encouraged, to be idle, they cannot expect a [parish maintenance] and therefore must depend only on what they bring with them, either their estates or industry, both which are equally profitable to the kingdom.

I would ask anyone, have we too many people already? That I think nobody will say. For in proportion to our produce and extent I think I may say we have not half so many as Holland. Have we then just enough? That can as hardly be said for we have not half so many as Holland and that country grows rich by it. But to put this past doubt this is certain: no country can by the accession of strangers grow too full of people, for those who bring estates to maintain them bring actually so much riches. And if you are so full of people already that handicraftsmen and labourers cannot live better here by their hands than at home you need not fear, they will not remove hither to be in a worse state here. You may therefore safely open your doors, and a freedom to them to settle here being secure of this advantage that you have the profit of all their labour, for by that they pay for what they eat and spend of yours, unless you think it should be given to them for nothing which is not much to be feared.

I have sometimes heard it objected that they eat the bread out of our own people's mouths. Which is no further true than it is a confession that they work cheaper or better, for nobody will leave his neighbour to use a foreigner but for one of those reasons, and can that be counted an inconvenience which will bring down the unreasonable rates of your own people or force them to work better? Want of people raises their price and makes them both dear and careless. Besides when they are once naturalised, how can it be said they eat the bread out of our people's mouths? when they are then in interest as much our own people as any. The only odds is their language, which will be cured too in their children, and they be as perfect Englishmen as those that have been here ever since William the Conqueror's days and came over with him. For 'tis hardly to be doubted but that most of even our ancestors were foreigners.

The other great part of trade is carriage. This is that whereby the Dutch make so great advantage to themselves by employing so many hands in navigation and transporting the several commodities of the world from one country to another. This they could not do without the great plenty of people which being once crammed into any country will endeavour there to find a livelihood and be content with what they can get in any employment at home before they will look abroad into other countries for it. The want of language and other difficulties that everywhere attends strangers keeping ordinary people from easily venturing on such changes. You need not fear therefore that you have opened such an inlet to them by an easy naturalisation that you shall be overrun with them. But since people are so valuable a commodity and this may be a means to invite some and to retain others whom any change has brought hither, it cannot but be for our advantage.

Another objection very apt to be made is that it will increase the number of the poor.

If by poor are meant such as have nothing to maintain them but their hands, those [who] live by their labour are so far from being a burden that 'tis to them chiefly we owe our riches.

If by poor are meant such as want relief and being idle themselves live upon the labour of others; if there be any such poor amongst us already who are able to work and do not, 'tis a shame to the government and a fault in our constitution and ought to be remedied, for whilst that is permitted we must ruin, whether we have many or few people. But if people have here no permission nor encouragement to be idle amongst us the more we have the better is it for us, and will abundantly satisfy for those whom age or any other accident shall make uncapable to get their livelihoods.

Labour

1693. 'Labor'. Adversaria 1661, pp. 310–11. Printed in Kelly 1991, II, 493–5; Wootton 1993, pp. 440–2. Locke discusses right conduct for the preservation of health; the moral value of practical labour; and offers a vision of a society of plenty without idleness. There are similar remarks in *Some Thoughts Concerning Education* and in 'Study'.

We ought to look on it as a mark of goodness in God that he has put us in this life under a necessity of labour not only to keep mankind from the mischiefs that ill men at leisure are very apt to do. But it is a benefit even to the good and the virtuous which are thereby preserved from the ills of idleness or the diseases that attend constant study in a sedentary life. Half the day employed in useful labour would supply the inhabitants of the earth with the necessaries and conveniences of life, in a full plenty. Had not the luxury of Courts and by their example inferior grandees found out idle and useless employments for themselves and others subservient to their pride and vanity, and so brought honest labour in useful and mechanical arts wholly into disgrace whereby the studious and sedentary part of mankind as well as the rich and the noble have been deprived of that natural and true preservative against diseases. And 'tis to this that we may justly impute the spleen and the gout and those other decays of health under which the lazily voluptuous, or

busily studious part of men uselessly languish away a great part
of their lives. How many shall we find amongst those who sit
still either at their books or their pleasure, whom either the
spleen or the gout does not rob of his thoughts or his limbs
before he is got half his journey? and becomes a useless member
of the commonwealth in that mature age which should make him
most serviceable whilst the sober and working artisan and the
frugal laborious country man performs his part well and cheerfully goes on in his business to a vigorous old age. So that when
we have reckoned up how much of their time those who are
intent on the improvements of their minds are robbed of either
by the pains and languishing of their bodies, or the observance
of medicinal rules to remove them, a very favourable calculation
will show that if they had spent four nay I think I may say six
hours in a day in the constant exercise of some laborious calling
they would have more hours of their lives to be employed in
study than in that languishing estate [condition] of a broken
health which the neglect of bodily labour seldom fails to bring
them to. He that exempts half his time from serious business
may be thought to have made no scanty allowance for recreation
and refreshment and if the other twelve hours of the four and
twenty are divided betwixt the body and the mind I imagine the
improvement of the one and the health of the other would be
well enough provided for. I make account that six hours in the
day well directed in study would carry a man as far in the
improvement of his mind as his parts are capable of and is more
I think than most scholars that live to any [considerable] age do
or are able to employ in study. For as I have said those who at
their first setting out eager in the pursuit of knowledge spare as
little as they can of their time to the necessities of life to bestow
it all upon their minds find it at last but an ill sort of husbandry,
when they are fain to refund to the care of their decayed body
a greater portion of their time than what they improvidently
robbed them of. Six hours thus allotted to the mind, the other
six might be employed in the provisions of the body and the
preservation of health. Six hours labour every day in some honest
calling would at once provide necessaries for the body and secure
the health of it in the use of them. If this distribution of the
twelve hours seem not fair nor sufficiently to keep up the distinc-

tion that ought to be in the ranks of men let us change it a little. Let the gentleman and scholar employ nine of the twelve on his mind in thought and reading and the other three in some honest labour. And the man of manual labour nine in work and three in knowledge. By which all mankind might be supplied with what the real necessities and conveniency of life demand in greater plenty than they have now and be delivered from that horrid ignorance and brutality to which the bulk of them is now everywhere given up. If it be not so it is owing to the carelessness and negligence of the governments of the world, which wholly intent upon the care of aggrandising themselves at the same time neglect the happiness of the people and with it their own peace and security. Would [that] they suppress the arts and instruments of luxury and vanity. And bring those of honest and useful industry in fashion. [Then] there would be neither that temptation to ambition where the possession of power could not display itself in the distinctions and shows of pride and vanity. Nor the well instructed minds of the people suffer them to be the instruments of aspiring and turbulent men. The populace well instructed in their duty and removed from the implicit faith their ignorance submits them in to others would not be so easy to be blown into tumults and popular commotions by the breath and artifice of designing and discontented grandees. To conclude, this is certain that if the labour of the world were rightly directed and distributed there would be more knowledge, peace, health and plenty in it than now there is. And mankind be much more happy than now it is. JL

Law

c. 1693. 'Law'. MS Locke, c. 28, fo. 141. Printed in Dunn 1969, p. 1.

The original and foundation of all law is dependency. A dependent intelligent being is under the power and direction and dominion of him on whom he depends and must be for the ends appointed him by that superior being. If man were independent he could have no law but his own will, no end but himself. He would be a god to himself, and the satisfaction of his own will the sole measure and end of all his actions.

Liberty of the Press

1694–5. MS Locke, b. 4, pp. 75–8; copies in PRO 30/24/30/30. A set of three papers: (A) Locke's criticisms of the Licensing Act of 1662, in Locke's hand (probably January 1695 or earlier); (B) a draft Bill for Regulating Printing, in John Freke's hand (February); (C) Locke's comments on B (March). Locke endorsed A 'Printing 94', and B and C 'Printing 94/5'. A and C are here printed in full; B is summarised. C is an incomplete document and there is evidence in Locke's correspondence of its further content. All three are printed in De Beer 1976–89, v, 785–96 (where B is misleadingly described as a 'Licensing Bill': it aimed to achieve the nonrenewal of the licensing system); extracts in *Journals of House of Commons*, x, 305–6; King 1830, I, 375–87; Fox Bourne 1876, II, 312–15. Discussed in Astbury 1978.

The Licensing Act of 1662 was a punitive measure against a press that had flooded the land with seditious tracts during the Civil War; it restricted the number of printing presses, and revived the pre-War censorship by which all publications had to be approved by a Licenser. The Act lapsed in 1679, was renewed in 1685 for seven years, and renewed in 1692 and 1693 for a further year at a time. Liberty of the press was not the only, perhaps not even the main, rallying cry of opponents of the Act, but rather the lucrative monopoly powers of the Stationers' Company. On 30 November 1694 the House of Commons appointed a committee to consider laws due to expire. On 9 January 1695 it recommended the renewal of the Licensing Act. On 11 February the House decided instead to appoint a committee to prepare a new Bill. Locke's friend Edward Clarke was a member and it was he who introduced a new Bill on 2 March: this Bill is document B. This was the first legislative collaboration between Locke and 'the College', whose main members were Clarke and John Freke. The Bill did away with the Licensing system but tried to offer sufficient regulation of the press to satisfy the pro-Licensers.

Despite the Bill's reassuring title, 'for regulating the press', Freke and Clarke told Locke that it was 'so contrived that there is an absolute liberty for the printing everything that 'tis lawful to speak' (Letter 1856). Locke was 'mightily pleased' that Clarke was introducing a Bill (Letter 1858); he was sent the Bill on 14 March, and in document C, which he sent on 18 March, he proposed further clauses designed to defend the rights of authors and the interests of scholars. The document is especially interesting on intellectual property, and prefigures the Copyright Act passed in 1709. In one letter to Clarke he mentioned a pamphlet, perhaps referring to Charles Blount's *Just Vindication of Learning* (1679, republished 1695; Letter 1856). The College was not hopeful that their Bill would pass. There were those who wanted a tougher Act, and those who wanted no Act. The College reported that the bishops, the stationers, and elements at court were hostile, though these opponents prudently, if vaguely, talked about the defence of (intellectual) property, because 'property [is] a very popular word, which Licenser is not'. The College of Physicians was also opposed, demanding the right to peruse new medical books, 'lest some new Sydenham should rise up and show they kill by the[ir] rules of art' (Letter 1860). The Bill made no progress, but nor did proposals to renew the Licensing Act: hence, from 1695 pre-publication censorship disappeared in England. The matter is regularly discussed in Locke's letters: the College series, January–April and December 1695.

A. Locke's criticisms of the Licensing Act of 1662
Anno 14 Car. II. Cap. xxxiii[81]

An Act for preventing abuses in printing seditious, treasonable and unlicensed books and pamphlets and for regulating printing and printing presses.

§2[82] Heretical, seditious, schismatical or offensive books, wherein anything contrary to Christian faith, or the doctrine or discipline of the Church of England is asserted, or which may tend to the scandal of religion or the church or the government or governors of the church, state, or of any corporation or particular person are prohibited to be printed, imported or sold.

Some of these terms are so general and comprehensive or at least so submitted to the sense and interpretation of the governors of

---

[81] Note that Charles II dated his reign from his father's execution in 1649 and not from his restoration in 1660.

[82] Locke begins by paraphrasing the text of the Act, followed by his commentary; later he omits the terms of the Act altogether, and just comments.

church or state for the time being that it is impossible any book should pass but just what suits their humours. And who knows but that the motion of the earth may be found to be heretical, etc., as asserting antipodes[83] once was?

I know not why a man should not have liberty to print whatever he would speak, and to be answerable for the one just as he is for the other if he transgresses the law in either.[84] But gagging a man for fear he should talk heresy or sedition has no other ground than such as will make gives [sic] necessary for fear a man should use violence if his hands were free and must at last end in the imprisonment of all whom you will suspect may be guilty of treason, or misdemeanour.

To prevent men's being undiscovered for what they print you may prohibit any book to be printed, published or sold without the printer's or bookseller's name under great penalties whatever be in it. And then let the printer or bookseller whose name is to it be answerable for whatever is against law in it as if he were the author unless he can produce the person[85] he had it from which is all the restraint ought to be upon printing.

§3 All books prohibited to be printed that are not first entered in the register of the Company of Stationers and licensed.[86]

Whereby it comes to pass that sometimes when a book is brought to be entered in the register of the Company of Stationers, if they think it may turn to account, they enter it there as theirs, whereby the other person is hindered from printing and publishing it, an example whereof can be given by Mr Awnsham Churchill.[87]

§6 No books to be printed or imported, which any person or persons by force or [by] virtue of any letters patents have the right, privilege, authority or allowance solely to print, upon pain of forfeiture, and being proceeded against as an offender against this present

---

[83] Locke has in mind the treatment of the Copernican system of astronomy as heretical, especially by the Catholic church in the case of Galileo.

[84] Locke's claim is that there should be no pre-publication censorship, but that the printed word should be judged by such other laws as those of libel and sedition.

[85] 'Person' substituted for 'author'.

[86] Books were required to be licensed by the Secretary of State's Licenser of the Press, or by church or legal authorities. They were also required to be registered with the guild of master printers, the Company of Stationers, by which was supposed to be established a copyright.

[87] Awnsham Churchill (d. 1728) was Locke's publisher.

Act and upon the further penalty and forfeiture of 6s 8d for every such book or books or part of such book or books imported, bound, stitched or put to sale, a moiety to the king and a moiety to the owner.

By this clause the Company of Stationers have a monopoly of all the classic authors and scholars cannot but at excessive rates have the fair and correct editions of these books and the comments [commentaries] on them printed beyond [the] seas.[88] For the Company of Stationers have obtained from the crown a patent to print all or at least the greatest part of the classic authors, upon pretence, as I hear, that they should be well and truly printed, whereas they are by them scandalously ill printed, both for letter, paper and correctness, and scarce one tolerable edition made by them of any one of them:[89] whenever any of these books of better editions are imported from beyond [the] seas, the Company seize them and make the importer pay 6s 8d for each book so imported or else they confiscate them, unless they are so bountiful as to let the importer compound with them at a lower rate. There are daily examples of this: I shall mention one which I had from the sufferer's own mouth. Mr Sam Smith two or three years since imported from Holland Tully's [Cicero's] works of a very fine edition with new corrections made by Gronovius who had taken the pains to compare that which was thought the best edition before, with several ancient MSS and to correct his by them.[90] These Tully's works, upon pretence of their patent for their alone printing Tully's works, or any part therefore and by virtue of this clause of this Act, the Company of Stationers seized and kept a good while in their custody,

---

[88] This paragraph recapitulates points made by Locke in Letter 1586 (2 January 1693). The Stationers' Company had a monopoly in certain classical texts. Locke himself collided with the Company over his project to publish a new edition of *Aesop's Fables* as a Latin–English primer. He worked on the project in 1691, but it was not published until 1703; the Company had refused to allow it. See Letters 1431, 1586, 3383.

[89] Locke was vehement about the failures of English printers in Letter 3556; he also complained about the botched printing of the *Two Treatises*.

[90] Samuel Smith, bookseller in St Paul's Churchyard. Jacob Gronovius's edition of Cicero was published at Leyden in 1692. Locke probably spoke from personal experience: Jean Le Clerc told him about this edition (Letter 1541); Smith imported Locke's *Epistola de Tolerantia* in 1689; hence, Locke probably asked Smith to import the Cicero. See also Letters 951, 955.

demanding 6s 8d per book, how at last he compounded with them I know not. But by this Act scholars are subjected to the power of these dull wretches who do not so much as understand Latin, whether they shall have any true or good copies of the best ancient Latin authors, unless they will pay them 6s 8d a book for that leave.

Another thing observable is that whatever money by virtue of this clause they have levied upon the subject either as forfeiture or composition I am apt to believe not one farthing of it has ever been accounted for to the king or brought into the Exchequer, though this clause reserves a moiety to the king, and 'tis probable consider-able sums have been raised.

Upon occasion of this instance of the classic authors I demand whether if another Act for printing should be made it be not reason-able that nobody should have any peculiar right in any book which has been in print fifty years, but any one as well as another might have the liberty to print it, for by such titles as these which lie dormant and hinder others many good books come quite to be lost.[91] But be that determined as it will in regard to those authors who now write and sell their copies to booksellers. This certain[ly] is very absurd at first sight that any person or company should now have a title to the printing of the works of Tully's, Caesar's or Livy's, who lived so many ages since, exclusive of any other, nor can there be any reason in nature[92] why I might not print them as well as the Company of Stationers if I thought fit. This liberty to anyone of printing them is certainly the way to have them the cheaper and the better and 'tis this which in Holland has produced so many fair and excellent editions of them, whilst the printers[93] all strive to outdo one another which has also brought in great sums to the trade of Holland. Whilst our Company of Stationers, having the monopoly here by this Act and their patents, slubber[94] them over as they can cheapest, so that there is not a book of them vended beyond [the] seas both for their badness and dearness nor will the scholars beyond seas look upon a book of them now printed at London, so ill and false are they, besides it would be hard to find

---

[91] The Copyright Act of 1709 first established authorial copyright.
[92] 'In nature' is an interlinear insertion.
[93] Locke first wrote 'the publishers'.
[94] To perform hurriedly and carelessly.

how a restraint of printing the classic authors does any way prevent printing seditious and treasonable pamphlets which is the title and pretence of this Act.

§9 No English book may be imprinted or imported from beyond the sea. Nor foreigner or other, unless stationer of London, may import or sell any books of any language whatever.

This clause serves only to confirm and enlarge the Stationers' monopoly.

§10 In this paragraph, besides a great many other clauses to secure the Stationers' monopoly of printing, which are very hard upon the subject, the stationers' interest is so far preferred to all others that a landlord who lets a house forfeits £5 if he know that his tenant has a printing press in it and does not give notice of it to the master and wardens of the Stationers' Company. Nor must a joiner, carpenter or smith, etc., work about a printing press without giving the like notice under the like penalty.

Which is greater caution than I think is used about the presses for coinage to secure the people from false money.

By §11, the number of master printers were reduced from a greater number to twenty and the number of master founders of letters reduced to four, and upon vacancy the number to be filled by the Archbishop of Canterbury and Bishop of London and to give security not to print any unlicensed books.

This hinders a man who has served out his time[95] the benefit of setting up his trade, which whether it be not against the right of the subject as well as contrary to common equity deserves to be considered.

§12 The number of presses that every one of the twenty master printers shall have are reduced to two, only those who have been masters or upper wardens of the Company may have three and as many more as the Archbishop of Canterbury or Bishop of London will allow.

§13 Everyone who hath been master or upper warden of the Company may have three. Everyone of the livery two, and every master printer of the yeomanry but one apprentice at a time.

By which restraint of presses and taking of apprentices and the prohibition in §14 of taking or using any journeymen except

[95] I.e. as an apprentice.

334

Englishmen and freemen of the trade, is the reason why our printing is so very bad and yet so very dear in England. They who are hereby privileged to the exclusion of others working and setting the price as they please, whereby any advantage that might be made to the realm by this manufacture is wholly lost to England and thrown into the hands of our neighbours. The sole manufacture of printing bringing into the Low Countries great sums every year. But our ecclesiastical laws seldom favour trade, and he that reads this Act with attention will find it *upse*[96] ecclesiastical. The nation loses by the Act, for our books are so dear and ill printed that they have very little vent amongst foreigners unless now and then by truck [exchange] for theirs, which yet shows how much those who buy here books printed here are imposed on. Since a book printed at London may be bought cheaper at Amsterdam than in [St] Paul's Churchyard notwithstanding all the charge and hazard of transportation. For their printing being free and unrestrained they sell their books at so much a cheaper rate than our booksellers do ours, that in truck valuing ours proportionably to their own, or their own equally to ours which is the same thing, they can afford books received from London upon such exchanges cheaper in Holland than our stationers sell them in England. By this Act England loses in general, scholars in particular are ground [down] and nobody gets [anything] but a lazy ignorant Company of Stationers, to say no worse of them. But anything rather than let mother church be disturbed in her opinions or impositions, by any bold enquirer from the press.

§15 One or more of the Messengers of his majesty's chamber, by warrant under his majesty's sign manual, or under the hand of one of his majesty's principal Secretaries of State, or the master and wardens of the Company of Stationers taking with him a constable and such assistance as they shall think needful, has an unlimited power to search all houses and to seize upon all books which they shall but think fit to suspect.

How the gentlemen, much more how the peers, of England came thus to prostitute their houses to the visitation and inspection of anybody, much less a Messenger, upon pretence of searching for books, I cannot imagine. Indeed, the houses of peers and others not

---

[96] A Dutch word for 'highly'.

of the trades mentioned in this Act are pretended to be exempted from this search, §18, where 'tis provided they shall not be searched but by special warrant under the king's sign manual or under the hands of one of the Secretaries of State. But this is but the shadow of an exemption for they are still subject to be searched, every corner and coffer in them, under pretence of unlicensed books, a mark of slavery which I think their ancestors would never have submitted to. Thus to lay their houses which are their castles open not to the pursuit of the law against a malefactor convicted of misdemeanour or accused upon oath, but to the suspicion of having unlicensed books, which is whenever it is thought fit to search his house and see what is in it.

§16 All printers offending [in] any way against this Act [are] incapacitated to exercise their trade for three years. And for the second offence perpetual incapacity, with any other punishment not reaching to life or limb.

And thus a man is to be undone and starve for printing Dr Bury's case or the history of Tom Thumb unlicensed.[97]

§17 Three copies of every book printed are to be reserved, whereof two to be sent to the two universities by the master of the Stationers' Company.

This clause upon examination I suppose will be found to be mightily if not wholly neglected, as all things that are good in this Act, the Company of Stationers minding nothing in it but what makes for their monopoly. I believe that if the public libraries of both universities be looked into (which[98] this will give a fit occasion to do) there will not be found in them half, perhaps not one in ten, of the copies of books printed since this Act. Vide 17 Car. II, c. 4. [1665].

§ Last. This Act, though made in a time when everyone strove to be forwardest to make court to the church and court by giving whatever was asked, yet this was so manifest an invasion on the trade, liberty, and property of the subject that it was made to be in

---

[97] Dr Arthur Bury, Rector of Exeter College, Oxford, published *The Naked Gospel* (1690), which was charged with heresy, condemned and burnt by the University. Locke's friend Le Clerc published *An Historical Vindication of the Naked Gospel* (1690). *Tom Thumb*, illustrated with woodcuts for the non-literate, was a popular 'penny merriment'; this favourite ancient story was registered as the property of a particular publishing partnership. See Watt 1991.

[98] 'The endeavour to renew this' [Act] deleted.

force only for two years. From which 14 Car. II it has by the joint endeavour of church and court been from time to time revived and so continued to this day. Everyone being answerable for books he publishes, prints, or sells containing anything seditious or against law makes this or any other act for the restraint of printing very needless in that part and so it may be left free in that part as it was before 14 Car. II. That any person or company should have patents for the sole printing of ancient authors is very unreasonable and injurious to learning. And for those who purchase copies from authors that now live and write it may be reasonable to limit their property to a certain number of years after the death of the author or the first printing of the book as suppose 50 or 70 years. This I am sure, 'tis very absurd and ridiculous that anyone now living should pretend to have a property in or a power to dispose of the property of any copies or writings of authors who lived before printing was known and used in Europe.

B. *Summary of 'A Bill for the Better Regulating of Printing'*

It begins: 'For preventing the mischiefs that may happen in church or state for want of a due regulation of printing'. Its terms are as follows.

[1] Printing presses in London to be registered with the Lord Chancellor, Lord Chief Justice, or Secretary of State; in Cambridge and Oxford with the Chancellor or Vice-Chancellor; and in other cities or corporate towns with the chief magistrate. No other presses permissible.

[2] A copy of every book, pamphlet, 'portraiture', or paper to be deposited with a bishop or university Vice-Chancellor (in the case of books concerning divinity), with the Lord Chancellor or a judge (for law books), or with one of the Secretaries of State (for books concerning affairs of state or the history of the realm).

[3] Nothing to be printed contrary to the laws, 'or contrary to the Christian religion as it is established by law', under penalty of suspension from the trade and confiscation of equipment.

[4] All printed books, pamphlets, etc., shall include the name and place of abode of the printer and publisher, under the same penalties. These names not to appear without the written authority of

those named. Such persons whose names appear will be answerable at law as if they were the author.

[5] A copy of every book to be lodged with his Majesty's library and the libraries of the two universities.

[6] Law officers and magistrates may have printers' premises searched 'where they shall be informed upon oath that there is any private printing press and to seize and take away all or any copies or prints of any treasonable, seditious, atheistical, or heretical book, pamphlet, or paper'.

[7] No prosecution to occur beyond an [unspecified] period after an alleged offence.

[8] This Act to lapse after an [unspecified] number of years.

C. *Locke's amendments to the draft Bill*

And be it further enacted that no printer shall print the name of any person as author[99] or publisher of any book, pamphlet, portraiture, or paper without authority given in writing for so doing under the penalty of forfeiting the sum of [blank] to the party whose name shall be so printed as author or publisher and the further, etc.

To secure the author's property in his copy, or his to whom he has transferred it, I suppose such a clause as this [following] will do, subjoined to the clause above written:

And be it further enacted that no book, pamphlet, portraiture or paper printed with the name of the author or publisher upon it shall within [blank] years after its first edition be reprinted with or without the name of the author to it without authority given in writing by the author or somebody entitled by him, for so doing under the penalty of the forfeiture of all that shall be so reprinted to the author his executors, administrators or assigns.

Or thus: after these words in the Bill – 'For the use of the public libraries of the said universities' [§5], add as followeth:

And for the better encouragement thereof be it further enacted that upon delivery of three copies as aforesaid for the use of the said three libraries, a receipt under the hand of the king's library

---

[99] This clause repeats the second part of clause 4 in the Bill, but Locke has added 'author' to 'publisher'.

keeper and under the hand of the Vice-Chancellor of each university to whom they are delivered who are hereby required to give such receipts, for the said books, shall vest a privilege in the author of the said book, his executors, administrators, and assigns, of solely reprinting and publishing the said book for [blank] years from the first edition thereof, with a power to seize on all copies of the said book reprinted by any other person which by virtue of this Act shall be forfeited to the said author, his executors, administrators and assigns.[100]

Punitive Justice

1695. 'Justitia'. Adversaria 1661, p. 24. Printed in Dunn 1968, n. 84.

Punitive justice consists in not exceeding, solutive[101] in not coming short. And both for the same reason, viz. because [in] neither of these ways can we entrench on another's right, for punishment consists in taking away a good from another, payment in conveying or doing good to another, as [for example] money, praise, etc. He that keeps within these bounds to every person will not be unjust. JL

Venditio

1695. 'Venditio'. Adversaria 1661, pp. 268–9. Printed in Dunn 1968, pp. 84–7; Kelly 1991, II, 496–500; Wootton 1993, pp. 440–

---

[100] This document is either incomplete or was supplemented in a covering letter of 18 March 1695 which is not extant. Letter 1862, from Freke and Clarke to Locke on 21 March, begins: 'The College is obliged to you for your compliment in that of the 18th and to ease your mind a little about the words "heretical" [§6] and "as it is established by law" [§3] they crave leave to inform you that by a statute made in Queen Elizabeth's time [1 Eliz. I, c. 1] 'tis enacted that nothing shall be adjudged heresy but what is declared such by the Holy Scriptures or by the first four General Councils or by other General Councils by the express words of Scripture, so that we think the word "heresy" being thus determined as to its signification by a statute it can do no hurt in the printing Bill, and as to the other words [you] yourself observe how the words "Christian religion" influences them, but let us observe to you that as the words are penned 'twill be incumbent on the prosecutor to show not only that what he prosecutes for, is contrary to the Christian religion as he understands that religion, but that what he so understands is established by law as he understands it. So that we think those words some of the best words in the Bill.'

[101] Relaxing, releasing, setting free; merciful.

6. Locke's Greek letters are here replaced by P, Q, and R. Venditio = selling or sale. Locke here discusses market price and value,
justice and charity, necessity and subsistence, and the criteria for
legitimate merchandising. By implication he continues the long
Scholastic debate about the just price, usury, and the taking of
interest. The text is related to *Some Considerations of the Consequences of the Lowering of Interest* (1692).

Upon demand what is the measure that ought to regulate the price
for which anyone sells so as to keep it within the bounds of equity
and justice, I suppose it in short to be this. The market price at the
place where he sells. Whosoever keeps to that in whatever he sells
I think is free from cheat, extortion and oppression or any guilt in
whatever he sells, supposing no fallacy [fault, fraud] in his wares.

To explain this a little.

A man will not sell the same wheat this year under 10s per bushel
which the last year he sold for 5s. This is no extortion by the above
said rule because it is this year the market price, and if he should
sell under that rate he would not do a beneficial thing to the con-
sumers, because others then would buy up his corn at his low rate
and sell it again to others at the market rate and so the[y] make
profit of his weakness and share a part of his money. If to prevent
this he will sell his wheat only to the poor at this under rate, this
indeed is charity but not what strict justice requires. For that only
requires that we should sell to all buyers at the market rate, for if
it be unjust to sell it to a poor man at 10s per bushel it is also unjust
to sell it to the rich at 10s a bushel, for justice has but one measure
for all men. If you think him bound to sell it to the rich too who is
the consumer under the market rate but not to a jobber or ingrosser
[speculator or middleman]. To this I answer, he cannot know
whether the rich buyer will not sell it again and so gain the money
which he loses. But if it be said 'tis unlawful to sell the same corn
for 10s this week which I sold the last year or week for 5s because
it is worth no more now than it was then having no new qualities
put into it to make it better, I answer, it is worth no more 'tis true
in its natural value because it will not feed more men nor better
feed them than it did last year, but yet it is worth more in its
political or marchand value, as I may so call it, which lies in the
proportion of the quantity of wheat to the proportion of money in
that place and the need of one and the other. This same market rate

governs too in things sold in shops or private houses, and is known by this that a man sells not dearer to one than he would to another. He that makes use of another's ignorance, fancy, or necessity to sell ribbon or cloth, etc., dearer to him than to another man at the same time, cheats him. But in things that a man does not set to sale this market price is not regulated by that of the next market but by the value that the owner puts on it himself.

E.g. P has a horse that pleases him and is for his turn [suitable to his purpose]; this Q would buy of[f] him. P tells him he has no mind to sell; Q presses him to set him a price and thereupon P demands and takes £40 for his horse which in a market or fair would not yield above twenty. But supposing Q refusing to give £40, R comes the next day and desires to buy this horse having such a necessity to have it that if he should fail of it, it would make him lose a business of much greater consequence and this necessity P knows. If in this case he makes R pay £50 for the horse which he would have sold to Q for £40, he oppresses him and is guilty of extortion, whereby he robs him of £10, because he does not sell the horse to him, as he would to another, at his own market rate which was £40, but makes use of R's necessity to extort £10 from him above what in his own account was the just value, the one man's money being as good as the other's. But yet he had done no injury to Q in taking his £40 for a horse which at the next market would not have yielded above £20 because he sold it at the market rate of the place where the horse was sold, viz. his own house where he would not have sold it to any other at a cheaper rate than he did to Q. For if by any artifice he had raised Q's longing for that horse, or because of his great fancy sold it dearer to him than he would to another man he had cheated him too. But what anyone has he may value at what rate he will and transgresses not against justice if he sells it at any price provided he makes no distinction of buyers but parts with it as cheap to this as he would to any other buyer. I say he transgresses not against justice; what he may do against charity is another case.

To have a fuller view of this matter, let us suppose a merchant of Danzig sends two ships laden with corn whereof the one puts into Dunkirk where there is almost a famine for want of corn and there he sells his wheat for 20s a bushel whilst the other ship sells his at Ostend just [near]by for 5s. Here it will be demanded whether it be not oppression and injustice to make such an advantage of their necessity at Dunkirk as to sell to them the same commodity at 20s per bushel which he sells for a quarter the price but twenty miles off? I answer no. Because he sells at the market rate at the place where he is, but sells there no dearer to Thomas than he would to Richard. And if there he should sell for less than his corn would yield he would only throw his profit into other men's hands, who buying of[f] him under the market rate would sell it again to others at the full rate it would yield. Besides, as there can be no other measure set to a merchant's gain but the market price where he comes, so if there were any other measure [such] as 5 or 10 per cent as the utmost justifiable profit, there would be no commerce in the world, and mankind would be deprived of the supply of foreign mutual conveniencies of life. For the buyer not knowing what the commodity cost the merchant to purchase and bring thither could be under no tie of giving him the profit of 5 to 10 per cent and so can have no other rule but of buying as cheap as he can, which turning often to the merchant's downright loss when he comes to a bad market, if he has not the liberty on his side to sell as dear as he can when he comes to a good market. This obligation to certain loss often, without any certainty of reparation, will quickly put an end to merchandising. The measure that is common to buyer and seller is just that if one should buy as cheap as he could in the market the other should sell as dear as he could there, everyone running his venture and taking his chance, which by the mutual and perpetually changing wants of money and commodities in buyer and seller comes to a pretty equal and fair account.

But though he that sells his corn in a town pressed with famine at the utmost rate he can get for it does no unjustice against the common rule of traffic, yet if he carry it away unless they will give him more than they are able, or extorts so much from their present necessity as not to leave them the means of subsistence afterwards, he offends against the common rule of charity as a man and if they perish any of them by reason of his extortion is no doubt guilty of murder. For though all the selling merchant's gain arises only from the advantage he makes of the buyer's want, whether it be a want of necessity or fancy that's all one, yet he must not make use of his necessity to his destruction, and enrich himself so as to make another perish. He is so far from being permitted to gain to that degree, that he is bound to be at some loss and impart of his own to save another from perishing.

Dunkirk is the market to which the English merchant has carried his corn and by reason of their necessity it proves a good one and there he may sell his corn as it will yield at the market rate, for 20s per bushel. But if a Dunkirker should at the same time come to England to buy corn, not to sell to him at the market rate, but to make him because of the necessity of his country to pay 10s per bushel when you sold to others for five would be extortion.

A ship at sea that has an anchor to spare meets another which has lost all her anchors. What here shall be the just price that she shall sell her anchor to the distressed ship [for]? To this I answer, the same price that she would sell the same anchor to a ship that was not in that distress. For that still is the market rate for which one would part with anything to anybody, who was not in distress and absolute want of it. And in this case the master of the vessel must make his estimate by the length of his voyage, the season and seas he sails in, and so what risk he shall run himself by parting with his anchor, which all put together perhaps he would not part with it at any rate, but if he would, he must then take no more for it from a ship in distress than he would from any other. And here we see, the price which the anchor cost him which is the market price at another place makes no part of the measure of the price which he fairly sells it for at sea. And therefore I put in 'the place where the thing is sold', i.e. the measure of rating anything in selling is the market price where the thing is sold. Whereby it is evident that a thing may be lawfully sold for 10, 20, nay cent per cent [100%] and ten times more in one place than is the market price in another place perhaps not far off. These are my extempore thought[s] concerning this matter. JL

Sacerdos

1698. Adversaria 1661, p. 93. Printed in King 1829, pp. 285–6; 1830, II, 82–92; extract in Fox Bourne 1876, I, 156–60. Fox Bourne and others incorrectly date this to the 1660s. King conflated this passage with two others that occur elsewhere (1829, pp. 287–91; Adversaria 1661, pp. 125, 270–1): see 'Toleration A' (*c.* 1675). Locke begins with an account of ancient religion, out of Cicero, and then turns to stress the essential character of Christianity as lying in holy living, and not in ritual. The passage is a commentary on Pierre Bayle's *Pensées diverses* (1682), §127.

There were two sorts of teachers amongst the ancients: those who professed to teach them the arts of propitiation and atonement, and these were properly their priests, who for the most part made themselves the mediators betwixt the gods and men, wherein they performed all or the principal part, at least nothing was done without them. The laity had but a small part in the performance, unless it were in the charge [cost] of it, and that was wholly theirs. The chief, at least the essential, and sanctifying part of the ceremony, was always the priests', and the people could do nothing without them. The ancients had another sort of teachers, who were called philosophers. These led their schools, and professed to instruct those who would apply to them in the knowledge of things and the rules of virtue. These meddled not with the public religion, worship, or ceremonies, but left them entirely to the priests, as the priests left the instruction of men in natural and moral knowledge wholly to the philosophers. These two parts or provinces of knowledge thus under the government of two distinct sorts of men, seem to be founded upon the supposition of two clearly distinct originals, viz. revelation and reason. For the priests never for any of their ceremonies or forms of worship pleaded reason; but always urged their sacred observances from the pleasure of the gods, antiquity, and tradition, which at last resolves all their established rites into nothing but revelation.[102] The philosophers, on the other side, pretended to nothing but reason in all that they said, and from thence owned to fetch [claimed to derive] all their doctrines; though how little their lives answered their own rules whilst they studied ostentation and vanity, rather than solid virtue, Cicero tells us, *Tusculanarum Quaestionum*, bk II, ch. 4.

Jesus Christ, bringing by revelation from heaven the true religion to mankind, reunited these two again, religion and morality, as the inseparable parts of the worship of God, which ought never to have been separated, wherein for the obtaining the favour and forgiveness

---

[102] In a footnote Locke reproduced a quotation by Bayle from Cicero's *De Natura Deorum*, bk III.

of the deity, the chief part of what man could do consisted in a holy life, and little or nothing at all was left to outward ceremony, which was therefore almost wholly cashiered out of this true religion, and only two very plain and simple institutions introduced, all pompous rites being wholly abolished, and no more of outward performances commanded but just so much as decency and order required in the actions of public assemblies. This being the state of this true religion coming immediately from God himself, the ministers of it, who also call themselves priests, have assumed to themselves the parts both of the heathen priests and philosophers, and claim a right not only to perform all the outward acts of the Christian religion in public, and to regulate the ceremonies to be used there, but also to teach men their duties of morality towards one another and towards themselves, and to prescribe to them in the conduct of their lives.

Error

1698. 'Error'. Adversaria 1661, pp. 320–1. Printed in King 1829, pp. 281–4; 1830, II, 75–81; Fox Bourne 1876, I, 306–9. Paragraph breaks added. Locke attacks elaborate doctrinal confessions of faith, unquestioning belief, and the tyranny of religious orthodoxy. He affirms the priority of sincerity in belief and of morality in conduct.

The great division amongst Christians is about opinions. Every sect has its set of them, and that is called orthodoxy. And he who professes his assent to them, though with an implicit faith, and without examining, he is orthodox and in the way to salvation. But if he examines, and thereupon questions any one of them, he is presently suspected of heresy, and if he oppose them or hold the contrary, he is presently condemned as in a damnable error, and [in] the sure way to perdition. Of this, one may say, that there is, nor can be, nothing more wrong. For he that examines, and upon a fair examination embraces an error for a truth, has done his duty, more than he who embraces the profession (for the truths themselves he does not embrace) of the truth without having examined whether it be true or no. And he that has done his duty, according to the best of his ability, is certainly more in the way to heaven than he who has done nothing of it. For if it be our duty to search after truth, he certainly that has searched after it, though he has not found it in some points, has paid a more acceptable obedience to the will of his maker, than he that has not searched at all, but professes to have found truth, when he has neither searched nor found it. For he that takes up the opinions of any church in the lump, without examining them, has truly neither searched after, nor found truth, but has only found those that he thinks have found truth, and so receives what they say with an implicit faith, and so pays them the homage that is due only to God, who cannot be deceived, nor deceive.

In this way the several churches (in which, as one may observe, opinions are preferred to life [conduct] and orthodoxy is that which they are concerned for, and not morals) put the terms of salvation in that which the author of our salvation does not put them in. The believing of a collection of certain propositions, which are called and esteemed fundamental articles, because it has pleased the compilers to put them into their confession of faith, is made the condition of salvation. But this believing is not, in truth, believing, but a profession to believe; for it is enough to join with those who make the same profession; and ignorance or disbelief of some of those articles is well enough borne, and a man is orthodox enough and without any suspicion, till he begins to examine. As soon as it is perceived that he quits the implicit faith, expected though disowned by the church, his orthodoxy is presently questioned, and he is marked out for a heretic. In this way of an implicit faith, I do not deny but a man who believes in God the Father almighty, and that Jesus Christ is his only Son our Lord, may be saved, because many of the articles of every sect are such as a man may be saved without the explicit belief of. But how the several churches who place salvation in no less than a knowledge and belief of their several confessions, can content themselves with such an implicit faith in any of their members, I must own I do not see. The truth is, we cannot be saved without performing something which is the explicit believing of what God in the Gospel has made absolutely necessary to salvation to be explicitly believed, and sincerely to obey what he has there commanded. To a man who believes in Jesus Christ, that he is sent from God to be the saviour of the world, the first step to orthodoxy is a sincere obedience to his law.

Objection: But 'tis an ignorant day-labourer that cannot so much as read, and how can he study the Gospel, and become orthodox that way? Answer: A ploughman that cannot read, is not so ignorant but he has a conscience, and knows in those few cases which concern his own actions, what is right and what is wrong. Let him sincerely obey this light of nature, it is the transcript of the moral law in the Gospel; and this, even though there be errors in it, will lead him into all the truths in the Gospel that are necessary for him to know. For he that in earnest believes Jesus Christ to be sent from God, to be his Lord and ruler, and does sincerely and unfeignedly set upon a good life as far as he knows his duty; and where he is in doubt in any matter that concerns himself he cannot fail to enquire of those better skilled in Christ's law, to tell him what his Lord and master has commanded in the case, and desires to have his law read to him concerning that duty which he finds himself concerned in, for the regulation of his own actions; for as for other men's actions, what is right or wrong as to them, that he is not concerned to know; his business is to live well himself, and do what is his particular duty. This is knowledge and orthodoxy enough for him, which will be sure to bring him to salvation, an orthodoxy which nobody can miss, who in earnest resolves to lead a good life; and, therefore, I lay it down as a principle of Christianity, that the right and only way to saving orthodoxy, is the sincere and steady purpose of a good life.

Ignorant of many things contained in the Holy Scriptures we are all. Errors also concerning doctrines delivered in Scripture, we have all of us not a few: these, therefore, cannot be damnable, if any shall be saved. And if they are dangerous, 'tis certain the ignorant and illiterate are safest, for they have the fewest errors that trouble not themselves with speculations above their capacities, or beside their concern. A good life in obedience to the law of Christ their Lord, is their indispensable business, and if they inform themselves concerning that, as far as their particular duties lead them to enquire, and oblige them to know, they have orthodoxy enough, and will not be condemned for ignorance in those speculations which they had neither parts [ability], opportunity, nor leisure to know. Here we may see the difference between the orthodoxy required by Christianity, and the orthodoxy required by the several sects, or as they are called, churches of Christians. The one is explicitly to believe what is indispensably required to be believed as absolutely necessary to salvation, and to know and believe in the other doctrines of faith delivered in the word of God, as a man has opportunity, helps and parts; but to inform himself in the rules and measures of his own duty as far as his actions are concerned, and to pay a sincere obedience to them. But the other, viz. the orthodoxy required by the several sects, is a profession of believing the whole bundle of their respective articles set down in each church's system, without knowing the rules of everyone's particular duty, or requiring a sincere or strict obedience to them. For they are speculative opinions, confessions of faith that are insisted on in the several communions; they must be owned and subscribed to, but the precepts and rules of morality and the observance of them, I do not remember there is much notice taken of, or any great stir made about a collection or observance of them, in any of the terms of church communion. But it is also to be observed, that this is much better fitted to get and retain church members than the other way, and is much more suited to that end, as much as it is easier to make profession of believing a certain collection of opinions that one never perhaps so much as reads, and several whereof one could not perhaps understand if one did read and study (for no more is required than a profession to believe them, expressed in an acquiescence that suffers one not to question or contradict any of them), than it is to practise the duties of a good life in a sincere obedience to those precepts of the Gospel wherein his actions are concerned. Precepts not hard to be known by those who are willing and ready to obey them. JL

Some Thoughts Concerning Reading and Study for a Gentleman

1703. BL, MS Sloane 4290, ff. 11–14. 'Mr Locke's Extempore Advice &c': Samuel Bold's title, to whom it was dictated. Usually known as 'Some Thoughts Concerning Reading and Study for a Gentleman', Pierre Desmaizeaux's title, who first printed it, imperfectly. Printed in Locke 1720, pp. 236–9; *Works* 1801, III, 269–76; Axtell 1968, pp. 397–404; Yolton and Yolton 1989, pp. 319–27. Cited by Laslett, Second Treatise, §239. For the politics of Locke's educational writing see Tarcov 1984; Anderson 1992. The books Locke cites are identified in 'Locke's Reading List', below. The essay is important especially for the books on politics and ethics which he recommends. Compare Letters 844, 1921, 2320, 3326,

3328 and 3339. Also this passage in *Some Thoughts Concerning Education* (Yolton and Yolton 1989, pp. 239–40):

'§185. The knowledge of virtue, all along from the beginning, in all the instances he is capable of, being taught him, more by practice than rules; and the love of reputation instead of satisfying his appetite, being made habitual in him, I know not whether he should read any other discourses of morality, but what he finds in the Bible; or have any system of ethics put into his hand, till he can read Tully's *Offices* [*On Duties*], not as a schoolboy to learn Latin, but as one that would be informed in the principles and precepts of virtue, for the conduct of his life.

'§186. When he has pretty well digested Tully's *Offices*, and added to it Pufendorf, *De officio hominis et civis*, it may be seasonable to set him upon Grotius, *De jure belli ac pacis*, or which perhaps is the better of the two, Pufendorf, *De jure naturali et gentium*; wherein he will be instructed in the natural rights of men, and the original and foundations of society, and the duties resulting from thence. This general part of civil law and history, are studies which a gentleman should not barely touch at, but constantly dwell upon, and never have done with . . .

'§187. It would be strange to suppose an English gentleman should be ignorant of the law of his country . . . And to that purpose, I think the right way for a gentleman to study our law, which he does not design for his calling, is to take a view of our English constitution and government, in the ancient books of the common law; and some more modern writers, who out of them have given an account of this government. And having got a true idea of that, then to read our history, and with it join in every king's reign the laws then made. This will give an insight into the reason of our statutes, and show the true ground upon which they came to be made, and what weight they ought to have.'

Reading is for the improvement of the understanding. The improvement of the understanding is for two ends: first, for our own increase of knowledge; secondly, to enable us to deliver and make out that knowledge to others. The latter of these, if it be not the chief end of study in a gentleman, yet it is at least equal to the other, since the greatest part of his business and usefulness in the world, is by the influence of what he says, or writes to others.

The extent of our knowledge cannot exceed the extent of our ideas. Therefore he who would be universally knowing, must acquaint himself with the objects of all sciences. But this is not necessary to a gentleman, whose proper calling is the service of his country; and so is most properly concerned in moral, and political knowledge; and thus the studies which more immediately belong to his calling, are those which treat of virtues and vices, of civil society, and the arts of government, and so will take in also law and history.

It is enough to be furnished with the ideas belonging to his calling, which he will find in the sorts of books above mentioned. But the next step towards the improvement of his understanding must be to observe the connection of these ideas in the propositions, which those books hold forth, and pretend to teach as truths; which, till a man can judge whether they be truths or no, his understanding is but little improved; and he does but think and talk after the books that he hath read, without having any knowledge thereby. And thus, men of much reading are greatly learned, and but little knowing.

The third and last step therefore in improving the understanding, is to find out upon what foundation any proposition advanced bottoms; and to observe the connection of the intermediate ideas by which it is joined to that foundation, upon which it is erected, or that principle from which it is derived. This, in short, is right reasoning, and by this way alone true knowledge is to be got by reading and studying. When a man by use hath got this faculty of observing and judging of the reasoning and coherence of what he reads, and how it proves what it pretends to teach, he is then, and not till then, in the right way of improving his understanding, and enlarging his knowledge by reading.

But that (as I have said) being not all that a gentleman should aim at in reading, he should further take care to improve himself in the art also of speaking, that so he may be able to make the best use of what he knows. The art of speaking well, consists chiefly in two things, viz. perspicuity and right reasoning. Perspicuity consists in the using of proper terms for the ideas or thoughts which he would have pass from his own mind into that of another man's. 'Tis this, that gives them an easy entrance, and 'tis with delight that men hearken to those whom they easily understand; whereas, what is obscurely said, dying as it is spoken, is usually not only lost, but creates a prejudice in the hearer, as if he that spoke knew not what he said, or was afraid to have it understood.

The way to obtain this, is to read such books, as are allowed to be writ with the greatest clearness and propriety in the language that a man uses. An author excellent in this faculty, as well as several other, is Dr Tillotson, late Archbishop of Canterbury, in all that is published of his. I have chosen rather to propose this pattern, for the attainment of the art of speaking clearly, than those who give rules about it, since we are more apt to learn by example, than by direction. But if anyone hath a mind to consult the masters in the art of speaking, and writing, he may find in Tully [Cicero] *De Oratore*, and another treatise of his, called *Orator*, and in Quintilian's *Institutions*, and Boileau's discourse, *Du Sublime*, instructions concerning this, and the other parts of speaking well.

Besides perspicuity, there must be also right reasoning; without which perspicuity serves but to expose the speaker. And for the attaining of this, I should propose the constant reading of Chillingworth, who by his example will teach both perspicuity, and the way of right reasoning better than any book that I know; and therefore will deserve to be read upon that account over and over again, not to say anything of his argument. Besides these books in English, Tully (the best edition of Tully is by Gulielmus and Gruter, printed at Hamburg 1618; Elzevir's edition of Tully in nine volumes in duodecimo is also an excellent good one), Terence (the late edition at Cambridge), Virgil (at the same place lately), Livy (Elzevir's edition), and Caesar's *Commentaries* (Stephen's edition), may be read to form one's mind to a relish of a right way of speaking and writing. The books I have hitherto mentioned have been in order only to writing and speaking well, not but that they will deserve to be read upon other accounts.

The study of morality I have above mentioned as that, that becomes a gentleman, not barely as a man, but in order to his business as a gentleman. Of this, there are books enough writ both by ancient and modern philosophers; but the morality of the Gospel doth so exceed them all, that to give a man a full knowledge of true morality, I should send him to no other book, but the New Testament. But if he hath a mind to see how far the heathen world carried that science, and whereon they bottomed their ethics, he will be delightfully and profitably entertained in Tully's treatises *De Officiis*.

Politics contains two parts very different the one from the other. The one containing the original of societies, and the rise and extent of political power, the other, the art of governing men in society.

The first of these hath been so bandied amongst us for this sixty years backward, that one can hardly miss books of this kind. Those which I think are most talked of in English, are the first book of Mr Hooker's *Ecclesiastical Polity*, and Mr Algernon Sidney's book of government; the latter of these I never read. (Let me here add, *Two Treatises of Government*, printed 1690. And a treatise of *Civil Polity*, printed this year.) To these one may add Pufendorf, *De Officio Hominis et Civis*, and *De Jure Naturali et Gentium*, which last is the best book of that kind.

As to the other part of politics, which concerns the art of government, that I think is best to be learned by experience and history, especially that of a man's own country. And therefore I think an English gentleman should be well versed in the history of England; taking his rise as far back as there are any records of it; joining with it the laws that were made in the several ages, as he goes along in his history, that he may observe from thence the several turns of state, and how they have been produced. In Mr Tyrrell's *History of England* he will find all along those several authors which have treated of our affairs, and which he may have recourse to concerning any point which either his curiosity or judgement shall lead him to enquire into.

With the history he may also do well to read the ancient lawyers (such as are Bracton, Fleta, Henningham, *Mirror of Justice*, my Lord Coke on the second *Institutes*, and *Modus Tenendi Parliamentum*, and others of that kind, whom he may find quoted in the late controversies between Mr Petyt, Mr Tyrrell, Mr Atwood, etc., with Dr Brady, as also I suppose in Sadler's treatise of the *Rights of the Kingdom, and Customs of our Ancestors*, whereof the first edition is the best) wherein he will find the ancient constitution of the government of England. There are two volumes of *State Tracts* printed since the Revolution, in which there are many things relating to the government of England.

As for general history Sir Walter Raleigh, and Dr Howell are books to be had. He who hath a mind to launch further into that ocean may consult Wheare's *Methodus Legendi Historias* of the last edition, which will direct him to the authors he is to read, and the method wherein he is to read them.

To the reading of history, chronology and geography are absolutely necessary. In geography we have two general ones in English,

Heylyn and Moll; which is the best of them, I know not, having not been much conversant in either of them; but the last I should think to be of most use, because of the new discoveries that are made every day, tending to the perfection of that science; though I believe that the countries which Heylyn mentions are better treated of by him, bating [excepting] what new discoveries since his time have added. These two books contain geography in general; but whether an English gentleman would think it worth his time to bestow much pains upon that, though without it, he cannot well understand a gazette, this is certain, he cannot well be without Camden's *Britannia*, which is much enlarged in the last edition. A good collection of maps is also very necessary.

To geography, books of travel may be added. In that kind the collections made by our countrymen, Hakluyt and Purchas, are very good. There is also a very good collection made by Thévenot in folio in French, and by Ramusio in Italian, whether translated into English or no I know not. There are also several good books of travels of Englishmen published, as Sandys, Roe, Browne, Gage, and Dampier. There are also several voyages in French which are very good, as, Pyrard, Bergeron, Sagard, Bernier, etc., which, whether all of them are translated into English I know not. There is at present a very good *Collection of Travels* never before in English, and such as are out of print, now printing by Mr Churchill. There are besides these, a vast number of other travels; a sort of books that have a very good mixture of delight and usefulness. To set them down all, would take up too much time and room; those I have mentioned are enough to begin with.

As to chronology, I think Helvicus the best for common use, which is not a book to be read, but to lie by, and be consulted upon occasion. He that hath a mind to look further into chronology may get Tallent's *Tables*, and Strauchius's *Breviarium Temporum*, and may to those add Scaliger, *De Emendatione Temporum*, and Petavius, if he hath a mind to engage deeper in that study.

Those who are accounted to have writ best particular parts of our English history are Bacon of Henry VII. And Herbert of Henry VIII. Daniel also is commended, and Burnet's *History of the Reformation*. Mariana's *History of Spain*, and Thuanus his *History of his Own Time*, and Philip de Comines are of great and deserved reputation. There are also several French and English memoirs and collections, such as Rochefoucauld, Melville, Rushworth, etc., which give a great light to those who have a mind to look into what has passed in Europe this last age.

To fit a gentleman for the conduct of himself whether as a private man, or as interested in the government of his country, nothing can be more necessary, than the knowledge of men; which though it be to [be] had chiefly from experience, and next to that, from a judicious reading of history, yet there are books which of purpose treat of human nature, which help to give an insight into it. Such are those which treat of the passions and how they are moved, whereof Aristotle in his second book of *Rhetoric* has admirably treated, and that in a little compass. I think this *Rhetoric* is translated into English, if not, it may be had in Greek and Latin together. La Bruyère's *Characters* are also an admirable piece of painting, I think, it is also translated out of French into English. Satirical writings also, such as Juvenal, and Persius, and above all, Horace, though they paint the deformities of men, yet thereby they teach us to know them.

There is another use of reading, which is for diversion, and delight. Such are poetical writings, especially dramatic, if they be free from profaneness, obscenity, and what corrupts good manners; for such pitch should not be handled. Of all the books of fiction, I know none that equals Cervantes his *History of Don Quixote* in usefulness, pleasantry, and a constant decorum; and indeed no writings can be pleasant which have not nature at the bottom, and are not drawn after her copy.

There is another sort of books, which I had almost forgot, with which a gentleman's study ought to be well furnished, viz. dictionaries of all kinds. For the Latin tongue, Cole[s], Cooper, Calepino, and Robert Stephen's *Thesaurus Linguae Latinae*, and Vossius' *Etymologicum Linguae Latinae*. Skinner's *Lexicon Etymologicum* is an excellent one of that kind for the English tongue. Cowell's *Interpreter* is useful for law terms. Spelman's *Glossary* is a very useful and learned book. And Selden's *Titles of Honour*, a gentleman should not be without. Baudrand has a very good geographical dictionary. And there are several historical ones which are of use; as Lloyd's, Hofman's, Moreri, and Bayle's *Dictionary* is something of the same kind. He that hath occasion to look into books written in Latin since the decay of the Roman Empire, and the purity of the

Latin tongue, cannot be well without Du Cange's *Glossarium*. Among the books above set down, I mentioned Johannes Gerardus Vossius' *Etymologicum Linguae Latinae*: all his works are lately printed in Holland in six tomes, they are very fit books for a gentleman's library, as containing very learned discourses concerning all the sciences.

Appendix

Draft B of *Human Understanding* (Extract)

1671. MS Locke, f. 26. Headed 'Intellectus', 'De Intellectu Humano', and 'An Essay concerning the Understanding, Knowledge, Opinion & Assent'. Now known as Draft B of the *Essay Concerning Human Understanding*. The authoritative edition is Nidditch and Rogers 1990. The following extract comprises §157. §§151 and 155–62 concern morality. Locke explains that we derive moral ideas in two ways: either from cultural mores (§157) or from the will of lawmakers (§160). §160 occurs almost verbatim in the essay 'Of Ethic in General', printed above. Compare *ECHU*, bk II, ch. 28. The passage opens with the 'either' of cultural mores; §160 contains the 'or' of the will of lawmakers.

Either by the common consent and usage of the country and those men whose language we speak. For if there were no law, no punishment, no obligation human or divine, yet there must and would be in the societies of men notions of virtues and vices, justice, temperance, and fortitude, etc., consisting in certain collections of simple ideas without which notions all those words which express moral things would in all languages be perfect jargon and insignificant. But all the knowledge of particular virtues and vices which a man attained to this way would amount to no more than taking the definitions or significations of the words of any language, either from the men skilled in that language or the common usage of the country, to know how to apply them and call particular actions in that country by their right names, and so in effect would be no more but the skill how to speak properly or at most to know what actions in the country he lives in are thought laudable, i.e. are called virtues and vices, the general rule whereof and the most constant that I can find is that those actions are esteemed virtuous, which tend absolutely to the preservation of society, and those that dissolve the bonds of society are everywhere esteemed ill and vicious, which would necessarily fall out so were there no obligation or superior law at all besides that of society, since it cannot be supposed that any men should associate together and unite in the same community and at the same time allow that for commendable, i.e. count it a virtue, nay not discountenance and treat such actions as blameable, i.e. count them vices, which tended to the dissolution of that society in which they were united. But all other actions that have not such an immediate influence on society I find not (as far as I have been conversant in history) but that in some countries, i.e. societies, they are virtues, in others vices, and in others indifferent, wherein the inclination or fashion of the people seems wholly to have established them virtues or vices. So that the ideas of virtues taken up this way teach us no more than to speak properly according to the fashion of the country we are in, without any great improvement of our knowledge more than what men meant by such words. And this is the knowledge contained in the common ethics of the schools.

A Letter from a Person of Quality (Extract)

1675. *A Letter from a Person of Quality, to his Friend in the Country*. No place of publication or name of publisher is given; there is no extant manuscript. The tract was included in Pierre Desmaizeaux's *Collection of Several Pieces of Mr John Locke* (1720) and in later editions of Locke's *Works*. Desmaizeaux wrote that the Earl of Shaftesbury 'desired Mr Locke to draw up this relation; which he did under his lordship's inspection, and only committed to writing what my Lord Shaftesbury did in a manner dictate to him'. This is the sum of the evidence for Locke's authorship. Ashcraft defends this attribution (1986, pp. 120–3). Whatever the case, there is little doubt that the tract reflected Locke's views. It attacked the growth of absolute monarchy and marked a turning point in Restoration political thought. It was condemned by the government and publicly burned.

Pocock treats the tract as indicative of the emergence of a 'neo-Harringtonian' emphasis upon the nobility as the 'balance' of the constitution (1975, pp. 406–16). But most of the tract, which is thirty-four quarto pages long, is an attack on the political role of the church hierarchy, and is a narrative of recent political events. The immediate provocation was the attempt by Lord Treasurer Danby to impose an oath upon members of parliament requiring them to swear that 'I will not at any time endeavour any alteration of government either in church or state.' After prolonged parliamentary debate 'Danby's Test' was defeated. The following extracts comprise the beginning and the end of the tract (pp. 1–3, 32–4).

The opening passage refers to several Acts passed early in the Restoration: the Act of Oblivion (1660), which provided a general amnesty from prosecution for actions committed during the Civil War and Interregnum; the Corporation Act (1661), which purged the boroughs of Puritan officeholders, and which included new doctrinal oaths renouncing a right to take up arms against the ruler and repudiating the Parliamentary Covenant of 1643; the Militia Act (1661); the Uniformity Act (1662), which re-established the Church of England, based on episcopacy and the old Prayer Book, and which caused some two thousand Puritan clergy to be driven out of the established church, who rued the 'Black Bartholomew Day' upon which the Act took effect; and the Five Mile Act (1665), which drove Puritan ministers from their former parishes and towns, and introduced the 'no alteration' oath which, in 1675, the Earl of Danby was proposing to extend to members of parliament.

This session being ended, and the Bill of Test near finished at the Committee of the Whole House, I can now give you a perfect account of this state masterpiece. It was first hatched (as almost all the mischiefs of the world had hitherto been) amongst the great churchmen, and is a project of several years standing, but found not ministers bold enough to go through with it, until these new ones,[1] who, wanting a better bottom to support them, betook themselves wholly to this, which is no small undertaking, if you consider it in its whole extent.

First, to make a distinct party from the rest of the nation of the high episcopal man, and the old Cavalier, who are to swallow the hopes of enjoying all the power and office of the kingdom, being also tempted by the advantage which they may receive from overthrowing the Act of Oblivion, and not a little rejoicing to think how valiant they should prove, if they could get any to fight the old quarrel over again; now they are possessed of the arms, forts, and ammunition of the nation.

Next they design to have the government of the church sworn to be unalterable, and so tacitly owned to be of divine right, which though inconsistent with the Oath of Supremacy;[2] yet the churchmen easily break through all obligations whatsoever, to attain this station, the advantage of which, the prelate of Rome hath sufficiently taught the world.

[1] Between 1673 and 1675 Shaftesbury was driven from office and Danby consolidated his power in alliance with the 'old Cavaliers' and the Anglican hierarchy.
[2] I.e. inconsistent with the crown's supremacy over the church, established at the Reformation.

Then in requital to the crown, they declare the government absolute and arbitrary, and allow monarchy as well as episcopacy to be *jure divino* [by divine right], and not to be bounded or limited by human laws.

And to secure all this, they resolve to take away the power and opportunity of parliaments to alter anything in church or state, only leave them as an instrument to raise money, and to pass such laws, as the court and church shall have a mind to: the attempt of any other, how necessary soever, must be no less a crime than perjury.

And as the topstone of the whole fabric, a pretence shall be taken from the jealousies they themselves have raised, and a real necessity from the smallness of their party, to increase and keep up a standing army, and then in due time the Cavalier and churchman will be made greater fools but as errant slaves as the rest of the nation.

In order to this, the first step was made in the Act for Regulating Corporations, wisely beginning that, in those lesser governments, which they meant afterwards to introduce upon the government of the nation, and making them swear to a declaration and belief of such propositions as themselves afterwards upon debate were enforced to alter, and could not justify in those words; so that many of the wealthiest, worthiest, and soberest men, are still kept out of the magistracy of those places.

The next step was in the Act of the Militia, which went for most of the chiefest nobility and gentry, being obliged as lord lieutenants, deputy lieutenants, etc., to swear to the same declaration and belief, with the addition of these words, 'in pursuance of such military commissions', which makes the matter rather worse than better; yet this went down smoothly as an oath in fashion, a testimony of loyalty, and none adventuring freely to debate the matter, the humour of the age, like a strong tide, carries wise and good men down before it; this Act is of a piece, for it establisheth a standing army by a law, and swears us into a military government.

Immediately after this, followeth the Act of Uniformity, by which all the clergy of England are obliged to subscribe, and declare what the corporations, nobility, and gentry had before sworn, but with this additional clause of the Militia Act omitted: this the clergy readily complied with, for you know that sort of men are taught rather to obey than understand, and to use that learning they have to justify, not to examine, what their superiors command: and yet that Bartholomew Day was fatal to our church and religion, in throwing out a very great number of worthy, learned, pious, and orthodox divines, who could not come up to this, and other things in that Act . . .

But this matter was not complete until the Five Mile Act, passed at Oxford, wherein they take an opportunity to introduce the oath in the terms they would have it: this was then strongly opposed by the Lord Treasurer Southampton, Lord Wharton, Lord Ashley,[3] and others, not only in the concern of those poor ministers that were so severely handled, but as it was in itself, a most unlawful and unjustifiable oath; however, the zeal of that time against all nonconformity easily passed the Act . . .

Thus our church became triumphant, and continued so for divers years, the dissenting Protestant being the only enemy, and therefore only persecuted, whilst the papists remained undisturbed, being by the court thought loyal, and by our great bishops not dangerous, they differing only in doctrine, and fundamentals; but as to the government of the church, that was in their religion in its highest exaltation . . .

* * *

Thus Sir, you see the standard of the new party[4] is not yet set up, but must be the work of another session. Though it be admirable to me, how the king can be induced to venture his affairs upon such weak counsels, and of so fatal consequences; for I believe it is the first time in the world, that ever it was thought advisable, after fifteen years of the highest peace, quiet, and obedience, that ever was in any country, that there should be a pretence taken up, and a reviving of former miscarriages, especially after so many promises, and declarations, as well as acts of oblivion, and so much merit of the offending party, in being the instruments of the king's happy return,[5] besides the putting so vast a number of the king's subjects in utter despair of having their crimes ever forgotten; and it must be a great mistake in counsels, or worse, that there should be so much pains taken by the court to debase, and bring low the House

---

[3] Who became Earl of Shaftesbury in 1672.
[4] I.e. Danby's Test.
[5] It was widely held, with good reason, that the Presbyterian party had been instrumental in Charles II's restoration in 1660, but had thereafter been outmanoeuvred.

of Peers, if a military government be not intended by some. For the power of peerage and a standing army are like two buckets, the proportion that one goes down, the other exactly goes up; and I refer you to the consideration of all the histories of ours, or any of our neighbour northern monarchies, whether standing forces military, and arbitrary government, came not plainly in by the same steps, that the nobility were lessened; and whether, whenever they were in power and greatness, they permitted the least shadow of any of them: our own country is a clear instance of it; for though the white rose and the red[6] changed fortunes often to the ruin, slaughter and beheading of the great men of the other side; yet nothing could enforce them to secure themselves by a standing force: but I cannot believe that the king himself will ever design any such thing; for he is not of a temper robust and laborious enough to deal with such a sort of men, or reap the advantages, if there be any, of such a government; and I think, he can hardly have forgot the treatment his father received from the officers of his army, both at Oxford, and Newark; 'twas an hard, but almost an even choice to be the parliament's prisoner, or their slave;[7] but I am sure the greatest prosperity of his arms could have brought him to no happier condition, than our king his son hath before him whenever he please . . .

I shall conclude with that [which], upon the whole matter, is most worthy your consideration, that the design is to declare us first into another government more absolute, and arbitrary, than the oath of allegiance, or old law knew, and then make us swear unto it, as it is so established: and less than this the bishops could not offer in requital to the crown for parting with its supremacy, and suffering them to be sworn to equal with itself. Archbishop Laud was the first founder of this device; in his canons of 1640 you shall find an oath very like this, and a declaratory canon preceding, that monarchy is of divine right,[8] which was also affirmed in this debate by our reverend prelates, and is owned in print by no less men that

---

[6] The Yorkists and Lancastrians in the Wars of the Roses of the fifteenth century.
[7] After his defeat in the Civil War, Charles I was by turns a captive of parliament and the army, who were now divided among themselves.
[8] Canon 1 of the Convocation of 1640 pronounced that 'the most high and sacred order of kings is of divine right', and specified a 'no alteration' oath for all clergy; these canons were never ratified.

Archbishop Ussher and Bishop Sanderson;[9] and I am afraid it is the avowed opinion of much the greater part of the dignified clergy: if so, I am sure they are the most dangerous sort of men alive to our English government, and it is the first thing ought to be looked into, and strictly examined by our parliaments, 'tis the leaven that corrupts the whole lump; for if that be true, I am sure monarchy is not to be bounded by human laws, and the 8th chapter of 1 Samuel[10] will prove (as many of our divines would have it) the great charter of the royal prerogative, and our Magna Charta, that says, 'our kings may not take our fields, our vineyards, our corn, and our sheep', is not in force, but void and null, because against divine institution; and you have the riddle out, why the clergy are so ready to take themselves, and impose upon others, such kind of oaths as these; they have placed themselves, and their possessions, upon a surer bottom (as they think) than Magna Charta, and so have no need of, or concern for it: nay what is worse, they have trucked away the rights and liberties of the people in this, and all other countries wherever they have had opportunity, that they might be owned by the prince to be *jure divino*, and maintained in that pretension by that absolute power and force, [which] they have contributed so much to put into his hands; and that priest and prince may, like Castor and Pollux,[11] be worshipped together as divine in the same temple by us poor lay subjects; and that sense and reason, law, properties, rights, and liberties, shall be understood as the oracles of those deities shall interpret, or give signification to them, and ne'r be made use of in the world to oppose the absolute and free will of either of them.

Study (Extracts)

1677 (26 March to early May). MS Locke, f. 2, pp. 87–140. Printed in King 1829, pp. 92–109; 1830, I, 171–203; Axtell 1968, pp. 405–22; partly in Fox Bourne 1876, I, 360–4. Locke discusses the snares

---

[9] James Ussher, *The Power Communicated by God to the Prince*, written *c.* 1640, and published by James Tyrrell in 1661, with an introduction by Robert Sanderson. Locke drew heavily on Sanderson's works in his writings in the 1660s.

[10] The people of Israel asked for a king and God granted them one; in the subsequent chapters Saul is anointed king.

[11] Two heroes of classical mythology, worshipped in early Rome, usually pictured as twin brothers on horseback.

in the way of acquiring truth, and the proper methods of study. He incorporated some of these ideas into *The Conduct of the Understanding*. The total length is about 7000 words. The following extracts derive from the whole essay; they include discussion of the value of history and of ancient exemplars, and a remark on Hobbes. Compare remarks on historical study elsewhere: *Some Thoughts Concerning Education*, §§182, 184 – 'history, which is the great mistress of prudence and civil knowledge'; 'as nothing teaches, so nothing delights more than history'. Also *ECHU*, bk IV, ch. 16, §11; Letter 2320; Knowledge B (1681).

The end of study is knowledge, and the end of knowledge practice or communication. 'Tis true, delight is commonly joined with all improvements of knowledge; but when we study only for that end, it is to be considered rather as diversion than business, and so is to be reckoned amongst our recreations.

The extent of knowledge or things knowable is so vast, our duration here so short, and the entrance by which the knowledge of things gets into our understandings so narrow, that the time of our whole life would be found too short, without the necessary allowances for childhood and old age (which are not capable of much improvement), for the refreshment of our bodies and unavoidable avocations, and in most conditions for the ordinary employments of their callings, which if they neglect, they cannot eat or live. I say that the whole time of our life, without these necessary defalcations [deductions], is not enough to acquaint us with all those things. I will not say which we are capable of knowing, but which it would not be only convenient, but very advantageous for us to know. He that will consider how many doubts and difficulties have remained in the minds of most knowing men after long and studious enquiry, how much, in those several provinces of knowledge they have surveyed, they have left undiscovered, how many other provinces of the *mundus intelligibilis* [intelligible world], as I may call it, they never once touched on, will easily consent to the disproportionateness of our time and strength to the greatness of this business of knowledge taken in its full latitude, and which, if it be not our main business here, yet it is so necessary to it, and so interwoven with it, that we can make little further progress in doing, than we do in knowing – or at least to little purpose; acting without understanding being at best but lost labour.

It therefore much behoves us to improve the best we can our time and talent in this respect, and since we have a long journey to go, and the days are but short, to take the straightest and most direct way we can. To this purpose, it may not perhaps be amiss to decline some things that are likely to bewilder us, or at least lie out of our way, as:

(1) As all that maze of words and phrases which have been invented and employed only to instruct and amuse people in the art of disputing, and will be found perhaps, when looked into, to have little or no meaning; and with this kind of stuff the logics, physics, ethics, metaphysics, and divinity of the schools [Scholasticism] are thought by some to be too much filled . . .

(2) An aim and desire to know what hath been other men's opinions. Truth needs no recommendation, and error is not mended by it; and in our enquiry after knowledge, it as little concerns us what other men have thought, . . . Interest hath blinded some, and prejudiced others, who have yet marched confidently on; and however out of the way, they have thought themselves most in the right. I do not say this to undervalue the light we receive from others, or to think there are not those who assist us mightily in our endeavours after knowledge, perhaps without books we should be as ignorant as the Indians, whose minds are as ill-clad as their bodies. But I think it is an idle and useless thing to make it one's business to study what have been other men's sentiments in things where reason is only to be judge, on purpose to be furnished with them, and to be able to cite them on all occasions. However it be esteemed a great part of learning, yet to a man that considers how little time he has, and how much work to do, how many things he is to learn, how many doubts to clear in religion, how many rules to establish to himself in morality, how much pain to be taken with himself to master his unruly desires and passions, how to provide himself against a thousand cases and accidents that will happen, and an infinite deal more both in his general and particular calling; I say to a man that considers this well, it will not seem much his business to acquaint himself designedly with the various conceits of men that are to be found in books, even upon subjects of moment. I deny not but the knowing of these opinions in all their variety, contradiction, and extravagancy may serve to instruct us in the vanity and ignorance of mankind, and both to humble and caution us upon that

consideration; but this seems not reason enough for me to engage purposely in this study, and in our enquiries after more material points we shall meet with enough of this medley to acquaint us with the weakness of man's understanding . . .

(3) [The third snare is stylishness of expression when not subservient to truth and virtue.]

(4) Antiquity and history, as far as it is designed only to furnish us with story and talk. For the stories of Alexander and Caesar, no further than they instruct us in the art of living well, and furnish us with observations of wisdom and prudence, are not one jot to be preferred to the history of Robin Hood, or the Seven Wise Masters.[12] I do not deny but history is very useful, and very instructive of human life; but if it be studied only for the reputation of being an historian, it is a very empty thing; and he that can tell all the particularities of Herodotus and Plutarch, Curtius and Livy,[13] without making any other use of them, may be an ignorant man with a good memory, and with all his pains hath only filled his head with Christmas tales. And which is worse, the greatest part of history being made up of wars and conquests, and their style, especially the Romans, speaking of valour as the chief if not almost the only virtue, we are in danger to be misled by the general current and business of history; and, looking on Alexander and Caesar and such like heroes, as the highest instances of human greatness, because they each of them caused the death of several hundred thousand men, and the ruin of a much greater number, overran great parts of the earth, and killed their inhabitants to possess themselves of their countries, we are apt to make butchery and rapine the chief marks and very essence of human greatness . . .

(5) [The fifth snare is 'nice questions and remote useless speculations'.]

But if it were fit for me to marshal the parts of knowledge, and allot to every one its place and precedency, thereby to direct our studies, I should think it were natural to set them in this order:

(1) Heaven being our great business and interest, the knowledge which may direct us thither is certainly so, too; so that this is without peradventure the study which ought to take up the first and

---

[12] A popular and ancient fable sold by the chapmen (itinerant peddlars).

[13] Greek and Roman historians, the least known of whom is Curtius Rufus (*c.* first century AD), historian of Alexander the Great.

chiefest place in our thoughts. But wherein it consists, its parts, method, and application, will deserve a chapter by itself.

(2) The next thing to happiness in the other world is a quiet prosperous passage through this, which requires a discreet conduct and management of ourselves in the several occurrences of our lives. The study of prudence, then, seems to me to deserve the second place in our thoughts and studies. A man may be, perhaps, a good man (which lives in truth and sincerity of heart towards God) with a small portion of prudence, but he will never be very happy in himself, nor useful to others without. These two are every man's business.

(3) If those who are left by their predecessors with a plentiful fortune are excused from having a particular calling, in order to their subsistence in this life, 'tis yet certain, by the law of God, they are under an obligation of doing something; which, having been judiciously treated by an able pen,[14] I shall not meddle with, but pass to those who have made letters their business; and on these I think it is incumbent to make the proper business of their calling the third place in their study . . .

[There follows an exhortation to have a healthy mind in a healthy body.]

Our first and great duty, then, is to bring to our studies and to our enquiries after knowledge a mind covetous of truth, that seeks after nothing else, and after that impartially, and embraces it, how poor, how contemptible, how unfashionable soever it may seem. This is that which all studious men profess to do, and yet it is that where I think very many miscarry. Who is there almost that hath not opinions planted in him by education time out of mind; which by that means come to be as the municipal laws of the country, which must not be questioned, but are here looked on with reverence as the standards of right and wrong, truth and falsehood; when perhaps these so sacred opinions were but the oracles of the nursery, or the traditional grave talk of those who pretend to inform our childhood, who receive them from hand to hand without ever examining them? This is the fate of our tender age, which being thus seasoned early, it grows by continuation of time, as it were, into the very constitution of the mind, which afterwards very difficultly

---

[14] Probably Richard Allestree, *The Gentleman's Calling* (1659).

receives a different tincture. When we are grown up, we find the world divided into bands and companies, not only as congregated under several polities and governments, but united only upon account of opinions, and in that respect combined strictly one with another, and distinguished from others, especially in matters of religion. If birth or chance hath not thrown a man young into any of these (which yet seldom fails to happen), choice, when he is grown up, certainly puts him into some or other of them; often out of an opinion that that party is in the right, and sometimes because he finds it is not safe to stand alone, and therefore thinks it convenient to herd somewhere.

Now, in every one of these parties of men there are a certain number of opinions which are received and owned as the doctrine and tenets of that society, the profession and practice whereof all who are of their communion ought to give up themselves, or else they will be scarce looked on as of that society, or at least be thought but lukewarm brothers, or in danger to apostatise. 'Tis plain, in the great difference and contrariety of opinions that are amongst these several parties, that there is much falsehood and abundance of mistakes in most of them. Cunning in some, and ignorance in others, first made them keep them up, and yet how seldom is it that implicit faith, fear of losing credit with the party, or interest (for all these operate in their turns), suffers anyone to question any of the tenets of his party; but altogether in a bundle he receives, embraces, and without examining, professes, and sticks to them, and measures all other opinions by them. Worldly interest also insinuates into several men's minds diverse opinions, which, suiting with their temporal advantage, are kindly received, and in time so riveted there, that it is not easy to remove them.

By these, and perhaps other means, opinions come to be settled and fixed in men's minds, which, whether true or false, there they remain in reputation as substantial material truths, and so are seldom questioned or examined by those who entertain them; and if they happen to be false, as in most men the greatest part must necessarily be, they put a man quite out of the way in the whole course of his studies; and though in his reading and enquiries he flatters himself that his design is to inform his understanding in the real knowledge of truth, yet in effect it tends and reaches to nothing but the confirming of his already received opinions, the things he meets with in other men's writings or discourses being received or rejected as they hold proportion with those anticipations which before hath taken possession of his mind. This will plainly appear if we look but on an instance or two of it.

'Tis a principal doctrine of the Roman party to believe that their church is infallible. This is received as the mark of a good Catholic, and implicit faith, or fear, or interest, keeps all men from questioning it. This being entertained as an undoubted principle, see what work it makes with scripture and reason; neither of them will be heard – though speaking with never so much clearness and demonstration – when they contradict any of her doctrines or institutions; and though it is not grown to that height barefaced to deny the scripture, yet interpretations and distinctions evidently contrary to the plain sense and to the common apprehensions of men are made use of to elude its meaning, and preserve entire the authority of this their principle, that the church is infallible. On the other side, make the light within our guide, and see also what will become of reason and scripture. A Hobbist, with his principle of self-preservation, whereof himself is to be judge, will not easily admit a great many plain duties of morality. The same must necessarily be found in all men who have taken up principles without examining the truth of them.

It being here, then, that men take up prejudice to truth without being aware of it, and afterwards, like men of corrupted appetites, when they think to nourish themselves, generally feed only on those things that suit with and increase the vicious humour – this part is carefully to be looked after. These ancient preoccupations of our minds, these revered and almost sacred opinions, are to be examined, if we will make way for truth, and put our minds in that freedom which belongs and is necessary to them. A mistake is not the less so, nor will ever grow into a truth, because we have believed it a long time, though perhaps it be the harder to part with. And an error is not the less dangerous, nor the less contrary to truth, because it is cried up and had in veneration by any party, though 'tis likely we shall be the less disposed to think it so. Here, therefore, we had need of all our force and all our sincerity; and here 'tis we have use of the assistance of a serious and sober friend, who may help us sedately to examine these our received and beloved opinions. For they are those that the mind, by itself being prepossessed with them, cannot so easily question, look round, and argue against. They are the darlings of our minds, and 'tis as hard to find fault with them as for a man in love to dislike his mistress. There is need, therefore, of the assistance of another; at least it is very useful impartially to show us their defects, and help us to try them by the plain and evident principle of reason or religion . . .

[Most of the remainder concerns techniques of study.]

'Tis time to make an end of this long overgrown discourse. I shall only add one word and then conclude; and that is, that whereas in the beginning I cut off history from our study as a useless part, as certainly it is, when it is read only as a tale that is told; here, on the other side, I recommended it to one who hath well settled in his mind the principles of morality, and knows how to make a judgement on the actions of men, as one of the most useful studies he can apply himself to. There he shall see a picture of the world and the nature of mankind, and so learn to think of men as they are. There he shall see the rise of opinions, and find from what slight and sometimes shameful occasions some of them have taken their rise, which yet afterwards have had great authority, and passed almost for sacred in the world, and borne down all before them. There also one may learn great and useful instructions of prudence, and be warned against the cheats and rogueries of the world, with many more advantages, which I shall not here enumerate.

And so much concerning study. JL

Critical Notes on Stillingfleet (Extract)

1681. Untitled. Generally referred to as 'Critical Notes' on Edward Stillingfleet's *Mischief of Separation* (1680) and *The Unreasonableness of Separation* (1681). MS Locke c. 34. Brief extracts printed in King 1829, pp. 346–58; 1830, II, 195–218; Fox Bourne 1876, I, 457–60 (entitled 'A Defence of Nonconformity'). The relative contribution of Locke and James Tyrrell has been questioned but Locke is now held to be the author (Marshall 1994, pp. 96–110). The manuscript is 167 pages long and is a point-by-point refutation of Stillingfleet's defence of the legislative imposition of Anglican conformity. It is the most important of Locke's works not yet published. Besides the extract below, I confine myself to two quotations: 'If the papists are punished for anything but for being subjects to a prince that hath a declared enmity and war to us I think they have hard usage' (p. 26); and, 'What is done in parliament in civil things may be truly said to be the consent of the nation because they are done by their representatives who are empowered to that purpose' (p. 118). The following extract has not hitherto been printed. It occurs at pp. 101–3 and is a discussion of religious reformation and resistance. The text is hard to follow: Tyrrell was probably writing to Locke's dictation.

When the temporal authority came to be mixed with ecclesiastical jurisdiction, and force was made use of, contrary to the nature of the thing, to make men Christians, or of this or that church whether they would or no, religion became a business of state, and the ecclesiastical government depending upon the secular arm, neglecting the true discipline of Christ, which was either by preaching and persuasion to make men truly Christians, or else by expulsion to shut them out from church communion and disowning them to be of their religion, those who were the ecclesiastical governors would force men by compulsion to that which they were pleased to call true religion, though not at all to be found in the Gospel, but indeed were often such opinions as pleased at court, and best suited the designs and interest of secular domination, and thus the ministers of the Gospel, to the shame of their function, became the great persecutors for religion, and all this upon this false ground that the magistrate's power ought to join with and back their authority and execute their decrees; by which means the church being removed from its true foundation, and that discipline which is only proper to convey into the minds of men the truths of faith and religion, viz. instruction, argument, and persuasion, has become a scene of popular commotions, blood and confusion, whilst men in defence of their natural and evangelical right of taking care of their own salvation, and not owning the belief of what they did, or could not believe, often resisted that force which would unreasonably, and contrary to the methods of the Gospel, compel them to a profession of that religion and those doctrines, which they did not believe or could not assent to, or to join in that way of worship which they thought displeasing and provoking to that God they served. For were the Christian religion left still as it was in the beginning, left to the real convictions of men's minds and their free submission to the doctrine and discipline that they judged right without any force or compulsion, there would not be room for those dangerous questions about reformation which have so shaken the governments of civil states, for [the question] when it is right whether the people may reform if the magistrate does not? it in the bottom means this: whether the people may use force against the magistrate to alter either the doctrine or discipline of the church which he by force has established or maintained; nor can indeed reformation in the church be well set up without disorder and commotion in the state while the magistrate's power interests or concerns itself in the discipline and government of the church, nor do usually such reformations much mend the matter, nor help much to the peace and purity of the church, whilst the reformers, commonly proceeding upon the same ground, desire only to have the secular arm (which they think belongs to the church) only of their side, and so did not only by force withdraw themselves (which is unavoidable in such a state of affairs) from that church they think corrupted and which the power of the magistrate compelled them to be of, against their consciences, but use the same force to compel others to quit the church they were of before and embody with them, when perhaps these converts of the sword they are not convinced of the goodness of the change, and were better satisfied of that way they were of before; these mischiefs both with or without reformation doth a mixture of secular power with matters of religion, and the arm of flesh, produce when it meddles with things belonging to the spirit, whereas were the church left to the bare exercise of that power which our Saviour (who had no kingdom of this world) put into it, reformations (when there are need) would be wrought in the world with that quiet and peace which the Gospel requires; every man (which is the only true reformation) might quietly reform himself, that is upon contrition of conscience, quit his errors, and amend his miscarriages and betake himself to that way of public worship which he wishes, found purest and best suited to the ends of religion, or could get others to join with him in: and to all this there would be no bustle, for there would need no force for a man to get out of that corrupted church where there were none to keep him in; and until this great and fundamental popish doctrine of using force in matters of religion be laid aside there is little hopes of peace, and truth in the world; it as necessarily following from thence that the king of Spain should burn Lutherans, the king of France destroy the Huguenots, as we in England punish fanatics, or the Presbyterians persecute the episcopate when they had power, and the Independent and Quaker think they ought to use the magistrate's power or have any temporal ties to force men to keep them in their churches. I know not whether they would not be as dangerous reformers as Germany found the Anabaptists; all the mischiefs, of want of reformation on the one side, and the commotions and disorders which the pretences and desires of reforming on the other have produced in the Christian world, have all followed from a complication of the civil and ecclesiastical power, and that force which hath been used both to keep men in, or get them out, of the nationally established forms of religion, in the several kingdoms and commonwealths of Christendom.

Locke's reading list

This list identifies the books recommended in Locke's 'Some Thoughts Concerning Reading and Study for a Gentleman' (1703). Classical authors are identified by name only, unless Locke specifies a particular work. For fuller bibliographical details see Yolton and Yolton 1989, pp. 319–27. Items which Locke had in his library are cited by their catalogue numbers in Harrison and Laslett 1965 (HL). For commentary on some of the items: on Sidney see Scott 1991; on Paxton see Gunn 1968 and Letter 3326; on Tyrrell see Gough 1976; on the Ancient Constitutionalist writings see Pocock 1957, Resnick 1984, Greenberg 1989, Weston 1991; on Cowell see Chrimes 1949; on the travel literature see Bonno 1955, Batz 1974.

Speaking well: for perspicuity and right reasoning

Nicolas Boileau-Despréaux, *Traité du sublime* (1675) (HL 371, 1806)
Caesar, *Commentaries* (HL 561)
William Chillingworth, *The Religion of Protestants* (1638) (HL 685–6)
Cicero ('Tully'), *Works* (HL 711)
Cicero, *De Oratore* (HL 721)
Cicero, *Orator*
Livy (HL 1770–2a)
Quintilian, *Institutiones Oratoriae* (HL 2424–5)
Terence (HL 2852–6b)
John Tillotson, *Works* (1696) (HL 2902–20a)
Virgil (HL 3089–95)

Morality

Cicero, *De Officiis* (*On duties*) (HL 714–17, 721h–i)
The New Testament (HL 302–30c)

Politics: the origin of society and extent of political power

Richard Hooker, *Of the Laws of Ecclesiastical Polity* (1593–7) (HL 1490–2)
John Locke, *Two Treatises of Government* (1689) (HL 1293)
Peter Paxton, *Civil Polity* (1703) (HL 725)
Samuel Pufendorf, *De Officio Hominis et Civis* (1673) (HL 2403)
Samuel Pufendorf, *De Jure Naturae et Gentium* (1672) (HL 2401, 2407)
Algernon Sidney, *Discourses concerning Government* (1698; written *c.* 1681–
3) (HL 2666)

Politics: the art of government

Anonymous, *Fleta, seu Commentarius juris Anglicani* (*c.* 1290; printed 1647)
(A summary of Bracton)
William Atwood, *Jus Anglorum ab Antiquo* (1681) (HL 145)
Henry de Bracton (d. 1268), *De Legibus et Consuetudinibus Angliae* (printed
1569)
Robert Brady, *A Full and Clear Answer* (1681)
Robert Brady, *An Introduction to the Old English History* (1684)
Robert Brady, *Complete History of England* (1685, 1700)
Sir Edward Coke, *The Second Part of the Institutes of the Laws of England*
(1642)
William Hakewill, *Modus Tenendi Parliamentum, or the Old Manner of Hold-
ing Parliaments* (1641, 1659)
Ralph Hengham (Henningham) (d. 1311), *Registrum Cancellarie* (printed
1531)
Andrew Horne, *The Mirror of Justices* (1646)
William Petyt, *The Ancient Right of the Commons of England Asserted* (1680)
John Sadler, *The Rights of the Kingdom* (1649) (HL 2525)
State Tracts (1689) (HL 2759) (another edn, 2 parts, 1692–3)
James Tyrrell, *Patriarcha non Monarcha* (1681)
James Tyrrell, *Bibliotheca Politica* (1694)
James Tyrrell, *General History of England* (1697–1700) (HL 3002)

General History

Francis Bacon, *The Historie of the Raigne of King Henry VII* (1622) (HL
162)

Gilbert Burnet, *The History of the Reformation of the Church of England* (1679)

Phillipe de Comines (Commynes), *Mémoires* (1524)

Samuel Daniel, *The Historie of England* (1612)

Edward Herbert (Lord Herbert of Cherbury), *The Life and Reigne of King Henry VIII* (1649)

William Howell, *Elementae Historiae* (1671)

Juan de Mariana, *Historiae de Rebus Hispaniae* (1592) (HL 1905)

Sir James Melville, *Memoirs* (1683)

Sir Walter Raleigh, *History of the World* (1614) (HL 2435)

François de La Rochefoucauld, *Mémoires* (1662) (HL 2492–3)

John Rushworth, *Historical Collections of Private Passages of State* (1659–1701) (HL 2514)

Jacques Auguste de Thou (Thuanus), *Historiae sui Temporis* (1604–6)

Diggory Whear, *De Ratione et Methodo Legendi Historias Dissertatio* (1623)

Chronology

Helvicus, *Chronology*

Dionysius Petavius (Denys Petau), *Rationarum temporum* (1662)

Joseph Scaliger, *De Emendatione Temporum* (1593) (HL 2558)

Aegidius Strauchius, *Breviarum Chronologicum* (HL 2793–a) (English edn, 1699)

Francis Tallents, *A View of Universal History* (1685) (HL 2829)

Geography

William Camden, *Britannia* (1586) (HL 574–5)

Peter Heylyn, *Cosmographie* (1652)

Hermann Moll, *A System of Geographie* (1701) (HL 2009)

Travel

Pierre Bergeron, *Relation des voyages en Tartarie* (1634) (HL 280)

François Bernier, *The History of the Late Revolution of the Empire of the Great Mogul* (1671); *A Continuation of the Memoirs* (1672); and other travel writings (HL 284–9)

Edward Browne, *A Brief Account of Some Travels in Hungary, Servia, Bulgaria* (1673) (HL 498)

A Collection of Voyages and Travels (1704) (HL 3118)

William Dampier, *A New Voyage Round the World* (1697) (HL 910)

Thomas Gage, *A New Survey of the West Indies* (1648) (HL 1205)

Richard Hakluyt, *The Principal Navigations . . . of the English Nation* (1589) (HL 1374)

Samuel Purchas, *Purchas his Pilgrimage* (1613) (HL 2409)

François Pyrard, *Discours du voyage des françois aux Indes orientales* (1611) (HL 2411)

Giovanni Battista Ramusio, *Navigationi e viaggi* (1595–1665) (HL 2438)

Sir Thomas Roe, *Mémoires de T. Rhoe* (1663) (HL 3118)

Gabriel Sagard, *Histoire du Canada* (1636) (HL 2526)

Gabriel Sagard, *Les Grand voyage du pays des Hurons* (1632) (HL 2527)

George Sandys, *A Relation of a Journey* (1615) (HL 2553)

Melchisédech Thévenot, *Recueil de voyages* (1681) (HL 2890)

For an understanding of human nature

Aristotle, *Rhetoric* (HL 118)

Jean de La Bruyère, *Les Caractères de Théophraste* (1688) (HL 505)

Horace (HL 1494–1512a)

Juvenal (HL 1604–8b)

Persius (HL 2263–4)

For diversion and delight

Miguel de Cervantes, *Don Quixote* (1605) (HL 651, 2428)

Reference books

Michel Baudrand, *Geographia Ordine Literarum Disposita* (1671) (HL 224)

Pierre Bayle, *Dictionnaire historique et critique* (1697) (HL 237)

Ambrosio Calepino, *Dictionarium Septem Linguarum* (1516) (HL 569–a)

Elisha Coles, *A Dictionary English-Latin and Latin-English* (1677) (HL 808–a)

Thomas Cooper, *Thesaurus Linguae Romanae et Britannicae* (1565) (HL 842)

John Cowell, *The Interpreter* (1607) (HL 868)

Robert Estienne (Stephens), *Thesaurus Linguae Latinae* (1573)

Charles du Fresne, sieur du Cange, *Glossarium ad Scriptores Mediae et Infimae Latinitatis* (1678) (HL 579)

Johann Jacob Hofmann, *Lexicon Universale Historicum* (1677) (HL 1468–9)

Nicholas Lloyd, *Dictionarium Historicum Poeticum* (1671) (HL 1773)

Louis Moreri, *Le Grand Dictionnaire historique* (1674) (HL 2051)

John Selden, *Titles of Honour* (1614) (HL 2608)

Stephen Skinner, *Etymologicon Linguae Anglicanae* (1669) (HL 2689)
Sir Henry Spelman, *Glossarium Archailogicum* (1626) (HL 2739)
Johannes Gerardus Vossius, *Etymologicon Linguae Latinae* (1662) (HL 3107–8)

Checklist of Lockeana in print

This list provides a guide to those of Locke's manuscripts which have been printed in this volume or elsewhere, arranged according to their archival provenance. It will also serve to decode the footnotes of Locke scholars who refer to texts by their manuscript number rather than by title. Items with asterisks are printed in this volume (earlier printings are indicated in the headnotes); items printed here for the first time have two asterisks. The list is not exhaustive: see, more fully, Long 1959, Attig 1985, Schankula 1973. In particular, Locke's medical writings are not included (see Dewhurst 1963 and 1966; Long 1959, pp. 36–8; Romanell 1984). There are also a number of brief entries in Locke's journals printed in King 1829 and 1830. Locke's journals during his period in France are printed in Lough 1953. His library lists are in Harrison and Laslett 1965.

Bodleian Library: MSS Locke

b. 3, p. 48	Guineas, *c.* 1695 (Kelly 1991, II, 363–4)
b. 3, p. 64	Paper for Sir William Trumbull, 1695 (Kelly 1991, II, 365–73)
b. 3, p. 68	Proposals to the Lords Justices, 1695 (Kelly 1991, II, 374–80)
b. 3, p. 70	Answers to the Lord Keeper's Queries, 1695 (Kelly 1991, II, 381–97)
b. 4, pp. 75–8	*Liberty of the Press, 1694–5
b. 4, pp. 169–14	Memoir of Shaftesbury (*Works*, IX, 266–81)

b. 5, item 14	Locke's Will (De Beer 1989, VIII, 419–27)
c. 25, fos. 56–7	Rules of the Dry Club, *c.* 1692 (*Works*, X, 312–14)
c. 27, fo. 29	*Civil and Ecclesiastical Power, 1674
c. 27, fo. 30	**The Particular Test for Priests, *c.* 1674
c. 27, fo. 30	*Philanthropy, 1675
c. 27, fos. 32–3	*Catholic Infallibility, 1675
c. 27, fos. 69–71	De S. Scripturae Authorite, 1685 (Sina 1972, pp. 64–8)
c. 27, fos. 73–4	An Inward Inspiration or Revelation, 1687 (Sina 1972, pp. 68–73)
c. 27, fo. 80	*Pacific Christians, 1688
c. 27, fo. 112	Redemption, Death, *c.* 1697 (Sina 1972, pp. 400–1)
c. 27, fos. 131–7	Spirit, Soul and Body, 1690s (Sina 1972, pp. 403–8; Wainright 1987, II, 675–8)
c. 27, fo. 143	Who Righteous Man, 1696 (Sina 1972, pp. 408–9)
c. 27, fo. 143	Critique of Richard Bentley, *c.* 1696 (Sina 1972, pp. 409–12)
c. 27, fos. 147–50	Observations on Mr Bold's Papers, 1698 (Sina 1972, pp. 412–16)
c. 27, fos. 162–75	The Resurrection (Wainright 1987, II, 679–84)
c. 27, fos. 213–14	Christianae Religionis Synopsis, 1702 (Sina 1972, pp. 416–18; Wainright 1987, II, 686–8)
c. 27, fos. 217–19	An Essay for the Understanding of St Paul's Epistles, *c.* 1703 (Sina 1972, pp. 418–24; Wainright 1987, II, 672–4)
c. 27, fos. 221–3	Synopsis of St Paul's Epistles (1703–4) (Wainright 1987, II, 689–90)
c. 27, fos. 238–9	Volkelii Hypothesis Lib. de Vera Religione, n.d. (Sina 1972, pp. 424–7)
c. 28, fos. 1–2	*Preface, First Tract on Government, 1661
c. 28, fos. 3–20	*Second Tract on Government, *c.* 1662
c. 28, fos. 21–32	*Essay on Toleration, 1667
c. 28, fos. 33–40	Draft B of *ECHU*, 1671, Contents List (Nidditch and Rogers 1990)
c. 28, fos. 42–4	On Pierre Nicole (Von Leyden 1954, pp. 252–4)
c. 28, fos. 83–96	**On William Sherlock, 1690–1
c. 28, fos. 107–11	Answer to John Norris, 1692 (Acworth 1971)
c. 28, fo. 113	*Ethica B, 1693
c. 28, fo. 113	**Homo ante et post Lapsum, 1693
c. 28, fo. 114	*Voluntas, 1693
c. 28, fos. 115–16	Method (Farr 1987, pp. 70–2)

c. 28, fos. 121–37	The Conduct of the Understanding (*Works*, III, 185–265, and various edns)
c. 28, fos. 139–40	*Morality, *c.* 1677–8
c. 28, fo. 141	*Law, *c.* 1693
c. 28, fos. 143–4	*Thus I Think, *c.* 1686–8?
c. 28, fos. 146–52	*Of Ethic in General, *c.* 1686–8?
c. 28, fo. 157–8	**Adversaria C, *c.* 1681
c. 30, fo. 18	*Trade, 1674
c. 30, fos. 87–8, 94–5	*Draft of Essay on the Poor Law, 1697
c. 33, fo. 10	**Pietas, 25 March 1679
c. 33, fo. 11	**Justitia, 25 March 1679
c. 33, fo. 11	**Politia, 25 March 1679
c. 34	[*extract only] Critical Notes on Stillingfleet, 1681
c. 39, pp. 7–9	*On Samuel Parker, 1669–70
c. 42B, p. 36	**Atlantis, 1679
c. 42B, p. 224	*Ethica A, 1692
d. 1, p. 5	Conformitas, 1679 (Harris 1994, p. 365)
d. 1, pp. 53, 57	*Love of Country, 1679
d. 1, p. 57	**Love, 1679
d. 1, pp. 125–6	*Toleration D, 1679
d. 2	Some Considerations of the Consequences of the Lowering of Interest (draft), 1691 (Kelly 1991, II, 503–612)
d. 3, pp. 1–88	An Examination of Malebranche (*Works*, X, 211–55)
d. 3, pp. 89–112	Remarks on Mr Norris's Book (*Works*, X, 247–59)
d. 10, pp. 43–4	*Ecclesia, *c.* 1682
d. 10, p. 161	*Superstition, *c.* 1682
d. 10, p. 163	*Tradition, *c.* 1682
e. 6, fos. 63–90	[*]Essays on the Law of Nature, 1663–4
e. 6, fos. 91–69	[*]Second Tract on Government, 1660–1
e. 7	*First Tract on Government, 1660
e. 8, pp. 3–37	Some of the Consequences . . . upon Lessening of Interest (Essay on Money and Interest, 1668) (Kelly 1991, I, 167–202; Letwin 1963, pp. 295–323)
e. 9, pp. 1–38	The Grievances of Virginia, 1697 (Kammen 1966, pp. 153–69)
e. 18	*On Allegiance and the Revolution, 1690
f. 1, pp. 123–6	*Obligation of Penal Laws, 25 February 1676
f. 1, pp. 173–4	Spacium, 27 March 1676 (Aaron and Gibb 1936, p. 77)

f. 1, p. 280	**Atlantis, 12 June 1676
f. 1, pp. 289–95	Extension, 20 June 1676 (Aaron and Gibb 1936, pp. 77–80)
f. 1, pp. 313–14	Extension, 9 July 1676 (Von Leyden 1954, pp. 258–9)
f. 1, pp. 317–19	Simple Ideas, 13 July 1676 (Aaron and Gibb 1936, pp. 80–1)
f. 1, p. 319	**Atlantis, 14 July 1676
f. 1, pp. 320–5, 354–5	Idolatry, 15 and 20 July 1676 (Von Leyden 1954, pp. 259–63)
f. 1, pp. 325–47	*Pleasure, Pain, the Passions, 16 July 1676
f. 1, pp. 367–70	*Atheism, 29 July 1676
f. 1, p. 392	Simple Ideas, 3 August 1676 (Aaron and Gibb 1936, p. 83)
f. 1, pp. 402–6	Spelling, 15 August 1676 (Von Leyden 1954, pp. 256–7)
f. 1, pp. 412–15	*Toleration B, 23 August 1676
f. 1, pp. 415–21	*Faith and Reason, 24–6 August 1676
f. 1, pp. 421–9	Transubstantiation, 26–8 August 1676 (Von Leyden 1954, pp. 277–81)
f. 1, pp. 430–2	*Knowledge A, 1 September 1676
f. 1, pp. 442–3	Species, 19 September 1676 (Aaron and Gibb 1936, p. 83)
f. 1, pp. 445–7	*Happiness A, 26 September 1676
f. 1, p. 469	**Politica, 14 October 1676
f. 2, pp. 42–55	*Understanding, 8 February 1677
f. 2, pp. 57–9	Arguments Positive and Negative, 12 February 1677 (Aaron and Gibb 1936, pp. 90–1)
f. 2, pp. 87–101, 114–40	[*extracts only] Study, March–May 1677
f. 2, pp. 226–7	Cartesii Opera, 8 August 1677 (Aaron and Gibb 1936, p. 91)
f. 2, pp. 247–52	*Adversaria B, 4 September 1677
f. 2, pp. 265–9	Space, 16 September 1677 (Aaron and Gibb 1936, pp. 94–6)
f. 2, pp. 280–2	Sensation, Delight, 1 October 1677 (Aaron and Gibb 1936, pp. 96–7)
f. 2, p. 289	**Atlantis, 4 October 1677
f. 2, pp. 296–8	**Atlantis, 14 October 1677
f. 2, pp. 319–20	Madness, 5 November 1677 (King 1829, p. 328)
f. 2, pp. 347–8	Error, 11 November 1677 (Aaron and Gibb 1936, pp. 97–8)

f. 2, pp. 356–8	Species, 19 November 1677 (Aaron and Gibb 1936, pp. 98–9)
f. 3, pp. 5–16	Relation, Space, 20 January 1678 (Aaron and Gibb 1936, pp. 99–103)
f. 3, pp. 16–21	Memory, Madness, 22 January 1678 (Aaron and Gibb 1936, pp. 103–5)
f. 3, pp. 21–2	Discourse, 23 January 1678 (Cox 1960, p. 32)
f. 3, pp. 24–5	Space, 24 January 1678 (Aaron and Gibb 1936, p. 105)
f. 3, pp. 49–60	Descartes, 7 March 1678 (Aaron and Gibb 1936, pp. 105–11)
f. 3, pp. 69–79	Scrupulosity, 20 March 1678 (King 1829, pp. 109–13; De Beer 1976, I, 555–60: Letter 374)
f. 3, p. 107	**Toleration C, 19 April 1678
f. 3, pp. 111–12	*Law, 21 April 1678
f. 3, pp. 142–3	*Atlantis, 26 May 1678
f. 3, pp. 198–201	**Atlantis, 15 July 1678
f. 3, pp. 201–2	*Law of Nature, 15 July 1678
f. 3, pp. 205–6	Infinitum, 16 July 1678 (Aaron and Gibb 1936, pp. 111–12)
f. 3, p. 263	Modes Complex, 25 August (Aaron and Gibb 1936, p. 112)
f. 3, pp. 266–7	**Virtue A, 26 August 1678
f. 3, pp. 304–5	*Happiness B, 1 October 1678
f. 3, pp. 351–7	Recreation, 2 December 1678 (King 1829, pp. 323–5, Fox Bourne 1676, I, 388–90; De Beer 1976, I, 473–5: Letter 328)
f. 3, pp. 358–78	Scrupulosity, 2 December 1678 (part in King 1829, pp. 113–15; part in De Beer 1976, I, 646–50: Letter 426)
f. 3, pp. 381–2	*Reputation, 12 December 1678
f. 4, pp. 145–51	*Of God's Justice, 1 August 1680
f. 5, pp. 33–8	*Religion, 3 April 1681
f. 5, p. 59	*Reason, Passion, Superstition, 16 May 1681
f. 5, pp. 77–83	*Knowledge B, 26 June 1681
f. 5, pp. 86–7	*Laws, 28 June 1681
f. 5, pp. 113–14	Perfect Ideas, 19 August 1681 (Aaron and Gibb 1936, p. 118)
f. 6, pp. 19–20	Cudworth, 18 February 1682 (Aaron and Gibb 1936, p. 118)
f. 6, pp. 20–5	*Enthusiasm, 19 February 1682

f. 6, pp. 25–33	Proof, 20 February 1682 (Aaron and Gibb 1936, pp. 121–3)
f. 6, pp. 33–8	Enthusiasm, 21 February 1682 (Aaron and Gibb 1936, pp. 123–5; De Beer 1976, II, 488: Letter 687)
f. 8, pp. 114–21	**The Labadists, 22 August 1684
f. 26	[*extract only] Draft B of *ECHU*, 1671 (Nidditch and Rogers 1990)
f. 30, pp. 122–84	[*]Essays on the Law of Nature, *c.* 1663–4
f. 31	*Essays on the Law of Nature, *c.* 1663–4
f. 31, pp. 120–38	Valedictory Speech, 1664 (Von Leyden 1954, pp. 220–43)

British Library: Sloane 4290

fos. 11–14	*Some Thoughts Concerning Reading, 1703

British Library: Add. MS 15,642 (Also available in Bodleian Library, MS Film 424.)

pp. 13–14	*Atlantis, 14 February 1679
p. 18	**Carolina, 20 February 1679
pp. 18–22	*Atlantis, 20–1 February 1679
p. 22	**Marriage, 22 February 1679
p. 101	*Opinion, 17 June 1679
pp. 108–11	Unity, 3 July 1679 (Aaron and Gibb 1936, pp. 112–13)

British Library: Add. MS 38,771

Draft of 'Some Thoughts Concerning Education' (1684) (Kenyon 1933)

Public Record Office: Shaftesbury Papers

30/24/30/30	[*]Liberty of the Press, 1694–5
30/24/42/62	Memoir of the Life of the Earl of Shaftesbury (*Works*, IX, 266–81)
30/24/47/1	[*]Essay on Toleration, 1667
30/24/47/2	De Arte Medica (1669) (Dewhurst 1966, pp. 79–84)

30/24/47/3	*Fundamental Constitutions of Carolina, 1669
30/24/47/7	Draft A of *ECHU*, copy
30/24/47/30	*Selecting the Grand Jury, 1681
30/24/47/33	*Infallibility, 1661–2
30/24/47/34–5	Observations upon the Growth and Culture of Vines and Olives (*Works*, x, 323–56)

Public Record Office: Colonial Office Papers

CO/388/5/86–95	*Essay on the Poor Law, 1697
CO/5/286/266–303	The Grievances of Virginia (Ashcraft 1969)

Adversaria 1661 (1661 Commonplace Book)
(Also available in Bodleian Library: MS Film 77. The opening folios are not paginated.)

fos. 1–3	*Adversaria A, *c.* 1670?
pp. 10–11	*Virtue B, 1681
p. 20	Religio, 1699 (King 1829, p. 285; 1830, II, 81)
p. 24	*Punitive Justice, 1695
pp. 56–89, 94–5	Draft A of *ECHU*, 1671 (Aaron and Gibb 1936; Nidditch and Rogers 1990)
p. 93	*Sacerdos, 1698
pp. 106–25	[*]Essay on Toleration, 1667
p. 125	*Toleration A, *c.* 1675
p. 268–9	*Venditio, 1695
pp. 270–1	*Toleration A, *c.* 1675
pp. 310–11	*Labour, 1693
pp. 320–1	*Error, 1698

Huntington Library, California: MS HM 584
(Also available in Bodleian Library: MS Film 151.)

[*]Essay on Toleration, 1667

Houghton Library, Harvard University: MS Eng. 818

pp. 1–5	*General Naturalisation, 1693

Bibliography

Aaron, R. I. (1937). *John Locke* (Oxford; 3rd edn, 1971).

Aaron, R. I. and Gibb, J., ed. (1936). *An Early Draft of Locke's Essay, together with Excerpts from his Journals* (Oxford).

Abrams, P., ed. (1967). *John Locke: Two Tracts on Government* (Cambridge).

Acworth, R. (1971). 'Locke's first reply to John Norris', *Locke Newsletter*, 2:7–11.

Anderson, C. (1992). ' "Safe enough in honesty and prudence": the ordinary conduct of government in the thought of John Locke', *History of Political Thought*, 13:587–630.

Appleby, J. O. (1978). *Economic Thought and Ideology in Seventeenth-Century England* (Princeton, 1978).

Ashcraft, R. (1969). 'Political theory and political reform: John Locke's essay on Virginia', *Western Political Quarterly*, 22:742–58.

(1986). *Revolutionary Politics and Locke's 'Two Treatises of Government'* (Princeton).

(1987). *Locke's 'Two Treatises of Government'* (London).

(ed.) (1991). *John Locke: Critical Assessments*, 4 vols. (London).

Astbury, R. (1978). 'The renewal of the licensing act in 1693 and its lapse in 1695', *The Library*, 33:296–322.

Attig, J. C. (1985). *The Works of John Locke: A Comprehensive Bibliography* (Westport, Conn.).

Axtell, J. L., ed. (1968). *The Educational Writings of John Locke* (Cambridge).

Bastide, C. (1907). *John Locke, ses théories politiques et leur influence en Angleterre* (Paris; repr. Geneva, 1970).

Batz, W. G. (1974). 'The historical anthropology of John Locke', *Journal of the History of Ideas*, 35:663–70.

Beier, A. L. (1988). ' "Utter strangers to industry, morality and religion": John Locke on the poor', *Eighteenth-Century Life*, 12:28–41.

Biddle, J. C. (1977). 'John Locke's Essay on Infallibility: introduction, text and translation', *Journal of Church and State*, 19:301–27.

Blaug, M., ed. (1991). *The Later Mercantilists* (Aldershot, Hants.)

Bonno, G. (1955). *Les Relations intellectuelles de Locke avec la France* (Berkeley, Calif.).

Brandt, R., ed. (1981). *John Locke Symposium* (Berlin).

Brennan, J. (1957). 'A Gallican interlude in Ireland: The Irish Remonstrance of 1661', *Irish Theological Quarterly*, 24:217–37, 283–309.

Burns, J. H. and Goldie, M., eds. (1991). *The Cambridge History of Political Thought, 1450–1700* (Cambridge).

Chappell, V., ed. (1994). *The Cambridge Companion to Locke* (Cambridge).

Chrimes, S. B. (1949). 'The constitutional ideas of Dr John Cowell', *English Historical Review*, 64:461–87.

Christophersen, H. O. (1930). *A Bibliographical Introduction to the Study of John Locke* (Oslo).

Clarke, G., ed. (1987). *John Bellers: His Life, Times, and Writings* (London).

Colman, J. (1983). *John Locke's Moral Philosophy* (Edinburgh).

Cox, R. H. (1960). *Locke on War and Peace* (Oxford).

Cranston, M. (1957). *John Locke: A Biography* (Oxford; repr. 1985).

Daly, J. (1979). *Sir Robert Filmer and English Political Thought* (Toronto).

De Beer, E. S., ed. (1976–89). *The Correspondence of John Locke*, 8 vols. (Oxford).

De Marchi, E. (1955). 'Locke's Atlantis', *Political Studies*, 3:164–5.

Dewhurst, K. (1963). *John Locke (1632–1704), Physician and Philosopher* (London).

(1966). *Dr Thomas Sydenham (1624–1689)* (London).

Driscoll, E. A. (1972). 'The influence of Gassendi on Locke's hedonism', *International Philosophical Quarterly*, 12:87–110.

Dunn, J. (1967). 'Consent in the political theory of John Locke', *Historical Journal*, 10:153–82.

(1968). 'Justice and the interpretation of Locke's political theory', *Political Studies*, 16:68–87.

(1969). *The Political Thought of John Locke* (Cambridge).

(1980). *Political Obligation in its Historical Context* (Cambridge).

(1984). *Locke* (Oxford).

Dworetz, S. M. (1990). *The Unvarnished Doctrine: Locke, Liberalism and the American Revolution* (Durham, N.C.).

Farr, J. (1986). ' "So vile and miserable an estate': the problem of slavery in Locke's political thought', *Political Theory*, 14:263–90.

(1987). 'The way of hypotheses: Locke on method', *Journal of the History of Ideas*, 48:51–72.

Farr, J. and Roberts, C. (1985). 'John Locke on the Glorious Revolution: a rediscovered document', *Historical Journal*, 28:385–98.

Fox Bourne, H. R. (1876). *The Life of John Locke*, 2 vols. (London).

Franklin, J. H. (1978). *John Locke and the Theory of Sovereignty* (Cambridge).

Glausser, W. (1990). 'Three approaches to Locke and the slave trade', *Journal of the History of Ideas*, 51:199–216.

Goldie, M. (1980). 'The Revolution of 1689 and the structure of political argument', *Bulletin of Research in the Humanities*, 83:473–564.

(1983). 'John Locke and Anglican Royalism', *Political Studies*, 31:61–85.

(1991). 'The theory of religious intolerance in Restoration England', in *From Persecution to Toleration*, eds. O. P. Grell, J. I. Israel and N. Tyacke (Oxford).

(ed.) (1993). *John Locke: Two Treatises of Government* (London).

Gough, J. W. (1950). *John Locke's Political Philosophy* (Oxford; repr. 1973).

(1976). 'James Tyrrell, Whig historian and friend of John Locke', *Historical Journal*, 19:581–610.

Grant, R. (1987). *John Locke's Liberalism* (Chicago).

Greenberg, J. (1989). 'The Confessor's laws and the radical face of the ancient constitution', *English Historical Review*, 104:611–37.

Gunn, J. A. W. (1968). 'The *Civil Polity* of Peter Paxton', *Past and Present*, 40:42–57.

Haley, K. H. D. (1968). *The First Earl of Shaftesbury* (Oxford).

Hall, R., and Woolhouse, R. (1983). *Eighty Years of Locke Scholarship* (Edinburgh).

Harris, I. (1994). *The Mind of John Locke* (Cambridge).

Harrison, J. and Laslett, P. (1965). *The Library of John Locke* (Oxford Bibliographical Society; repr. 1971).

Hartogh, G. A. den (1990). 'Express consent and full membership in Locke', *Political Studies*, 38:105–15.

Hooker, R. (1989). *Of the Laws of Ecclesiastical Polity*, ed. A. S. McGrade (Cambridge).

Horne, T. A. (1990). *Property Rights and Poverty: Political Argument in Britain, 1605–1834* (Chapel Hill, N.C.).

Horton, J. and Mendus, S., eds. (1991). *John Locke: 'A Letter Concerning Toleration' in Focus* (London).

Horwitz, R., Clay, J. S. and Clay, D., eds. (1990). *John Locke: Questions Concerning the Law of Nature* (Ithaca, N.Y.).

Hundert, E. J. (1972). 'The making of homo faber: John Locke between ideology and history', *Journal of the History of Ideas*, 33:3–22.

Inoue, K., ed. (1974). *John Locke: An Essay Concerning Toleration, and Toleratio* (Nara, Japan).

Jolley, N. (1975). 'Leibniz on Hobbes, Locke's *Two Treatises* and Sherlock's *Case of Allegiance*', *Historical Journal*, 18:21–35.

Kammen, M. G. (1966). 'Virginia at the close of the seventeenth century: an appraisal by James Blair and John Locke', *Virginia Magazine of History and Biography*, 74:141–69.

Kearney, H. F. (1959). 'The political background to English mercantilism, 1695–1700', *Economic History Review*, 11:484–96.

Kelly, P. (1988). ' "All things richly to enjoy": economics and politics in Locke's *Two Treatises of Government*', *Political Studies*, 36:273–93.

(ed.) (1991). *Locke on Money*, 2 vols. (Oxford).

Kenyon, F. G., ed. (1933). *John Locke: Directions Concerning Education* (Oxford).

Kenyon, J. P. (1977). *Revolution Principles: The Politics of Party, 1689–1720* (Cambridge).

King, P. (1829, 1830). *The Life and Letters of John Locke* (London). New edition, with additions, 1830, in 2 vols.

Klibansky, R. and Gough, J. W., eds. (1968). *John Locke: Epistola de Tolerantia: A Letter on Toleration* (Oxford).

Knights, M. (1993). 'Petitioning and the political theorists: John Locke, Algernon Sidney and London's 'monster'' petition of 1680', *Past and Present*, 138:94–111.

Laslett, P., ed. (1960). *John Locke: Two Treatises of Government* (Cambridge; repr. 1967, 1988).

Letwin, W. (1963). *The Origins of Scientific Economics* (London).

Locke, J. (1720). *A Collection of Several Pieces of Mr John Locke* (London).

(1801). *Works*, 10th edn, 10 vols. (London).

Long, P. (1959). *A Summary Catalogue of the Lovelace Collection of the Papers of John Locke in the Bodleian Library* (Oxford Bibliographical Society).

(1964). 'The Mellon donation of additional MSS of John Locke from the Lovelace Collection', *Bodleian Library Record*, 7:185–93.

Lough, J., ed. (1953). *Locke's Travels in France, 1675–1679, as related in his Journals* (Cambridge).

Macfarlane, S. M. (1982). 'Studies in poverty and poor relief in London at the end of the seventeenth century' (Oxford D.Phil. thesis).

McGuinness, C. (1990). 'The Fundamental Constitutions of Carolina as a tool for Lockean scholarship', *Interpretation*, 17:127–43.

McNally, D. (1988). *Political Economy and the Rise of Capitalism* (Berkeley).

Macpherson, C. B. (1962). *The Political Theory of Possessive Individualism* (Oxford).

Marshall, J. (1992). 'John Locke and latitudinarianism', in *Philosophy, Science and Religion in England 1640–1700*, ed. R. Kroll, R. Ashcraft, and P. Zagorin (Cambridge).

(1994). *John Locke: Resistance, Religion, and Responsibility* (Cambridge).

Mason, M. G. (1962). 'John Locke's proposals for work-house schools', *Durham Research Review*, 4:8–16.

Mehta, U. D. (1992). *The Anxiety of Freedom: Imagination and Individuality in Locke's Political Thought* (Ithaca, N.Y.)

Milton, J. R. (1990). 'John Locke and the Fundamental Constitutions of Carolina', *Locke Newsletter*, 21:111–33.

(1993). 'Locke's *Essay on Toleration*: text and context', *British Journal of the History of Philosophy*, 1:45–66.

(1996a). 'Lockean political apocrypha', *British Journal of the History of Philosophy*, 4:248–67.

(1996b). 'Locke manuscripts among the Shaftesbury papers in the Public Record Office', *Locke Newsletter*, 27: 109–30.

Milton, J. R. and Milton, P. (1997). 'The selection of juries: a tract by John Locke', *Historical Journal*, 40:185–94.

Montuori, M., ed. (1963). *John Locke: A Letter Concerning Toleration* (The Hague).

Nidditch, P. H., ed. (1975). *John Locke: An Essay Concerning Human Understanding* (Oxford).

Nidditch, P. H. and Rogers, G. A. J., eds. (1990). *John Locke: Drafts for the 'Essay Concerning Human Understanding', and Other Philosophical Writings* (Oxford).

Parker, M. E. E., ed. (1963). *North Carolina Charters and Constitutions, 1578–1698* (Raleigh, N.C.).

Parry, G. (1978). *John Locke* (London).

Pateman, C. (1988). *The Sexual Contract* (Cambridge).

Phillipson, N. and Skinner, Q., eds. (1993). *Political Discourse in Early Modern Britain* (Cambridge).

Pocock, J. G. A. (1957). *The Ancient Constitution and the Feudal Law* (Cambridge, 1957; repr. 1987).

(1975). *The Machiavellian Moment* (Princeton).

(1985). *Virtue, Commerce, and History* (Cambridge).

Rand, B., ed. (1931). *An Essay Concerning the Understanding* (Cambridge, Mass.).

Raphael, D. D., ed. (1969). *British Moralists, 1650–1800*, 2 vols. (Oxford).

Resnick, D. (1984). 'Locke and the rejection of the Ancient Constitution', *Political Theory*, 12:97–114.

(1987). 'John Locke and the problem of naturalization', *Review of Politics*, 49:368–88.

Riley, P. ed. (1988). *Leibniz: Political Writings* (Cambridge).

Robbins, C., ed. (1969). *Two English Republican Tracts* (Cambridge).

Rogers, G. A. J., ed. (1994). *Locke's Philosophy: Content and Context* (Oxford).

Romanell, P. (1984). *John Locke and Medicine*, Buffalo, N.Y.

Sainsbury, W. N. (1872). *Annual Report of the Deputy Keeper of the Public Records*, 33:211–69.

Sargentich, T. (1974). 'Locke and ethical theory: two MS pieces', *The Locke Newsletter*, 5:24–31.

Saxby, T. J. (1987). *The Quest for the New Jerusalem: Jean Labadie and the Labadists, 1610–1744* (Dordrecht).

Schankula, H. A. S. (1973). 'A summary catalogue of the philosophical manuscript papers of John Locke', *Bodleian Library Record*, 9:24–35, 81–2.

Schochet, G. J. (1975). *Patriarchalism in Political Thought* (Oxford).

Schouls, A. J. (1992). *The Lockean Theory of Rights* (Princeton).

Scott, J. (1991). *Algernon Sidney and the Restoration Crisis, 1677–1683* (Cambridge).

Seliger, M. (1963). 'Locke's natural law and the foundation of politics', *Journal of the History of Ideas*, 24:337–54.

(1968). *The Liberal Politics of John Locke* (London).

Sheasgreen, W. J. (1986). 'John Locke and the charity school movement', *History of Education*, 15:63–79.

Simmons, A. J. (1992). *The Lockean Theory of Rights* (Princeton).

(1993). *On the Edge of Anarchy: Locke, Consent and the Limits of Society* (Princeton).

Sina, M. (1972). 'Testi teologico-filosofici Lockiani dal MS Locke c. 27 della Lovelace Collection', *Rivista di filosofia neo-scholastica* 64:54–75, 400–27.

Singh, R. (1961). 'John Locke and the theory of natural law', *Political Studies*, 9:105–18.

Skinner, Q. (1978). *The Foundations of Modern Political Thought*, 2 vols. (Cambridge).

Slaughter, T. P. (1981). ' "Abdicate" and 'contract" in the Glorious Revolution', *Historical Journal*, 24:323–37.

Snyder, D. C. (1986). 'Faith and reason in Locke's *Essay*', *Journal of the History of Ideas*, 47:197–214.

Spellman, W. M. (1988). *John Locke and the Problem of Depravity* (Oxford).

Spurr, J. (1988). ' "Latitudinarianism" and the Restoration Church', *The Historical Journal*, 31:61–82.

Statt, D. (1995). *Foreigners and English Nationalism: The Controversy over Immigration and Population, 1660–1760* (Newark, N.J.).

Stewart, M. A. (1992). Review of R. Horwitz *et al.*, 1990, *Locke Newsletter*, 23:145–65.

Tarcov, N. (1984). *Locke's Education for Liberty* (Chicago).

Thirsk, J. and Cooper, J. P., eds. (1972). *Seventeenth-Century Economic Documents* (Oxford).

Tuck, R. (1979). *Natural Rights Theories: Their Origin and Development* (Cambridge).

Tully, J. (1980). *A Discourse on Property: John Locke and his Adversaries* (Cambridge).

(ed.) (1983). *John Locke: A Letter Concerning Toleration* (Indianapolis).

(1993). *An Approach to Political Philosophy: John Locke in Contexts* (Cambridge).

(1994). 'The *Two Treatises* and aboriginal rights', in Rogers 1994.

Viano, C. A., ed. (1961). *John Locke: scritti editi e inediti sulla tolleranza* (Turin).

Von Leyden, W., ed. (1954). *John Locke: Essays on the Law of Nature* (Oxford).

(1956). 'John Locke and natural law', *Philosophy*, 21:23–35.

(1981). *Hobbes and Locke: The Politics of Freedom and Obligation.*

Wainright, A. W., ed. (1987). *John Locke: A Paraphrase and Notes on the Epistles of St Paul*, 2 vols. (Oxford).

Waldron, J. (1988). *The Right to Private Property* (Oxford).

Watt, T. (1991). *Cheap Print and Popular Piety, 1550–1640* (Cambridge).

Western, J. R. (1972). *Monarchy and Revolution: The English State in the 1680s* (London).

Weston, C. C. (1991). 'England: ancient constitution and common law', in Burns and Goldie 1991.

Wood, N. (1983). *The Politics of Locke's Philosophy* (Berkeley).

(1984). *John Locke and Agrarian Capitalism* (Berkeley).

Wootton, D., ed. (1993). *John Locke: Political Writings* (London).

Yolton, J., ed. (1956). *John Locke and the Way of Ideas* (Oxford).

(ed.) (1969). *John Locke: Problems and Perspectives* (Cambridge).

(ed.) (1976). *John Locke: An Essay Concerning Human Understanding* (London).

(1993). *A Locke Dictionary* (Oxford).

Yolton, J. and J. W. (1985). *John Locke: A Reference Guide* (Boston, Mass.).

(eds.) (1989). *John Locke: Some Thoughts Concerning Education* (Oxford).

Index

396

Index

Cambridge Texts in the History of Political Thought

Titles published in the series thus far

Aristotle *The Politics* and *The Constitution of Athens* (edited by Stephen Everson)

Arnold *Culture and Anarchy and other Writings* (edited by Stefan Collini)

Astell *Political Writings* (edited by Patricia Springborg)

Austin *The Province of Jurisprudence Determined* (edited by Wilfrid E. Rumble)

Bakunin *Statism and Anarchy* (edited by Marshall Shatz)

Baxter *A Holy Commonwealth* (edited by William Lamont)

Beccaria *On Crimes and Punishments and other Writings* (edited by Richard Bellamy)

Bentham *A Fragment on Government* (introduction by Ross Harrison)

Bernstein *The Preconditions of Socialism* (edited by Henry Tudor)

Bodin *On Sovereignty* (edited by Julian H. Franklin)

Bolingbroke *Political Writings* (edited by David Armitage)

Bossuet *Politics Drawn from the Very Words of Holy Scripture* (edited by Patrick Riley)

The British Idealists (edited by David Boucher)

Burke *Pre-Revolutionary Writings* (edited by Ian Harris)

Christine de Pizan *The Book of the Body Politic* (edited by Kate Langdon Forhan)

Cicero *On Duties* (edited by M. T. Griffin and E. M. Atkins)

Constant *Political Writings* (edited by Biancamaria Fontana)

Dante *Monarchy* (edited by Prue Shaw)

Diderot *Political Writings* (edited by John Hope Mason and Robert Wokler)

The Dutch Revolt (edited by Martin van Gelderen)

The Early Political Writings of the German Romantic (edited by Frederick C. Beiser)

Early Greek Political Thought from Homer to the Sophists (edited by Michael Gagarin and Paul Woodruff)

Erasmus: *The Education of a Christian Prince* (edited by Lisa Jardine)

Ferguson *An Essay on the History of Civil Society* (edited by Fania Oz-Salzberger)

Filmer *Patriarcha and other Writings* (edited by Johann P. Sommerville)

Sir John Fortescue *On the Laws and Governance of England* (edited by Shelley Lockwood)